COME SAVE SOMEONE LIKE ME

Christy Gerrell

Copyright © 2025 Christy Gerrell

All rights reserved.

No part of this book may be reproduced, stored in a retrieval system, or transmitted by any means, electronic, mechanical, photocopying, recording, or otherwise, without written permission from the author.

ISBN (Paperback): 979-8-9989661-1-8

COME SAVE SOMEONE LIKE ME

I saw her cold and lonely,
Standing by the door.
Her hair the color of twilight,
I wanted to touch her more.

Her eyes were filled with tears,
As she called out my brother's name.
She did not belong to me,
She was never mine to claim.

My hand reached out to her,
But she wasn't mine to touch.
I saw her back away,
I knew I loved her far too much

I cast my eyes downward
I would leave her cold and alone
But my heart begged me to stay
I had to make her my own

I raised my eyes to see her,
One last and longing look
My hand reached out for her
My heart in her hand she took

The war destroyed my soul,
My plea was for her to see,
I needed her to come,
Come and save someone like me.

Come Save Someone Like Me

Dedicated to:
My little lost girl – my Amy – and
My beautiful Grandparents
Spencer Thomas and Merrill Celeste
Who inspired me to always have a story to tell
and to tell that story well
And to my own sweet Charlotte –thank you
For caring for my child

Don't miss – **the Blackburn Legacy** – you can read them in any order:
Allen and Alicia's love story in – Come Love Someone Like Me
Lang and Holly's love story in – A Return of Innocence
Levi and Cecily's love story in – No Sound the Silence Makes
Tucker and Jessie's love story in – Come Tame Someone Like Me
Christian and Jordan's love story – Beyond a Certain Surrender
The Legacy begins with Levi's parents
Ethan and Lilliana's love story – Cherish the Light Burning Low

Prologue

September 1916
Rockhaven, Florida

Sarah Cartledge stood alone on the banks of the Saint Marks River and looked out at the water flowing over the large limestone rocks. The river was violent here where she stood. The river was beautiful. The river was deep and dark and seemed to hold secrets that the depths of that river would never tell anyone. She leaned back against a large cypress tree, and she watched as an alligator slide off the bank on the other side of the river and into the water. Sarah didn't move. She knew that if she left the ancient beast alone, that beast would not bother her.

A light rain had begun to fall only a few moments ago, and now Sarah was damp, though she was not soaking wet. Her long hair had come down from the pins that held it in place and was hanging to her waist, her thick hair was her vanity as her hair framed her beautiful face in a way that made her appear innocent and sweet, both of these things were just what she was. Sarah glanced down at herself and she saw that her dress was clinging to her slender body. She felt almost wild out here on the river, free to roam like the squirrels, the birds, and even the alligators that were a threat to her. She felt as though she were able to do anything that she wanted to do. She was happy here, Sarah thought. She belonged here. This little space on the earth had been created just for her.

Taking a deep breath of the fresh clean air, Sarah closed her eyes thinking of her dilemma, and she had a dilemma, there was no doubt in that fact. She was worried over what she might do. She was worried over hurting someone's feelings in her choice for the future.

Shane and Shaun Blackburn were identical twin brothers, no one could tell them apart, and everyone loved them for their playful nature and happy, carefree ways. Shane was serious-minded and laid back. Shane was the calm in a storm, while his twin brother, Shaun was the one that was always competing with Shane. Shaun was strong-willed and confident, secure in what he wanted out of his life. and always on the go. The twins personality was the only way the two brothers differed, and even in that, they were both so loving and good that they could still be easily confused.

Sarah pushed herself away from the tree that she was leaning against and she walked down to the edge of the river. She loved them both. Sarah honestly, and with all of her heart, loved Shane and Shaun Blackburn, and knowing this, Sarah was unafraid to admit to herself, or to anyone else, that she loved the brothers dearly, and she always would. For Sarah, she knew that she never wanted to hurt either of the Blackburn boys; they were a huge part of her world.

She picked up a rock and skipped it across the surface of the water six times, and she knew that if Shaun were here with her, he would have to outdo her throw, whereas Shane would praise her for the throw and never throw a rock of his own. A sigh escaped her as she bent for another stone and threw it thinking of how she loved Shane. He was good and so kind. Shane was always protective and caring of her, and she adored the way he was with her. But she was in love with Shaun. Shaun, who was always in motion, always confident, self-assured, and in his way, he was overprotective of her and she was content and happy that he was.

Both brothers were in love with her, and Sarah knew that they were. Shaun was openly courting her, and he had been doing so for months with her father's blessing. Her mother and father liked him and had high hopes for her as one day becoming his wife. While Sarah watched as Shane gave her shy glances, within those glances Sarah saw Shane's feelings for her. Shane was as Shane had always been with her, quick to come help her, and he was always polite, and she knew, even though he didn't say how he felt, that he was in love with her too, maybe more so than his brother.

"Sarah, whatcha doing?" her brother Edward bounced to her side, and he really did bounce, Edward rarely walked anywhere. His hands, they were always moving, and he was smiling no matter what, even when he was hurt, Eddie was smiling.

"I'm not doing anything, Eddie," Sarah said and turned to look up at her older brother, a grown man that had the mind of a young boy. He was her best friend. They were closer than any other brother and sister ever, and if anyone picked on Eddie, they picked on Sarah. She had learned to throw rocks at the children in school who bullied her brother when they were young, and she threw a rock now knowing that she would always look out for him. She loved him unconditionally.

The accident had happened so quickly, Sarah thought as she remembered a day long ago. She reached out and she brushed her brother's long hair back away from his face thinking how beautiful he was. He had been beautiful that day in her memory as well.

Her family had gone to the Blackburn home of Riverbend for the Fourth of July picnic. All the children had been playing down by the natural pool that was near the river's edge, a pool of water that was often referred to as a spring. Eddie had been almost twelve years old then, a happy young boy waiting impatiently to become a man, and she had only been a nine years old little girl unaware of the dangers of the river's current only feet beyond that pool of spring water.

Sarah closed her eyes as she drifted back to that day that Eddie had accidentally swum out too far and been caught in the river's current knowing that the accident had happened so fast, without any warning. One second Eddie was in control of his future, laughing and having fun. Within the next second, Eddie was crying out for help as he was pulled under and down the river. Sarah remembered Uncle Allen had jumped into the river wearing all of his clothes, even his boots, and Uncle Allen had gone into the current after Eddie. Sarah could still hear in her head Aunt Alicia's scream from the bank of the river, Alicia seeing her husband fight to grab Eddie, but Eddie disappeared into the deep dark river, and then so had Uncle Allen.

Sarah hugged her brother now with the memory of that day as she thanked God that Eddie had lived. Uncle Allen had resurfaced downriver and fought his way back to shore pulling Eddie out by the foot, Eddie more dead than alive. With their Mama screaming and her Daddy holding her Mama's hand, everyone had run along the banks to where Eddie lay. And then Uncle Heath picked Eddie up and shook him hard and beat him on the back while everyone was praying for Eddie to breathe, and after what seemed to be a long time, Eddie did breathe, he grabbed a quick breath of air, and Eddie survived the river's violence that day.

Sarah pulled away from her brother, and she saw him smiling down at her with the eyes of total innocence that held trust and love that she could depend on never wavering. Eddie had lived that day, but he had never been the same again.

"I don't know what to do, Eddie," she said knowing that she could tell him anything and he wouldn't say a word to anyone else. Even if he did say a word of what she told him, almost no one would listen to him. Eddie often kept to himself, and Eddie always smiled. "I love Shaun," she said to her brother and turned back to look at the river seeing in her mind's eyes Shane's pretty face.

"Shane loves you," Eddie stated simply as he picked up a rock that he handed to his sister. "Throw it like you can, Sarah. I wanna see it skip." Sarah gave a laugh and threw the rock knowing that if Eddie knew Shane was in love with her, then she hadn't misjudged her situation.

"I love them both," she sighed as the rock skipped across the river nine times. She had never had a rock skip that many times. Even Shaun couldn't beat her in that throw.

"You belong to Shaun," Eddie said and reached down for another rock that he put in his sister's small hand. "Shane isn't for you." He almost sounds like he used to before the accident, Sarah thought as she looked up into her brother's wide innocent eyes.

"Why do you say that Eddie?" He was only a boy in his mind, and she knew this, she had known this for years. Some people called him halfwit, other people called him the town idiot, but in this conversation, he seems to be firm in his mind of what he was saying.

"Cause you're too much like Shane, you're calm and don't fuss. But Shaun, you're nothing like Shaun. Mama told Ellen not to marry Deputy Nichols cause they were like-minded, and Ellen is going to marry Deputy Nichols anyway. Mama says they're gonna be bored to tears together. Mama's right cause Mama knows everything." Sarah laughed and hugged her big brother. "I don't want you bored to tears, Sarah." Eddie returned her hug quickly and stepped back from the river's edge. Sarah knew that Eddie was afraid of getting too close to the river and she understood why.

"You're a good big brother Eddie," she said and walked beyond the bank with Eddie holding her hand feeling comfortable with her life and more confident in her choice for her future.

"Oh look, here comes Shane now," Eddie pointed off in the distance with his sister telling him that wasn't Shane coming toward them seconds before Eddie broke into a run to greet Shaun. Sarah laughed as she saw her brother bounce around Shaun with her having a fleeting second of doubt as to this being Shaun, or was this Shane? She was unsure of which twin was coming toward her until she got close to him and saw the sly look that he gave to her, and then the wink. Shane would never be playful with her in that way. Shane would have come to her and given to her his undivided attention. Shane would have treated her as though she were made of glass.

"Eddie," Shaun was saying to her brother, "here's a nickel, go up to the general store and get yourself a drink." He laughed when Eddie started jumping again and watched the young man run off in the direction of the store. A lot of people didn't really know Eddie, Shaun thought. Eddie was a good man, kind of heart and special in every way. Most people thought that Eddie Cartledge was a burden, but those that knew him best, knew him to be an angel you just wanted to protect and love.

"I've got you to myself," Shaun said and reached for Sarah who laughed as he pulled her close. Shane would never be this way. Shane would have asked her before he touched her. And she grieved that she would hurt Shane, but her heart belonged to Shaun and it always would. Shaun was her sweetheart.

"I skipped a rock on the river nine times," she said proudly and saw he looked impressed. "But I don't want to skip rocks right now," she breathed as she saw him lowering his head, his huge grass green eyes looking into her eyes. "I love you, Shaun Blackburn," she said softly before his mouth covered her mouth and she molded her body into his. He made her melt like butter on a hot potato, Sarah thought, and she melted into him now as his tongue plunged into her open mouth, her heart pounding hard in her chest as she wanted more, yet she was unsure of what more she wanted.

"You make me forget myself," Shaun said as he held Sarah close feeling his body wanting her too much and afraid that she would know how much he wanted her if he didn't pull away from her now. But then Shaun thought of how innocent she was, and he pulled her back to his body, and she cried out as he kissed her again. His hands lost in her long loose hair, and he loved the feel of her hair in his fingers as he covered her mouth with his own.

"You'll think me forward if we don't stop," Sarah said wishing they never had to stop. "You make me want something with your kisses, and I don't know what that something is."

"I know how to fill you up," Shaun breathed into her hair as his mouth found her ear and he plunged his tongue there hearing her gasp and cling to him. "Sarah, I can't wait any longer. You have to tell me if you've made up your mind." He pulled away from her, and he looked down at the beautiful woman that he held in his arms. "Are you going to marry me?"

Sarah looked up at him, their eyes locked for a long few seconds. She knew inside her answer to this question, and she laid her head against his chest, her face turned toward the river, and she saw him, she saw Shane. Her answer to Shaun would hurt his brother, but she knew who she belonged with. The brother that she loved with all of her heart was Shaun, and she knew that she had known for years that he was meant for only her.

"Do you love me, Shaun?" she asked innocently as she turned and looked back up into his eyes.

"With all my heart Sarah. Before God and man, I love you with all my heart, body, and soul. I want only you forever." His voice was serious, and she smiled because she knew he did love her that much and she loved him that much right back.

She glanced down toward the river where Shane was and saw Shaun followed her eyes. Shaun had no idea that his twin brother was in love with Sarah. If someone had told Shaun that Shane was in love with her and wanted her for his wife, Shaun wouldn't have believed them.

"I'll marry you," she said softly, and Shaun looked away from his brother and down into Sarah's eyes. "I love you so much, Shaun. I think I would marry you a million times over if you'll have me." He laughed and lifted her up into his arms before calling out to Shane,

"Come congratulate me, brother! This beautiful girl has finally agreed to put up with me forever!!" Sarah laughed and held on to Shaun as he twirled her around knowing Shane, always good-natured, always doing the right thing, would come and be happy for them.

"You're a very blessed man," Shane said seriously as Shaun put Sarah down and shook his brother's hand. "You're blessed as well, Sarah. My brother is the very best." He reached down and pulled her into his arms to hug, and she hugged him back. So like Shane to be loving and caring and kind, to never show his brother his real feelings so he wouldn't hurt Shaun or anyone.

"Why are we hugging?" Eddie jumped around Shane, Shaun, and Sarah. "Can I get hugs?" The three laughed as they each gave Eddie a hug.

"Run up to the house and tell Mama that Shaun just asked me to marry him and I've said yes." Eddie waved his hands and danced around.

"I'm gonna tell Daddy and Ellen too," he called out, and Sarah laughed as she watched her brother run toward the town and the general store that her father ran.

"Everyone he meets along the way will know we're engaged," Shaun laughed and pulled Sarah close. "But the one I wanted to know first is my brother." Shaun looked at Shane and smiled. "You've been my best friend all my life. And the three of us are always going to be a close family." He looked up seeing Eddie in the distance before revising what he had said. "The four of us are going to be a close family."

"Always together," Sarah said and she reached for Shane's hand. "Now you'll be my brother too." She saw Shane force a smile and she reached up and touched his cheek. "No girl could ask for a better brother." She hoped that her words gave him comfort. Sarah never wanted to hurt Shane. She loved Shane too.

PART ONE

Shaun and Sarah

Chapter One

Early December 1916
Riverbend, Florida

"Those boys are wild," Mary Blackburn said as she came into the house and saw her sister-in-law standing at the window watching her sons ride by on their horses yelling to the top of their lungs. "They're always competing," Mary said shaking her head seeing her husband Seth was egging the boys on in their race. Her husband's older brother, Allen was waving his hat and yelling at the boys to both go faster.

"It's because they're twins," Alicia Blackburn said as she watched her husband throw his hat down when one of the twins lost, and she knew the one that lost was Shane. Her husband Allen was always cheering on Shane, offering that twin encouragement because Shane needed the encouragement more than his brother Shaun. Shane was insecure and lacked confidence, Shaun was full of both of those traits that were missing from his brother Shane, though not many noticed this difference in the twins.

The twins were just alike physically. It was almost impossible to tell them apart unless you knew them well, and often they fooled the family as to which one was which because they were so identical, and yet in personality, they differed, though very slightly.

Shane was more gentle. He felt things more deeply than Shaun did. Shane was kind and good, whereas Shaun was the one that was more outgoing and carefree.

"Shaun won again, pay up," Seth Blackburn turned to his brother Allen and held out his hand for the money his brother owed in the bet they had on the race between the twins.

Shane galloped his horse into the yard stopping before he reached his father and uncle and he laughed with a good nature. That was Shane's way, he was laid back, easy going, and serious, whereas his brother Shaun, who always had to win at everything, and if the truth were known, Shane often let Shaun win, was more confident and secure in himself. Shaun more certain of the direction that his life was going in.

"You're good with a horse, Shane," Allen Blackburn said to his nephew. "It doesn't matter if you win or not, you have a real talent breaking these animals."

"I don't care so much for winning like Shaun does," Shane confessed as he got down off of his horse and walked the animal slowly around the yard to cool down. "Hey mother!" he yelled into the house and saw his mother come out onto the porch. Mary Blackburn leaned over the rail and when he walked by she reached out and ruffled his hair. "Shaun said to tell you he's ridden into Rockhaven and won't be home until after dinner."

"We all know why Shaun's gone to Rockhaven," Seth said to his wife, and they exchanged a knowing look along with a smile.

"Sarah Cartledge," Shane said and started with his horse to the barn, his Uncle and his father watched him leave them as the older gentlemen joined their wives on the porch.

Allen Blackburn stood quiet as he watched his nephew Shane slowly walk away. Allen felt badly for the young man that was good with horses. And Allen knew, no one knew Shane's secret. No one would have believed his secret if he had shouted it to the top of the cypress trees down by the river. But Allen knew. Allen knew because Allen loved his wife more than life itself, and he knew what the look of unreturned love looked like. He saw that look every time Shane was with Shaun's fiancée Sarah.

Allen Blackburn reached for his wife Alicia and he held her close thankful to God that he had won her love. He might have lost her once, but she had found him, and forever they had been all right. "It's starting to get cold," he spoke to his family standing on the porch. "Let's get inside and talk in front of the fire. Are Heath and Emily coming to join us tonight for dinner?" he asked his wife, and he saw her nod her head. "And the girls?" he looked at the stairwell expecting his daughters to come bouncing down the stairs along with his niece, Heather at any given moment.

"It's quiet, Allen," Alicia said as she too looked to the stairwell. "I think our girls are outside somewhere." She went to the window and looked out and saw her daughters, Bethany, Jenny, and Julie running to the barn, and she knew the girls were going to be with Shane. Everyone wanted to be with Shane. He had grown into a nice man who treated everyone like they were his little sister, even her, Alicia thought with a smile. "Yes, the girls are with Shane," Alicia sighed.

"I wish Shane would find a girl and settle down like his brother," Seth poured himself and Allen a drink and then sat next to his wife in front of the fire.

"Shane will find the right girl in his own time and in his own way, Seth," Mary said and looked at Allen. Mary knew that her brother-in-law, Allen, knew Shane's secret. The right girl for Shane was engaged to Shane's brother Shaun.

Allen nodded his head to Mary as he took his wife Alicia's hand. He should have known that a mother would have seen in her child what Allen had seen in Shane. He thought of the time that he had loved Alicia more than anything in this world and Alicia had not loved him. Alicia had rejected him, and he had ached in an agony he wouldn't wish anyone to know. And now he saw his nephew Shane was hurting just as he had been, only for Shane there was no hope of winning Sarah's love. Sarah's heart belonged to Shane's brother Shaun.

Bethany Blackburn raced her sisters and her cousin Heather into the barn knowing that she would win the race even if she were shorter than the others. "I get to ask him because I reached him first," she called out to the girls with her and laughed when she did so.

"Ask me what?" Shane Blackburn turned his attention from his horse to his cousins. Heather was the oldest and the leader of their little pack. Heather was also taller than Bethany, Jenny, and Julie and most would refer to Heather as willowy. Heather also differed from the other girls as her hair was golden in color and Heather had the Blackburn grass green eyes. Shane knew that Heather was a beauty, but to him, she was often cold and cruel, and he had to work hard to like her.

Bethany, Jenny, and Julie all favored their mother, Alicia Blackburn. All three girls were small with a mass of curly hair that hung in long ringlets and all three had deep, dark red hair like his Aunt Alicia. Jenny and Julie had his Uncle Allen's grass green eyes, but Bethany was the very image of his Aunt Alicia with a unique color of eyes like his Aunt, a color that his Uncle Allen called aqua.

"Is it true that we're going to go into the war? That they are drafting men now to go to Europe and fight?" He stopped brushing his horse and looked at his small and beautiful cousin, Bethany. Talk of war was everywhere, and he knew it was possible that soon the United States would enter the war. Shane hoped that they wouldn't get involved. He would have to go, and he never wanted to leave his home. He never wanted to leave his river. His father owned a place upriver that was called Riverview. His Uncle Allen owned this place known as Riverbend, and his Uncle Heath and Aunt Emily owned Riversedge. He and Shaun had built a house that was just like his Uncle's here at Riverbend only they split the house in two, and one of them lived in one half, and the other lived in the other half. They named their home Twin River.

Shaun was going to bring Sarah home to his half of the house when they married, and Shane knew he probably wouldn't be able to continue living there. He had already found a place where he was going to build his own home. Shane had made up his mind that his brother, nor anyone else, would ever know that he was in love with Sarah.

"I hope we don't get involved in this war, Bethany," Shane said trying to smile at the girls. "I don't want to leave you girls. You make me the best cookies." He tousled Bethany's long curls and ran toward the house knowing the girls were behind him. He was trying to be light-hearted because Shane knew, there was every possible chance that this country was going to join the war, and he would be leaving his home, his family, and everything in life that mattered to him. He wanted only to stay here, right here with his family on this river for the rest of his life. This place was in his blood as his father often said. He belonged here running from his cousins and laughing and happy, this was the best life anyone could ask for even if Sarah hadn't returned his love.

Shaun Blackburn knocked at the door of the Cartledge home in Rockhaven and hoped Sarah would answer. He had known Sarah all of his life, he had fallen in love with her in Sunday school when he was eleven years old, and she was only seven, and he was happiest when he was with her. Her father owned the general store in Rockhaven, and their families had grown close over the years. She was more than his friend, more than the woman that he loved, Sarah was his family.

"Shaun," Edward Cartledge said his name as the young man opened the door causing Shaun to laugh out loud when Eddie hugged him close. "I missed you," Eddie said in his childish voice, and Shaun laughed and tugged at Eddy's long hair.

"I was just here this morning buddy," he used his nickname for Sarah's only brother. Eddie was a grown man older than Shaun, but in Eddie's mind he was a boy, and he would always be a boy. Almost everyone in and around Rockhaven was very protective of Eddie Cartledge, and everyone loved him because he was a very gentle person.

"Sarah is helping Mama and Daddy in the store," Eddie pulled Shaun into the house and through the dining room door that connected the Cartledge home the store where they all worked. "Look who I found," Eddie called out, and everyone in the room turned to see Shaun.

"You came," Sarah looked at her fiancée and gave him a smile before reaching out her hand toward him. Shaun went to Sarah and smiled down into her eyes. She reminded him of his Aunt Alicia as she was very small. The Blackburn men towered over all their women, Shaun thought with a smile knowing that Sarah fit in with his family. Her eyes were a pale light blue, the color of a cloudless sky on a clear fall day. Her hair was the shade of the night sky just before sunset, a golden brown. Shaun picked up a lock of her hair from her shoulder and thought how shiny and silky smooth her hair was. He knew he was blessed. He loved her, and he knew that she returned his feelings. She was everything any man could want in a woman. She was everything that he wanted in a wife.

"Did Shane come with you?" Sarah asked, and Shaun frowned wishing that she would think of just him alone and not always as a pair with his brother. They had grown up together, Shane, Sarah, and Shaun, best friends, and he knew he shouldn't be jealous of his brother spending time with them. He just wanted Sarah to himself some of the time, and if he were honest, he wanted Sarah all to himself most of the time.

Shaun almost laughed thinking of how he wanted to kiss her and mold her into his body, and he couldn't do that with her brother hanging around. And tonight he wanted her all to himself to do just that. She fit into him perfectly, he thought, and he ached to be alone with her, he couldn't wait until they were married and he could fill her up with himself every day for the rest of their lives. They would be the perfect couple with no problems ever, of that, Shaun Blackburn was certain.

"Is Shane coming tonight or not?" Sarah pushed on Shaun to get his attention seeing that he was daydreaming and knowing that she did that the better part of the days, her dreams all being with him in their new home.

"No, Shane stayed at Uncle Allen's house with the girls tonight," Shaun finally answered Sarah's question before moving across the room to help close up the store by bringing in barrels of crackers, and pickles and then helping Eddie lock the door securely.

"I wish Shane had come. Mama got the new Victrola, and we're going to listen to the new John McCormack record tonight." Shaun rolled his eyes and knew; he wouldn't get the time alone with Sarah that he craved.

"I thought we could take a walk down to the river before it gets dark," Shaun suggested, and he saw Sarah smile at him shyly before looking at her parents. He was more hopeful that the evening might go his way after all.

"Mama, may I go for a walk with Shaun before dinner?" Shaun saw Mrs. Cartledge look at him and the older woman gave a nod of her head, and then she smiled at him. He knew that Sarah's mother liked him and that the older woman was very aware that he loved her daughter more than anything in this world.

"No staying out until dark you two," Sarah's father called after them.

Sarah laughed as she ran out the door with Shaun behind helping her pull on her coat after he closed the door behind them.

The twilight was beautiful. The sun was sinking low in the western sky causing the clouds to be a vibrant orange, pink, and almost a gray-blue in color off in the distance. The air was crisp and clear and clean and felt good against Shaun's cheeks as it wasn't too cold, but cold enough to want to be close to Sarah.

"Bet you can't get me," Sarah yelled over her shoulder to Shaun as they left the house and she heard him laugh as she looked back to see him chasing her.

"Bet you I can!" Shaun loved to compete and to win. He rushed ahead of her and caught her in his arms feeling her giggle as she clung to him. "You'll never get away from me Sarah Cartledge. You belong to me for life." She fell against him and hugged him close knowing that he was hugging her just as close. He was right; she would belong to him for life. He was made just for her.

"No argument here, Shaun. Forever I'll love you. I don't want to get away from you. I want to crawl inside of you." She let him go and twirled around on the white sandy road seeing the sun sinking low and lower still and appearing to be swallowed up by the earth. "I love this time of year Shaun. I love the winter birds calling out in the night, and the cool wind in my face. I love the sound of the river rushing by, and the way the leaves seem to dance on the trees, the noise the leaves makes almost sound like angels whispering to God. I want to stay right here with you just like this forever."

Shaun stood looking at Sarah, her long hair had come loose and was down to her hips. Her skin was a creamy white with her light eyes that seem to be pools of clear blue. She was lovely, and he knew that she was his, and he wanted her always. Even in eternity, Shaun Blackburn knew that he would only want Sarah.

"You're beautiful," Shaun said softly, and Sarah turned to look at him, her hand held out toward him, and he pulled her to him. "June can't come soon enough," he said seriously as he looked down into her beautiful eyes. They would be joined together by the Reverend Farmer in the Shady Grove church on June ninth of nineteen hundred and seventeen, and he couldn't wait. He wanted her now as he told himself that he wasn't a patient man.

"You're beautiful," Sarah looked up at Shaun's face, he was like all of the Blackburn men, dark hair with a cowlick in front, grass green eyes, and a smile that could make the rain stop falling. She felt tiny in his arms. She felt safe in his arms. She always wanted to be in his arms.

"I don't know if I can wait," Shaun pulled Sarah into his arms and lowered his head, his mouth only an inch from her mouth. "I want you so badly," he breathed, and she melted into him letting him know he wasn't alone in what he was feeling. "Shane and I almost have the house finished, we could push up the wedding date and be moved in by Christmas," there was a plea in his voice, and he felt Sarah go stiff in his arms at this suggestion.

"Mama wants me to wait until after Ellen is married," she said softly, her lips only an inch still from his. "Ellen is the oldest, and her wedding has been planned much longer than mine."

"Why don't we get married in April since Ellen is getting married in March?" Shaun suggested, and he hoped Sarah would agree.

"We'll see," she whispered as his lips touched hers. "It's so hard to wait. Six months feels like a lifetime away Shaun."

"I agree," he let his lips touch hers. "If I start kissing you, I might not be able to stop," he said gently while he pulled her closer.

"I want you to kiss me, Shaun." Sarah leaned even more into her fiancée. "Please," she breathed, and his mouth covered her mouth as she clung to him.

Their kiss might have gone on forever except for Eddie who came running up to them, and out of breath Eddie innocently asked, "What are ya'll doing?" Shaun and Sarah both laughed as they parted their lips and watched Eddie bounce around them.

"Waiting on you to come get us so we can go listen to the new music your Mama got," Shaun said hearing Sarah laugh as she broke into a run toward the house with Eddie chasing her. Shaun fell in with them running to the house and he beat them both to the door laughing as he caught Sarah up into his arms and spun her around and into the house. Soon they would be married, and he would be with her every free minute that he had. Soon, Shaun thought knowing that soon couldn't come quick enough. Shaun loved Sarah. Shaun needed Sarah.

Shane lay in his bed in the house that he and Shaun were building together and he listened to his brother stumble into the room in the dark. They had just put in gas lighting, something they both had wanted for their new home together. Shane sat up in his bed seeing his brother's smile when Shaun turned on their new lights and spoke to him. "Sarah missed you tonight. And I really like having lights in this place."

"When you turn them on it's easy to see," Shane laughed softly as he said this sitting up with a smile. "We need to put in a bathroom like Uncle Allen and Aunt Alicia have," Shane said noting the smile on Shaun's face. "Sarah would be happier here with both hot and cold running water and that new central gas heat Uncle Allen is having put in next month, we should think about getting installed here as well." Shaun hit his brother's leg and smiled.

"You're always so good to think of my Sarah," he laughed. "When we're done with this place it'll be a grand home for the three of us. We just need to find you your own girl." Shane turned his face to the wall and knew that he would never tell his brother the truth of his life. For Shane, if he couldn't have Sarah, then he didn't want anyone. "Don't you want a wife and children someday, Shane?" Shaun turned serious with his brother, he wanted Shane as happy as he was.

"Maybe I just want to grow old with you and Sarah and Eddie and a passel of your kids," Shane said coolly and looked at his brother, a brother that everything came to with ease. Shaun was like their Uncle Allen and their father, Seth. Shaun was fun to be with always finding the humor in life, and he was very responsible and confident. Shane was more serious, he was more accepting of things, he had a healthy dose of his mother's sweet ways, and he knew that too, and he didn't mind. He loved easy, he loved well, and he didn't mind giving of himself if it would please another.

The brothers were identical. When they looked into a mirror, they each saw their brother and not themselves. But in personality, though similar in some ways, they were also very different in other ways. Shane knew that those differences were what made them best friends.

Shaun reached out a hand, and he messed up his brother's hair before moving to the doorway. "Sarah says hi, she wanted you to come listen to their new music machine tonight," Shaun said and looked back to see his brother, Shane sitting still on the bed.

"How was the music?" he asked, and he saw Shaun shrug his shoulders.

"All right, I guess. Eddie was excited." Shane laughed at his brother's answer. Everyone knew how Eddie could be when he was excited about something – Eddie bounced.

"I'll come next time," Shane said knowing that he wouldn't go to Sarah's unless his life depended on it. Being around her was an agony. He knew he was going to move back in with his parents when she and Shaun married. Sometimes when he thought of her, Shane wanted to cry, and he hated that weakness within himself. "Bethany and the girls are worried we're going to war," Shane changed the subject and saw his brother go stiff and still.

"If we do, I'll join up. They won't have to draft me. I'm no coward. But I hope we don't go to war. I want to stay right here on this river all my days." Shaun saw Shane sit up nodding his head.

"We agree on that, brother. I don't ever want to leave this river. Do you wanna get up and go hunting at dawn with me before we start working at the sawmill?"

"If we're getting up early, I better get to bed." Shaun turned away from his brother and almost ran over his cousin Bethany who was standing behind him. He cried out sounding almost like a girl when he did so reaching for her, and he grabbed his little cousin by the arms keeping them both from falling. "Good grief Bethany, what are you doing here this late? Did you come alone?" Both Shane and Shaun saw their cousin nodding her head.

"I need to talk to you both about something, and I don't want Mama and Daddy to know," she said seriously as she went and sat down on the foot of Shane's bed.

"Must be serious for you to be out this late at night alone, aren't you afraid in the dark?" Shane asked in his concerned way and saw little Bethany Blackburn shaking her head in a negative fashion.

"No, silly, I grew up on this river. I'd never be afraid here, and besides, I brought a lantern with me to show me the way. And I knew you both would walk me back home." Shaun laughed out loud at his little cousin and patted her on the head thinking she was growing up too fast. She was too tiny to be old.

"You did? What if we won't walk you home?" Shaun asked Bethany and saw her roll her eyes up at him.

"We don't have time to be walking you home, little girl. We're going hunting in the morning at dawn. We need our sleep," Shane teased, and Bethany rolled her eyes again at both brothers.

"You two are enough to drive me to distraction. I don't know why I come to you with my problems.

But despite how we tease one another boys, I'm here now on a serious matter. And I need your help," she sat up straight seeing both of her cousins leaning toward her.

"And you also know that we'll do anything for you," Shane spoke the truth, and he saw Bethany nod her head and smile.

"I'm fifteen years old, and Mama and Daddy treat me like I'm still a baby," she pouted not seeing the brothers exchange serious looks.

"Well, you are awfully young," Shaun teased her, and she slapped at him.

"I'm trying to be serious," she said and smiled at her cousins. "Last month I went with Daddy when he met with a man named

Levi Tucker in Tallahassee. Mr. Tucker has a successful sawmill business over in Madison County. He and Daddy are talking about Mr. Tucker opening a sawmill here on our river because Daddy and Uncle Seth own all this land and all these trees."

"We know all about Uncle Allen going into business with some Yankee from over in Madison County, Bethany. We're the ones that helped plant another 600 acres in longleaf pines and clear cut 200 acres last year. The trees are our money making crop. The trees are our business too." Shane said seriously.

"I don't care about any old tree or timber or longleaf anything," Bethany said seriously and jumped up to pace the room. "I met the man Daddy's going to become partners with, Mr. Tucker, and he has a son." Shaun shook his head as Shane spoke for them both,

"You're too young Bethany."

"He knows how young I am," Bethany sat back down. "His name is Ethan Tucker, and he's so handsome. While our daddies talked business we sat and had an ice cream and talked for hours, he even held my hand." She didn't see her cousins roll their eyes. "He asked me if I'd wait for him, he's going to join up as soon as he can for the war. I told him I'd wait for him forever and I meant it too. We've been writing letters to one another every single day. I'm keeping a secret from Mama, and I never keep secrets from Mama, but I don't know how to tell her. You, boys, know how gentle and sweet my Mama is. Won't you help me tell her?"

"So you want us to tell Aunt Alicia for you about this boy Ethan that you're writing to every day?" Shane was shaking his head as he spoke and saw his cousin Bethany nodding her head. "That won't happen," he laughed. "We love Aunt Alicia, but she's sort of delicate. If we tell her you've given your heart to some rich man's son and that son is joining the army before we're even in the war, she'll faint and bump her head. And Uncle Allen will kill us both for causing her harm. You're on your own in this little one." Shane patted Bethany on the head with a gentle smile.

"Shane is right," Shaun agreed. "And best you just tell Uncle Allen and let him tell Aunt Alicia. I want to meet this Ethan Tucker. He sounds like the stuff heroes are made of joining the army before we're even in the war."

"I think he's wonderful, and he's not joining the army, he's joining the marines," Bethany said looking up at the ceiling with a dreamy smile. "He has eyes that are crystal clear blue, so clear they almost have no color. He's taller than you boys, and you're both sky high. He's coming here in the spring with his Daddy, and he wants to ask my Daddy if he can write me while he's gone to war. I want you both to be there and meet him when he comes." Bethany took Shane by one hand and Shaun by the other. "You two are my best friends, you've been with me while I grew up. and I really want you to walk me home now." She giggled, and her cousins both tried to pull her close thus pulling her in two different directions.

"We'll walk you home, Bethany," Shane said, and Shaun fell in with them grabbing the lantern. "So, he's tall huh? Taller than us?" The brothers didn't see the smile on Bethany's face, but they heard the teasing in her voice,

"And he's as good looking as any of our Blackburn clan," she assured them and heard them laugh. "Maybe better looking, he's got the prettiest face." Shane and Shaun laughed at her words knowing that they loved her like a little sister. They had no memories of their life before her. She put a smile on everyone's face.

"We're keeping the lantern, Bethy," Shane said using the nickname the family had for her as they left her on the porch of her home, "We'll see you tomorrow. Get to bed, its cold out here." Bethany turned to go into the house and stopped short, her father was at the doorway looking at her, and her mother stood beside him, both of her parents were looking firm, her mother's face held a hint of disappointment.

"What are you doing out this late?" Alicia Blackburn demanded to know, and Bethany looked in the direction of Shane and Shaun, they were disappearing beyond the trees, and she knew she was alone with her mother and father.

"I needed to talk to the boys," Bethany said seriously as she joined her parents on the porch. "I'm sorry, I shouldn't be out in the dark, but I had the lantern, and you can see they brought me home," she walked into their living room and toward the stairwell.

"What did you need to talk to the boys about that couldn't wait until morning, young lady?" Allen Blackburn demanded to know of his oldest daughter as he followed close behind her.

"I can't talk about it right now, Daddy. We'll talk next week. I need to think." Allen Blackburn watched his oldest daughter go up the stairs seeing that his wife watching Bethany leave them as well.

"Why do we have to wait until next week," Allen asked his Alicia and she shrugged her shoulders. "And what does she need to think about? She's all of fifteen years old, still a child. Children don't think because their parents think for them."

"Allen, you know Bethany was born old. She's so serious-minded. What you and I view as nothing, she sees as earth-shattering." Alicia spoke while still looking up the stairwell where her child had gone.

"She's just like her mother," Allen turned to his wife and pulled her into his arms. He had fallen in love with her years ago, she was everything to him, and they had three beautiful daughters and no son to carry on in his place when he passed on. He turned and looked back out into the darkness of night, he might not have sons, but he had two nephews that watched out for his family, and he could rely on those two young men to carry on the family business. Shane and Shaun were Allen's male legacy, and he was thankful his brother and sister-in-law shared the boys with him and Alicia.

The twins were wonderful young men to be admired. Their younger brother Michael was away at college and following in

Allen's footsteps of getting a law degree. Allen knew that Michael would watch out for his girls if anything happened to him. Their family was secure and complete and very large, and they were made of sturdy stock. Allen lifted his wife into his arms and started up the stairs laughing as he held her close knowing that as long as God allowed, he would hold his wife close.

"The other day in the general store the Sheriff Deputy came in to pay court to Ellen Cartledge, and she told Deputy Nichols that her sister Sarah was now engaged to one of the Blackburn Twins. Deputy Nichols said that all of us Blackburns are hell on an ax handle." Allen saw his beautiful wife frown and shake her head.

"What a terrible thing to say. Only the Blackburn men are hell on an ax handle," Alicia said seriously as her husband lowered her onto their bed. "And Bethany is nothing like me except in appearance. She's your daughter and just like you, and I'm so thankful because you're the most wonderful man in the world." She felt her husband touch her and knew he was beyond wonderful.

"I love you, Alicia," Allen said softly as he lowered himself onto his wife and heard her response,

"Forever Allen, forever…."

Late February 1917
Rockhaven, Florida

"Shaun," Sarah breathed as she pushed up and opened her bedroom window. "What are you doing here?"

"It's not Shaun, it's me, Shane," Sarah backed up from the window and pulled her nightgown up to her chin. "I wanted you to see this." He pointed out a picture from the Sears and Roebuck catalog of a brand new, top of the line stove. "I want to surprise Shaun by getting this for our house, but since you'll be doing all the cooking, I thought it best to check with you first. Don't tell Shaun though. I want it to be a surprise." Sarah leaned out the window and looked at the catalog.

"That's a nice stove, Shane. It's going to be your house too, you can pick out the stove if you want," Sarah said seriously knowing that the three of them would be living in the house together after she and Shaun were married. The house was built for two families; the boys had planned it that way. The kitchen and dining room were in the middle of the house with a living area on each side for them both and four bedrooms on each side of the house making it eight bedrooms. They had been working on the house since they were eighteen years old, for almost five full years and it was almost complete.

The twins new house sat right at the mouth of the river where the current was fastest, and the banks were highest, it was the most beautiful spot on the river as it looked like a mill pond before the current picked up, and then it became a flowing river. The calm before the rush is what Shaun said of the place they chose to build their home. Sarah also knew that the spot the boys had chosen to live on the river had the clearest water. On any given sunny day, even at the deepest part of the river, you could see the bottom of limestone and sand and the fish swimming by.

She smiled thinking of her future home, she didn't have long to wait, and she almost lost her breath knowing that soon she would be with Shaun every day for the rest of her life. The boys hadn't meant for the house to turn out like it had, but it looked just like their Uncle Allen's home. A breezeway ran right through the middle on both the upstairs and downstairs floors. And like their Uncle's home, both homes had covered porches upstairs and downstairs on the front and on the back of the house. The front of the homes faced the river, and the back of the home faced the road that led to the main road which went to Rockhaven and beyond to Woodville. She felt blessed to be moving into the house, a house where she knew she would grow old looking out at the river that she had grown up with the twins as her best friends.

"Sarah," Shane said her name in a serious voice looking from her to the book in his hands. "I won't be able to live there with you and Shaun. The house is for you and Shaun. I'll visit from time to time, but I plan on building my own place down river. You both need your privacy."

"Shane Blackburn, that house is huge, way big enough for all of us, and you know it. Why, one day you'll have your own wife,"

"No, Sarah, I won't," Shane cut her off and his grass green eyes collided with her clear blue eyes.

"Shane, you'll find the right woman someday, I know you will."

"Sarah," he breathed her name, "the right woman for me is going to marry my brother. We both know that. And that's all right. I'm happy for you, and for Shaun. But I can't live in that house with you both, and I won't." Shane saw the sadness on Sarah's face. "Don't feel bad, Sarah," he spoke the truth before turning away. "You'll have a wonderful stove to cook on, and Shaun loves you, and I love Shaun."

Sarah Cartledge watched Shane Blackburn lift his hand as he walked away from her bedroom window before sat down on her unmade bed. She had known how he felt for her for a long time now. His feelings had her conflicted over Shaun for years. She loved them both. They were almost the same. But Shaun was the one meant for her, he was confident and strong-willed, he knew what he wanted in life, and he went after what he wanted in life. He was brave, and he would provide for her always. Sarah would be happiest with him. Shane was wonderful and the best friend she could ask for, but there was something missing with Shane, he wasn't her lover. Shane was her friend.

"Mama says come to breakfast, Sarah," Eddie said beyond the door, and she could hear him hopping from one foot to the other excited for her to come out.

Come Save Someone Like Me

"Let me get dressed sweetie, and I'll be right there. Maybe we can take a walk later this morning," she called through the door and heard him hopping even more. If only everyone were as happy and as easy to please as Eddie, the world would be a better place.

The first Sunday in March, the good Reverend Farmer joined in holy matrimony Ellen Cartledge and the Deputy Sheriff, Clayton Nichols. Sarah, dressed in a light blue dress, and wearing a beautiful straw hat on her head, stood by her sister holding flowers, she kept glancing back at Shaun knowing they would be next to marry. Her parents still wanted them to wait until June, but now that it was March, the month of June didn't seem so far away.

Everyone laughed when Eddie bounced down the church aisles when the Reverend told Clayton he could kiss the bride and Eddie kissed the bride; his sister, and then Eddie kissed Clayton. Sarah saw how furious Clayton was and heard him tell Ellen that he would see that dummy locked away for good and all in the tool shed someday. Sarah had gasped at these horrible words seeing her sister Ellen's face, and she knew that Ellen agreed with Clayton. The newly wedded couple wanted Eddie locked away.

Sarah hadn't known. She hadn't had one clue that Ellen was ashamed of Eddie and embarrassed by their brother until right now. Hot tears burned her eyes with the reality of how cruel her sister was. As she blinked hard, an expression of gratitude came upon her face when she saw Shane, who had been sitting in the third row of the church, hurrying to come forward and take a gentle hold of Eddie's hand encouraging Eddie to come sit with him. Eddie, always close to Shane and Shaun, and because he was close to them, went agreeably with Sarah's fiancée's brother, doing as Shane wanted.

"Everyone loves our Eddie," Ester Cartledge said of her son and smiled after the services were over totally unaware that her own daughter Ellen wanted Eddie locked away. "I'm so grateful he's loved here, he's a very special man." Sarah heard her mother saying, and she knew that she could hate Ellen for not seeing what a blessing their brother was to their family.

"He certainly is a sweetheart," Alicia Blackburn said watching her three daughters run after Eddie and making him laugh in the churchyard. Alicia thought of how Allen had almost drowned saving Eddie from the river years ago, since that event a special bond had been formed between the families. Allen felt like Eddie was one of their own and he told the Cartledge children to always refer to him as their Uncle. Ester and Thomas Cartledge knew that Allen was Eddie's savior and they adored the man for saving their only son. Even if Eddie was left harmed by the river that day, he was alive and happy and bringing joy to his family. "He's such a happy person. He makes us all smile," Alicia said of Eddie and laughed as he turned and waved to his Mama.

Eddie wasn't just happy, Alicia Blackburn thought. Eddie was beautiful. His light brown hair fell over his forehead, his fair face always appeared childlike with deep dimples in each cheek as he smiled, and he had light blue eyes that always held a happiness that only Eddie would know. It was a shame the river had damaged him that day. No matter what, Alicia held true to her feelings for the young man, Eddie was one of their own, and they would all protect him always and care for him. Allen wouldn't let anything bad happen to him.

Alicia looked at Clayton Nichols and made a vow that the Sheriff Deputy would never lock up Eddie and the reason she knew the Deputy wanted Eddie locked away was because Clayton had come out to Riverbend to talk to Allen about Eddie a week ago. The disgusting Deputy believed that Allen would support him in forcing Eddie's parents to either lock Eddie in the tool shed or send Eddie away to a place where they hide people like Eddie. Allen had remembered what Deputy Nichols had said of all Blackburns being hell on an ax handle in that moment, and Alicia had watched in supportive shock as her husband went outside and grabbed the ax he used to chop firewood and come back into the house telling the Deputy "no body, no crime." The Deputy had acted confused for all of a minute when Allen looked at him and assured him that he was hell on an ax handle and when he was done the Deputy would be in one inches pieces. "Nobody, no crime," Allen spoke in the way of an attorney.

Alicia looked at her husband now standing in the churchyard, and she pinched her lips to keep from smiling in her memory of last week and his behavior. He had taken that ax and shoved it in the deputy's face and told the Deputy that if anything ever happened to Eddie, he would make that Deputy sorry he ever heard the Blackburn name. Allen had then raised the ax, and the Deputy ran to the door, the ax beat Deputy Nichols to the door as Allen threw it and it lodged in the heavy wood.

"You stay away from Eddie," Allen had growled as the Deputy hurried out the house. Then her loving husband, red in the face, turned back to her and said he was sorry that she had to see what she had seen seconds before he called the Deputy a very ugly word, which he apologized for that to his wife as well. Allen may be hell on an ax handle, Alicia thought now as he winked at her, but he also had very good manners.

"I just worry about what will happen to him when I'm passed over," Ester said watching her beautiful son bounce around to all the families and get hugs.

"When Sarah and Shaun marry, that'll make Eddie a Blackburn by marriage," Allen said as he walked up to his wife and Ester hearing what Ester was saying to Alicia. "And we Blackburn's are known for taking care of our own. Nothing bad will happen to Eddie, he'll be a Blackburn." Ester looked at Allen with gratitude. "Besides, Ester," he leaned in close to her. "Haven't you heard? We Blackburn's are hell on an ax handle."

"That's what Clayton said about you," Ester touched Allen's hand. "We all know you Blackburns take care of one another."

"We sure do, Ester." Allen looked at Clayton and saw the younger man look back at him, but only for a moment. "Clayton knows better than anyone what I'm capable of doing with an ax." Allen looked back down at Ester with tender care in his eyes. "If your family ever needs anything, we're here for you." He hugged his wife who was looking up at him with trusting eyes.

They had their own rocky start years ago. Allen thought of the beginning of his marriage to Alicia. Everything had been hard for them. He had almost lost her. But they had gotten through that time, and their marriage was strong. Their marriage was on solid grown and as sturdy as cast iron. There was no way that Shaun and Sarah would suffer as Alicia and Allen had, and of that fact, Allen was relieved. Things were different for the young couple, he thought, and he saw Shaun pulling Sarah into the woods, Sarah's soft laughter easily heard before she disappeared in the trees with his nephew. Allen was more than certain that the young couple would never know the pain that he and his Alicia had known, and for that, he was thankful.

"Where are we going?" Sarah asked out of breath as Shaun pulled her along behind himself running down to the river where he and Shane had built their house. "I think Eddie is following us," she said with a laugh as they jumped up onto the front porch of the house known as Twin River.

"He's not following us, Sarah. Shane was taking him to show him the new colt, and you know how Shane loves being with Eddie. Plus Dad has Shane going to look at the new trees we planted out in the east pasture, and he'll take Eddie for sure when he goes. So we are all alone." Shaun pulled Sarah into the house and showed her around.

"You boys have done a lot of work on this place," she said turning around seeing that wallpaper had been hung in the dining room, and the walls in the kitchen painted since the last time she had been here. The floors were stained a light color and shining with a heavy coat of wax. The furniture that she had helped pick out and order had been delivered and was in place in each room. "I'm so blessed to be coming to live here." She looked up at Shaun, and he smiled down into her eyes. "Thank you."

"I'm the one that is blessed, and thank you," Shaun spoke in a deep voice filled with passion before lifting Sarah up into his arms. "I want you," he said as he carried her into his bedroom and laid her on the bed. "I need you, Sarah. Please."

"No, Shaun, we mustn't. We're not married." Sarah tried to move to the far side of the bed, but he caught her in his arms and looked down into her eyes.

"We're just going to kiss," he pleaded with her, feeling her relax and knowing that he didn't want to frighten her. "Just kiss me, nothing more, I promise." He saw her give in to him and become still on his bed. "I ache for you," he confessed to her as he came over her and began to kiss her mouth very gently at first and with an ease of familiarity as he often kissed Sarah.

Sarah might not want this, she might want to keep herself pure for their wedding night, but with the soft bed beneath her, Shaun above her, and him kissing the very breath from her lungs, she knew that she was helpless to stop whatever might happen. And Sarah loved Shaun. She desired him as much, if not more than he desired her. Soon, very soon, they were going to be married.

"Oh my God," he breathed in a prayer like fashion as he kissed her neck and fondled her breasts, "you're so soft, Sarah." He undid the buttons of her dress and kissed her neck and lower.

"Shaun, do you know what you're doing?" she asked him seeing his head nod.

"I read a book, with pictures," he confessed, and she knew he was as innocent as she was.

"What kind of book was that?" she asked and sucked in her breath as he covered her ear with his mouth and plunged his tongue there. "Where did you get this book?" she asked trying to catch her breath as he was seducing her.

"Found it," he said. "I met a man in Tallahassee, and he was selling books out of a bag at the train station. And none of this matters Sarah other than I learned from the book. I want to try some of what the book taught me with you. On our wedding night, we'll read the book together." He saw Sarah's head nod before his mouth covered her mouth again kissing her in a way she had never been kissed by him before.

"This is all right to do, Shaun? Before we marry?" Shaun lifted himself up and over her and undid all the buttons on the front of her dress.

"Sarah, we aren't doing what makes us man and wife right now, we're just kissing," he bared both of her small breasts, and she gasped that he had done so without her knowing. "You're so beautiful," he spoke on a sigh as he looked at her breast, his hand touching first one and then the other. If she had thought to protest with her lover, the protest died on her lips as his mouth covered one of her breasts and he made her not able to think.

"Shaun, I can't breathe," Sarah gasped as he moved to the other breast, his tongue touching her breast in a teasing way making her want more. "Shaun, you're killing me," she pleaded as his leg went between her legs and he pushed upward while she pushed downward.

"I don't know if I can wait until our wedding night," Shaun was gasping as he rubbed Sarah with his knee as he had read in the book to do, and then she was crying out his name and falling back onto the bed shaking all over, and he was relieved he had made her happy.

"What did you do to me?" Sarah's voice broke, and she started to cry, Shaun hadn't expected her to react like this.

"I hurt you?" he begged to know, and he saw her head shake from side to side. "What's wrong, Sarah?" He rolled over onto his back and pulled her with him.

"I don't want you to think badly of me for the way I behaved," she cried and laid her head on his chest.

"Dear God, Sarah," he held her tightly in his arms. "I could never think badly of you, and you just made me the happiest man alive." He felt her pull free of him and lift up and look down into his beautiful eyes with wonder on her face clear for him to see.

"How did I make you the happiest man alive?" She was so sweet, so innocent, so open, and so honest, everything about her, Shaun knew he adored.

"Sarah, it's important to a man that he pleases a woman in their bed. I know it sounds stupid, but I don't have any experience, and I've worried a lot that I'd not be able to make you feel like a woman feels when she's with her man in bed. You just felt something nice with me, didn't you?" He saw her head nod, and he sighed in relief. "I love you, Sarah. I want to make love to you, and you to be happy while I do so." He rolled her back onto her back and lowered his head to her breast again. Sarah's hand came up and held the back of his head to her breast. She wanted more of what he was doing to her. She didn't want this that he was making her feel come to an end.

"That feels so good Shaun," she gasped as he moved to the other breast, her eyes closed as he made his love to her and she ached all over, for what she ached, she didn't know.

"I need to touch you," Shaun said, and he saw her head nod giving him permission in her innocent trust of him, a trust that Shaun knew that he would never betray.

With gentle care, Shaun slipped his hand up under her skirt and found where he knew he was supposed to touch her and he heard her cry out. If he didn't stop, he knew he would do now what they were supposed to wait for the wedding night to do.

"Shaun," Sarah cried out his name as he touched her and he had to fight to not go further when all he wanted to do was to go further.

"I can't wait, Sarah," he lifted her skirt and felt her tense up. "I'll stop if you want me to," he almost cried not wanting to stop.

"I can't wait either." Sarah was gasping for breath as he came up over her and started removing her clothes, she saw he also removed his own clothes, and she was amazed at how he had done this, undressed them both in only a few moments. "I don't know what is going to happen," she cried out seeing his nude body in the light of day that was coming in through the window. "And you're so beautiful." She went very still looking at him while he came back between her legs. "I don't know what's going to happen," she cried out again, and he lowered his head to her breast causing her to relax against him again as he reached down and joined their bodies together.

Shaun moved gently and slowly seeing the pain on Sarah's face. He couldn't hurt her, so he became very still above her. "I love you," he said and hoped she would open her eyes and look at him. She didn't. Still holding still inside of her, he kissed her eyes, her cheeks and then plunged his tongue into her mouth feeling her become less tense when he did so. Then he moved to her breast still not moving within her but wanting to move so badly that he ached all over in the worst way he had ever known. The more he touched her, the more relaxed she became, and he knew, soon he would make her his in every way.

"Shaun," she cried his name when he moved and again he stopped holding deathly still above her when all he wanted to do was move inside of her.

"Am I hurting you, Sarah?" he saw her shake her head and felt her lift her hips and come up to him. "Don't do that," he pleaded, and she held still again. "Yes, do that Sarah," he said, and she moved upward again, and he arched his back. "I have to pull out of you," he did so, and she wondered why. "The book says if you stay in a woman that you'll make her become with child," Shaun said as he found his release lying next to her on the bed. "I want a lot of babies with you Sarah, but not until after we're married." He saw her nodding her head, and then he heard her crying.

"We shouldn't have done this Shaun, it was for our wedding night." He cradled her in his arms and kissed her head.

"As far as I'm concerned, today was our wedding day. Sarah, you've always been mine, we were meant to be together all our lives. This joining we did today just made our love more solid. I love you. I want to marry you now. I don't want to wait. I've waited too long for you already." He sat up and grabbed for his clothes throwing her clothes at her. "Get dressed," he ordered, and Sarah moved quickly to pull on her clothes.

"What's wrong Shaun?" he grabbed her hand and pulled her from the house.

"Nothing is wrong, Sarah. We're going to Woodville right now." Sarah let him pull her into his barn and watched him saddle his horse.

"What's in Woodville?" Sarah asked of the town that was only about six miles away from where they were.

"The justice of the peace. You and I are going to get married today, and we won't tell anyone. We can have days and nights in secret here until after June and then we'll have Reverend Farmer marry us. But you're mine, and I'm going to make you mine today. No more waiting." Sarah gasped as he lifted her onto his horse.

"My hair, Shaun, it's a mess." Sarah fussed with her hair while Shaun mounted the horse. He pulled the last of the pins from her hair, and it fell free down her back.

"I love your hair, Sarah; it's like a cloudless twilight sky." He kicked his horse hard and started down the road. "We need Shane," he said and looked down the road for his brother. "But he has Eddie with him," he breathed, and then he saw Eddie in the distance running toward Rockhaven. "Looks like Eddie is going home, let's go find Shane." Sarah held on to his arm wrapped around her waist as he turned the horse to find his brother.

"I see him," Sarah pointed into the near distance, and Shane, having seen them turned his horse to gallop toward them.

"What's wrong," Shane asked seeing Sarah's hair down and his brother looking flushed.

"I need you brother," Shaun said and turned his horse knowing Shane would fall in riding fast beside him.

"Talk to me Shaun," Shane demanded and looked at Sarah looking pale and almost frightened.

"We're eloping," Sarah said in a weak voice. "We have to Shane," she caught his eye, and knew he understood her meaning.

"We're in love and can't wait any longer," Shaun said firmly holding his Sarah close.

"I understand," Shane said knowing his brother didn't see how jealous and hurt he was, he hid his pain well, and he wanted to. Shane never wanted Shaun to know how much he wanted Sarah for himself. Shane then looked at Sarah and seeing the look she gave to him, he knew she knew his feelings. He wasn't hiding anything from her.

"I can't get married without you beside me Shane," Shaun said openly knowing they were making good time, they would reach Woodville in a few hours.

"Actually," Shane pulled in his horse to a stop just outside the smaller city of Rockhaven, "Reverend Farmer is still in town. He didn't leave after Ellen's wedding today. The Reverend said he was going to spend a few days out here resting before he went home." Shaun smiled, this was the best news of the year, he thought. "We can circle around behind the church and go in the back way," Shane was being supportive and helpful, and Sarah smiled in relief, her smile was just for him.

"You're so good to us, Shane," she said softly and felt Shaun guide his horse beside Shane's horse to the back of the church.

"Now if only the Reverend will marry us," she said in a softer voice.

"He will," Shane said firmly and watched his brother dismount his horse and reach for Sarah. "I'll go see if he's inside, if he's not, I'll go hunt him down," Shane went up the back steps of the church and disappeared inside while Sarah finger brushed her long hair.

"Brother Blackburn," the Reverend Farmer said as he came to Shane standing in the doorway of his church. He didn't call him Shane as he wasn't sure if this were Shane or Shaun. "How can I help you today?"

Shane glanced back at the open door, and he saw his brother helping Sarah pull her hair into a braid. "It's good to see you Reverend. It's Shane, by the way. We need a favor," he looked back again at his twin brother standing with Sarah. "We need you to marry Shaun and Sarah today, sir. Private, please." Shane saw the look on the Reverend's face and nodded his head. "Sir, it's vital that they are married today," he cocked his head back to the door where his brother and Sarah were standing, and the Reverend saw Sarah's hair down, the front buttons on her dress done up wrong and the old gentleman knew what needed to be done.

"You know I don't approve of elopement," he said firmly while looking at the young couple and then to Shane. "Unless the situation is warranted?" he said this as a question and saw Sarah blush and Shaun nod his head.

"We'll marry now," Shaun said in a low voice, "and only the people here right now need to know. And then in June, when we're scheduled to get married, we'll marry again." He saw the Reverend Farmer pull out his bible and move to the front of the church.

"I understand," the Reverend said and looked at both Shane and Shaun. "I married your Uncle Allen and your Aunt Alicia twice. Maybe this is something that runs in the family."

"I didn't know that," Shane and Shaun said at the same time.

"Oh yes. Your Uncle and Aunt didn't marry with the ease of most young couples. In fact, their first attempt at marriage was awful. Do not follow their path," the Reverend said firmly to the couple before him. "Work at being happy, work at communicating, and never miss church."

"We won't," Sarah said very seriously looking at Shane, then Shaun, and then back at the Reverend. "None of us will miss church ever."

"Then let's get you two married," the Reverend Farmer smiled and began the vows seeing Sarah holding Shaun's hand and looking up at Shaun. The Reverend saw Shane next to Sarah, and Shane's hand was in Sarah's other hand. And then he saw Shane holding Shaun's hand and that they made a circle and the Reverend felt like he was joining the three of them in marriage. They were certainly a family, and he hoped they would always be happy.

Chapter Two

"We can't tell mama," Sarah said to Shaun as she climbed out of her bedroom window and into his arms.

"She'll never find out we're married until we are married in June," Shaun assured his sweet wife as he helped her onto his horse. The moon was high, and he knew it would guide him home. Shane was with their Uncle Heath waiting on a new colt to come in the night. Shaun knew that he and Sarah had their house to themselves.

"I'm afraid Shaun. Will we do what we did the last time?" "

"You said I didn't hurt," his voice shook as he spoke and he felt her lean into him.

"No, you didn't hurt me. I'm just afraid because this is all so new." She felt his hand come up and cup her breast.

"I finished reading the whole book, Sarah. I feel confident I know what I'm doing." Shaun smiled as he kissed the back of Sarah's neck.

"I haven't read this book," she gave a nervous laugh and felt his mouth cover her ear before she gasped and leaned back into his arms.

"I'll teach you everything I learned from the book, Sarah." They had reached his house, and he slid off his horse before reaching back for her. "Graze in the yard old Dixie," he patted his horse and swung Sarah up in his arms. "I love you, Sarah Blackburn," he said these words to her as he carried her up the steps and into the house laying her on the bed they had laid upon only the day before.

"I don't know what to do," Sarah almost cried as Shaun reached up and started unbuttoning her dress and helping her slide out of it and then yank his shirt off and then his pants.

"I know what to do," he said confidently as she laid still while he used his mouth to make her ache all over and cry out his name.

Sarah never knew of anything like this. She was unprepared for what they were doing, but Shaun was right, he could teach her. He was making her body throb and ache all over for him. He came up over her, and in a half teasing very husky voice he said, "I told you I know what to do." She felt him come into her and she gasped, again he held still until she was no longer tense. "I can't get enough of you," he said as he looked down at his new wife, her twilight hair fanned out on his pillow, the moonlight falling on her soft white skin.

"I love you, Shaun," Sarah cried out, and he pulled her up toward him as he lost himself inside of his wife and she heard him say he loved her too over and over with each move he made within her.

"Shaun," Bethany breathed his name from his bedroom doorway seeing him and Sarah under the covers in the pre-dawn light.

"Sarah, I have to get you home." Shaun went to jump out of bed as his eyes slammed into Bethany's eyes, his little cousin's face a blood red. In a hard voice filled with shock and surprise, he ordered Bethany to turn around.

"We have to hurry. Mama can't find out," Sarah's voice held panic as she pulled on her clothes seeing Bethany in the doorway. "Don't tell Bethany, please don't tell," she begged her husband's cousin.

"I won't tell, Sarah," Bethany said in a reassuring voice.

"We're married," Shaun said seeing his brother Shane standing still in the hallway.

"Whatcha doing here Bethy?" Shane spoke while watching Sarah braid her hair and look at the covers which were a mess on the bed. "Oh boy, you both are caught," Shane said seriously.

"Bethany isn't going to tell," Shaun pulled on his shoes, "I'll have Sarah home before the sun is all the way up." He grabbed Sarah's hand and pulled her to the door searching the yard for his horse.

"Bethany is going to ride with me," Shane said. "She and Sarah can be out in front of the general store talking. Sarah's folks will think Bethany is there to shop early, and it'll appear as though Sarah just came out to visit with our little cousin."

"I didn't know you were so sneaky," Shaun said to his brother as he found his horse roaming the yard and lifted Sarah into the saddle, and watched Shane lift Bethany onto a horse.

"Well, after we do this," Bethany said holding on to Shane as he kicked his horse, "I need you two to come with me to my house. Ethan and his family are arriving today to talk to Daddy and Uncle Seth about the timber and the sawmill. Ethan is going to ask Daddy about courting me."

"You're only fifteen years old," Shaun said and looked at his very beautiful younger cousin.

"You're only twenty-one," Bethany shot back at Shaun.

"Let's just meet this Ethan fellow before anyone decides anything," Shane said seeing the store come into sight. "Bethy, how old is this Ethan anyway?"

"He's twenty-one," she said as though he were almost her age.

"An old man," Shaun teased her, and she smiled at him.

"Sarah," Shane called her name before they reached the store, "are you all right?" She looked small, and pale, and worried.

"I don't like sneaking around on Mama," she started to cry. "I feel evil and wrong, and bad." She leaned back into her husband and felt him hold her tight.

"I guess your Ethan won't be the center of attention at Riverbend today, Bethany," Shaun said as he dismounted his horse and reached up for Sarah. "No use in being sneaky now Shane, my wife isn't dishonest, and I won't make her so. Come on with me while I face her folks." Sarah gasped and felt Shaun's arm go around. "You'll be fine Sarah. I won't let anything hurt you ever." Shaun stood by his brother Shane with his wife on the other side of him, Bethany stood next to Shane as they entered the store.

"Mr. Cartledge," Shaun went to Sarah's father, and the man looked at the group that came into his store. "I made Sarah elope with me this past week, and I need to be honest with you about that now because my wife is not happy about keeping this from her parents." Shaun saw the smile start and then spread on Thomas Cartledge's face as Thomas's wife, Ester peeked out from the back room where she was stocking shelves and Shaun her sweet face.

"Well, I feel a sight better," Ester Cartledge said, "after seeing you two go into the back door of the church with him," she pointed to Shane, "we knew the June ninth wedding wasn't going to be needed. And the noise you made leaving here on your horse last night, well, we knew where our girl was and with whom." Ester was smiling now for her daughter. "You don't think the Reverend Farmer was able to keep this from us, do you?"

Sarah rushed to her mother and gave her a hug. "Mama, I was so worried you would be mad at me."

"Sarah, I've seen you mooning after those two," Ester waved her hand at Shaun and Shane, "since you were a little thing. I knew you were going to marry one of them someday. And I'm happy you're happy."

"You take good care of my daughter," Thomas Cartledge said in a firm voice to Shaun knowing that all the Blackburn men took the best of care of their women.

"We need to get to my house," Bethany said looking at her cousins and then Sarah.

"Let me change and put up my hair, and I'll come with you," Sarah let go of her mother and turned to her husband.

"I won't leave without you, Sarah. Where I go, you go." His tender eyes held hers, and she knew she had chosen the right brother. She was deeply in love with Shaun.

"Where you go, I go," she said softly back to him before she turned and ran to her room.

"Bethy's here, Bethy's here," Eddie came bouncing into the room, and Bethany rushed to hug him. "You're so pretty," Eddie said and bounced around her even more.

"You're pretty too Eddie," Bethany said, and he hugged her again. "And we're cousins now. Your sister married Shaun."

"That makes us brothers," Shaun said as Eddie bounced around him smiling from ear to ear.

Pointing to Shane, Eddie laughed and said, "You're my brother too."

"I sure am," Shane said and then chased Eddie out into the yard hearing his laughter. Everyone just wanted to protect Eddie Cartledge, he was a sweet man, and now he was part of the Blackburn clan for real. Nothing bad would ever happen to him.

"Oh Bethany," Sarah breathed, "he's even more beautiful than a Blackburn," she spoke on looking at Ethan Tucker standing in the living room before the fireplace at Riverbend. The young man had a serious look on his handsome face, and he did not look up right away when Shane, Shaun, Sarah, and Bethany entered the room.

"Hello," Bethany said softly, and that was when Ethan Tucker looked up from the empty fireplace and turned toward Bethany. Within a few short seconds, the young man had moved across the room, and he had both of Bethany Blackburn's hands held in his own as he looked down into her eyes. "You look so different in this," she said touching his olive gray uniform. Ethan had all of her attention, and she knew that she had all of his.

"I told you I wasn't waiting for the draft," Ethan smiled down into Bethany's beautiful and unique eyes. "I'll be leaving for camp Leon in a week. I know I'll be gone a long time. When I get back, you'll be all grown up." Ethan was aware of the others around them, but he kept his eyes on Bethany. "You'll be more beautiful than you are now when I return from this war."

"Ethan," she spoke his name wishing that he never had to leave her. She might be young, but Bethany knew that this man was the only man that she would ever love. "I'm forgetting my manners." She looked away from him to her cousins. "These are the twins, Shane and Shaun, and Shaun just got married. This is his wife, Sarah." Ethan shook hands with the brothers before he bowed to Sarah.

"It's a pleasure to meet you," Ethan spoke in a certain voice before turning to Bethany again. "I believe all our parents are on the porch." And holding Bethany's hand, he led the way outside with the others following him.

"Shane, Shaun," Mary Blackburn said and stood to go to her sons, "do not get any ideas about joining this war," she said firmly looking at Ethan Tucker with a frown.

"Mother, Father," Shaun said seriously and saw his parents, Aunts, and Uncles turn to look at him. "Sarah and I eloped," he said simply, and within a moment Sarah was being hugged, and he was as well by all of the Blackburn family.

"No church wedding," Mary moaned, and her son Shane took her hand and pulled her close.

"Actually mother, the Reverend Farmer did marry them in the church." His mother sagged against him, she was aware that her Shane loved Sarah, and her heart broke that there weren't two Sarahs as there were two of her boys.

"Things would be bad had you both signed up to join the war. An elopement is a cause of joy," Seth said in an almost grateful tone that his boys were safe. He prayed that this war never came to their door.

"Where are my manners?" Alicia Blackburn asked and moved to Ethan's parents. "Levi and Cecily Tucker, this is our daughter Bethany, our two nephews Shane and Shaun, and Shaun's new wife, Sarah." Alicia reached and hugged Sarah again.

"I'm Shane, he's Shaun," Shane corrected his Aunt as she had called him by his brother's name.

"It doesn't matter," Alicia said with a laugh and a quick wave of her hand. "A rose by any other name would smell as sweet," she quoted Shakespeare.

Shaun looked at Cecily Tucker, Ethan's mother as he bowed toward her. She was almost as beautiful as his Aunt Alicia he thought as Cecily Tucker moved closer to her husband. Levi Tucker was, in fact, taller than any of the Blackburn men, and they all were at least six feet tall. Shaun saw the older man put an arm around Ethan's mother and he knew in that gesture that Ethan had been raised in a loving home.

Turning his attention to Ethan, Shaun felt right away that he liked the young man his cousin was sweet on. He could only be hopeful that his Uncle Allen and his Aunt Alicia would allow Bethany to write to the young soldier while he was away at war.

"I'd like to talk with you Ethan," Shaun said and left Sarah on the porch with Bethany. When they entered the house, they passed his Uncle Heath and Aunt Emily, and their daughter Heather, that family walking toward the front porch. "So, can you tell me about signing up for this war?"

"Shaun, you just got married. You can't leave Sarah to go off and fight in some war we're not even a part of yet," Shane said in a rough, harsh voice as he grabbed his brother's arm and looked him in the eye not seeing their cousin Heather had come up to him and whisper in a cruel voice to Shane

"Coward."

"Heather," Shaun pushed Shane aside and faced their beautiful cousin. "Go away," he ordered her, and he watched her leave the house with a scowl on his face before turning back to face his twin brother. "They're going to draft us, Shane," Shaun argued once Heather was out of the room. "They're going to make us go. If we join up first, maybe we'll have some say in what regiment we join."

"He's right," Ethan said firmly. "We're going into this war at a fast pace, best to join up now and get it over with – do our duty and come home to our women."

"What if you're killed and don't come home?" Shane demanded of his brother ignoring Ethan Tucker. "What about Sarah? She'll be all alone if we join." Shaun smiled and patted his worried brother's arm.

"I'll come home to my wife," he looked at Sarah beyond the doors. "Because my brother will keep me safe and see I get home well and sound." Shane and Shaun's eyes locked and held for a long moment. "We have to go, brother," Shaun said. "We have always been raised to help others. France is in trouble. All of Europe is in trouble. There are innocent women and children there dying every day because of some maniac. What if that were happening here at Riverbend? We'd fight to protect our home, and we'd fight to the death. I'm going to sign up, and when Ethan goes, I'm going with him."

"I know better than to argue with you," Shane said, and his shoulders slumped forward. "You're telling Mama. And you're right. I'd want someone fighting for my family if they were being threatened." Shaun patted his back, and the three men sat together for a long time discussing their future together and growing close.

"So we're partners now," Allen took Levi Tucker's hand and shook it firmly. "I'll keep your sawmill supplied with trees for years to come." Levi nodded his head and then shook Seth's hand to seal the deal. "I think our partnership is going to have a problem early on," Allen nodded to his daughter Bethany walking in the yard hand in hand with Ethan Tucker.

"I don't know what to tell you, Allen." Levi turned and looked at the young couple that was his son and Allen's daughter. "My wife and I had a similar situation. I knew at nineteen years of age that I loved her and I was going to wait for her to grow up. Cecily was only fourteen years old at the time. I waited for her. And then I had to wait longer for her to fall in love with me. She was worth that wait." Levi looked at his Cecily across the porch, and he saw her smile at him, and he nodded his head toward their son. "Like father, like son."

"I can see that you're accepting of this situation," Allen spoke while seeing the exchange between Levi and Cecily Tucker. "I think you would feel differently if it were your daughter that was fifteen and my son that was much older paying her court," Allen said seriously.

"Probably," Levi laughed, "since I have four daughters at home with my sister and her husband while I'm here with you, I can certainly empathize. That being said, what is it going to hurt for them to write while he's away at war? It's just letters. They'll probably lose interest in a week, and that'll be the end of that."

"Or he'll come home and elope with her like Shaun just did with Sarah," Alicia said seriously. "But you do make a point Mr. Tucker. If we keep those two young people apart, they'll find some way to be together. Best to allow them to write and we all watch over them closely." Alicia was embraced by her husband who felt she was smarter than him in this situation. Right now he had the urge to run into the yard, grab his daughter and lock her in her room until she was twenty-one.

"Alicia," Cecily Tucker came forward and took Alicia Blackburn's hand. "Our son is a good and honorable man. He won't take advantage of your daughter. He'd die to protect her." Levi was nodding his head in agreement.

"Well, he certainly has devoted parents," Alicia laughed and looked at Shaun holding Sarah's hand. That couple hadn't been married long, and she could see that Shaun was ready to take his bride home. "Why don't we go in and eat so Shaun can take Sarah to her new home?" Alicia opened the double doors leading to the dining room. "The Tuckers are staying here in our home," she said and gave her husband a pointed look which he understood completely.

"Shane!" Allen called out to his favored nephew. "Come here." The younger man hurried to his uncle and stood aside where they could talk privately. "You're staying the night here with that Ethan Tucker fellow and making sure he doesn't go near my daughter after dark." Shane nodded his head in understanding and smiling at his Uncle who he knew was being serious with him.

"Uncle Allen," Shane said in a low voice. "Might I speak with you away from the family for a few moments?"

"Alicia," Allen called to his wife, "we'll be back in a few minutes." His wife looked up at him as he moved with Shane back onto the porch alone. "What's the problem, son?" Allen asked seeing Shane looking back inside the house at his brother Shaun.

"Shaun doesn't want to wait to be drafted. He's going to sign up and leave with Ethan Tucker. And I'm going with them." Shane saw his Uncle look at him hard and long. "I'm worried about telling Mama and Daddy and Sarah."

Allen grabbed his nephew Shane in a hug knowing that he viewed the twins as his own sons. He loved the boys that much, and he always had. "I admire what you and your brother are doing," Allen said pulling away from Shane. "Shaun has always been headstrong and too much like me. He'll run into battle without one thought for his life. Keep him safe Shane, and yourself. I need you boys to take over this place for me one day. Hear me well Shane. It's on you to keep you and Shaun safe, you're the one with the level head on his shoulders."

"And we both know I'm not the hero type, Uncle Allen," Shane said in a serious voice. "I always look before I leap. You have my word that I'll watch out for Shaun. I'll bring him home safe, and myself too. We'll be all right with everyone here praying for us and loving us."

"When are you going to tell your parents?" Allen put his arm around Shane as they re-entered the dining room together.

"Tomorrow. Shaun says he wants a real wedding night with Sarah." Shane smiled and nodded to his brother keeping his voice low.

"I'm sorry Shane," Allen said before they sat down and joined the family. "I know you have feelings for Sarah." Shane looked at his Uncle with shocked eyes. "I keep things to myself Shane, and you know that son. I will always love and support you unconditionally. As I said, you and your brother are like my sons."

"We'll be home soon," Shane spoke softly where only Allen Blackburn could hear his words. His eyes met Sarah's eyes, and Shane knew in that glance that he would die to make certain Shaun came home to her.

A screech owl screamed long and loud as Shaun walked with his wife to the home they would call their own, Twin River. He held her hand and felt her come closer to him when the owl cried out, and he assured her it wasn't a panther or bobcat. "The crickets are sure loud this afternoon," he added as he hugged his new wife close feeling her soft in his arms, she belonged in his arms. "They won't sound so loud in the house. Shane and I put on the latest type of glass in the windows, and we made the walls twice as thick as we had planned. It's a good and sound house Sarah, one we can grow old together in." He heard the birds out in the trees near the river calling out, and he felt peaceful inside.

"That's what I want, Shaun," Sarah hugged him closer, "to grow old with you. I want to sit out on our front porch and watch the river flow by and shell peas with our babies at my feet and the company of all the water birds and the crickets with me." She felt Shaun stop walking and pull her into his arms.

"I just want to thank you, Sarah. Thank you for marrying me. You're so beautiful. You could have had any man in the county, and you chose me." In the late afternoon, early evening light, he could only see the shadows cast on her face by the trees surrounding them, and he was glad, he was thankful to be alone with her.

"I only wanted you, Shaun. For as long as I can remember, I only wanted to be with you." She saw his head lower, and his lips cover her lips, the kiss was deep and filling, and she sighed as she leaned closer to him. "Can we go and do some more things from your book?" she pulled from him, and he laughed before taking her hand and pulling her quickly to the house.

"I finished reading the whole book," Shaun laughed, "and I was thinking of something it taught I'd try tonight." At the front door, he lifted her into his arms and carried her into the house. "Shane is staying at Uncle Allen's tonight with that fellow Ethan, so we have the whole place to ourselves."

Sarah watched Shaun turn on the overhead gas lamp, the light guiding her to the bed where she pulled back the covers and plumped up the pillows. "I don't have a nightgown," she said in a whisper, "all my clothes are at Mama and Daddy's house." She saw her new husband staring at her from across the bed. She noticed that he was breathing hard, and her own breath caught in her throat.

"I need to see you. You do not need a nightgown with me," Shaun said coming around the bed that was no longer his alone. "No clothes," he said and helped her slowly take off her dress, their eyes locked while her clothes fell into a heap onto the floor. "You're so beautiful," he touched her breast and heard her suck in a deep breath. "So small," he ran his hand down her body, and then both hands touching all of her. Shaun lowered his head and took her breast in his mouth; Sarah's arms went around his head and pulled him closer.

"Shaun," she breathed his name as he lifted her up into his arms before placing her onto the bed. "You're fully dressed," she said, and she heard him laugh, and she laughed too. With innocent hands she unbuttoned his shirt, her eyes locked with his. "Should we turn out the light?" She watched him push his shirt off of his shoulders.

"Oh no," he moved down to her breast again still wearing his trousers. "I want to see all of you," he touched her softness and felt her tense, and he looked back into her eyes. "Am I hurting you?" he pleaded to know, and she shook her head.

"It feels like I need more," she cried as he kept touching her.

"The book tells how to bring your wife to fulfillment," he said and looked away from her eyes going down her body and following the instructions he had read in a book that he was certain his mother would have forbidden he read. Right now, Shaun was happy that he had purchased that book. Because of that book, he knew how to make love to his wife.

Sarah was holding on to her husband's hair as he did what he knew he had to do. She was lifting up to him, and he heard her gasping for every breath that she took. Within minutes she was crying out his name and falling. It felt as though she was falling far and fast as he had made her feel the most wonderful feeling to ever consume her in this life.

"The book was right," Shaun came back up and over his wife before undoing his trousers and pushing them off, kicking them to the floor. "You liked what I just did. And now, I need you," he cried out as he came into his wife and felt her lift up for him. "We fit so well together," he pulled her closer and heard her moaning into his ear.

"I'm so glad you found that book," were the last words Sarah said to her husband before she fell asleep with him by her side.

As she knew that her whole family was coming to breakfast at Riverbend, Alicia had the long dining table set, the doors and windows open wide to let in the cool air, and the food prepared on the long sideboard against the dining room wall. Emily, her husband's sister, was the first to arrive with her husband Heath, and their daughter Heather. Heath was always up before the sun as he ran the whole farm and oversaw everything from the cattle to the planting of the fields and the trees.

Alicia saw Cecily Tucker come down the stairs with her son Ethan beside her and Bethany following behind them. Cecily offered to help Alicia and taking the linen napkins Alicia gave to her, she placed one at each place on the table seeing her husband Levi, was on the porch talking with Alicia's husband, Allen.

"Here comes Mama and Daddy," Shane said looking out the dining room window. "Everyone is here now except for Shaun and Sarah." Shane ruffled the hair of his two cousins, Julie and Jenny as they came by carrying platters of bacon and sausage, and ham. He grabbed a slice of bacon and both girls laughed at him. Shane knew that he was part of a loving family. And then he saw Heather looking at him, and he moved away from her while looking away from her stare.

"We won't wait for Shaun and Sarah," Seth said as he sat down at the table. "I'm sure they'll be late." Just as the father said this, his son Shaun appeared pulling Sarah behind him and laughing because he was so happily married to the girl that he had long wanted.

"We're here," Shaun said and sat down in the chair next to his cousin Heather pulling his wife down in the empty seat beside him. "Everything looks good, Aunt Alicia," he said with a smile and grabbed for the platter of eggs.

"Someone is starving to death," Alicia said giving her nephew a look before bowing her head, and he put the platter down.

"Sorry, Aunt Alicia, my stomach out thought my brain," Shaun said in his teasing manner knowing his aunt could never be angry at him or Shane. They were the spitting image of their Uncle Allen, and they knew Aunt Alicia looked at them and thought of her husband. "Want me to say grace?" he saw his Aunt nod her head and he looked around at everyone with their heads bowed. "Thank you Lord for this food we're about to receive and please; watch over my brother Shane, our new friend Ethan and I as we prepare to go off to war."

"What?" almost every person at the table spoke this one worded question as all eyes turned to Shaun.

"Shane and I talked it over yesterday," Shaun said in a lighthearted way not blind to the horror on his parents' faces even as he put bacon on his plate and reached for the sausage. "We can't let our new best friend Ethan go off to war and come home a hero by himself. And I need to go to protect my brother." Shaun grinned at Shane who, as the serious one, made no joke about joining the war.

"We'll be fine mother," Shane said looking across the table at his mother noting that she had never looked so frail and fragile before. "Shaun is right, he and I will take care of one another, and we'll come back home to you after the war. Signing up now is better than waiting on the draft. And the sooner we get there, the sooner this war will end, they need more men."

"Shaun," Sarah spoke quietly to her husband, and he looked down at her, "you're going to leave me?" he took her hand under the table and held her hand tight.

"Just for a little bit, sweetheart," he playfully kissed her nose. "I'll be home before you notice I'm gone. I need to do this. I need to serve my country. I won't be labeled a coward."

"Some might label you a fool," his Uncle Heath said without looking at him. The older man was staring at his plate not touching his food. "I'm proud of you boys," Heath continued. "But I'm afraid for you as well." Heath looked up and met Shaun's eyes.

"You twins have been all of ours, not just your mama and daddy's. And besides, with Michael away at school, you're the men we're depending on to take over for us older fellows someday soon," Heath looked at Allen and Seth. "You're both the Blackburn legacy." Everyone was quiet as Emily reached and took her husband's hand. Together they only had Heather, their second child had died at the age of two, and no other children had come to the couple. The boys meant the world to them both, and to everyone at the table.

"Heath has spoken for me," Allen said seriously. "I have these girls," he indicated Julie, Jenny, and Bethany. " I know they'll marry and carry on our family, but they probably won't stay on this river, and I know you boys will."

"We'll all stay on the river, Daddy," Bethany interrupted her father. She didn't like this conversation. She didn't like the thought of her cousins and Ethan going away to war.

"Even if you stay on the river, Bethany," her father looked into her beautiful aqua eyes, "which I doubt you will if you marry this young man," he nodded his head toward Ethan. "He has a sawmill in Madison County to run for his daddy, Our twins are the oldest. They've done well supporting us and worked hard here. They do a man's job every single day, and we depend on them. I've always been comfortable with the thought of dying. I know I'll leave you girls cared for by our twins." Allen turned and looked at Shane and Shaun equally. "Heath's right, you belong to all of us. Seth and Mary are your parents, but I think they've known you two were not just theirs." He turned and saw Mary looking pale and frightened. "Don't cry, Mary," Allen said firmly. "We'll pray these two home."

"I don't want you to leave," Sarah said again softly to Shaun, and he leaned into her.

"You can stay with my folks or with your folks while I'm gone. Time will pass quickly, sweetheart. Trust me. I'll come home to you safe and sound." He looked up at his mother and saw her looking at him and Sarah. "I promise Mama. Both Shane and I will be back soon." Mary nodded her head to her son, she trusted both of her boys, if they said they were going to do something; then they did that something. "Let's eat," Shaun smiled at everyone, "Aunt Alicia makes the best breakfast in three counties."

"Why didn't you tell me last night?" Sarah asked as she sat on the horse in front of her husband.

"Because it was really our wedding night Sarah, and I wanted you focused on me. Shane, Ethan, and I are going to Tallahassee in two days, and we'll get enlisted, and I might not be back. With us joining up, this war can't last too long. I'll write you as often as I can. And you write me," he said only now realizing that he was leaving behind something he wanted to take with him. "I'm going to miss you, more so now that I know what we can do together."

Sarah snuggled closer to her husband. "Is Shane coming home tonight?" she asked aware that it wasn't even noon yet.

"He'll stay again at Uncle Allen's, I already asked him too. You and I are going home. We'll see the family at breakfast tomorrow." He reached Twin River and got off the horse. "There is only one thing I'm going to do today," he said in a husky voice while lowering his wife to the ground in front of him, his mouth covering her mouth knowing he could make her want what he wanted with his kisses.

"You will come back to me, won't you Shaun?" Sarah leaned into him and held him tight. "I'm frightened," she almost cried, and he lifted her up into his arms and carried her into the house unaware that his brother Shane stood beside a tree near the edge of the river watching him carry his wife into the house.

"Don't worry, Shane will take care of me, you know that," Shaun said as he kicked the door to their home closed and spent the day making love to his wife.

Shane turned away from the tender scene of his brother carrying Sarah into their home, and he walked along the banks of the river toward Riverbend, his Uncle Allen's home. He bent and picked up a rock and then threw it into the river watching the rock bounce off the water several times.

"So, how long have you been in love with your brother's wife?" Ethan Tucker asked from a tree he was leaning against near to where Shane stood. Shane spun around and faced the younger man dressed in a marine uniform.

"I'm not in love with Sarah," he said seriously. "We've all been friends since we were little. I just wish I had what those two have," he nodded back to his house.

"I understand," Ethan said seriously. "You're related to some of the most beautiful women I've ever seen." Ethan bent and picked up two rocks handing one to Shane. "How in the world are you going to find a bride of your own to measure up to all these women?" Ethan laughed when he said this and threw his rock, Shane did as well, and he laughed harder when Shane's rock skipped four times and his only three.

"I hope we're going to be together since we're all joining at the same time and the same place and as marines," Shane said walking back toward Riverbend and seeing Bethany walking toward them.

"We will be," Ethan said and waved at Bethany. "I think when we get home from this war that I'll be related to you if I can get her Daddy to see. I'm the best man for her."

"Well," Shane saw Bethany bounce up to Ethan and give him a smile, "I'm going to think of you as family now. You'd like that wouldn't you Bethy?" he used his cousin's nickname, "me thinking of Ethan as another brother?"

"Yes," Bethany said seriously, "and that is really good to hear. You'll take care of Shaun and Ethan because that's what you do Shane. You take care of everyone that you love," she said these words with a smile. "Can you chaperone us, please? Mama and Daddy don't want us alone together?" Shane laughed and nodded his head to his little sweet cousin.

"It must be my day to watch lovers kiss," he teased. "I'll go sit down on the bank of the river, you two stick close by and kiss or talk doesn't matter to me which you do. Come get me when you're ready to go up to the house."

"Ethan," Bethany watched her tall kind cousin walk away, "I really need you to please watch out for my twins." Her eyes turned up to the handsome young man she was in love with, his eyes so crystal clear she felt like he could see inside of her, that he could read her mind. "Shane is level headed and calm, he thinks things through and won't give you any trouble. But Shaun, he's different. He goes into things head first, no thought, and he laughs while he does so. Shane will follow Shaun, and that'll put them both in danger." She saw Ethan nod his head before he took a gentle hold of both of her hands.

"Bethany, I'll do all I can to keep them both safe. And myself also, because all I want to do is come home to you. I want us to marry and start our lives together as soon as your Daddy agrees." Bethany allowed Ethan to pull her close after looking to be sure no one, including Shane sitting on the bank facing the river, was watching them. "May I kiss you?" he asked her in a gentle way, and she smiled up at him.

"Yes, but we have to get one thing clear first," she said with a twinkle in her eyes.

"And what's that darlin'?" he asked sounding older than he was.

"That when we marry, if we move to your Cherry Lake, we come back here to Riverbend for a week stay every other month. I don't think I can be away from Mama for too long." Ethan pulled her close, and before his mouth covered her mouth he spoke against her lips,

"I'll build us a house here too, Bethany," we can live half the year here and half the year at Cherry Lake. I'll even build a sawmill right on this river to harvest the trees here with. And that way, neither of us has to leave our body of water that is in our blood for too long. As your Daddy said to me this morning when I told him my plan," he was smiling down at her when she pulled away from him and gasped, "you're a part of this river, and that makes me a part of this river too."

"You spoke to Daddy?" she searched his face for affirmation and saw him slowly nod his head.

"He said we could become engaged, but it would be a long engagement, at least a year depending on how long I'm gone, it might be two years. I was going to ask you to marry me tonight, but I couldn't wait. So here we are, standing on the banks of your beloved Saint Marks River and me begging you to make me the happiest man alive by becoming my wife." Ethan saw her head nodding, and he moved quickly covering her mouth with his own and remembering that her Daddy had told him she was only fifteen years old and could change her mind. But Ethan prayed that her mind was set on him, he never wanted anything more than he wanted Bethany Blackburn. "Honestly Bethany, you are too young, and I know that too, but I know what love is, and I love you. You'll make me happy forever being my wife."

"Ethan, I'm not fickle. I'm like my Daddy, I make up my mind to something, and I don't change my mind. I'll wait for you, and I'm certain I love you too. Just come home to me. Please, come home to me, and I'll be waiting."

Shane looked back from the river and saw his new friend Ethan devouring his little cousin, and his little cousin was molded into Ethan like she was a part of the young man's uniform. "Good grief," he groaned as he stood up knowing his Aunt Alicia would skin his hide if she walked up on this scene.

Shane walked toward where Bethany and Ethan were standing together, and he saw them kissing, arms wrapped tightly around one another. He shook his head hard, ran a hand through his hair, and turned to walk away thinking that he didn't really care that much for his skin. He wished he could have that kind of love for himself. For a brief moment, Shane closed his eyes, and he thought of Sarah, and he knew that he never would know this sort of love. The only woman for him was Sarah, his brother's wife.

The sun was setting when Shaun got up out of bed and dressed and urged his wife to do the same. "We forgot to talk to your Mama and Daddy about my leaving for the war and where the best place for you is, Sarah. I can't leave you here at Twin River alone, it's close to Uncle Allen's house, but you can't stay out here by yourself. You either stay with my folks, or you stay with your own." He turned and saw Sarah sitting up in the bed, her knees pulled up to her chin and her hair down and around her body like a blanket.

"I'm going to stay at my parent's house, Shaun. Working in the store will help pass the time while you're gone." Sarah got up on her knees, and he came to her. She wrapped her arms around his neck and allowed him to lift her out of bed. "With Ellen and Clayton married, mama and daddy will need my help at the store and with Eddie. And I'll need to keep busy," she said softly as he kissed her again. "Don't let's waste time going to my house to talk. Let's stay here, stay here and you teach me more you learned from that old book you bought in Tallahassee."

"You sure worked hard to convince me not to leave this room," Shaun laughed and let his wife help him get out of his clothes that he had just put on. "What about something to eat?" he asked her as she pulled him back down into the bed.

"I'm only hungry for you," she said as he lay down on top of her. "Teach me to kiss you like you kiss me," she pleaded, and he smiled because that he could do.

"You use your whole mouth," he said softly, you cover the whole ear," and he did so breathing into her ear and making her shiver. "Then you plunge in your tongue," he did this, and she gasped as she always would when he kissed her this way. "Then you circle the outside and the inside," he did this to her, and she was lifting her body up toward his. "The book gives detailed instructions," he said as he moved down to her breast again.

"That's good Shaun," she said in a raspy voice, "but what about me? I want to do to you what you do to me." She saw him look up at her with a questioning look and she nodded her head.

"When I get back from the war, I'll teach you how to touch me. I promise. But now, I give to you, sweetheart." He joined himself to her and felt blessed that he had her, more blessed than he had felt in the past. She wanted him as much as he wanted her, no man could ask for more from his wife.

An hour later Shane knocked on the front door of his Twin River home. He didn't give Shaun and Sarah time to think of coming to the door as he came inside and called up the staircase. "It's just me Shaun," he called out. "Aunt Alicia and Mama fixed dinner for you both, and I'm leaving it in the kitchen. Mama says be at breakfast at Aunt Alicia's early tomorrow. She wants her family together before we leave to catch the train to Tallahassee."

The couple heard Shane in the kitchen and then the front door close and his footsteps fade away from the porch. "I have the best brother a man could ask for," Shaun said hugging his wife close. "And my family is feeding us tonight," he smiled and jumped from the bed. "Race you to the kitchen," he pulled on his trousers and threw Sarah her slip. "Hurry up slowpoke. I'm starving to death."

Chapter Three

"This house is too quiet," Shaun complained over breakfast seeing around him too many long faces. "We're just going off to war," he spoke in a teasing fashion and felt his father punch him in the shoulder.

"It's our last breakfast together for a long while," Seth said to his son without looking at Shane or Shaun. "This war has been going on for a while. And now that Russia is having its own revolution, troops from the United States were needed.

"Dad," Shaun spoke in a confident way. "As soon as we arrive in France, we'll take control, and this war will be over for Ethan, Shane, and I before it even begins."

"I hope your right son," Seth said this giving his son a worried glance. Shaun was wild, Seth knew that about the man that would always be his little boy. "Just be careful, Shaun. I know Shane will be with you to do the thinking. I just need you to be careful." Seth looked at his older brother, Allen knowing that all of his life, his brother had solved many of the family's problems. But this, this war his brother couldn't fix, and Seth was scared. He was scared for his children as any loving father would be. "Allen, Levi, and I are going to ride into town with you boys. We'll see you off at the train station in Woodville then we'll bring your horses home."

"I have to see Sarah's folks first," Shaun said and took his wife by the hand. "Y'all stop by the general store and pick me up."

"Wait," Seth called, and he and his wife Mary stood walking Shaun to the door.

"So much has happened so quickly, we've not had time to even talk," Mary said to Sarah. "Are you going to come and stay with us while Shaun is gone? We'd love to have you."

"I know Mama will need my help in the store, Aunt Mary," Sarah said, and Mary wrapped the younger woman in her arms.

"No, you mustn't call me Aunt Mary any longer," she laughed. "You're my daughter now. You have to call us Daddy and Mama too, or if you can't do that then Papa Seth and Mama Mary." She let Sarah go and saw the younger girl smiling.

"I've known you both all my life, it'll be easy calling you Mama and Daddy," Sarah said sweetly while Shaun held her hand.

"We'll watch over her for you while you're gone, son," Seth said before he grabbed a hold of his son that was always confident and secure and happy, and hugged Shaun close. "You be safe," the father ordered his son. "You're a lot like me with your humor, and you're more like your Uncle Allen in your strong will. I need you to come home and your brother as well. Don't let Shane get hurt."

"I give my word Dad," Shaun said as he bent to kiss his mother who was crying.

"Me as well, Dad," Shane said coming up to stand with his family. "I'll take good care of Shaun, and we'll be back in no time."

"I love you both so much," Mary cried, and her sons wrapped her in their arms. The Blackburns weren't just a family; they were a tapestry woven together. They all were incomplete without the other. One missing thread of the tapestry meant the tapestry had a hole, a hole that no other thread could fill.

"I'm going to Rockhaven with Shaun, Mama. Best to have only one farewell. And Ethan is on the porch kissing Bethany goodbye now, he's going with us to Rockhaven."

"What will we do without our boys?" Mary put her face in her hands and burst into tears, her husband Seth pulling her close in his arms.

"They'll be home soon Mary," Seth lied to his wife as these were the only words that he could think to say.

Shane went into the yard where he had three horses saddled, and he mounted up looking back at his family standing on the porch. "I'll see you in Rockhaven, Uncle Allen." He lifted his hand high and waved to his family. "I'll want breakfast when I get home from the war Aunt Alicia. And mama, you'll need to make your rolls that we all love so much."

"I'll be waiting on you, son!" Mary cried out to her sweet twin that was so like her.

Ethan was right, Shane thought. The Blackburn women were the most beautiful women in the world. And then he saw her, his cousin Heather and she was mouthing the word 'coward' and pointing at him. He shook his head at her. She had been this way toward him all their lives, and if he were honest, he would tell that he couldn't stand being around her. Every family has one member that's a difficult person, and Shane knew Heather was this family's difficult person. Poor Uncle Heath and Aunt Emily, their only child and she was so hate-filled. All Shane could think to do was pray for her and hope that she would change, if not for her sake, then for her Mother's sake.

Shaun helped Sarah onto his horse, mounted behind her, and turned the horse in the yard waving his hand and giving a loud yell as he galloped down the road. Bethany had walked with Ethan and watched him mount his own horse. He looked to his mama on the porch, and he smiled.

"I love you, Mama. Just in case I never told you, you're the best Mother a man could ever ask for." Bethany saw his mother cover her face at his words before she looked up at her lover.

"Promise me," she pleaded, and he touched her sweet face.

"I'll come home to you, darlin'. We'll build our homes, and I'll keep you warm every night of my life." He held her hand until Shane came to him and together the two men turned their horses, and like Shaun before them, they gave out a loud yell and galloped down the road.

"I can't believe we let this happen," Alicia said softly to her husband Allen as he pulled her close kissing the top of her head gently.

"They would have been drafted soon, Alicia. Going off like this is for the best. Hopefully, they'll receive better training." Allen looked at his eldest daughter standing in the yard looking heartbroken, her eyes still looking in the direction that young Ethan Tucker had disappeared.

"I wasn't talking about our twins going off to war," Alicia said looking up at her husband. "I was talking about our daughter being engaged."

"You were seventeen when I married you," Allen said gently. "She'll turn sixteen tomorrow Alicia. By the time that young man returns from war, she'll be seventeen. And I need to say this. She looks just like you. She's you made over outwardly. But our daughter is like me." He saw his wife nod her head. "She's determined, strong-willed, sometimes too serious, hardheaded," Alicia put her hand over her husband's mouth to silence him.

"And I love her for all those things and more," Alicia said and leaned into her husband. "You need to get your horse saddled. Seth and Levi are headed to the stable. Heath is going with you as well." Allen nodded his head and kissed his wife as he always did, as though it were the first time he had ever kissed her. "Right now, I'm glad we had all girls," she said as she clung to him, "no boys to send off to war."

"You're doing what, son?" Thomas Cartledge asked Shaun as he and Sarah went into the store and talked to Sarah's parents for a few moments. "I knew some of our boys would have to go to war, and a few have, but I just thought with Florida being so sparsely populated none of our local boys would have to go. You're needed at home. Shaun you just got married."

"I want to do my duty, Mr. Cartledge," Shaun said and saw the look of concern on his new mother-in-law's face. "I'll be all right Mrs. Cartledge. Shane will take care of me," Shaun assured her, and she came and gave him a hug.

"Both of you boys have grown up underfoot," Ester Cartledge said. "Just come home, any way you can. We'll keep Sarah with us until you get back."

"Thank you, Mrs. Cartledge," Shaun looked at his new mother-in-law. "Sarah can't stay out at Twin River alone. The house is finished and nicely done, but the nearest house is Uncle Allen's, and it's a twenty-minute walk." Both of Sarah's parents were shaking their heads and agreeing she couldn't stay there alone when Eddie bounced into the room and hugged Shaun.

"I saw Shane in the yard," he smiled in his very innocent way, "Can I come with you?" His mother grabbed a hold of him and pulled him to her while Shaun answered.

"Not this time, buddy. You take care of my wife while I'm gone," Shaun looked at Sarah who was sobbing silently across the room.

"I will, Shaun. And she'll take care of me." Eddie went to his sister and took her hand. "Let's go watch them leave, Sarah. The yard is full of Blackburns," he said, and Sarah went with him into the yard to see Allen, Seth, Levi Tucker, and Heath Ferrell had joined Ethan and Shane. This is really happening she thought, her new husband was leaving her, and she had no idea if or when he would be back.

"I have to go," Shaun said, and he kissed her long and hard one last time. "Thank you for the last week, Sarah, I'll live on the memories of our lovemaking until I get home to you," he whispered into her ear. "Know I'll be dreaming of you always."

"Shane," Sarah cried her brother-in-law's name and saw him turn his horse and come near to her and his brother. "Shane, bring my husband home to me safe, please. I need him, Shane. Please, please bring him home to me. Don't let anything bad happen to him." Shane looked down at Sarah, she was so beautiful, those clear blue eyes so shockingly blue were staring up at him with pain, and with fear, and he knew he would do anything for her, promise her anything to give her peace. He had loved her all of his life.

"I'll bring him home to you, Sarah. I promise," Shane said seriously, and he felt Sarah kiss his hand.

"God bless and keep you both," she sobbed, and looking at Ethan she asked God to bless him too.

"And I'll bring Shane home safe too," Shaun said meeting his wife's eyes one last time. "We'll all take care of one another. Pray for us. Pray every day."

This is happening, Sarah thought to herself again as she watched her husband ride away with the men in his family. They were married, they were happy, and she was now alone, and there was no idea how long she would be alone. Then she turned, and she saw her mother crying, and she knew that she wasn't the only one feeling cold and empty right now. Everyone around her was feeling that way. The twins were a large part of this community. They really breathed life into the community. Things would be empty without them. Sarah would be empty without her Shaun.

She saw him look back and she ran toward him, her hand raised in a wave, tears covering her face and she yelled as loud as she could, "I love you, Shaun Blackburn, I love you." She had to stop running, and she grabbed a hold of a tree to steady herself as she sobbed and heard thin in the air his reply,

"I love you always Sarah! Always Sarah!" And she knew, she would live on those words until he returned home to her.

July 1917
Marine Corps Base Quantico, Virginia

Ethan, Shaun, and Shane became a part of the Sixth Marines, an infantry regiment that was with the American Expeditionary Force. They were preparing to leave for France with Shane the only one not prepared to go and become a part of the Great War. Shane just wanted the war to be over with so that he could go home. He missed the river, he missed the sounds on the river, and he missed his loving family, the peaceful life that he was used to living. Shaun and Ethan wanted to go into this war, There plan was to make the United States and other countries safe from a destructive enemy, and they encouraged Shane to become strong in the training alongside of them, and he did become strong with his urge to go home stronger.

"I heard a rumor going around camp that we're the smartest bunch of men in the military," Ethan said with a laugh to his friends Shane and Shaun.

"If I were smart, I would have stayed home with Sarah," Shaun tried to laugh, though he found no humor in his words as they were true. He was missing his Sarah more than he had ever imagined he would. And Shaun was worried that this war wasn't going to end soon as every moment away from Sarah was beginning to feel like a million years instead of a brief moment. The training for battle that they had to do was daily exercise with long hours that seemed to be endless. His uniform made him miserable, the wool causing him to break out in a rash and itch in the worst way. Being from the south, the three men were not used to wool material that was standard Army issue, and Shaun insisted to anyone willing to listen that he would never get used to these clothes he was made to wear.

"Word is more than sixty percent of the fellows here are college educated," Ethan said, and Shane gave him a look that said clearly what his mouth wasn't saying, and that was that he didn't care. "The commander is saying for us to write home now," Ethan continued. "We'll be leaving for France by the end of this week. I never dreamed I would ever see anything of the world beyond Florida, and look at me now, going to Europe."

"I would be happy just to be home in Florida," Shane said pulling out pencil and paper to write home to his mother and he saw Shaun had turned his back on him and Ethan to write home to Sarah.

"Dear Sarah," Shaun started his letter wishing he had better penmanship, but he knew Sarah would read his words no matter how he wrote. "We've been training here in Virginia for a while. The summers up here are as hot as they are down in Florida, though people up here don't call them the 'dog days' like we do at home. We're leaving for France soon. Word is, we'll have more training when we arrive there before we join the fighting. I don't know if I'll be able to send you letters from over there. I have no idea what the postal service from France to home is like. So what I'm going to do is write to you Sarah, and once I get back to you, then I'll give you all the letters, and we can read them together. If I'm able, I will post them to you, but don't worry if you don't hear from me. I just don't know what to expect in the near future.

"Sarah, I can honestly say I'm glad to be here with Shane and Ethan, Ethan had become a good friend, and Shane, well you know how we are together. But the truth be told Sarah, I'm sorry I joined up. I'd rather be home with you. Don't miss me too much. Stay as busy as you can. It might be a year before I get back to you. Tell Eddie I said hello and if you see the family, tell everyone I'll be home as fast as I can. Oh, and Ethan just came and told Shane and me that we're the smartest group of men going into battle with sixty percent of the men here college educated. I wish I had obtained a higher education sometimes. Maybe my writing would be better if I had, but then, maybe not.

"I love you, Sarah. I'll be home as fast as I can. Always you're loving husband, Shaun."

"I'm done," Ethan said with a smile. "And I don't have a twin that will write to my Mama while I write to Bethany like you two can do for one another. Let's go post these and then let's get some sleep; it's getting late."

"Listen to him giving orders," Shaun laughed and hurried to do like Ethan had said.

"That won't last long when he gets home. Bethany is really bossy. She'll have Ethan under her thumb just like she has Uncle Allen." Shane laughed, and he saw Ethan smile.

"When we're married, she can boss me all she wants, and I'll let her. She's a pretty little thing." Ethan saw her cousins nod their heads in agreement, and he wished this war was over now. He wished they were all headed home to Florida instead of off to France to join in a war that needed to end.

Early June 1918

Shaun marched next to his brother Shane and best friend Ethan aware that they were only fifty miles from Paris, France. It had taken them weeks to get here to this country. On the voyage over Shaun had been horribly seasick, something that he never dreamed would happen to him. And he had not just been a little seasick. He had struggled almost every minute of the day on the ship while Shane and Ethan seemed to have no problem with the waves and the rocking motion of the ship that he had. He had worked very hard to hide how sick he was from everyone as he didn't want to be viewed as weak. It wouldn't do for him, Shaun, the strong-willed and brave brother to be seen as weak in any way or to show weakness, but he feared his brother knew how hard the trip had been on him.

Once they had arrived in France they spent the late winter and early spring training with the French as they joined up with other Regiments preparing for battle. They finally entered the trenches near Verdun in March of 1918 and sadly experienced their first combat casualties. There were more than thirty-three men killed in the trenches and not by gunfire, but by poison gas. They had just spent weeks helping to strengthen the French lines near Chateau Thierry, and the battle there had changed Shane. He was nervous for the next battle, and he didn't want to kill anyone again. All three of them had to use their bayonets in the battle, and at times they were forced to use their fists and fight hard to survive. Shane just wanted to win the war and go home. Shaun was watching his brother closely knowing that Shane was trying to be brave and strong, but the battles were overwhelming for all three of them. They weren't in Florida anymore. They weren't safe on the Saint Mark's River fishing with their fathers. They were in danger and facing a threatening force that meant to destroy them.

Shaun closed his eyes, and he spoke a quick prayer as they were going into a place known as the Belleau Wood with orders to seize the town of Bouresches. They had to clear out the southern half of this area that they were in and they needed to do so quickly. Shaun felt that this battle was going to be bigger and last longer than any other battle they had been in. They were surrounded by more troops than he ever imagined he would see in one place, and the generals in charge were all working together. They were on the Western front, and word had come to them that the Eastern front had fallen to the Germans and that Russia was now having a civil war. If they lost here, the war would end with the Germans the victor. This battle they were fixing to engage in was going to be the battle that put an end to the war, Shaun thought as he kept looking at his brother who had changed so much in the past month. Ethan seemed stronger than ever. Ethan seemed to take the battles in stride. When they were in hand to hand combat, Ethan had plowed through like he was a tank and he told Shaun and Shane later that he was fighting for his country. He was patriotic to the core, and he was on a mission, a mission not to fail himself or their commanding officers.

Shaun had done what he was trained to do, what was good and right, and then when it was over and he had survived to tell about it, he sat and thought of his wife, of Sarah. He missed her more with each passing day. He hadn't seen her in more than a year, and he hadn't read a letter from her in months. There was no mail here. There was no way to send word home or to get word from home. He bowed his head as they marched onward and he knew, once they left the shores of the United States, they were gone from everything they had ever known. Their families may have well been on the moon. And now here he was ready to face the German soldiers in France again.

"This isn't going to be a little battle like we've been facing," Ethan said softly. "If I don't make it home boys, tell Bethany I never stopped loving her, and I'll see her again in heaven."

"You'll make it home," Shaun said firmly as he stared straight ahead.

"They're saying we're going to bed down for the night, boys," a soldier called out from the front of the line, and everyone seemed to relax.

"It'll be tomorrow before we see any fighting," Shaun said to Shane who was looking like Shaun had felt while on the ship over here – horribly sick to his stomach. "You all right, brother?" he asked, and he saw Shane nod before looking out over the wheat fields and the woods beyond.

"The wheat fields would be beautiful," Shane said looking across the golden world, "if there weren't Germans hiding there with machine guns and sharpshooters. And those woods," Shane nodded his head off to the thick trees. "Daddy and Uncle Allen would love the timber here. So would your Daddy, Ethan." Shaun agreed silently with his brother and glanced over at Ethan who was nodding his head as well. Looking at the woods made them all homesick, more than they had been.

Near dark, the men were told to bunk down in the fields, and the twins with their friend Ethan lay down together. "I can't eat," Shane said as he pulled out some of his hard bread and canteen of water. "I never wanted to go home so badly as I do right now in my whole life."

"We're going to clean out the Belleau Woods fellows. The Germans won't get to Paris without going through us," one of the officers that passed them was saying this loud for all the men to hear. "Sleep while you can. Tomorrow we enter hell, boys. And have your gas masks ready, word is the Germans have gassed another battalion."

Shaun pulled out what was left of his pencil; it was only a nub now. He saw Ethan writing, probably to Bethany and he knew their letters would never be mailed. Instead, Shaun was keeping his letters as though they were a journal he'd give one day soon to his wife.

"We had to dig our own trenches last week, sweetheart and mine was like a rabbit hole back home. I cannot tell you the things I've seen here, Sarah. This sure isn't our river banks back home. What I've seen here would make an alligator look friendly, and nothing I've seen here has been good. I don't know when you'll read this, if you'll ever read this, but I want you to know, our few days together has sustained me here in this horrible place. I've done things I won't ever get out of my head, and I'm afraid for Shane, he's not handling this well at all, he's withdrawn from Ethan and I. As for Ethan, he's the hero we expected him to be. He'll make Bethany a fine husband. He's made me a good and true friend."

The sun was setting, and the light was fading. Shaun put away his letter, and he laid back and tried to get comfortable hoping tomorrow's battle would end the war. He wanted to get home to Sarah. He wanted for his brother Shane to get home to their river.

"Whatcha thinking about Shane?" he asked when he turned and saw his brother's face. Shane was staring up at the night sky and looked almost peaceful for the first time in weeks.

"Of Sarah," Shane said softly, and Shaun set up looking down at his brother.

"My Sarah?" Shaun asked seeing Ethan had sat up along with several other men to hear the conversation.

"Yes," Shane said softly not looking at Shaun. "If you hadn't spoken up for her, I was going to court her," Shane confessed. "I've loved her since we were kids too." He turned his identical eyes onto his brother, and he blinked hard to see if Shaun was mad at him. He hoped in a way that Shaun was mad at him. Shane needed his brother to be mad at him. "I never told anyone," he said softly. "But I dream about her all the time."

"Well stop," Shaun said firmly and almost in anger. "She's my wife."

"Don't you think I know that Shaun? Don't you think I torment myself every day for loving my brother's wife?" Shane saw Ethan sitting up straighter.

"Fellows, this isn't a really good conversation to be having right before we go into battle," Ethan said. "Shane, you're not really in love with Sarah, you just admire her. Right?"

"I love her, and she knows I do," Shane said looking back up at the night sky not seeing his brother was beyond mad.

"Sarah knows you love her?" Shaun said, and Ethan grabbed his shoulders before he made a physical move on his brother.

"I told her I couldn't live at Twin River with you two, I know she knew why. I won't ever settle on any other girl, Shaun. You're married to the only girl I'll ever love."

"Stop saying that," Shaun ordered and Shane shook his head hard when he looked again at his brother with grief-stricken eyes.

"Now you see why I have to be the one that doesn't make it home, Shaun," he looked very serious, and his brother calmed down and went still. "You've always been the best of us two. You put me behind you in that last skirmish, but you won't tomorrow. Tomorrow I'm in front of you. You have to go home, Shaun. You have to go home to our Sarah, and the sad truth is, one of you Shaun, is worth ten of me."

"We're both going home Shane, so just shut up." Shaun realized Shane was only saying that he loved Sarah to make Shaun mad, to make Shaun hide behind Shane so Shaun wouldn't get hurt in tomorrow's battle. "We're all going home," Shaun said firmly to everyone around him. "We are going through this wheat field and into those woods, and we're going to make the Germans sorry they ever met a Marine. And then, we're getting back on those big boats, and we're going home."

"He's right," Ethan said, and several others agreed. "Let's get some rest boys, tomorrow we have a job to do, and then we're going the hell home."

Shaun lay back down and on his side looking at his brother Shane. Shane was the nice one, the calm one, the one that never did anything wrong, his best friend, his twin brother. "Shane," he said his brother's name, "I love you, brother," he said, and Shane turned his head to look at him. "I would lay down my life for you. You're more than my brother; you've always been my best friend. Without you, I'm only half the man I am when I'm with you. We're both going to survive this war, and we're both going home to Twin River and to Sarah and Mama and Dad."

Shane lifted his hand and reached for his brother's hand, and they clasped hands for a long few minutes. "I really do love Sarah," Shane said and then laughed. "I wasn't lying."

"Everyone loves Sarah," Shaun said and laughed as well.

"Go to sleep," Ethan said rolling on his side away from the twins. "Tomorrow is going to come on us quick. You two can talk on the way home to our girls."

"Any word Uncle Allen?" Sarah rushed to Allen Blackburn's side as he pulled his horse to a stop in front of the general store. Allen had been to Tallahassee, and he had heard the latest news. The latest news wasn't good. He looked down at his nephew's wife. He knew that she was afraid for his nephews as much as he was, probably more so since Shaun was her husband.

"Sarah," Allen said while getting off of his horse and putting his arm around her shoulders. She was as small as his wife and his daughter Bethany, he thought, and he felt he had to be protective of her as he could see that she was too fragile and anxious in wanting word from her husband.

"I'm sorry Uncle Allen. I'm just so worried I can't think straight. All I keep thinking of is news of the war?" She saw his head nod as he entered the general store with her beside him.

"I only want to tell this one time, Sarah so I'll tell here in the store where your folks can hear and spread the word." Allen saw Thomas and Ester Cartledge come to him along with several other men that were in the store, including Deputy Nichols. "The Eastern front has fallen," Allen said. "The Germans have won the Eastern front, and now Russia is at war with itself. The latest word is that the Germans are fifty miles away from Paris and bearing down fast. But," he looked at Sarah, "our Marines are bearing down on them as I tell you this. If our boys can take the Germans on the western front, this war is at an end. And yes, Sarah, Shaun, Shane and Ethan's regiment is there, near Paris fighting with the Germans as I tell you this."

"We need to pray for our boys hard, all of us," Ester said

"When will we know if they've won and kept Paris safe?" Thomas asked, and Allen shook his head wishing he had the answer to that question.

"No one can say, Tom. All we can do is wait. Battles like this can last hours, or they can last days. I did find out that our Shaun and Shane and Ethan are still alive, they've been in several battles. Some men in their regiment were gassed by the Germans and died, but our boys weren't among them. Why don't we all hold hands now and pray for our boys?" Allen reached out for Sarah and saw the small crowd all gather together and bow their heads.

"You pray Allen, you are better at praying in public than any of us," Thomas Cartledge said.

"Dear Father in Heaven, thank you for hearing our prayer. Please, Father, be with our boys in France as they go to war. Be with them all and guard and guide them. Bring our Shaun and Shane and Ethan home, Lord. This family needs them. In Christ's holy and loving name I pray."

"Thank you, Uncle Allen," Sarah said before she walked outside. Everyone in the store knew that Sarah needed to be alone and cry, and everyone understood. She was too young to be waiting for her husband in this way and not knowing if he was safe or not. And when the boys had left, no one really believed they would be gone longer than a couple of months. And now more than a year had passed since they had all been together having breakfast and no one had any idea when or if the boys would soon be home.

"Uncle Allen," Eddie bounced into the store and up to Allen Blackburn, the older man reaching out and hugging the man that was the sweetest man in town. "I found a snake down by the river, but I didn't touch it because Sarah said not to touch snakes."

"She's right Eddie. You need to listen to Sarah and do as she tells you to do at all time." Allen patted Eddie on the back and looked at Ester. "I have a new colt at my house. Mind if I take Eddie home and show him? Sarah can come too."

"Please, Mama," Eddie begged. "Please, let me see the new horse?" His mother laughed and nodded her head seeing the joy on her son's face, joy over seeing a new horse.

"Be sure to be home by dark and take care of your sister," his mother said and watched him bounce out the door to. "Thank you, Allen. Eddie loves running wild in these woods. He never goes near the edge of the river, close, but never near. He's afraid he'll fall in again." Allen nodded his head, he understood. When Eddie Cartledge had fallen in the river long ago as a little boy, and the river had almost kept him and Allen had to battle that river to get Eddie free. They both learned what the river could do that day, and Allen had a healthy respect for that river's current and he always would.

Sarah walked down the road with Shaun's uncle beside her watching her brother run ahead of them. "I know you're frightened Sarah," Allen said to her before they both laughed when Eddie jumped from one side of the road to the other side of the road in a playful way. "We're all worried." He stopped and looked down at Sarah seeing her stop and look up at him. "I really asked you to come home with me so you can visit with Bethany. I'm going to have to tell her where the boys are, and she's not going to handle it as well as you are. Bethany is too much like me; she wants to fix everything that's broken, and this war is something neither one of us is going to fix."

"I understand Uncle Allen," Sarah said as Riverbend came into view. "Let me tell Bethany."

"Thank you," he said simply. "While I show Eddie my new colt, why don't you tell Alicia as well," he laughed softly and smiled down at her.

"So that's why I got invited to your home," he reached an arm down and hugged her. Sarah hugged him back.

"Yes, I don't think I can handle both Alicia and Bethany when they hear of this major battle. And I have to tell Seth, Mary, Emily, and Heath." They reached the porch steps, and Allen saw his sister Emily at the door with Mary beside her, he wasn't expecting Mary to be at his home today.

"Any news?" Mary asked anxiously, and Sarah hurried up the steps to her mother-in-law.

"Go show Eddie that colt, Uncle Allen. I'll give the news." She smiled down at him and saw the relief on his face. Allen Blackburn was a strong, confident, and capable man. But he loved his boys, and Shane and Shaun were as much his as they were his brother Seth's. The worry for him of them being in harm's way was heavy on his shoulders. He wanted to go to France and bring them home to their river where they belonged. This war couldn't end soon enough. There shouldn't be wars, Allen thought as he turned seeing his brother Seth, and his brother-in-law Heath, standing at the stable door with Eddie, the three of them waiting on him, and two of them waiting to hear the news of the ongoing war.

June 6th, 1918
Belleau Wood, France

"Orders are we're going to take the woods boys," A man walked back to where all the troops were lined up. Shaun looked up at the night sky before he looked over at Ethan and his brother Shane and he wondered if they would live out the day. With only an hour away from dawn breaking Shaun wished there would be light before they made this attack, but he knew, this attack would be made in the darkest hour before dawn. "We're going through the wheat field boys, and the Germans have machine guns, do the best you can and put on your gas mask. This is it. We have to win this war."

A loud roar came up from the troops right before the gas masks went on and Shane looked at his brother Shaun stepping in front of Shaun. "Keep behind me. I was telling you the truth last night.

I love Sarah, I always have loved her and I always will." Shane needed Shaun to listen to him. He needed to protect his brother. He would say anything to make Shaun use him for cover and stay safe and go home to Sarah. Shane had promised Sarah that Shaun would come home safely to her. "If you die, I'll marry Sarah. I'll love her better than you ever would have." Without any warning to Shane, Shaun punched him in the face and watched him fall. A full minute passed before Shane got up from the ground and yelled at his brother. "Hate me you son of a bitch. You die. She's mine." Shaun went to punch him again, and Shane grabbed his brother and got into his face. "So stay behind me and live, or as God as my witness, I'll love your wife better than you ever could have! You're half the man I am Shaun because you're selfish. You'll never put Sarah first and I will!"

"Go to hell!" Shaun yelled at his brother. "You'll never touch my wife."

"You die here, she's mine," Shane spat these last words as he pulled on his gas mask and watched Shaun do the same. He had achieved what he knew he must achieve, Shane thought with confidence, Shaun would stay behind him. Shaun would be safe. Shaun would go home to Sarah. Tears welled up into his eyes, from the heat inside the mask or from the agony he was in at making his brother hate him, he wasn't sure which, but the tears burned and stung like fire, and he blinked hard to keep them away. Shane only knew that what he had done was the right thing to do. The only thing that he could do. Shaun was a hothead and always had been. Shaun would have protected Shane and died for him with no thought to Sarah. With the words he had just said to his brother, Shaun wouldn't protect Shane. Now Shane could protect Shaun as he had promised Sarah that he would.

Shane turned, and he ran into the field in front of his brother Shaun knowing that he was right where he needed to be. He heard someone yelling nearby, and he focused on the words being said keeping his identical twin brother behind him.

"Come on you sons of bitches!" A man yelled, and Shane saw Ethan run ahead of him, in that moment he knew that Ethan had to go home to Bethany. He somehow had to protect Ethan too.

Within a matter of seconds, things became unreal for Shane. The Germans did have machine guns, and it felt like everyone was being shot down. Shaun saw everyone falling around him, and he pushed to get in front of Shane, the fear for Shane's life outweighed what Shane had just told him about loving his wife. He shoved Ethan out of the way as they rushed across the field waist high in wheat and it was only by the grace of God they were still moving when all around them men were falling. Shane was in front of him one second then beside him the next, and then he was gone. Shaun didn't have time to look for his brother, the minute he and Ethan reached the woods they were in hand to hand combat, their bayonets fixed and in full combat move with the Germans that were everywhere around them. His gun spent, Shaun started using his bayonet and then he was even punching and kicking and growling his way past the Germans. And he couldn't find Shane, and he had also lost Ethan as well.

Something hit him hard, and he fell, as he was going down. Shaun saw Shane off in the distance through the fog of smoke and gas, and Shane turned, saw him falling, and was running to Shaun, his hand held out to try and catch him, and then Shane was hit. Shaun saw Shane get blown backward and away just as Shaun hit the ground, and he couldn't breathe, he couldn't move, all he could do was feel the horrible pain and scream his brother's name inside his gas mask. And then someone was over him yelling medic and the world was getting dark. The last thing he saw was her, the last face in his mind was of Sarah. He tried to reach out to her, but he couldn't reach her, she was slipping away. And Shane, his brother Shane was shot and killed too. Shane had seen him shot dead only a few feet from where Shane lay. And Ethan, he tried so hard to turn his head but he couldn't. He wondered if Ethan would be in Heaven with him right before he heard gunfire only a few feet away from him and he wondered, how many times would he be shot before he died. With this thought, everything went black, darker than a moonless sky over the Saint Mark's River back home. Shaun Blackburn would never see home again. Shaun was dead...

June 11th, 1918
France

"What's your name son?" someone kept asking him over and over again, and he couldn't talk, he couldn't open his eyes. He felt like something was sitting on him and it wouldn't get off. "Son, I need to know your name," the man pleaded, and he sat up on the cot he was laying on and cried out,

"Shane!" and the man patted his arm and helped him lay back down.

"That's a good fellow. Do you know your last name, Shane?" The man was relentless in knowing his name, Shane thought, everyone knew who he was. He was one of the identical twins from Riverview.

"Same as it's been all my life?" Shane didn't see the man's frown. "Blackburn," He lay still. He was in so much pain, and he couldn't tell for sure where the pain was coming from. He couldn't get his eyes open. And then he saw in his mind what he knew to be true. He remembered the battlefield and the battle. He had seen his brother shot. He was falling to the ground at the same time because he had also been shot. "No!" he cried out and tried to sit up again. This was a bad dream. Shane had to wake up.

"They spent half the night digging that bullet out of you, Shane. If you don't lie still, you're going to start bleeding again," the man that had insisted on hearing his full name said pushing Shane down on a cot and holding him still.

"My brother," he spoke in a pleading voice. "I saw him get shot."

"Shane," he heard his name called out, and he turned his head to see Ethan on a cot nearby. "I saw Shaun get shot too," Ethan almost cried looking at the man that was trying to get their names for the list he was making, and Ethan hoped they would know Shaun was here in this hospital tent with them soon enough. "Sir, his brother, my friend, Shaun Blackburn, he looks just like him sir, they're identical twins. Have you seen him?"

"Not yet, son," the man spoke to Ethan as Shane looked up at the ceiling breathing hard and fast.

"We have to find my brother," Shane cried out as he tried again to get up.

"You need to lie down son," the man ordered. "We have too many hurt men here to have to work on you a second time. Now your brother could be here, or in another field hospital, or already taken to an infirmary. You just need to settle down."

"We had a fight. I have to find him. I have to talk to him." Shane was frantic, and he knew that he was frantic. His last words to his brother Shaun had been awful and untrue, and he had to tell Shaun that his words weren't true.

"Lay still and start to heal, and I'll let you know if I find him. You're in bed forty-seven, I'll be back." The man patted his shoulder, and Shane closed his eyes. He felt sick, and he rolled over to his side and vomited onto the floor.

"He's dead. Oh God help me, my brother's dead," Shane cried and held on to the side of the bed remembering his brother falling, remembering that he hadn't been able to reach him. There had been gunfire all around them, endless machine guns going off, and he knew that it was a miracle that he and Ethan were still alive.

Ethan Tucker lay still on his cot, he was afraid that Shane was right. He had seen Shaun running, using the bayonet, fighting as hard as Ethan was fighting. Then there had been a blast and Shaun had been thrown backward and away from them. That was the last thing he saw of his friend.

"Shane, can you look and tell me how bad my face is?" Shane glanced at Ethan and saw a bandage on one whole side of Ethan's face. "I got hit in the face with a bayonet. Bethany's too beautiful to be with a man heavily scared. I might as well have died on that battlefield. Shaun should be here alive, not me."

"Ethan, I can't see anything but a big white bandage on your face. The thing covers you from your forehead to your chin. Are you hurt anywhere else?"

"Shot in the upper shoulder, but they say it went clean through me. You got shot in the thigh and the ribs. They say we're both going home now." Shane saw Ethan look away from him with the one eye that wasn't covered. "Word is the Germans gave us Marines a name," Ethan said, and Shane thought the only name he wanted to hear was his brother's name followed by the words that Shaun was alive.

"What name did they give us?" Shane took a few calming breaths and asked this of Ethan.

"Devil dogs or something like that because we chased them like dogs to hell. I hope Shaun is found soon. I want us all to go home together. They say we lost more than ten thousand men in one day." Shane heard Ethan's voice go weak and knew he was hurting badly, they both were.

"Let's get some sleep, devil dog. Maybe when we open our eyes Shaun will be here with us," Shane said and closed his eyes feeling certain when he woke up that his brother would be looking down at him, and everything would be all right. He had lived, he had been shot twice, and he was here alive. They just had to wait for that man to come back and tell them what bed number Shaun was in and then they would all go home and everything could go back to the way it was before this Great War.

July 18th, 1918
Rockhaven, Florida

"Daddy?" Bethany ran to her father who held a newspaper he had gotten while in Woodville. "Is there any word on the boys?" she pleaded to know as her father shook his head.

"Damn war continues," Allen said softly watching Sarah come closer. "Our Marines won a major battle girls. There were a lot of casualties though. No word on our boys."

The general store was full of people as it was a Saturday and they knew Allen went to town every week for the war news. Heads bowed, prayers were said, and the women worried while the men tried not to worry. "Shane is taking care of Shaun," Sarah said with certainty in her voice before she went to help her mother put jars of tomatoes on a shelf for sale.

"And Shaun is taking care of Shane," Bethany said looking at her father. "And they're both watching out for my Ethan."

"I'm going to ride into Woodville every day and meet the train, if one of them were wounded in battle, they might be coming home any time now," Allen said as he helped Bethany up onto his horse before he mounted behind her. "And no, you can't come with me," he said firmly putting a stop to Bethany's question before she asked.

"May I come with you, Uncle Allen?" Sarah called from the doorway of the store. "I have my own horse, but I don't want to ride so far alone." She saw Allen nod his head and she lifted a grateful hand in a wave. "I'll see you in a couple of days, sir. Thank you."

"You can come with me Bethany," Allen said to his daughter as he started his horse toward home and he knew that his daughter was relieved in the words that he said. He could never refuse Bethany anything. Looking at her made him think of her mother who he always treated with tender care. Allen was blessed with the women in his family, and he knew that too.

"There's no sign of Shaun anywhere," Ethan said as he sat on the edge of his cot. "I've been everywhere Shane. He's not here. He's just gone." He saw Shane shaking his head. Shane was still determined to find his brother, but he was too hurt to get up and go looking.

"I can't go home without him," Shane almost cried, and Ethan touched his shoulder. "I just can't leave here without my brother."

"They're putting us on a ship in the morning. We're going home. Who knows Shane? Maybe Shaun was already put on a ship and will beat us home." In saying these words to Shane, Ethan knew this wasn't possible. They had checked everywhere for days, Shaun wasn't on any list of survivors. Right now he was on the missing in action list and presumed dead. Ethan was feeling hopeless, but he wasn't going to say this to Shane. Shane was injured badly and needed to stay calm. They both needed to stay calm until they reached home and had the support of their families.

"I'm so confused," Shane said and rubbed his head. "I keep thinking he's here. I keep hearing him. He's calling my name over and over. I can hear him in my head, 'Shane,' over and over. And then I see him shot and falling. I'm so confused. I was supposed to die. He was going home to Sarah."

"I know one thing," Ethan said softly, and Shane opened his eyes and looked at his friend. "The Blackburn women are all the most beautiful in the world. I left home a nice looking fellow, but now, like this," he pointed to the bandage, "I'm not going home to Bethany like this. Half my face is wrecked and ruined."

"Ethan, you don't know what your face looks like yet. And you're still a good looking fellow. Well, you haven't changed since I've known you other than a bandage over half of your face." Shane wanted to reassure his friend, but he hadn't seen what Ethan looked like without the bandage.

"Nurse," Ethan called out, and she came to him. "I need to know how bad this is." He pointed to his face, and she gave him an understanding look.

"No one has shown you your injury?" he shook his head and held her eyes pleading with her to allow him to see his face. "Let me check with the Doctor first." She walked away, and Ethan sat frozen until she came back.

"I didn't know you were so vain Ethan," Shane tried to tease, but Ethan stayed serious.

"The Doctor said you could look at it while I clean it and change the bandages. But you're to understand it's far from healed yet and will look much worse than it will once it's all healed up." She took the bandage off, and then the tape holding the bandages on before she gently cleaned the wound with warm water and turpentine which stung so bad that Ethan was fanning his face while the nurse was blowing on his cheek.

"I need to see now," Ethan pleaded, and the nurse held up a sliver of silver glass for him to look into. He closed his eyes and he remembered plowing into the German Soldier who used the knife to cut him from his forehead down to his cheek just barely missing his eye. His face looked much worse than Ethan had feared and he hung his head knowing he had lost his girl back home.

"I am vain," he said to Shane and turned his head so Shane could see his face and his tears, there was no way he was going home to Bethany Blackburn like this, he was ruined.

"Sir," the nurse said firmly, "the Doctor said it's not healed yet. Give this wound time to close, and you'll be as pretty as you've always been." She put the bandage back on his face and Ethan covered his exposed eye with his hand and fought not to break down in childish sobs of agony.

"Ethan, let's go home. We'll worry about your face later. Right now, let's just get home to our families." Shane saw his friend nod his head and Shane waited until Ethan lay down and went to sleep. He motioned for the nurse to come back to him.

"I need to send a telegram, can you help me?"

"It's wartime, sir. It won't be a cheap thing to do." Shane nodded his head in understanding.

"Look in my locker for money," Shane said, and he saw the nurse open up his locker by the bed, a locker that held his things.

"Sir, your locker is empty. I can't find anything that is of yours in here beyond your uniform."

"Someone stole my money," Shane said in an angry voice. Then he calmly looked at Ethan. "Look in his locker," he motioned toward his friend, and the nurse did as he said.

"There's only his things here, sir." The nurse held up Ethan's few belongings.

"Is their money there?" she nodded her head, and Shane said, "take what you need to send the telegram." He saw her take Ethan's money and he hoped that his friend wouldn't notice the money missing. Why would anyone take his personal belongings and leave Ethan's things alone when it was now apparent that Ethan had far more money than he had? Shane wondered for a moment and then turned his attention back to the nurse. "Send the telegram to Woodville, Florida to Seth or Allen Blackburn. Tell them that Shane and Ethan are wounded and coming home, notify Ethan's parents to come to Riverbend. And that Shaun is missing in action. Can you send it today?" He saw the nurse nod her head and he knew that someone in Woodville would get the telegram out to Riverbend. His family would know they were coming home soon. And Ethan's parents would be waiting with Bethany when they got there, and Ethan wouldn't be so upset about the damage done to his face.

They just needed to get home Shane kept thinking over and over, this taking up his every thought as before he had been focused on finding Shaun. "Where are you, brother?" Shane whispered to the stillness around him, and he felt tears slide from his eyes into his ears. Lying on his back all he could see was the ceiling, and he knew, Shaun was lost. Shaun was lost forever.

"Uncle Allen?" Sarah said with her hand over her mouth at the same time Bethany spoke the word, "Daddy," in the most pathetic voice Sarah had ever heard.

They had ridden into Woodville just after noon to await the train, and the telegraph agent ran out and told Allen that a telegram had come for him. Allen stood still reading the paper the telegraph agent had handed to him. He reread it before looking up at the women that were with him. His daughter and his nephew's wife and he wished he were alone. He shouldn't have ever thought of allowing them to come with him.

"Shaun is dead," Sarah cried out, and Allen rushed to her catching her just before she hit the ground. Bethany rushed to her father as he carried Sarah into a little café near the train station and sat her in a chair then asked for a glass of water.

"Daddy?" Bethany looked at her father, he wasn't an old man, he wasn't even forty years old yet, but right now Allen Blackburn looked and felt very old.

"Shane and Ethan have been wounded. They're coming home. Shaun is missing. Ethan is coming here. The telegram says to notify his parents and have them meet him here."

"My poor Ethan," Bethany said as she fanned Sarah. "Shaun is missing. What does that mean Daddy?"

"When they're missing, they're presumed dead," Allen said in a weak voice. "Damn war. Why do people want to fight?"

"We have to get home; we have to tell Aunt Mary and Uncle Seth and Mama. Does it say when Shane and Ethan will be home?" Bethany took her father's hand, and he looked up at her. "Does it say when they'll be home Daddy?" He shook his head and stood up slowly.

"They're still in France. It'll be weeks. I need to go send a telegram to Levi and Cecily. I'll invite them to come here. My God, Shaun's missing." He covered his face with his hand and tried not to cry remembering the times he ran around the yard with one boy under one arm and another boy under his other arm. The boys looked just like him, and he had always been proud of that fact. Seth was several inches shorter than Allen, but the boys were as tall as Allen was. He couldn't stand the thought that this family had lost one of their twins, and he had to go home, and he had to let the family know.

"Is she all right?" he moved his hand from his eyes, and he thought of Sarah. She was far too young to be a widow, and yet that's what she now was. She's just a girl, Allen thought himself.

"She's breathing, she'll come too in a minute. Go do what you must, Daddy. And then we'll pray. We'll pray for hope that Shaun is found."

Bethany rode Sarah's horse while her father took Sarah onto his horse. Sarah couldn't stop crying, and he held her feeling like he wanted to cry with her and at times he did. He saw that Bethany was being strong, fighting not to cry and he knew again that she was his child. She held up under pressure, but she fought for herself at the same time. She was tough and yet soft. She had been born at a time when he was missing, and he wasn't there for her birth. He had even been buried in the cemetery presumed dead. He knew Shaun wouldn't have the same fate that he had as a young man. The war had stolen one of their own from them that couldn't even be buried in the family cemetery.

"Sarah," Allen said as they stopped at her parent's store, "Bethany is going to tell your parents that you're coming home with us for a few days. We need you to be with your husband's family right now. She'll also get your Mother to pack you a few things." He felt his nephew's wife nod her head as he saw his daughter disappear into the store and within a few seconds, he heard Ester Cartledge cry out.

"Mama," Sarah sobbed, and her mother ran out to her. Allen lowered her to the ground and into her mother's arms. "He's missing, Mama. Shane's coming home without him. If Shane can't find him and is coming home without him, Mama my Shaun is dead." Allen listened to Sarah's words, and he knew they were true. If Shane was coming home and Ethan as well, without Shaun, then Shaun was dead. Shane would never leave his brother behind.

"We'll take care of her Ester," Allen said gently as he lifted Sarah back up onto his horse.

"Tom and I are so very sorry, Allen. Tell Mary and Seth we're praying for them." Allen nodded his head as he looked to his eldest daughter knowing that she had grown up a lot since Ethan had gone away. The waiting for Ethan to come home had changed Bethany. She was stronger than she had been before.

"Bethany, ride ahead and find Uncle Heath, tell him to bring Mary and Seth, and Emily to our house. Make an excuse that Alicia has fixed a big dinner or something. Any excuse will do, doesn't matter. Hell, tell them I have news of the boys, just don't say what the news is. We'll be together when we tell them." He saw Bethany kick her horse hard and gallop off leaving him behind with Sarah in his arms crying again.

"Shane promised he would bring Shaun home," she sobbed, and Allen took a deep breath. Shane was a good man, and Allen loved him more than most. No one needed to blame Shane for Shaun's death, if Shaun was, in fact dead. Missing means dead, Allen thought to himself. Their wild, competitive, confident, too much like his Uncle Allen, beloved Shaun was gone.

Alicia was standing on the porch steps. She was too small, Allen thought as he rode into his yard thinking that his wife looked frail. She had survived her own hell and come out happy and healthy, and very sensitive. She wore her heart on her sleeve. She loved everyone, and she clung to everyone. He wished her father were still alive, and thoughts of her father lead him to thoughts of their brother living in Tallahassee and running his wife's father's practice there becoming one of the finest medical Doctors in the state. If the boys were wounded badly, Allen would send for Andrew.

"Bethany didn't say anything other than to cook for a large crowd. I was thinking you were coming home with the boys," Alicia said while looking up into Sarah's face. "We've lost Shaun?" Alicia spoke on a sudden sob seeing her husband, Allen nodding his head, Allen knowing that his wife guessed the truth by seeing Sarah's face. "I'm so sorry, Sarah," she said as her husband lowered Shaun's wife to the ground and he saw Alicia guide a sobbing Sarah into the house. "This is going to kill Mary," Alicia said and sat down on the sofa with Sarah. "And Shane?" she asked her husband.

"He and Ethan are headed home now, both wounded. I know it'll be a few weeks before they get here, but I've sent word to Levi and Cecily and invited them to come stay with us for an extended period of time. We're going to need to all rally around these boys." Alicia nodded her head and agreed with her husband's words. "There's Bethany now," Allen said as Bethany ran into the house.

"Uncle Heath went for Aunt Mary himself. I did tell Uncle Heath, Daddy. I wish I hadn't. He was standing in the stables one minute brushing a horse and the next he was crying. I've never seen Uncle Heath cry before." Allen had seen his brother-in-law cry only one time before, and that was when he and Emily's second child had died.

"Bethany, come help me get dinner going," Alicia said and pulled Sarah up with her from the sofa. "Come, Sarah, you can sit in the kitchen with us. We're here for you." Allen watched the women leave him alone, and within a few moments he went out onto the porch and sat down thinking of Shaun and Shane, and Ethan. This war needed to end, he thought, again and again, knowing that for

Shane and Shaun and Ethan, the war had now come to an end with one of them dead and the other two wounded.

Sarah sat feeling small and still in Alicia Blackburn's kitchen. She kept thinking of the time she'd had with Shaun, how close they had been and she knew, she could live a lifetime plus two more on those memories. A part of her couldn't believe that he had died. Someone so full of life just couldn't die and leave her alone like this. She had hoped when he left that he had left her in the family way, but he hadn't, and now here she sat, alone and more alone than she had been because he was missing, and everyone knew missing in this war meant that he was buried somewhere with no name in a mass grave with other soldiers.

Sarah looked out the window and down the river; she knew their home was down the river. Her and Shaun's home was Shane's home alone now. She would never live there as a wife. There would be no babies at her feet while she sat on the porch shelling peas and looking out at the river rushing by and listened to the crickets as she and Shaun had planned. There would be no more nights of him touching her the way that he had learned to touch her from some book that he had bought in Tallahassee. She had no future beyond working in her parent's store with her brother alongside of her. Her life, as she had planned her life with Shaun, was over.

Heather Ferrell came into the kitchen and sat down beside Sarah. Heather was Heath and Emily's only child, and the young girl was beautiful, tall, and slender with long golden hair and the Blackburn grass green eyes. Heather laid her head on Sarah's shoulder, and they clung to one another, both having tears fall onto their cheeks, they each had loved Shaun, but then, everyone that knew him had loved Shaun.

"It should have been Shane," Heather whispered to Sarah and Sarah agreed. Shane should be the one not coming home. Shane wasn't loved like Shaun was. Shane wasn't perfect like Shaun was.

Sarah cried because she knew now that she had never loved Shane as she had loved Shaun.

Mary Blackburn stood at the kitchen door looking at Alicia. Emily was standing behind her. Somehow the two women had reached the house without seeing Allen. Only Heather had seen him and learned the news of Shaun. Alicia turned and faced her sisters-in-law, and she realized right away, Mary didn't know that one of her sons was missing.

Mary Blackburn looked at her daughter-in-law Sarah sitting with Heather and crying. She then looked at her niece Bethany standing at the sink looking out the window, and the girl's shoulders were shaking, and Mary turned back to Alicia afraid of what she was going to ask.

"Not one of my twins?" she saw Alicia turn quickly coming to her. Mary felt Emily taking hold of her shoulders from behind, and for a second she thought she might not be able to ever breathe again. "Which one?" she gasped and felt a panic coming over her. Looking again at Sarah crying and she knew. No one needed to tell this mother which of her sons wasn't coming home, Sarah's sobbing answered her question. "My Shaun," Mary screamed and fell forward, Alicia catching her and holding her close.

"No! No!" The words echoed throughout the house coming from the front porch, and within seconds, Seth Blackburn was there, in the kitchen holding his wife and reaching out to Sarah who came into his arms, Seth's crying loud in the room where the women all stood.

"Not my Shaun," Mary kept saying over and over again as her husband held her up and Sarah clung to them both in Allen and Alicia's kitchen. There could be no joy that one twin was coming home. There was not even a sense of relief that one twin had survived. The boys were a pair. The grief for the one would be grief for the two because Shane had now lost half of himself. Seth and

Mary knew how close their twins were and had always been. Their number was more than divided. Their family was destroyed.

Bethany went to the porch where her father was and leaned against the rail seeing the pain on her father's face. "When do you think Ethan's folks will arrive?" she asked her father and saw only his shoulders shrug in answer. "Daddy," he looked up at her from the rocking chair that he sat in, and she saw her younger sisters in the hallway out of earshot. Being alone with her father, Bethany dared to say what no one was saying, but what they were all acting like. "It's like everyone is sad because the wrong twin is coming home. It's like Shane doesn't matter. All that matters is that Shaun is gone."

Allen jerked his head up and looked at his daughter. She was right. The family was grieving over the loss of Shaun, and no one was rejoicing in the coming home of Shane. In fact, no one had said Shane's name other than to state he promised not to come home without Shaun.

"It's just right now the loss of Shaun is raw, Bethany. Give this a few days and the tide will turn. Shane is as loved as his twin brother by all of us." Allen saw his daughter nod her head and he leaned back again in his chair. They both knew Shaun was the popular one in the family. They both knew that Shane was the calm, quiet, easy going son that just fit in. Shaun busted into a room and made you notice him. Shaun was the light in the darkness with the two boys. With Shaun, you knew there would always be fun in every moment.

"Poor Shane," Bethany said deciding to stay out on the porch with her father. "He's like my Mama," Bethany said as she climbed onto her Daddy's lap and laid her head on his shoulder.

"What do you mean he's like your Mama?" Allen asked his daughter as he held her close and rocked in the chair as he often did when Bethany was a child. "Alicia is nothing like Shane."

"Mama and Shane are both sweet and gentle, Daddy. There is a part of them closed off to our family. My Mama is the most loving person on this earth, so is Shane. But she holds back with everyone, almost as though she's afraid for us to really know her. Her and Shane both appear to be reaching out to us and touching us, but only with the tips of their fingers Daddy. Mama only grabs a hold of you."

"Bethany," Allen said his daughter's name in a shocked and surprised tone of voice and amazed that she saw more than anyone else besides himself. "Your mother loves you and your sisters from bits to pieces. She's grabbed a hold of all you girls."

"I didn't say Mama doesn't love us," Bethany snuggled closer in his arms wishing that she were three years old again and her Daddy could make everything in her world all right as he had done when she was only a child. "Mama holds a part of herself back from us. I can't explain what I know to you, Daddy. I just feel as though there's something within Mama that I don't really know. And there's something inside of Shane that keeps a part of him away from us."

Allen knew his daughter was right. He knew what his wife was hiding from her children, and he was protecting her secret and he always would. And Allen further knew what Shane was hiding from the world. Shane was hiding from everyone the fact that Shane loved Sarah. Shane was in love with Shaun's wife and always had been.

"Shane! Shane!" he was hearing his name while thrashing around on the small cot trying to reach his brother. And then he was seeing him. He was seeing his brother. "Shaun! Oh God, Shaun! Shaun!" he sat bolt upright in the bed, and he hurt his leg and side when he did. The nightmare had been so real. Every time that he had this nightmare, the nightmare had been real. "I saw him. I saw him Ethan, and he's alive. I've got to get well. I've got to find him. My brother needs me."

"Shane, calm down," Ethan said and helped his friend lay back down on the bed. "A lot of the men are having happen what you are. Me too. They're calling it shellshock. Some are saying they have ringing in their ears and others are even forgetting who they are for a time. One guy two beds over thought he was his best friend and then cried when he realized he wasn't. I've been having tremors in my legs and a headache. I'm not sleeping so good either. The Doctor came by and said all of this is normal and we'll get over it in time."

"This doesn't feel normal," Shane lay back down on the bed. "I keep seeing Shaun get shot and he's falling backward and then to the ground, Ethan. And I was supposed to be in front of him. He had Sarah to go home to. I made him mad so he'd stay behind me, and oh God, he didn't stay behind me." Ethan saw Shane put his hand over his eyes and look to be in horrible pain, a pain Ethan was helpless to help with in any way.

"You rest, Shane. I'll get the nurse and ask for something for the pain. We're getting put on a ship out of here tomorrow. They say first we'll be in England for a few days to a week; then we'll head home." Shane nodded his head and removed his hand from his face.

"You'll come to Twin River with me for a time, won't you? I don't think I can go there alone and face my family without my brother. Please, Ethan, come home with me." He saw Ethan shaking his head, and Shane nodded his head.

"I don't want to see Bethany. She deserves a normal looking husband. I'm going home to Cherry Lake, Shane. I'm not ever going near Riverbend ever again. I can't. Not like this." Shane grabbed his arm and pulled him close.

"You have to come with me," he pleaded. "I'm going home without Shaun. I promised everyone I would bring Shaun home. You have to come with me. I can't go alone. Swear to me. Swear to me now that you'll come home with me." Ethan saw the look in his friend's eyes, and he knew, he couldn't let Shane go home alone. He had to think of someone other than himself. Slowly, he nodded his head and patted Shane's shoulder in a comforting way.

"Calm down. It's going to be all right Shane. I'll see you get home safe, but I'm not staying there with you, not like this."

"Just get me home to my Uncle Allen. Uncle Allen won't hate me for not bringing Shaun home. Oh God, I'm going home without Shaun. Sarah will hate me. They'll all hate me."

Chapter Four

August 1918
Riverbend, Florida

Levi Tucker sat on the sawhorse near Allen Blackburn, both men were wiping their faces with handkerchiefs as it was the dog days of summer, the hottest time of the year in North Florida. "So we're building here, on this river, a house that's the same design as a home you built for our children on Cherry Lake?" Allen asked, and Levi nodded.

"I built Ethan and Bethany a nice little place, only four bedrooms looking right out over the lake, but far enough from the lake that if we have a rainy season, the house won't flood," Levi answered. "Building this place here for Ethan and Bethany fills up the time Allen while we wait for the boys to get home. Let's keep working." Allen agreed with Levi, and the two men went back to work with Seth and Heath joining them to help.

"We'll have this done in a week at the rate we're going," Heath said to Levi as he worked on the shingles for the roof.

For hours, and for days, these four men worked together in comfortable silence while Bethany, Sarah, and Heather sewed curtains for the windows and Alicia made a counterpane for the bed. Waiting on the return of their heroes was made easier by everyone keeping busy though Mary wasn't helping, and everyone was worried about her.

Mary didn't cry. Mary was silent, and she was still. Often she just sat and stared off in the distance like she would see Shaun coming down the road if she looked hard enough. But everyone knew Shaun wouldn't be coming down the road. Only Shane would be coming home alone.

"We're done for the day," Allen said to his wife. Alicia saw that he and the other men had gone down to bathe in the river before coming up to the house, and she knew, these men were now going to change clothes and go to Woodville. These men met every afternoon the train that came in from the east, and they had done so for three long weeks now. Each day they were all hoping that the boys would be on that train and they could bring Shane and Ethan home where they belonged.

Cecily Tucker came out onto the porch with a pitcher of sweet tea, and she handed each man a glass as she filled the glasses up with the amber liquid. The tea was ice cold and made from fresh water from the freezing cold sulfur spring. The spring water made everything taste better Alicia often said, and for the tea, these words were true.

"I hope today I come home with our son," Levi kissed his wife by the open dining room doors, and he saw her nod her head. Levi knew that his darling Cecily was worried about their son and she couldn't and wouldn't settle down until she had her son home and knew what Ethan's injuries were.

"All I keep thinking is that the telegram said he was injured, Levi. We don't know how badly he's hurt." Levi nodded his head. "We've been through so much together, you and I. Our love has seen us through some sad times, and we stayed strong. No matter what has happened to our eldest son, promise me, Levi, promise me, we'll make it together as a family." He tenderly touched her cheek, and Cecily closed her eyes and leaned into him. "I'm only strong because of you, Levi. Please, don't let me go weak on you or on our son."

"You don't have a weak bone in your whole body Cecily. You've always been far braver than I ever was. I love you, darlin', I am so thankful to God every single day for you. All I want is you and our children healthy and happy." he spoke these words against her lips before he kissed her hard, and long, and deep, not caring who was able to see him kissing his wife as he was.

"I pray our Ethan is on the train today," Cecily cried as she laid her head on Levi's chest feeling his arms holding her tight.

"I pray that prayer with you," Levi said remembering a time when he and his wife had been at odds, and he had very nearly lost her. Ethan had brought them back together. Because of Ethan, Cecily was here now in his arms.

"Daddy," Bethany said, and her father turned toward her, "I want to come with you today." She saw his head shaking, and she didn't argue with him. She had gone with him many times to Woodville, and the train had been empty of Ethan. She had been horribly disappointed, broken down into tears each time, and she knew her father didn't want her to be hurt. Her father would bring Ethan home and so would Mr. Tucker if Ethan were on today's train.

"You sew a beautiful seam, Bethany," Cecily sat down in a chair next to her, and they worked together on the new curtains for the house that was being built for her and Ethan here on the Saint Mark's River.

"What if he doesn't want me anymore?" Bethany said quietly looking at her mother. "What if he's changed his mind about loving me? He's been gone so long."

"You both love one another, Bethany." Cecily took her hand. "That's all that's important right now." She turned her attention back to the sewing and Alicia nodded her thanks to Cecily. They were all suffering weak moments at this time, and those weak moments were making them struggles all throughout the day. The waiting was hard. The not knowing how badly Ethan and Shane were wounded was an agony of the unknown. The wait seemed endless for the boys to come home, and still, there was no word of Shaun other than he was missing in action.

"You and your wife certainly have a strong marriage," Allen said to Levi Tucker as they rode together toward Woodville behind Seth and Heath who were both talking in low tones to one another.

"Allen, you want to know the truth about my marriage?" he saw his friend and business partner, Allen Blackburn meet his eyes as they rode side by side. "I treated my wife badly when we first married. I didn't honor her or cherish her. I wasn't nice to her. And then I turned, and she was still there, and I was damn lucky that she was still there." Allen nodded his head in complete understanding.

"I was similar. I didn't know what a gift God had given me in Alicia until I almost lost her. I wasn't always a gentle husband. She taught me how to be a gentle husband."

"I hope our children have an easier time than we did," Levi said, and Allen nodded in agreement. "Though the hardship Cecily and I dealt with early in our marriage has made our marriage strong."

"My daughter is a good person. She loves your son. Ethan and Bethany will be fine. We just have to get your boy home to her and see him well and strong. God will handle the rest through our prayers."

"Amen," Levi whispered feeling certain that Allen's words were true. "With God, all things are possible."

The trip home from Europe had not been easy for either Shane or Ethan. Before they left the hospital, the head nurse had come to Shane and told him that she had, at last, found his personal belongings. But what she gave to Shane were not his things. They were Shaun's personal items.

Shane saw the packet of letters Shaun had written to Sarah, and he very nearly had broken down knowing that this was all of his brother that he was taking home to Sarah. When he had seen Shaun's money belt, Shane was certain his brother was alive and here in this hospital. Shaun had been wearing the money belt when they went into battle, that money belt was secure around Shaun's waist.

Shane had fought to sit up sit up, and he couldn't, not with the wound in his side. Yet he knew that he had to get up and check each cot in this hospital. Shaun was here. Shaun had to be here because Shane now was in possession of Shaun's money belt.

"You're going to hurt yourself and miss our trip home Shane," Ethan said this as he pushed Shane back to laying down on the cot.

"Ethan," Shane grabbed his friend by the collar. "Ethan, with this money belt, we know Shaun's here. He's here Ethan because this money belt was around Shaun's waist when we went into those damn woods. He's alive Ethan, and you have to find him. You have to go look in every bed in this place. Shaun is here. I know he's here."

"You're right," Ethan said this while standing up from his own cot. "He was wearing this money belt. I'll be back." Ethan pushed his hair back out of his face. The bandage was no longer covering both of Ethan's eyes; only one side of his face was covered. Since he could see clearly, Ethan went from bed to bed searching each man's face looking for Shaun, but he never found Shaun. There were men who were so badly injured and their faces were completely ruined. The nurse had found the letters and Shaun's belongings near one of the men wrecked from the war, and Ethan had questioned that man before becoming certain that the man wasn't Shaun. He decided not to tell Shane this, and instead, he just told Shane that he couldn't find Shaun.

One of the men that worked in the hospital had told Ethan that someone probably took the belongings off of a dead body, and then put those things into the box to see them returned to the family. The man had told Ethan to have no hope in Shaun ever being found alive. Ethan felt that what the man was saying was what had happened, and he kept this information to himself — finding Shaun's belongings meant nothing. But Ethan knew the letters to Sarah would have value, and he knew those letters would go home with him and Shane.

The first part of the trip to England had been awful. Shane had been in a lot of pain, but the worst for them both was the shell shock they were living with. Ethan was suffering from this ailment in the worst way possible, nightmares in his sleep and tremors in his hands and legs that seemed to rock his whole body. Shane was also being tormented. Every night Shane would cry out his brother's name as well as his own name. Night after night he would relive his brother being shot, and some nights, he would only get an hour of sleep at most from the torment of this horrible aftermath of war known as shellshock.

After they left England the seas were calm, and finally, Shane settled down and was getting some real sleep, it was as though the ship was rocking him and soothing him in a way being on dry land hadn't been able to do. For this calm, Shane was more than grateful as he remembered how ill Shaun had been on the trip over here months ago.

Ethan slept a lot as well. Daily he would look in the small mirror in the common room that he shared with all the men at his wounded face. His face was healing up nicely, the ship's doctor had told him so, but from his forehead, down to his jaw was a jagged line that was an ugly scar. The scar wasn't bad when looking straight forward at himself in the mirror. But when he turned to the side, Ethan wanted to cry. He was disfigured. Half of his face was destroyed. He kept thinking of Bethany, the most beautiful woman in the world, and Ethan knew that he would end their engagement as soon as he got home.

Bethany Blackburn deserved a whole man, not a man marred and scarred, and suffering from shellshock. He would go to Shane's home, free Bethany from their courtship, and then head home to his mother. He was like a little boy again. Ethan needed, and he wanted his mother and his father. Ethan hated being seen as weak, but he knew inside that he was weak, and he hated himself for that weakness.

After they had arrived at the port in Jacksonville, Florida, Shane was taken off the ship by stretcher, Ethan walking beside him, and they boarded an eastbound train for home. It was in the late night that they were put on the train along with many other soldiers coming home from war, most of those soldiers were like Ethan and Shane, wounded and needing their families to care for them. Even here on the train, Shane begged Ethan to look for Shaun, and Ethan did so, every face he scanned he was looking for Shaun and hoping for Shane's sake that Shaun was here.

Shaun had been shot. Both Ethan and Shane knew that for a fact as Ethan swallowed hard seeing in his minds eyes again Shaun having been shot. Ethan saw his friend almost seem to fly through the air backward and hit the ground hard. Then Ethan had seen Shane going down. Ethan tried not to think about what he had seen that day in those woods because when he saw Shane go down, that was when the German soldier took him down and left him for dead, and with this scar that had ended any hope of a love between himself and the beautiful Bethany Blackburn.

The train went through Madison, Florida at noon and Ethan wanted to get off and run all the way to his parent's home on Cherry Lake. But he stayed on the train with his friend, determined to see Shane home, and determined to break his engagement with Bethany. They went through Monticello, Florida at two in the afternoon with the longest stop being in Tallahassee where they stayed for over an hour transferring Shane onto the train bound for Woodville, and for home.

The hour was well after four in the afternoon when they finally arrived in Woodville. Ethan had decided to stand instead of sit from

Tallahassee to Woodville as he worried and he wondered how he would get Shane home to the river.

Shane was still on the cot on the train. The young man wasn't well enough to walk yet on his wounded leg and with his shoulder and his side still not healed. There was no way his friend Ethan could carry him off of this train and to the stable where they might rent a horse. And Shane knew in his gut that there wasn't any way in this world that he could even sit on a horse in the state that he was in. He overheard several men talking to Ethan about his dilemma when Shane saw the conductor come and join the group of men and Ethan.

"You say this man is Shane Blackburn?" the conductor asked and Ethan nodded his head. "His family comes every evening to the station looking for him. They'll be there for certain today. And what's your name?" Ethan told the man his full name, and the conductor gave Ethan a smile. "Your Pa's with the Blackburn family every day, young man. They'll be thankful to have you heroes home. I'll find your family, and they'll come help you get this wounded soldier home where he needs to be." Ethan thanked the man before turning back to Shane and letting Shane know they were almost home and that their fathers were at the station waiting for them every day.

Allen pointed to the conductor on the train waving to him and Seth, and he pushed Seth in that direction of the conductor. "You have our boys on this train?" Allen called out seeing his brother Seth wasn't able to speak as he saw the conductor give him and Seth a firm nod.

"They need some help, Mr. Blackburn. Both are hurt," the train conductor called out as Levi, along with Heath hurried up and onto the train.

Ethan saw his father from a close distance, the father that he knew loved him more than life itself. His father was his best friend in this whole world, and the young man cried out, "Dad!" seconds before he was engulfed in strong, secure arms. "Dad, oh Dad," Ethan kept saying over and over again seeing Seth push past them and grab Shane's hand.

"I don't have Shaun," the younger man cried as his father embraced him and cried with him. "I lost him Dad, I lost Shaun. Please, forgive me. I'm so sorry."

"I have one of my boys back," Seth cried. "I love you, Shane. I love you, son. Let's get you home, to your Mama." Seth turned, and he saw Allen and Heath reach and lift the stretcher Shane was on and carry him out to Allen's car. Every soldier and man on the train stood up and applauded as Shane passed by them. Shane couldn't understand why they did that. He had failed his family. He had failed his brother. He had come home alone.

"Sir," Ethan pulled on Seth's shoulder when they were standing on the platform. "He's suffering from something the Doctors back in England are calling Shellshock." Ethan turned to his father. "We both are. It's pretty bad. We're having trouble sleeping. We're getting confused easily. I have a horrible ringing in my ears and terrible tremors. I just wanted you to know. Shane gets confused, and he's been very upset over his brother. We both have." Ethan found himself leaning against his father, and he felt his father's strong arms supporting him as he turned and put his face on his father's shoulder. "Dad, I saw him gunned down. Dad, Shaun was such a good guy. I saw them both just gunned down."

Levi felt his eyes fill with tears as he remembered his innocent son, how he had held Ethan in his arms as a baby, and how he had taught his son to swim and fish and hunt and go to church every Sunday. His beautiful son was changed. His beautiful son was scared and more than physically. For this wounded soldier, Levi had not been prepared.

"Heath rented a horse to get home on," Allen said as he helped put the stretcher with Shane laying still on the stretcher into the backseat of the car. "Seth can sit in the back with Shane and the rest of us fellows will ride up front."

"Dad," Ethan spoke in a fervent voice. "Dad, I promised Shane I would see him home, but I can't let Bethany see me like this. Please, let's just catch a train and go home now. I just want to be with you and Mom. Please Dad, please." Levi heard his son's pleading voice, and he looked at Ethan's bandaged face wondering how badly his son was scared. No matter what, Levi Tucker thought, Ethan was and always would be his beautiful son.

"Ethan, your mother and I received a telegram about a month ago that you both were coming here. We knew that you were coming home with Shane, so your mother and I both have been waiting with the Blackburn family for you to arrive." Levi held open the car door for his son to get inside, but Ethan refused to get in or to go home with the family.

"I can't go to Riverbend. I can't face Bethany. She can't see me, Dad," Ethan covered his eyes and lowered his head as he spoke.

"Because of your face?" Levi demanded to know.

"Bethany is beautiful; she's perfect. I'm not," Ethan said as though his refusal to be near Bethany were that simple.

"My daughter's beauty is on the inside, young man," Allen said in a firm hard voice. "If she loves you, it's not for how you look." Ethan raised his head and met Allen's eyes seeing Allen Blackburn motioning for him to get into the wagon. "Don't discount Bethany's love for you as being so fickle son. She deserves better than that from you after waiting faithfully for over a year for you to come home. She's grown up while you've been gone."

Levi gave his son a gentle shove toward the car and sighed in relief as Ethan entered that car. "You'll feel better once you've seen your mother and Bethany. We all will," Levi spoke in a confident voice as he followed his son into the car and they made their way home to Riverbend and to the women that loved them.

At dusk, Allen Blackburn's car passed through the small town of Rockhaven. Despite the late afternoon hour all of the people in the small community were out waiting where they had been waiting every day for over a week to welcome home their returning war heroes. And today was no different for these people. They were lined up along the street and waiting with the hope of seeing the car pass by with the young men inside. Today, at long last, they all shouted and cheered the boys through the town.

Eddie Cartledge ran alongside the car waving to Shane and causing Shane to cringe by calling him by his brother Shaun's name. But Shane knew, that was Eddie's way, as Eddie, like everyone else in Rockhaven, had loved Shaun the best.

"You're staying at Riverbend," Allen said to Seth and Shane, and he saw his brother Seth nod and give him a worried look. Allen and Seth both could see that Shane was very changed from the man that he had been before he had left for war.

Shane had always been quiet, but so far, the young man hadn't spoken one word on the drive home. Shane was too quiet. Shane wasn't looking at them. The young man kept his eyes cast downward and away as though he weren't really here. When they pulled up into the yard, Mary had fallen down the porch steps to get to him, and Shane never cried when he saw his mother. He just held her hand and let them carry him into the house and up to a bedroom. Shane almost appeared as though he were in a daze, not there with his family, not anywhere. Allen thought for a moment that Shane's mind had just shut down. The young man was lost without his identical twin brother.

Bethany saw Ethan from her upstairs bedroom window. He was getting out of her father's car on his own. He was able to walk, and for that, she was relieved. But there was something about the way he was standing, something about the way that he was holding himself that made her go cold inside. What if he didn't want her anymore? She thought this as she moved away from the bedroom window. What if he had changed his mind about marrying her?

She would make him want her; Bethany decided and turned to hurry down the stairs seeing her sisters Julie and Jenny watching her. "Are you going to kiss him?" Julie asked in a way only a little sister can ask, and Bethany waved a hand at her little sister knowing that she should just ignore Julie.

The family brought Shane into the house on a stretcher, and she saw Sarah watching from the kitchen doorway but not moving to show herself to Shane. And then Bethany made her way around the corner. She saw Ethan fall into his mother's arms, and his mother almost fall as Cecily held on to him before mother and son sat down together hugging still on the top porch step.

"I want to go home, Mom. I can't stay here and have Bethany see me," Ethan said in a broken voice, and Bethany took a step toward him wondering why she couldn't see him when all she had wanted for more than a year was to see him.

"You just need some good home cooking and sleep, Ethan. Then you'll be fine," Cecily said seeing Bethany out of the corner of her eye. "Let me up, son and I'll go help get dinner on the table. You're fine now. Everything is going to be just fine." Levi reached and helped his wife to her feet while knowing how hard it was for his wife to walk away from their hurting son. But Ethan needed Bethany right now, and Bethany needed Ethan right now, and it was right for this mother to let her so go.

Ethan sat on the porch alone with his face in his hands knowing that he couldn't go into the house. He couldn't see Bethany. She was so perfect, and he no longer was. One side of his face was wrecked. He didn't see his mother Cecily look at Bethany and mouth the words, "Help my son." Nor did he see Bethany move to the steps where he was and sit down beside him putting her hand on his shoulder.

"I waited," she said softly, and she saw Ethan remove his hand from his face and look at her.

"I have to free you," he said in a horribly serious tone. "I won't marry you. I'm breaking our engagement." Bethany pinched her lips together and slowly she nodded her head.

"All right," she said softly. "I'll agree to that on one condition," he looked down at her beautifully perfect face and into those unique eyes that she had, and he felt an intense grief that he must let her go. "You kiss me goodbye," she said softly. "Then I'll let you end our engagement."

"I won't kiss," she cut off his words by putting her mouth to his mouth, her arms around his neck, and even did what he had done when he kissed her that day by the river long ago by opening her mouth and forcing her tongue into the warm depths of his mouth. She heard Ethan gasp, felt him go weak against her, and then she was pulled close to him leaning back against the step with him laying over her. And that was how her father found them more than ten minutes later still locked in a kiss that seemed to have no end.

"Bethany, Ethan," Allen said in a hard voice, and the lovers came apart quickly. "Dinner is ready, and the mosquitoes are awful tonight. You both need to come inside." He watched his daughter stand, and then she reached out a helping hand to Ethan. "I told you my daughter was not a fickle person," Allen pulled Ethan up onto his feet seeing his daughter trying to help Ethan stand. "Five minutes, and we eat. Be inside the house by then." Bethany didn't watch her father go into the house. She turned into Ethan and held him tight before looking up at him and begging him to bend down so that she could kiss him again, and he did as she told him to do.

Sarah slowly went up the stairwell behind the men that carried Shane upstairs to a bedroom. She had seen him on the stretcher looking frail and pale and lost, and she burned inside that it was Shane coming home and not Shaun. His mother was holding his hand, and his father had one end of the stretcher while his Uncle

Heath had the other end. "I'm all right Mama," she heard Shane say to Mary Blackburn, and Sarah burned more inside that Shane sounded just like Shaun. He should be Shaun.

"You will be all right," Mary said to her surviving son. "Allen sent a telegram to Andrew in Tallahassee earlier, Andrew should be here tomorrow." Sarah knew that Andrew Martin was Aunt Alicia's brother and Andrew Martin was also a very well-known Doctor in Tallahassee. The doctor should be coming to help Shaun. Shane had promised her that he would bring Shaun home to her.

She watched as the men lifted Shane and put him into a bed in the spare room. He had cried out when they moved him, but only for a moment. Uncle Heath came out in the hall and saw Sarah standing there alone staring at the bed and Shane, and he patted her shoulder as though he knew how she felt. No one knew how she felt. Sarah thought as she watched Shane's mother change his bandages with his father standing nearby. And then she watched as his mother hugged him gently and his father stared down at him. Again, Sarah thought, this should be Shaun, not Shane.

No one in the room saw Sarah in the hall. No one noticed when she stepped into the room. She was thinking of Shaun, of the day that he had taken her to Twin River and made love to her, and then how he had married her. His secret book, the memory of his secret book made her smile despite the burning hot tears sliding down her face. She could see her husband, the man that she adored, riding away from her. He had looked back to her, and he had lifted his hand, and she thought he should have come home. Shaun was the one that was supposed to come home.

Sarah looked at Shane hard, and she saw him looking just like Shaun. Shane looking alive and well, while her Shaun was buried in some mass grave in France with no hope of ever seeing the river he loved so much again. Shaun would never see her again, and she would never see him again. She didn't even have a baby from her husband to remember him by. All she had was his identical twin brother who she hated for being alive while her husband was dead.

Shane, propped up by the pillows, opened his eyes and he saw Sarah at the foot of the bed. She looked broken in two. She looked crushed. He still loved her. She would always be precious to him. He wanted to go to her. He wanted to wipe the endless river of tears falling onto her face away. He wanted to hold her close and tell her he was sorry he wasn't Shaun. He wanted her to forgive him for his coming home alone. He should have had Shaun with him. There were so many things that he wanted to tell her, and he couldn't say a word. All Shane could do was watch her at the foot of his bed crying her heart out.

"Oh Sarah," Seth said when he saw what his son Shane was looking at, and he let his wife go going to his lost son's wife and handing her his handkerchief. "I'm so sorry." Seth realized what it must be like for this beautiful young woman to stand staring at the very image of her husband and this not be her husband.

Shane knew what Sarah was thinking. Shane knew what Sarah was going to say. He wanted to reach out to her. He wanted to nod his head and give her his permission to speak her mind to him, and all he could do was lay still and look at her beautiful face that he had adored all of his life and pray that one day she could forgive him and that he could forgive himself.

"Where's Shaun?" Sarah asked in a horribly broken and weak voice. "You said you would keep him safe. You weren't supposed to come back without him." Seth tried to pull Sarah close and give her a hug, but she pushed Seth away.

"Sarah, I know you're hurting, but this conversation isn't going to help anyone," Seth said in a gentle, yet firm voice and he saw Sarah shake her head hard while still looking at Shane with huge tears falling from her eyes.

"Shaun. I need him," she cried seeing Mary move to Shane, take his hand and Mary bowed her head crying as well. "Shaun was supposed to come home too," Sarah cried not seeing the agony on Shane's face, only feeling a horrible agony no one should ever know.

"Sarah," Mary cried her name and then moved from her son to the girl at the foot of the bed that was her daughter by way of her lost son. "Oh Sarah," she pulled her into her arms and felt Sarah crumbled against her in sobs.

"Shaun! Oh, Shaun!" Sarah cried out as she sank to the floor taking Mary with her and both women sitting on the floor clinging to one another. "We're supposed to grow old together on the front porch of Twin River and have a bunch of babies," Sarah cried harder unaware that Seth had bent down and his arms were around both women. Seeing Shane, identical to Shaun come home the reality that only one son was ever going to come home became more real. Seth bowed his head and sobbed with the women while Shane lay upon the bed dry-eyed. Every time he closed his eyes he saw his brother getting shot, saw his brother falling backward, saw the way Shaun had landed on the ground, and he was helpless to save his brother as he had been shot as well.

"Shane," Sarah cried his name from the foot of his bed with his parents holding on to her, and he closed his eyes in agony at the way she had said his name. "You should have saved him. You said you would keep him safe. You promised. And now he'll never come back to me. Only you're here."

Heath had been in the doorway, and he heard much of what was said by Sarah. After a few long moments, he turned and rushed down the stairs finding Allen near the front door, and he motioned for his brother-in-law to come. Allen would know what to do; Heath thought. Allen always knew what to do. Heath saw Allen following him upstairs and no words needed to be said, no explanation was needed to be given.

Allen knew what was happening and this wasn't unexpected to him. He went into the room, and he touched Seth's shoulder.

"Seth, take Mary to your room and help her calm down," Allen said gently. "Heath, stay with Shane," he turned to say this to his brother-in-law. And then he knelt down, and he gently picked up Sarah into his strong arms going for the door holding her close as she continued to sob out of control. He saw his little sister Emily in the hall and nodded for her to follow him as he took Sarah to Bethany's room and lay her on the bed. "She's inconsolable, Em," he said to his sister. "I'll get Heather; they've been friends forever. Heather can come sit with her."

"I'll stay as well, Allen. I cannot fathom what seeing Shane was like for her. Shane who is so like Shaun," Emily closed her eyes and shook her head. Allen agreed as he went to get his niece, but first stopping to check on Shane. Heath was sitting by the bed, and he nodded when Allen asked if Shane was all right, Allen knew that no one in this house was all right tonight.

Allen went past the room Seth and Mary used when they stayed here with him and Alicia. He saw his brother laying in the bed holding Mary close; both were wrapped up into one another and in their grief. They were rejoicing that one of their sons was home and in that rejoicing the reality that another one of their sons was never coming home.

"Heather," Allen called for his niece in the hall, and she came to him. She was different from all of them. Allen thought as he met Heather's eyes. She was shy and quiet and showed very little emotion. She rarely spoke to anyone other than Sarah and Bethany, and even they only heard a few words from her. "Can you go to Sarah? She's in Bethany's room." He saw her nod her head and wondered if she even talked to his sister Emily, her own mother. She was so quiet that he felt there was more to her than any in the family saw, but she had distanced herself from everyone, and no one knew how to reach her.

Dismissing his quiet niece Allen went down the stairs and into the dining room. Alicia had the table set, and in a glance, he saw

Levi and Cecily were at the table with his wife. His home was full of people, and only three people were now at the table, Allen thought and went back into the hall and out on the front porch to find that Ethan and Bethany weren't there. He hurried back into the dining room and stopped in the doorway. "Where are our children?" he asked looking at Levi.

"I saw them on the front porch a few minutes ago," Levi answered.

"The new downstairs bathroom," Alicia said calmly and lifted her tea glass to take a sip.

"They're both in the bathroom? Together?" Allen asked, and he saw Levi had stood up and passed him heading in the direction of the bathroom. "What are they both doing in our new downstairs bathroom?" he asked as he fell in beside Levi who reached the bathroom first pulling open the door.

"I told you it was nothing, Ethan," Bethany was saying as the light above the bathroom mirror showed the young man all of his face. The scar was pink and raised, but it was on the side of his face starting at his forehead and going down into the eyebrow and back toward his ear. Looking straight on into the mirror, he couldn't see the scar. He had to turn his head to the side to see the jagged tear that ran down the side of his face. "And it's not even healed yet. Give it time, and it'll be smaller and will fade away." Bethany hugged him from behind, and his hand covered her hand.

Ethan saw how small she was. Bethany wasn't even up to his chest in height. She was tiny, and he just wanted to protect her. And as he was now, returned from the war, he didn't feel that he was good enough for her. Not like this, he thought as he looked again at the scar on his face.

"You deserve someone good and perfect, Bethany," Ethan said softly, and he closed his eyes. "I've done horrible things." He felt himself go weak and he opened his eyes trying not to remember how he had killed men, trying not to see himself battling for his life and for the lives of others. Ethan saw in the mirror in this bathroom that he was tall and strong, and he was with her, he was with Bethany, she was by his side, and he grieved that he was so changed by this war. He wished that he were as innocent as he had been when he left her over a year ago.

"Ethan, you need time." Bethany held him closer. "Let's go have dinner with our parents, please. We'll talk more later, I promise." Just as she turned, Bethany gasped loud and long seeing Levi Tucker standing in the open doorway with her father beside him.

"You two shouldn't be in here alone," Levi said to his son and his friend's daughter. "What are you doing in here?" he asked thinking the bathroom was an odd place to be holding a conversation.

"We're looking at how ugly the war made me Dad," Ethan said and walked out of the bathroom letting go of Bethany who followed him with a defeated look on her face. "I'm as scared on the inside as I am on the outside. I can't let go of what I did over there." His shoulders slumped, and Levi stood looking eye to eye with his very tall son having no idea how to respond to Ethan's words. He knew better than anyone that keeping things inside, not talking things out, not sharing how you feel with loved ones would destroy you and here Levi stood, speechless before his most cherished son, the son that had saved his marriage to Cecily.

"Come," Allen ordered Levi, Ethan, and Bethany. "Jenny, Julie," he called his younger daughters, "we're going to have a grown-up conversation in the dining room tonight. Make me happy and eat in the kitchen," he said this in a demanding voice, and both girls disappeared into the kitchen knowing that tone of voice from their father was not one to argue with. "Sit," Allen said to Ethan, and he saw Alicia and Cecily looking at him and then to Ethan with questioning eyes.

"Daddy, can we just be calm and eat dinner right now? We can be serious later," Bethany begged not wanting to upset Ethan further. The scar on his face was really bothering him, and she was afraid she was going to lose him over that scar.

"Not talking things out makes things seem worse than they are," Allen said, and he took his wife's hand. "We certainly learned that," he nodded to Alicia and saw Levi reach for his Cecily's hand, their eyes met from across the table, and both men knew that they had knowledge that Ethan didn't yet have. "Ethan, it's more than the scar on your face that's bothering you, you need to talk son. We're here to support you." Allen leaned back and met Ethan's eyes. "Problems never got solved or any better by ignoring them or letting them eat away at you. Face the problem head on son."

"Allen's right son and we're all here for you right now, and we'll always be here for you and for Bethany," Levi added.

"We love you so much, Ethan," Cecily said when her husband fell silent, her gentle voice making Ethan want to come to her and lay his head in her lap and just stay there for a long time until he felt safe again.

"It's Shane," Ethan said quietly, "and Shaun." His voice broke, and he covered his eyes and looked down at the empty plate in front of him. "We went through several small battles that we thought were horrible," Ethan spoke on. "We also were in a few skirmishes, and the twins watched out for me, made sure I was safe and I kept up with the two of them. Shaun never let Shane or I out of his sight. The twins stuck together every inch of the way. The last skirmish we were in, Shaun kept in front of us. Shane was mad at him, Shane was mad all over because he kept saying to me that Shaun had to come home safe to Sarah, that he had promised her Shaun would come home safe, and Shaun wouldn't listen to Shane and stay behind him."

Ethan uncovered his eyes, and he had a faraway look in those eyes that he had covered, as though he were not in the room when he was in this room. With his eyes covered, he did not see that everyone around him at the table was looking at him and hanging on to his every word.

"Shane tried to pick a fight with Shaun the night before we entered the Belleau Woods. We were in this wheat field that night. The next day, we were standing up to our waist in wheat with the Germans shooting their machine guns at us. It was still dark, not yet dawn. And we couldn't dig down in holes like rabbits the way we had before. We were exposed and hopeful that we didn't get shot. Shane was still trying to make Shaun mad at him, so Shaun would stay behind him while we were heading into the battle. I knew Shane was trying to get Shaun's goat so Shaun would stay behind him. Shane was trying to keep Shaun safe. But nothing Shane did worked, he couldn't get Shaun mad at him, and Shaun wouldn't listen to either of us and stay safe for Sarah.

"Right before we marched into the field headed for the woods and the Germans, Shane stopped and told Shaun that he was in love with Sarah, that if Shaun didn't stay behind him and safe, that he, Shane would come home and love Sarah in a way Shaun never could have." Ethan covered his eyes again and fought not to cry. "Shane only told Shaun that to keep him safe. Shane didn't mean a word of what he said. He was just trying to get Shaun to stay safe behind him. Shane wanted to save Shaun for Sarah, and he didn't care in the least about his own safety, his own life. I've never seen a more selfless act by anyone ever.

"And then Shaun punched Shane in the face for what Shane had said to him. Shaun knocked Shane down, and I just stood watching knowing what Shane was up to, and I could have told Shaun, but I didn't. I honestly felt that Shaun had figured out what his brother was trying to do, that Shane was trying to keep him safe.

"The last words between the brothers were ugly," Ethan closed his eyes, and he heard Shaun telling Shane to go to hell. "And then we came out of that wheat field, all three of us together and we hit the dark woods. The moon was the only light really, and it came down casting shadows from the trees. I saw one of them, I didn't know for sure if it was Shane or Shaun, but he was nearest to me, and he wasn't behind his brother. They were separated. Shane's words and efforts to protect his brother were useless, and whichever that brother was nearest me, he was shot by a German only feet away from where I stood battling some soldier from Germany I didn't want to battle. I saw that twin, and he was flung into the air with the blast, and then I saw him falling, almost like he was gliding to the ground, and beyond him the other brother, which could have been Shane or might have been Shaun, I had no idea which was which, I'll never know. But the brother that wasn't shot was running to the one that was shot, his hand held out, and I could hear him screaming despite that gas mask he wore. I can sleep now and hear him screaming, and then he was shot and flung to the ground too.

"I was then shot in the shoulder and went down only feet away from them both." Ethan fell silent, and he looked back up, his eyes meeting his father's eyes. "Before I passed out, before the German sliced my face open, I saw them reaching for one another Dad. Shaun died that day, reaching for Shane that had used his last words to his brother to try and protect him." Ethan then looked at Allen. "I killed men like that. I killed men that had brothers and fathers and mothers and sisters waiting for them at home just like our family was waiting here. I didn't think of the men I killed as people. I just killed them to be safe and because it was what we were told to do. I killed men like Shaun, men that won't ever come home."

Sarah stood out in the hall with Heather, always quiet Heather that no one knew for sure what she was thinking. Sarah put a finger over her lips to make sure Heather would stay silent as they listened to Ethan tell of the moment her Shaun had died and how he died and how Shaun's brother Shane had tried to keep him safe to get him home to her.

Sarah closed her eyes and felt bad about what she had said to Shane upstairs earlier. Shane, poor Shane had suffered too, and he was still suffering. And he had tried his best, done everything that he knew to do, to protect Shaun. Shaun was the way that he was, Sarah knew that, and Shaun's wild ways were the reason that she had been in love with him. He was always in the lead, always confident and headstrong and certain of what he wanted out of life. He was like his Uncle Allen with his father Seth's sense of humor, the best of both of the older Blackburn men. And Shane, he wasn't the hero type that Shaun had been, but he knew his duty, and he always did what he knew was expected of him. And Shane loved Shaun if anyone knew that, it was their best friend Sarah who had grown up with both boys, who had grown up loving both boys with all of her heart.

"Ethan," Levi spoke his son's name in a serious voice after they all sat in silence for a time thinking. "I never went to war. I can't say what it's like to kill a man. And I wish you didn't know that either, son. But you do. And now, you have one of two choices. You can let what you saw and did ruin the rest of your life, or you can live life to the fullest. Live for Shaun who didn't get to grow old with his wife. Live for all those German soldiers that you had to kill that will never go home to their families. Live to grow old and love as best as you can. Do good things, walk with Christ, son. Make this moment the first moment of your life by accepting Christ and never going to war again, never hurting anyone ever again. That's done and behind you, son. You're safe, and with those of us, that love you. You're home now."

"Wise words," Allen said in agreement with Levi. "Bethany, make time to read with Ethan, Romans Chapter eight, I've found that helpful in difficult times." He looked at his daughter who had sat silent listening to her fiancée describe the death of her much-loved cousin. Her eyes weren't dry; it had been painful to hear, but also uplifting. The love that Shane and Shaun had for one another, nothing could destroy; not even anger or death itself.

"I will, Daddy." Bethany saw Ethan looking down at her and forced a smile. "Mama and I cooked and the food is probably cold now, but it's still good. Let's all eat," she tried to put a cheerful sound into her voice not seeing Sarah and Heather enter the room until Sarah spoke softly looking at everyone around the table,

"I want to take a plate up to Shane, please." She looked at Allen, and he gently nodded his head and gave her an encouraging smile. "I need to take a plate of food up to Shane, please."

She came back into his room; this time there were no tears streaming down her face. Her hair had come loose of the ribbon that had held it back away from her face, and her hair was covering half of her body. He hadn't known how long her hair was all of these years; she had kept it pinned up. She looked smaller than ever, lost inside of herself, and he grieved that he had hurt her as he had. He closed his eyes not wanting to see her hurt eyes and know that he had allowed his brother to die.

"Sarah," he spoke her name so softly that he almost had not heard himself say her name. "In my bag, I don't know where my bag is now. But in my bag are all the letters Shaun wrote to you that he couldn't mail. Ask Mama where they put my bag." He saw her nod her head and felt relieved that she would have something of his brother though he knew they would grieve the loss of Shaun forever.

"Here," she said swallowing hard while shoving a tray at him piled high with more food than he would ever eat in one meal. "I didn't know what you liked," her voice broke as he tried to sit up more in the bed and he cried out in pain. She almost dropped the tray at his cry, and he reached out a hand to steady the thing and held still while he waited for the pain to ease off. "I didn't know what you liked," Sarah said again in the same broken voice when he finally was able to sit up. Sarah didn't turn to see Seth and Mary now standing in the doorway watching the tender scene between brother and sister-in-law play out in the room.

"I'm sorry, Sarah," Shane struggled to say and couldn't look at her. "I hope one day you'll forgive me." Sarah looked down at him, her husband's identical twin on the bed wishing it was Shaun and knowing this wasn't Shaun. She tried to nod her head and then turned and ran for the door squeezing past Seth and Mary. "She use to be one of my best friends, now she'll hate me forever," Shane said and covered his eyes as his father came to him, and his mother held herself up by holding onto the bedroom doorframe.

"Shane," Seth said sitting in a chair by the bed and glancing back at his wife. "She brought you food, Shane. Shaun's wife, our sweet Sarah, she wants you to eat and get strong again. Actions speak louder than any words ever heard." He saw his son look at him with hopeful eyes, and then he reached a hand out to his wife and Mary came forward and took hold. "And Sarah brought you a packed plate of food. Look there's Aunt Alicia's wonderful fried chicken and roast turkey and sliced ham and look at those deviled eggs, I bet Bethany made those. If only your mother would have made her rolls," Seth reached for a piece of chicken and handed it to Mary. "There's enough here for us all to eat, sit up son. Let's do what Sarah wants us to do and have dinner."

"I don't want her to hate me." Shane said as he popped one of the eggs into his mouth, not because he was hungry or had a desire for the egg, but because he knew if he ate something, his sweet mother would be happy a little and he wanted her not to look as sad and heartbroken as she was looking now. "I forgot how good the women in our family cook," he said this also for his mother's sake. "I've been starving half to death for a year." Seth forced a laugh and sat back satisfied in the second. One of his sons would heal. Shane just needed time. And one of his precious sons was gone, Seth almost choked on air thinking of never again seeing Shaun, hearing Shaun's laughter, and seeing his son ride wild and free all over this land they loved so much. Shaun wasn't even buried here. Shaun was dead too far from home.

Mary came out of Shane's room with her husband and saw Sarah standing in the hall leaning back against the wall, her eyes red from crying. Anyone could see this was hard on Sarah and she needed understanding and compassion. And Mary knew, this sweet girl was her daughter, she always would be her daughter. Sarah was a part of Shaun. "Sarah," Mary said her name and went to pull her into her arms with Seth beside her putting a secure hand on Sarah's back and Mary's shoulder.

"Shane," Sarah choked on his name, it was hard to say when she wanted him so badly to be Shaun. "He told me that he had Shaun's letters to me," Mary pulled away and looked down at Sarah nodding her head. "He said the letters are in his bag."

"I'll get them," Seth said and went back into the room pulling Shane's bag out from under the bed. When he returned to the hall, he held a stack of sixteen letters addressed to Sarah and eleven addressed to himself and Mary. "Thank you for telling us about these," Seth handed Sarah her stack and handed another stack to Mary.

"Thank you," Sarah said and moved down the hall. "I'm glad he wrote to us," she turned and looked back at Mary with a heavy heart, this mother had lost her child, and she felt for Mary who stood holding Shaun's last words to his mother in her hand.

"Night, Sarah," Mary said gently and turned to her room along with Seth, they both knew they would be up for a while reading what their son wrote, and they knew Sarah wouldn't sleep for a while yet as well.

"Where are we going?" Ethan asked his father as they mounted horses in Allen Blackburn's front yard, it was early morning and already the day was hot. He saw Bethany's father mount his own horse and pull Bethany up in front of him, Ethan wished that

Bethany were in his arms, but he knew that her father wouldn't want that until after they were married.

"We have something to show you," Bethany said with a secret smile and held on to her father's hand when he kicked his horse into motion very aware that Ethan and Levi Tucker were following them.

"We're not done with this place yet," Levi said getting off of his horse in the small yard that was near the river, the yard of this new house that he and the Blackburn men had been building here for his son and Bethany when they married. "But we will finish this week now that you're here to help. Good thing it's your left shoulder that's hurt; you can still hammer a nail as you are." Ethan followed his father up the steps of what looked like a lake cottage, and he could see pretty curtains on the windows even from outside as he noted that Bethany smiling.

"You made those curtains?" he asked her and saw her nod her head.

"And she made them for the same exact cottage I built for you myself over on Cherry Lake," Levi said, and Bethany reached out for his hand and pulled him into the house. "Half the year here tending the timber and the other half in Cherry Lake tending the sawmill with me," Levi said from the porch of his son's new home on the Saint Marks River.

"We both get our children," Allen said when Bethany pulled Ethan inside the house before Allen reached and closed the door then walking to the edge of the porch with Levi. "How much time alone should we allow them?" Allen asked his friend and Levi laughed out loud thinking had that been he and Cecily, ten minutes was too much time. When Levi said this Allen laughed louder and confessed with himself and his Alicia, if he had been her father, he wouldn't have allowed two full minutes.

"Your Mama and Daddy are good people," Bethany said almost shyly as she showed Ethan the house and saw him touching the curtains and the bedding and then looking out at the river which they could hear flowing from what would soon be their bedroom.

"I've wanted you since the second I saw you," Ethan turned from the window, and Bethany rushed into his arms. "How long do you think your Daddy will make us wait before we can marry?" he asked before he started to kiss her and heard her sigh, she still wanted him despite the scar on his face.

"He's right out the door," Bethany said looking up into Ethan's beautiful crystal clear eyes. "We'll ask him after you finish kissing me." He lowered his head and pulled her close, and she held on tight. He was so tall that he had to bend almost in half to reach her and she laughed against his mouth and pulled him to the bed. "Sit," she ordered, and he did as she asked. Within a few seconds, Ethan was kissing her more with her only slightly standing taller than he was sitting. Within a moment Bethany was laying on the bed, and he was lying on top of her, she was crying out in his mouth, and he was giving her what she wanted which was more of him. "Don't stop," she begged when he pulled away, and he came back to her neither caring their fathers were standing on their front porch and might walk in on them any second.

"God help me," he more prayed than said his Lord and Savior's name in vain. "You make me want you too much. If only our fathers would go away," he breathed into her hair and heard her sigh several times, he knew then she agreed with him, and he held her closer.

"Less than five minutes," Levi said as he came into the room laughing. "Pay up," he ordered Allen and held out his hand.

"I said you two could last ten minutes alone," Allen stood shaking his head hard in disappointment. "It's not even been five full minutes." He looked at the two on the bed in disgust and Bethany was relieved he wasn't furious with them for being in the bed together.

"We weren't doing anything, Daddy," Bethany said as Ethan helped her up off of the bed. She saw her father staring hard at her and blushed, then blushed worse when Levi winked at her and began laughing out loud.

"Let's go back to the house and pull out a calendar," Allen said to his daughter and Ethan both. "That is if you're both ready to set a date?" He mounted his horse and looked down at his eldest child that so favored his beautiful wife, the child that he adored so very much. She had grown up on him while he was watching and he wanted her to be a baby in his arms again.

"We're ready, sir," Ethan said getting on his own horse.

"Ride home with him," Allen motioned to Bethany to go to Ethan. "You can ride the long way along the river. Levi and I will let you two alone for a bit. Just don't tell your mothers," he ordered and saw Ethan, with his one good arm reach down and pull Bethany up and onto the horse in front of him while smiling at Allen.

"You can trust me, Mr. Blackburn," Ethan said, and Allen nodded.

"Ethan, I've not met a lot of real men in my life. I've met men, but not men like you. I don't just like you, I admire, and I respect you. From here on out, you're to call me Allen. I want to be your friend, not your father." Allen winked at Levi who nodded in understanding. "You have a good father. What you need is a friend." Ethan smiled, even though his face hurt when he did so, he felt a peace that he'd not felt in over a year. He was part of something larger than himself, this Blackburn family was beyond close-knit, they took care of one another, they were the example of unconditional love, and he knew that was because they were all, in their own way, allowing Christ to lead them.

"I'm honored to call you my friend, sir," Ethan said before he watched Allen and his father gallop off toward Riverbend. "You're lucky to have this family Bethany," he said as she leaned back against him, her arm coming up and reaching behind his neck as she pulled him down to kiss her.

"It's your family now too. My Daddy is the head of the family, Uncle Seth and Uncle Heath support him and the three of them take care of us women and provide for us. Shane and Shaun were the ones that were going to take over someday for Daddy and them. It'll now be you Ethan, you, and Shane," Bethany said as he started his horse toward the river at a slow pace.

"Your Father approved us being alone," he said as he pulled her closer. He was going to get to be alone with the woman that was too beautiful for him now; the woman that he would love forever. "Help me forget the war," Ethan pleaded as he reached the grassy bank of the river and helped Bethany down from the horse. "My memories won't let me go," he confided and allowed Bethany to pull him down to sit on the grassy bank.

"Focus on me," Bethany said and lay back in the soft thick grass. "I need you to kiss me," she put her arms around his neck as he lowered his body onto her body. "I love you so much," she said as his mouth came down on her mouth and she lifted up molding her body to his.

"Your Daddy better find a date on that calendar of his for no later than next month," Ethan said as he lowered his head back to Bethany's and felt her tongue touch his lips. "Oh God, you're killing me," he whispered and took control making love to her body with his mouth on the banks of the river.

Doctor Andrew Martin, the only brother of Allen Blackburn's wife Alicia, arrived in the early afternoon the day following Shane's return home. Andrew's reason for coming here to Riverbend was to examine the injuries that both Shane and Ethan were trying to heal from, injuries that were easily seen, and other injuries that no one could see or understand.

"How are you?" Andrew asked Shane in a serious voice as the Doctor closed the door to the bedroom Shane was recovering in.

The young man lying on the bed looked as much like Andrew as he did his Uncle Allen. And Andrew and Shane had many things in common, besides the fact that they strongly favored one another in appearance. Andrew was quiet, calm, and always in control of his feelings. Shane was the same way as Andrew, very much unlike his Uncle Allen.

"I'm not all right, Uncle Andrew," Shane spoke in a low tone of voice while looking at the closed bedroom door. "If I tell you how I'm really doing, will you promise not to tell any of the folks downstairs?" Andrew nodded his head and sat on the edge of the bed to listen seeing Shane meet his eyes. "My head hurts, a lot. I feel sometimes like it's going to bust wide open. And my eyes ache like they're going to pop out of my head. It's an awful feeling. But the worst is the dreams I'm having." Shane looked into his Uncle's eyes and didn't fight the tears; nor did he feel less of a man for allowing the tears to fall either. "Ethan, Bethany's fiancé, said it's called shellshock." Shane saw his Uncle Andrew nod twice while patting his leg in a comforting way and he fell silent hoping this man that was a loved Doctor could help him heal from this injury as well as the physical ones that he was suffering from.

"Yes, the Brits are studying what you have happening to you right now. They think it's the explosives going off too close to a man's head or the rapid sound of machine gun fire. They really don't know what's causing you, young men, to suffer from these issues. But they know this is as real and disabling as a saber or gunshot wound." Andrew moved to lift up Shane's shirt and remove the bandages. "Talk to me while I look you over, son." While he examined his nephew, Andrew saw the tremor in Shane's hands and knew that this tremor also was a condition associated with what was being diagnosed in these returning war heroes as shellshock.

"I keep dreaming of Shaun's death. I was shot Uncle Andrew, and I lived. What if Shaun lived? What if he can't remember who he is? I get confused sometimes, lost inside myself. I can't remember things. What if Shaun is like that somewhere? What if he doesn't know his name? There were a couple of men in the hospital in France that didn't remember one thing of who they were. I keep thinking of him Uncle Andrew. He might be out there in France somewhere laying in a field hospital or in an infirmary in England. I keep dreaming. I have to find him." Andrew nodded his head in understanding of his nephew's words. He also heard the tremor in Shane's voice and how anxious the young man was with his words. Shane's speech wasn't natural, and Andrew knew that this young man was suffering in the worst way the loss of his identical twin brother.

"Shane," Andrew Martin spoke in a calm and comforting way, a way that held complete and total sympathy and understanding for this young man. "It's been almost two months since you were shot. And since your brother Shaun was shot. If he were going to be found, Shaun would have been found by now. I understand your hope son, and that's normal. But you need to start accepting that Shaun is dead."

Andrew looked at Shane, and he saw his nephew looking like the wind was knocked out of him by what Andrew was saying to him. A long few moments of silence passed while Andrew changed Shane's bandage before speaking again. "It's okay to dream for a time son. And it's okay to hope. But the more time that passes, the less hope you can have that Shaun is alive and you have to let him rest in peace. You have to allow yourself peace as well." Easier said than done, Andrew thought of his advice to Shane. This Uncle wanted to have certain answers that were healing for his nephew, but the reality was something they all had to face. Shaun was lost to them. Shaun was buried in a foreign country in a mass grave, and Shaun Blackburn wasn't coming home to his family that loved and missed him. Only time would make the grief less pain to bear.

"So am I healing?" Shane asked not wanting to believe yet that Shaun was gone. Andrew nodded and smiled patting Shane's arm.

"The leg looks good, Shane. You'll have a limp for a time because of the muscle loss, but once you get back to working with your father and Allen again, you'll recover the full use of this leg just fine. In your side, the bullet went right through, and it didn't hit any vital organs. It's going to take time to heal, maybe even a few more months. I want you to be careful, take it easy, and don't re-injure that wound because it'll start bleeding again. If it does begin to bleed, apply pressure and be still until the bleeding stops. I don't want you riding a horse for a while, Shane. I'll leave orders with this family that you're not to do anything for a few more weeks. The best news I can give to you is that there isn't any sign of infection."

"How's my friend, Ethan? He was shot in the arm, and his face was hurt." Shane looked at the closed door to be sure they were still alone. "Maybe you could talk to him for a bit Uncle Andrew. Since the battle, almost every night, he's waking up screaming his head off. He's bad off, really bad off."

"I've seen him already," Andrew said in a serious voice. "Bethany is going to have her hands full for a while. He's having night terrors and like you, he has a pretty bad tremor as well, only Ethan's tremor is worse in his legs when he's sitting still. His shoulder is like your leg son. He'll need to work hard to build it back like it was when it's finally healed. I told him to carry our little Bethany around, that will build his arm back up once it's healed completely." Andrew smiled and winked at Shane. "And making love to his new wife every night, he'll be healed up faster than he thinks." Andrew laughed and ruffled Shane's hair. "You need to find a girl to get well for."

"No, I need to find some way to take care of my brother's wife. I need to get well to provide for her. He would have wanted me to see her secure for life." Shane looked again at the door to be sure they were alone. "You aren't going to blab what we say to anyone?

Not Uncle Allen or Aunt Alicia?" Andrew laughed and sat down on the chair.

"I give you my word. I won't say a word. You're whispering into the ear of God, son."

Shane nodded his head before he trusted his Uncle with all of the truth of himself. He told the Doctor that was his Uncle just what he had done, what he had told Shaun to make Shaun stay behind him during the worst of the battle. Shane told Andrew how Shaun had punched him and what he had said about Sarah to Shaun. Shane bared his soul, he told his Uncle everything, and in the telling, Shane found no peace, only worse torment within his soul.

"In every lie, Shane, there's some small truth," Andrew spoke in a patient voice as he held his nephew's eyes seeing the torment within those eyes. "You do love Sarah. You wouldn't want to get well and take care of her if you didn't love her. You want to support her because she matters to you." He saw his nephew nod his head, and Andrew patted his leg while standing. "Shane, don't be so hard on yourself. You're human, we all have weaknesses and desires. Just take it one day at a time. Let God guide you, don't make any plans, just let life happen. You're going to get well. In time we'll know if your hopes that Shaun is alive are true. But I strongly caution you, do not look for Shaun to come home. Your brother is gone from this life, and he'd want you to have peace. We all will miss that wild man running around here in constant motion. It'll be hard not having that bright light in this family. But we have you, and for that, we thank God every day."

Shane thanked his Uncle and watched Andrew leave the room after assuring him everything they talked about wouldn't leave this room. He closed his eyes, and he listened to birds in the trees outside of his room, and he thought that he heard Shaun off in the distance calling for Sarah. He sat up in the bed, and he felt certain that he was really hearing his brother. He listened closer, and he listened harder, and he hoped it was Shaun coming down the road, coming home to their family, a family that loved Shaun so much and missed his brother more than anything in this world.

Shane listened on and on in the stillness of the early afternoon, and all he heard were the birds in the trees outside of his bedroom window. Only the birds were real to Shane Blackburn.

Sarah didn't see Shane again. She left the Blackburn house quietly only telling Heather she was going home. Home, Sarah thought with deep sorrow. Home was supposed to have been Twin River. Home was where Shaun was. There was no home for her now, just her parents' house with Eddie.

She loved her brother Eddie, and he needed her. At least she had something to live for, Sarah thought as she walked to her parent's home crying again for her lost Shaun. She had to be strong and carry on, for her brother's sake. If anything happened to her, then when her parents died Eddie would go to Ellen and Clayton. And that meant Eddie would be locked away in a tool shed. Sarah couldn't let that happen to her innocent brother. Eddie loved to roam free in this place on the river. Eddie never needed to be locked away. He was so gentle a soul, Eddie didn't deserve to be hidden away either.

When Sarah had reached her parent's home, her mother and father both handled her with gentle care. They watched out for her and acted like she was a china doll. At any given moment, she would fall and break all apart. But she wasn't falling apart. Sarah was going through the motions of getting through each day trying not to think of any of the Blackburns. Thinking of one Blackburn made her long for the one she had lost. And because of this, she grew apart from Heather and Bethany. She grew apart from Seth and Mary. She stayed in her room as soon as the store closed each night reading her letters from Shaun and she didn't come out of her room until she had to go to work in the store again the next day.

Before the return of Shane and Ethan and the loss of Shaun, Sarah had been working and praying and hoping for the time

Shaun would come home, and they would make babies and swim in the river and set up house at Twin River. For more than a year Sarah had waited and planned while Shaun was at war. She had been dreaming and planning and hoping for their future together and now, now she had no hopes, no dreams, and no future. She was living in some dark void, and she felt isolated and alone, cut off from the rest of the world, and not even Eddie could cheer her up.

Sarah looked at the stack of Shaun's letters on her bed, and she touched them knowing that he had touched them. These letters were all she had left him and what they were, were confessions of his feelings of war and being away from home and away from her. She read the regret that he had that he had joined the Marines, and she read the pride that he had in being a Marine. She read of his sorrow over missing her and the springtime and the winter and of longing for his mother's sweet rolls. The letters brought her comfort. The letters brought her pain. The letters showed her a side of Shaun that she had never known.

She lay on her bed holding the last letter he had written to her. The penmanship was the worst, and he wrote in this letter to her that he was actually writing by the light of the moon in a field where German machine guns were killing men all around him. She rolled over onto her stomach knowing that she had come to an end, this was the last letter, and then there would be only a deathly silence from her Shaun. He would never speak to her again in any way. He would really be dead.

"I don't think I'll survive the battle we're in right now, Sarah. Things are bad, worse than any other battle we've been in. Shane's hurting. He's not like he was at home when you knew him. He's more withdrawn and sad, not frightened like I am sometimes. Shane is far braver than I ever knew him to be. He's strong Sarah. My brother makes me proud to be a part of him." Sarah read this final letter aloud to herself, and she had to move toward the light coming in from her window as she saw how faded the writing was.

It was as though the pencil Shaun had been using was no longer sharp enough to write and she felt sad that this last letter was so short. "Take care of my brother for me if I die, Sarah. Don't let Shane hurt over losing me. The truth is, I'll never be lost to Shane anymore than I'll ever be lost to you. Shane and I are like you and I Sarah. He and I are a part of one another. Maybe Shane is more a part of me than you are Sarah. We were all best friends. We all grew up in one another's pocket. Please, stay close to my brother. Please always be his best friend. For me, love Shane for me. He'll need you. You'll need him. I have to go now. If I never see you again, I want you to know I am so thankful to you for marrying me, for loving me, you made my life full and complete. Even if I die right now, I had everything I ever wanted in this life, because I had you."

The letter ended, and Sarah broke into a sob that wracked her body as she held this last letter to her heart. He couldn't be dead, she thought. Shaun couldn't be dead because he was so full of life. She cried harder not knowing she could cry harder than she was, and found herself on her bed still crying even when she slept.

"You've missed three Sundays of church," Ester Cartledge said to her daughter. "Reverend Farmer is here today, and I'm insisting that you come and attend with us. There will be no argument in this Sarah." Her mother's words and tone of voice left no room for doubt within Sarah. She would attend church today with her family. She would do as her mother told her to do.

Sarah didn't want to go to church. She didn't want to do anything but hide in her room away from the real world until she died and was reunited with Shaun. But her mother wasn't going to allow her to do that, she had to attend church today, or her mother would throw a fit, and Sarah didn't want her mother to throw a fit.

Thomas Cartledge watched his youngest daughter come out of her room, and he wished that she was like she use to be. Ellen, his eldest daughter, was the one that was serious and unhappy. Ellen had been born fussy and never outgrown that mood. But Sarah, she had been the sunshine in the family. Even in the night, she was sunny and happy, and ready for the day. But not anymore, he grieved for her. Now his daughter was broken, and no one could fix her. She was lost without her best friend, without her husband, Shaun.

"Sarah," Thomas spoke his daughter's name in a tender way, and he saw her huge eyes look up into his own. Her eyes were full of tears.

"Mama ordered me to go to church," she said in a hoarse voice as she picked up her handbag going to the front door of their home. "I'm going early and getting settled in our pew. Maybe if I'm already there, no one will notice me and everyone will leave me alone." Her father thought of stopping her, but he knew he couldn't, he might hurt her if he stopped her and she was hurt enough already.

"Where is Sarah," Ester asked her husband, and he pointed out the door and toward the porch. "She's got to get over this," Ester said firmly. "Shaun is gone. He's not coming back. They weren't together that long." She turned when she heard her husband gasp and shake his head.

"Shaun and Shane and Sarah grew up together. The three of them were best friends. You saw one of the three; then you saw all of the three. Those boys were more to her than playmates or her very dearest friends. Our Sarah fell in love with both of them, and they fell in love with her." He pointed to the buggy that pulled up to the church, and he saw Shane getting out with the help of his father and his Uncle Allen. "She didn't choose him for a husband because he was too much like her, calm and level headed. She chose the wild one to fall in love with and take for a husband. Right there is the healing for our daughter that she needs. And in time, she'll know that and he will too. But first, she has to grieve for the one she lost before she can be found by the one that's still here." Thomas said these words while firmly pointing toward

Shane Blackburn. "Shane was always meant to be with our Sarah. Even now those two are alike. They're both grieving the loss of Shaun in the exact same way." Thomas saw his wife go to the front door and looked out at Shane being helped to his feet by his father and his Uncle. Shane was still pale but not deathly ill-looking as he had been when Ester had first seen him that day he came home.

"The rascal," Ester said with a smile, "he sure has Shaun's face, doesn't he? You're right Tom. Shane is the level headed one like our Sarah. He's the one I wanted her to choose from the start. I cried for days when she chose that wild one that rode his horse through town like he was going to a fire." Tom Cartledge laughed and pulled his wife close.

"That was our Shaun, always up to something. And he loved our Eddie most of all. I'm glad she chose Shaun when she did. He was a fine man, and he would have made Sarah happy all of her days on this earth. And he's gone from us all now. But his brother Shane is still here. I think we need to pray hard that Shane steps in and fills his brother's shoes for our daughter. Sarah deserves a happily ever after." At that moment Eddie came running up to his parents dressed for church and bouncing in eagerness to go.

"Shaun," he said bouncing to the doorway. "I wanna see Shaun. I miss him," Eddie said and then squealed out loud flapping his hands, and his parents tried to stop him, but it was too late. "Shaun!!!" Eddie was screaming to the top of his lungs as he raced to Shane in the churchyard, Shane leaning heavily on a cane and his father. "Shaun! You came home, Shaun!!"

Sarah heard her brother in the churchyard, and she knew all of this part of the county had heard him calling out for Shaun. She gasped realizing Eddie had mistaken Shane for Shaun as Eddie often did make that mistake, and she nearly burst into tears again. Eddie missed Shaun so much, and he didn't understand death. Sarah dropped her handbag in the family pew and rushed outside to stop her sweet and innocent brother from upsetting Shane and the Blackburn family too much with his mistake.

Shane saw Eddie Cartledge coming to him, and he smiled from ear to ear despite being called by his brother's name, and despite the pain of hearing his brother's name. He held out the arm on the side that he hadn't been shot and Eddie bounced into him nearly causing Shane to fall down. "Hey," Shane said feeling Eddie's head lay on his shoulder. "I missed you, buddy," he said seriously, and he lost his breath when Eddie wrapped both arms around his waist and squeezed him hard.

"I missed you, Shaun," Eddie cried as Shane fought to take a breath past the pain in his side. "You went away forever," Eddie cried and kissed his cheek before Allen distracted Eddie so that he would let Shane go.

"What about me, do I get a hug, Eddie?" Allen Blackburn asked of Eddie, and the young man quickly left Shane and grabbed Allen jumping up and down while hugging the older man.

"Shaun is home, Uncle Allen," Eddie said and looked up to see Sarah coming out of the church. "Sarah, look," he pointed to Shane. "Shaun's home." Sarah blushed and hurried to her brother trying to get Eddie off of Allen Blackburn, a man that seemed all right that her brother was trying to climb him as though he were a tree.

"It's not Shaun," Sarah said gently to her special brother. "Remember, I told you that Shaun went to be with Jesus in heaven? Shane came home," she pointed to her husband's brother, "this is Shane sweetheart." She saw Eddie look back at Shane with a frown on his face and then turn and look at her and Sarah saw that Eddie was going to cry again. "It's all right to be sad," she put her arm around her brother and guided him inside the church. "We both loved Shaun so much."

Sarah looked back over her shoulder at Shane, and she saw that he was watching her and Eddie closely. She couldn't read the expression that he had on his face. He seemed calm and accepting of Eddie's mistake, and he seemed hurt by it as well. She could never figure out Shane. All of their lives, he had been too quiet. Shane was like her. He kept everything inside. Shaun had been an open book. She knew Shaun like the back of her hand. If Shaun had come home, might her husband have been changed and been calm like Shane? What might that war have done to the man that she adored? It wasn't worth asking this question of herself Sarah thought. Shaun hadn't come home.

"Are you all right, son?" Seth asked Shane as Mary came to stand with them, both of his parents seeing that he was in physical pain.

"I'm fine, Dad," Shaun nearly whispered these words before he looked at his parents' concerned faces. "I wish, I wish for Eddie and Sarah's sake I were Shaun. But I'm not. I'm Shane." He looked sad over that fact, and Allen patted his back giving him a look of pride and love.

"And Shane is who we're happy to have with us at church today," Allen spoke in an overloud voice seeing the look of hurt on his brother, Seth's face. "Why don't we go inside? After finishing the house for Ethan and Bethany and planting the north field without my right-hand man," Allen punched Shane in the shoulder, "I'm feeling my forty years age." He laughed and bounced up the stairs knowing he was in good shape for his age. Hard work was making Allen solid and strong, and for his nephew and his brother, he needed to be strong.

"Where's Aunt Alicia?" Shane asked looking for his sweet small Aunt in the churchyard.

"Sick this morning," Allen said and went to their pew helping Shane to sit down. "Oh Lord, there's blood on your shirt son. I think Eddie might have hurt you when he gave you that bear hug outside." Allen saw Shane shake his head and sit down with a look of agony on his face.

Come Save Someone Like Me

"Uncle Andrew said it would bleed from time to time while it healed. I forgot my handkerchief Uncle Allen, can I use yours to apply pressure?" Allen reached and quickly gave his handkerchief to his nephew seeing Shane force a smile for his mother Mary as Mary was in the church aisle talking to Ester Cartledge. "Don't tell Mama, she'll overreact, and I can't take any upset right now. I need to be calm until this passes." Allen nodded his head and kept quiet against his better judgment. Shane was bleeding pretty heavily despite the fact that the handkerchief was being pressed against the wound in his side and Allen kept looking to see if the blood had stopped flowing.

"I'll give you five minutes, Shane. Then I'm raising an alarm." Allen looked at Mary calm and quiet next to his brother Seth, and he didn't want to upset her unnecessarily. Mary had been through enough worry these past weeks. "Five minutes," Allen repeated firmly as he watched his three daughters enter the pew in front of him and Shane and sit down. "How did these girls grow up so fast?" he asked Shane while looking at his daughters, Julie and Jenny with their hair up. One of the girls was only twelve years old, while the other girl had just turned fourteen years old. And Bethany, Allen saw her sitting next to her fiancé Ethan. How did his baby become grown up and engaged to be married? He was too young to be this old Allen thought glancing quickly to see Shane's wound was still bleeding. "Five minutes," he spoke again to his nephew seeing Mary still talking to Ester in the church aisle.

Allen looked toward his daughters again, and he thought of Ethan's parents, Levi and Cecily. The couple had gone home to Cherry Lake leaving Ethan behind with the Blackburn family. The young man's arm was nearly healed now, and the scar on Ethan's face wasn't as awful as it had been when he returned home from the war. Allen was all right with Ethan being here with the family as Shane and Ethan were close, and the two young men still seemed to need one another for support. The effects of the war and the healing of their wounds lingered on.

"It's been three full minutes," Allen whispered to Shane and saw that his handkerchief was bloody. "Two more minute boy and I'm raising the alarm to your mama."

"Daddy," Bethany said turning in the pew to face her father Allen as he was sitting behind her.

"What," Allen whispered leaning toward his daughter that had her mother's face.

"A whole week, every morning Mama's been sick," she whispered, and Allen nodded his head. He knew this without his daughter telling him.

"I'll ride into Woodville later this afternoon and send a telegram to Uncle Andrew to get out here," Allen said to Bethany now worried not just about his wife but also his nephew as he glanced again and saw Shane was still bleeding.

"Daddy," Bethany made a face showing him that she was disgusted with him and Allen frowned over such a look from his oldest child. "Three children and you don't know the signs yet? Mama's only thirty-five and you may be forty something years old, but you look younger. And everyone knows how you love mama." Allen gave his child a puzzled frown, and she shook her head hard before her two sisters turned and said at the same time,

"It better not be a boy," Julie and Jenny fell into one another laughing. The two girls thought too much alike. "We're a family of girls, you're the only boy in the bunch Daddy," Jenny spoke up, and the dawning of this conversation hit Allen like a rainstorm in the face. His little girls knew his wife was going to have a baby before he did.

"Congrats," Seth said with a laugh and shook Allen's limp hand as Seth sat down in the pew Allen was sitting in with Shane.

"What next?" Allen said looking at Bethany.

Come Save Someone Like Me

"We need a bigger family Daddy. Stop looking worried. Mama will be all right." The Reverend Farmer entered the pulpit just as Bethany finished talking and Allen turned to look at the Reverend trying to get over the shock that he was going to be a father again. A chance for a boy, Allen thought looking at his three girls and knowing they were right, they were a girl family. Allen Blackburn smiled and had hope, but he was still sending for Andrew.

"The bleeding has almost stopped," Shane spoke to his Uncle when he saw Allen looking down at his hand holding the handkerchief still over his wound.

"I'm still watching over this thing," Allen whispered and waved his hand at the wound seeing Shane's head nodding before they both turned to hear the Reverend Farmer preaching.

Shane heard the Reverend's words, but he couldn't make out those words. All he could do was look across the aisle and two pews up at Sarah. Her delicate profile looked more so now. She had lost weight, Shane thought. Waiting more than a year for her husband to come home, and then finding out that Shaun was missing and presumed dead and was never coming home was more reason for Sarah to appear delicate and fragile. Shane wondered if she hated him. He remembered what she had said to him when he first came home, and he had been staying with his Uncle. He then remembered how later she had brought him food. Shane hadn't seen her since that night. He used to see her at least three times a week their whole lives growing up on this river. He missed her friendship. He missed her conversation, and he missed swimming in the river and fishing on the river, and chasing after Eddie with her and Shaun. Shane had lost more than Shaun. Shane had lost Sarah as well.

While he was staring at his brother's wife Sarah turned in her pew, and she saw him looking at her. He couldn't look away even though he was caught looking at her. He felt like he wanted to cry. She should have Shaun next to her. As he held her eyes with his own, he couldn't look away from her. And then she was standing up, no one else in the church was standing up, he thought, and the Reverend had stopped speaking as she rushed around the front pew and over to the far side where he was, and he fell. Everything happened almost like it was a slow long fall with Sarah always in his view.

"Shane!" he heard Sarah cry out his name as she tried to grab him before he hit the floor. His Uncle Allen had reached for him too, but Allen couldn't stop him from going to the floor, and he heard his mother cry out and his father too.

"I'm all right Sarah," he said as he looked up at her, his head cradled in her lap. She looked frightened out of her mind, and he didn't want that for her.

"He's bleeding again," Allen said and begged Seth for a handkerchief and pushed that handkerchief against Shane's wound. "You should have told me," Allen said to Shane while his parents came to where Sarah was and looked worriedly at their son. He saw his three cousins, Bethany, Julie, and Jenny looking over the pew in front of where he lay with worried faces.

"I'm all right girls," he said reassuringly, and then he looked at Ethan who was next to Bethany. "At least it doesn't hurt like it did when I was shot," and on those words to Ethan Shane slipped into an unconscious state.

No one had noticed Sarah was crying and then she was sobbing almost hysterically and Allen put a calming hand on her shoulder. "He's going to be fine, this is expected. He needs to be still, and we need to put pressure on his wound. It'll stop bleeding in a few minutes."

"I don't want him to die," Sarah bowed her head and sobbed harder. "We already lost Shaun." Everyone in the church was looking at sweet little Sarah, the wife of Shaun Blackburn with pity and hurt, and sorrow in their eyes. She was so obviously heartbroken over the loss of her husband. Shaun should have come home. "I keep looking for him," Sarah said to Allen and Seth, and Mary with everyone in the church listening. "I keep thinking he'll come tearing down the road on one of your wild horses Uncle Allen, and he'll ride up to me and tell me he was just fooling with me. He never got shot. He never went off to war." She leaned back into Mary's arms, Mary, who was agreeing with her.

"That's our Shaun, just like his Daddy, always teasing and yet super confident and strong-willed like his Uncle Allen," Mary said this as she looked to see if Shane was still bleeding. "Thank you, Jesus," she breathed, "he's not bleeding any longer."

"Mary, you and Shane stay with us for a couple of days," Thomas Cartledge invited. "The last thing this boy needs is bouncing down the road and causing that to bleed more. And we would love to have you." Mary looked at her husband, and Seth nodded his head in agreement with Thomas Cartledge.

"I think it's a good idea, Mary," Seth said and thanked Thomas and Ester for taking his son in. Only Allen saw how stiff Sarah had gone at this invitation, and Allen knew, having Shane living in her house even for a few days would constantly remind Sarah of Shaun. She was being torn up by being near Shane. Shane was a constant reminder of her loss.

"You'll be all right?" Allen asked Sarah softly as others talked around them and Sarah looked up at him with tortured eyes.

"I don't want him to bleed to death," she said softly, and he knew she didn't. She had seen from across the church that Shane was in trouble and she had rushed to catch him before he had hit the ground. She was still cradling his head in her lap.

"He's too big for any of us to carry to your place, Tom," Sam Morris said as he looked down at Shane. "Heck, he's taller than Allen now, and Allen towers over almost all of us."

"I can walk," Shane said coming aware of his surroundings and not attempting yet to move.

"He's back with us," the Reverend said. "Let's all bow our heads and pray for this young man's health." Everyone followed the Reverend's lead and Sarah, still holding Shane's head on her lap, was unaware that she had thick hot tears coming from her eyes and that those tears were now falling on Shane Blackburn's face.

Shane looked up at Sarah. She had seen him, she had seen he wasn't all right, and she had rushed to him. She didn't let the fact that he hadn't brought her husband home stand in the way of trying to help him. Maybe she wouldn't hate him forever; Shane thought, and he remembered again that she had brought him food that first night. He reached up a hand and touched her tears. He had put those tears on her face. If he were Shaun, Sarah wouldn't be crying like this. He thought of when he was in France, and that man had kept asking him his name, if he had said the name Shaun instead of Shane everything right now would be different for him and for Sarah. No one would have known he wasn't Shaun. The war changed Ethan, and the war had changed him and his brother Shaun on the battlefield. No one would ever guess he wasn't his brother. If only he had said his name was Shaun instead of Shane, then Sarah wouldn't be crying right now. But he wasn't Shaun; he grieved, he was Shane. He had always been Shane.

Several of the men were able to get Shane up sitting in the pew and out of Sarah's lap. He watched her turn from him and within a moment she had faded away into the crowd, and he wasn't surprised to see her going away from him. He missed being her friend. He missed hearing her voice and her laughter, and he missed his brother more. Shane tried to find out where she went, but he couldn't see her in the crowd, though he saw Eddie bouncing around.

"Let's get you over to the Cartledge house," he heard his father say to him, and he looked at Seth with a confused frown on his handsome face. "You're going to stay with the Cartledge family today and probably tomorrow." Seth helped Shane to stand supporting him on one side while his Uncle Allen supported him on the other side.

"Why am I staying at the Cartledge house?" Shane asked still confused as he hadn't been conscious when this decision had been made for him and his mother to stay with Sarah's family while his wound re-healed.

"Your Mama doesn't want you bouncing in the buggy down the road, Shane. It might start you to bleeding again," his Uncle Allen's youngest daughter, Jenny Blackburn answered his question.

Shane shook his head hard and pulled against his father and his Uncle Allen. There was no way that he could stay with Sarah's family and be near Sarah. She couldn't want him there. He had come home. He had returned from the war without his brother. No matter what he did in this life, he would never forget how he had let Sarah down. The wrong twin had come home, and Shane knew, he had probably always known that to his family, to Sarah he was the wrong twin.

"I'll stay here with the Reverend," Shane said this in a certain voice before he saw his mother shaking her head. "I'll be fine here Mama."

"No, you won't,' Mary looked up at her tall and handsome son. "Ester will be much better at watching over you, and I'll rest easy if you're with her and Sarah. I'm going to stay the night as well Shae, so stop fretting about being a bother to anyone." His mother could see the frown on her son's face, and she wished that she knew what he was thinking. Shane had always kept a part of himself closed off from his family, whereas his brother Shaun had been open and easy to read.

"Three women fussing over me," Shane sighed and leaned on his father. "I have to get well and home to Twin River. The place has been empty for over a year. Have you checked on things out there Dad?" he saw his father nod his head as they entered Sarah's parents' home and Ester led them to the spare bedroom.

"Allen and I replaced several shingles on the roof in the spring. One of the porch steps was loose as well that we fixed up for you. That new stove you ordered from Sears before you left for the war was delivered way back months ago. Allen and I installed the thing which wasn't easy as it's one of those new gas stoves." Shane heard what his father was saying, and he was confused, he didn't remember ordering a stove. Why would he order a stove?

"Dad, I ordered a stove?" he looked at his father, and by the expression on Seth's face, Shane knew that he had ordered a stove. "I'm losing my mind. I don't remember doing that. But lately, I get confused so easily."

"You had Sarah pick the stove out of the catalog," his mother said as they helped Shane to lay down in the bed. "You came here and had her pick out the one that she wanted before you made the purchase."

"That sounds like something I would do," Shane said before he checked to see if he was bleeding again and he sighed in relief that he wasn't bleeding. "Shaun would have picked out the stove himself and not asked Sarah or me," Shane said with laughter in his voice before he settled back lying still on the bed.

"There's truth in that," Mary said. "Shaun was my sweet child, but he wasn't a considerate man like you are Shane. I'm not saying anything negative about Shaun. The truth is, I worshiped the ground he walked on. Allen is like Shaun, and I adore your Uncle Allen to bits and pieces." Mary didn't see the look of consternation her brother-in-law, Allen Blackburn, gave to her. She was more than implying that he wasn't considerate, and not being very complimentary to him. "Allen and Shaun both just know what they want and what's best for everyone else, so they go for what they want without any thought of others. But for us, we're more thoughtful."

"Mary Blackburn," Allen spoke from behind her and she turned around quickly to face him, a blush staining her whole face. "I didn't know you found me inconsiderate and thoughtless," the look on his sister-in-law's face made him burst out laughing. "I'm going to have to amend my ways because I want to always please you, Mary. And you've not made any of your rolls for me in a long time." Mary made a face at her handsome brother-in-law seeing that Allen was a copy of her Seth only several inches taller.

"I do love you very much Allen," Mary said while giving him a hug. "And you know I love you." Mary was surrounded by men that all strongly favored one another in looks and in personality, and she was proud of her family, she always had been.

"I love you too, sweet Mary," Allen said gently and hugged her back looking over her head at his brother Seth. "We are blessed with our wives. And on that note, I'm going home to my Alicia. Stay still, Shane. I'm going to Woodville tomorrow and send a telegram to Andrew. I want him to come out and check on Alicia as soon as he can, and he can check on you as well."

Shane watched his Uncle, and his father leave. Only his mother was staying with him at Sarah's house. He felt out of place. Shane felt like he didn't belong here. Shaun belonged here. Shaun, he thought again of the brother that he didn't save. Sarah was like him, Shane thought. She was looking for Shaun to come home. He was certain that she was. They both knew that Shaun was strong-willed and determined. If Shaun wanted to come home, no bullet would stop him.

"Mother," he said to Mary, and she came and sat down on the bed where he lay. "I don't feel right being here. As soon as we're sure the bleeding has stopped, get me home. I need to get away from this place." Mary both saw and heard how serious her son was, and she nodded her head in understanding. "Shaun belongs here Mama, not me. Shaun should have come home."

"I have you," Mary Blackburn said as she touched her sweet son's face. "I love you, Shane. I've always loved you. Your father does as well. Neither of us ever favored one of our twins over the other one. God brought you home to us, and for that, we're thankful to Him."

"But Sarah isn't," Shane said hearing his mother gasp. "What I say is true Mama, and I wish with all my heart, for Sarah's sake, that I was Shaun."

"Shane, you are as valuable as your brother Shaun. Hush now and get some rest." Mary lifted his hand up to her lips and closed her eyes as she pressed a kiss on his fingers. "Thank God you came home to me Shane. I have you. I want you. I love you."

Sarah left the church after the men had helped Shane into a pew and she went down to the river. She hadn't realized until she said it out loud that she was looking for Shaun to return. She hadn't known that she was in this state of denial of his death. She knew better than anyone, if her Shaun could have gotten home or found a way home, he would be here. Like her and Shane, this river was in Shaun's blood. He was a part of this river and a part of her.

She smiled remembering the book he had bought that told him how to do all the things he had done to her in their bed at Twin River. They had such a short time together, so little time as husband and wife. They had made the most of every moment, and now she was glad that they had. He had soaked her up, and she had done the same with him. They had been joined as one, and they were happy to be one. No Shaun, and no Sarah, but one whole person together. She had wanted more of that with him. Sarah had wanted a lifetime connected to the love of her life, and that was what Shaun was to her, the love of her life. Instead, she had only been given a few short days with him, days that she would remember for always.

Sarah had grieved when he left for the war, and she had grieved again knowing that he hadn't left his baby inside of her before he had gone away. She had wanted his baby more than anything in the world. If only he had left that part of himself behind, maybe she wouldn't be grieving as horribly as she was now. She had been so certain that he was coming home. She had been so certain he was alive and coming home to her that his death didn't seem possible.

She knew as she looked out at the river flowing by that she was not going to give up on him yet. She was going to give him a year to return to her. In a year she would accept he wasn't coming back. In the meantime, she would await the coming of winter, the cold nights to come, and the icy mornings to follow those nights. The winter was dead. Maybe in the spring, he would come home. Maybe in the spring, there would be new life.

In the meantime, Shane Blackburn was in her home where Shaun Blackburn should be. She didn't hate Shane or even dislike him. She loved Shane as a friend, she always had. Sarah was just mad inside of herself that Shane had broken his word to her and not brought his brother home. She had no right to feel the way she did, and Sarah knew that too. Shane was suffering as much as she was. But still, in the pit of her stomach, right under her heart, she was mad at Shane for surviving the war and coming home without Shaun. Shane could have at least found Shaun's body and brought her husband's body home for burial. Even though she knew this was unreasonable as well, she couldn't stop herself from feeling as she was feeling. She looked back at her house taking a deep breath. Her Mama would need her help with dinner. They had Shane in their home, and they would have to see that he was cared for and fed. Shane was there, not Shaun. With this thought crowding out all other thoughts from her mind, Sarah turned and slowly left the water's edge and headed for her parents' home.

Allen Blackburn walked into his home in the early afternoon looking for his wife in the kitchen. Within a few moments, Allen realized that his Alicia wasn't downstairs and there was no dinner on the stove in the kitchen. This wasn't like his wife. Alicia always had meals prepared after church for her family.

"You girls go find us something to eat," he said casually to his two younger daughters Jenny and Julie as he took the stairs two at a time to find his wife.

Alicia Blackburn lay on the bed on her side thinking that the wave after wave of nausea would soon come to an end, but the nausea and vomiting weren't coming to an end. She had never been this ill with any of her other pregnancies, and she was held captive where she was unable to move due to the violent morning sickness she was experiencing.

"Allen," she reached for his hand when her husband came into their bedroom, and she knew that he could see how very ill she was. "I think you need to send for Andrew," Alicia cried softly holding her stomach and rocking back and forth, her husband's hand held in her own and pressed against her flat stomach where their baby was.

"Ethan!" Allen screamed for his future son-in-law as he pulled free of his wife's grasp and ran down the stairs. "Ethan!" he screamed the young man's name again as he came to a stop on the front porch of his home.

"I'm here sir," Ethan waved from the yard hurrying to where Allen stood still.

"Take my fastest horse and get to the telegraph office in Woodville. Send a telegram to my brother Andrew, tell Andrew to get out here as fast as he can!" As Allen said this, he saw his daughter Bethany hurrying to stand with Ethan in the yard. She had never seen her father frantic as he was. Bethany knew her father to always be in control and confident.

"I ride faster than Ethan," Bethany said to her father as she turned and ran for the stable.

"We'll both go," Ethan said to Allen as he turned and ran after Bethany.

Allen knelt on the floor by the bed his wife laid upon as she rocked back and forth and moaned. He touched her face feeling helpless and knowing that he was helpless to her. "Please, be all right Alicia. Please. I don't want to live my life without you."

Alicia had seen her husband cry only a few times in the past. She knew his love for her had brought him to his knees again. His love for her was as deep as abiding as her love for him was. They were more than husband and wife, and they always had been.

"We should have had twenty babies by the way we behave, Allen," Alicia whispered these words to her husband and she saw him nodding his head in agreement with her. "But I keep losing our babies," Alicia cried. "I don't want to lose another one. I want to keep this baby." Alicia was crying, and he was holding her hand kissing her fingers when his sister came running into their bedroom.

"Julie came for me," Emily said and hurried to the bed and to Alicia with Mary coming into the room only a moment behind Emily.

"Bethany and Ethan stopped at the Cartledge home and told me you were sick," Mary said with Alicia looking up at her and Alicia knew that she had a good family. "Allen, go have something to eat, and let us take care of Alicia." Mary reached down her hand to Allen, and he took a hold of her hand as she helped him to his feet.

"Mary," Allen spoke his sister-in-law's name as Mary pushed him out of the door of his bedroom, Allen still looking at his wife on the bed and in pain.

"This baby is early Allen, if she loses this one too, well it won't be as bad as the ones that were stillborn," Mary whispered to him, and she saw the agony in his eyes. Allen and Alicia had lost too many babies in their marriage.

Allen went into the hallway and leaning back against the wall he slowly slid down that wall to the floor where he clasped his hands and prayed to his God. He and Alicia were the perfect couple. They never argued or fussed or fought. They were both devoted to one another. They had three healthy daughters, and together they had buried three stillborn babies. Since the last stillborn baby, Alicia had suffered many miscarriages, but they kept hoping that they might yet have another baby. Allen wanted four girls. His plan was his fingers, Allen thought now. With Alicia as his wife and with four daughters to call his own, Allen would have a full hand of girls.

"Allen," Mary said from the doorway. "She's not losing this baby," Mary said and helped him to stand up. "Not yet anyway." Allen went back into the room, and he found Alicia on the bed lying on the pillows, and though she was pale, she wasn't crying in pain any longer.

"I'm sorry," she reached out her hand for her husband, and Allen climbed into the bed with her putting his head on her stomach and looking up at her. She reached down and smoothed his hair, and he clung to her hand.

"I'm afraid I'll lose you," he confessed his greatest fear as he pulled her hand to his lips and saw his sister and sister-in-law leave the room, leaving him alone with his wife.

"God's will be done, Allen. You and I know that better than anyone. God's will be done. I've loved you for a long time. I will love you even in eternity and beyond. And I know you love me." She felt him move up to her and cradle her into his arms.

"I look at Sarah missing Shaun, and I know I never want to understand what she's going through," Allen said to Alicia as she curled up into his arms.

"You saved my life long ago, Allen. We have a good marriage. We always have." Alicia felt better, her stomach wasn't cramped up as it had been and she thought that she was going to get past this. Each pregnancy had been difficult after Bethany, but she had three beautiful daughters, she couldn't give up that she and Allen may have more children. This house, this Blackburn home needed children.

"You saved me right back, Alicia. We went through some difficult days at the start of this marriage," he snuggled closer to her, and he was thankful that all the days since the difficult ones had come easy for them. "You rest now. I'll just stay here and hold you." Allen breathed in her scent, and he thought of them together, how he had been without her one minute, and then in the next minute, she had turned and found him sitting on the upstairs porch right outside this room one night. He had never been without her since.

"I love you, Allen Blackburn," Alicia said softly before she dozed off in his arms safe and secure and right where she belonged.

"Sarah," Shane called her name as she walked past his room. He was sitting up on the edge of the bed trying to get his boots on knowing that without his mother here to wait on him, he had to leave. He had to go home.

"What are you doing?" Sarah asked as she came into the room Shane was in. "Where do you think you're going?" she asked him. For a moment, Sarah thought to herself that she sounded just like her mother.

"I heard Bethany telling Aunt Mary that my Aunt Alicia is in trouble. Bethany and Ethan were going for Uncle Andrew." He tried to pull on his boot, but before he could do so, Sarah had come into the room and pushed him back and down onto the bed.

"Stay still, Shane," she ordered him while she picked up his boots thinking that if she took his boots, then he wouldn't attempt to get up again. "Your Aunt Alicia is going to be fine. But if you bleed to death then she'll grieve herself sick." Sarah started walking toward the door carrying his boots with her. "It's so sad that Aunt Alicia and Uncle Allen keep losing their babies. I wish Shaun had," she quickly fell silent and blushed to realize just what she was going to say to Shane. This wasn't a fit conversation for her to have with him.

Shane saw Sarah blush, and he felt awkward. He knew what she had been on the verge of saying, and he wished that she had Shaun's baby as well. "Sarah, did I have you pick out a stove for

Twin River?" he asked her hoping that by changing the subject she wouldn't be embarrassed any longer.

"Yes. Don't you remember?" Sarah saw his head shaking as she remembered the day he had her pick out the stove for Twin River.

"Since the war, I get confused. I forget things," he said seriously, and Sarah turned her eyes to look into his.

"I'm glad you forgot that day," Sarah said remembering how he had come to her bedroom window. How he had shown her the stove in the catalog, and how he had said the right woman for him was marrying his brother. She had known that he felt for her more than she felt for him, but she was meant for Shaun. She loved Shaun.

"Did I say something wrong to you that day, Sarah?" he saw her back out of the room shaking her head. "Are you sure?" he asked, and she started nodding her head. "I'm sorry, Sarah," she saw him close his eyes, while she stood still. When he opened his eyes, those huge grass green eyes identical to Shaun's eyes, met her eyes and she saw his sorrow for her. "I wish with all my heart that I was Shaun right now and that he was in this bed holding you. I'm so sorry I didn't bring him home to you." He saw Sarah move further out of the room again and she looked like she wanted to cry.

"I'm sorry you didn't bring him home too, Shane. Get some rest. I'll let you know if we hear anything about Aunt Alicia." Shane watched Sarah leave walking down the hallway as he laid still. He wished again that when that man in the hospital had asked his name that he had said Shaun and not Shane. Shane wanted to be Shaun.

Chapter Five

"We have a problem, Bethany," Ethan said after they had sent the telegram from Woodville to her Uncle Andrew in Tallahassee and were now waiting for a reply that Doctor Andrew Martin would be in on the morning train. "It's going to be dark in an hour. There is no way we're going to make Rockhaven by dark, much less Riverbend." He saw Bethany chewing on her lower lip aware that they were stuck here for the night.

"Daddy's going to skin me alive," Bethany said softly looking around the town thinking they should go to the boardinghouse. "We're going to have to stay here the night. We'll go back home with Uncle Andrew in the morning."

"All right," Ethan agreed. "The train gets in at nine o'clock in the morning. I'm sure your father will know that I'll take care of you." Ethan took her hand and together they ran across the street and to the boardinghouse.

"We only have one room left for the night," Mrs. Jerald, the owner of the boardinghouse said to Bethany and Ethan, and Ethan knew that he was going to be sleeping in a chair on the front porch of this place.

Bethany looked around and she saw Clayton Nichols, the deputy sheriff married to Ellen, Sarah's sister, and smiled at him.

"What are you doing here, Deputy Nichols?" she asked the man as he looked at her and then Ethan with a very hard stare.

"I should be asking you that question, Bethany Blackburn," Clayton said still looking hard at Ethan.

"Mama's in trouble with a baby again. Ethan and I came to town and telegraphed Uncle Andrew, he'll be here in the morning," she said seriously, and the Deputy nodded his head still staring hard at Ethan Tucker.

"Sorry about your Mama," Bethany heard Clayton Nichols say to her and to Ethan. "You two aren't married," the Deputy pointed to Ethan and Bethany saw her fiancé had narrowed his eyes. She was unaware that Ethan was feeling as though the Deputy was treating them like they were doing something wrong when they weren't doing anything wrong. Ethan was a former Marine, and an independent man. He was also a gentleman, and he knew how to treat a lady. With Bethany, Ethan would never do anything wrong. He loved her too much to disrespect her.

"Bethany is getting the only room left here, sir. I'm sleeping on the porch," Ethan spoke in a firm and serious voice. "I'm a gentleman sir, and I'll always treat Bethany as the lady that she is." Someone laughed from nearby and Ethan turned to find the Reverend Farmer was standing only a few feet beyond him.

"I was heading home on the morning train," the Minister said as he took Ethan's hand in a firm shake while dismissing the deputy with a slight turn of his body. "You can share my room here with me young man since it has two beds and we're both fellows." Tom Farmer saw Bethany smile and he patted her head as though she were a child. And for the Reverend to view her as a child made perfect sense as he had known Bethany all of her life.

"Thank you, sir," Ethan said following the Reverend into the dining room of the boardinghouse where they all sat down to have something to eat. Before their meal arrived the Reverend prayed for Bethany's mother, father, and the unborn baby with all three very aware that Alicia Blackburn might right now have miscarried. The Reverend also included Shane in his prayer, praying for the young former marine to have complete healing, and to grow strong again for his family.

"So, you two have been engaged a long time," the Reverend casually said as they ate roast beef and potatoes and drank sweet tea together in the dining room of the boardinghouse in Woodville, Florida.

"A really long time," Ethan said, then blushed when he saw Bethany blush reminding himself that he was talking to the Reverend. "We plan on marrying in October, sir. But to be honest, we would have married already except for the loss of Shaun. Everyone has been hurting so badly over that." Ethan fell silent looking down at the roast on his plate. He picked at the meat for a moment before covering Bethany's small pale hand with his free hand.

"I'm not trying to tell you what to do," the Reverend said softly looking from Bethany to Ethan, "But I married Shaun to Sarah before he left for the war. They eloped, and it was the best thing I could have done considering that now we've lost our Shaun. Sarah had those few hours together with Shaun, and those few hours are now cherished for her." Tom Farmer looked at Ethan seeing Bethany beside the young man. "You two could have that one room tonight," the Reverend said seriously. "I don't know why you're waiting to start your forever. You both know you love one another. Bethany is a sturdy girl, and she's full of heart and soul like her daddy. You won't go, wrong son, tying yourself to her. And I think you know that."

Ethan looked down at Bethany, and he knew the only reason he was waiting to marry her was with the hope that the shellshock he was dealing with would wear off. He didn't want her to know just how badly he was suffering in silence of what the war had done to him. She knew about his legs shaking beyond his control. The truth was that he was sitting here now with both legs shaking and she understood. She supported him, and often she would put her hand on his legs when the shaking was at its worse. Her beautiful, unique eyes were looking into his right now, and he knew he didn't want to waste another minute of his life without her as his wife.

"The marriage license?" Ethan asked the Reverend while looking down into Bethany's eyes.

"I can file one for you tomorrow in Tallahassee. You know I can marry you," the Reverend said seriously, and he saw Ethan look over at him.

"I know we should wait for our folks. But I don't want to waste any more time waiting before we begin our lives together. I belong with her." Ethan took Bethany's hand and kissed her hand gently.

"So you take her for your wife?" the Reverend saw Ethan nod his head while the young man looked at Bethany. "And you?" he saw Bethany's eyes were swimming in tears as she too nodded her head while she leaned her head onto Ethan's shoulder. "Finish your pot roast. I pronounce you man and wife. And get up to that room." Bethany gasped and gasped again as she looked to the Reverend Farmer.

"It was that easy?" she asked him, and he laughed at her while picking up his fork full of the roast.

"Painless too," the good Reverend teased her as he filled up his mouth with his food and watched the two young ones leave the table, their roast barely touched. The last Tom Farmer saw of Ethan and Bethany was Ethan looking up from the stairwell landing into Bethany's eyes, her hand in his hand before the young man swung her up into his arms and carried her to the room they would share for the night as husband and wife.

"Alicia," Allen said her name when he saw her sitting up in the bed not looking as pale as she had been earlier. He knew that she had eaten some chicken broth Mary had made for her and she had managed to keep that broth down for over an hour. "You're going to kill me," Allen made this statement as he paced out onto the porch just beyond their bedroom doorway. He then turned, and he came back inside to see her eyebrows raised and staring at him as though he had two heads instead of one.

"Allen, all these years together and I've never wanted to harm you. I seriously doubt your words that I have any intention to kill you." She watched him come back to the bed amazed at how much better she felt than she had earlier in the day, and too, thinking how handsome a man he was and how he belonged only to her.

"I had Ethan go to Woodville to send a telegraph to Andrew to get out here right away. I know Andrew will be on the morning train." Alicia watched Allen as he again paced back out onto the porch, he ran his hand through his thick dark hair before turning back to her, and she saw he was seriously worried over something.

"Allen, just tell me why you think I might bring you harm, and stop looking so tormented. You're making me feel ill again." Alicia saw him stop and stand still and she waited patiently to hear what he had to say as she had always been the patient one in their family.

"I let Bethany ride to Woodville with Ethan," he blurted out all at once. "And there's no way they are going to make it home before dark, and now it's getting late." He saw his wife wave her hand at him in a careless fashion, and he frowned.

"Bethany is a sensible young woman. She's like you that way. Our daughter is in a room in the boardinghouse right now sleeping hard and ready to get up in the morning to meet her Uncle Andrew. Stop fretting Allen, and come to bed." Alicia patted the side of the bed seeing that her husband was looking at her and that he was obviously upset, and Alicia knew, Allen was upset because she wasn't upset.

"She's with Ethan," Allen said this as though their daughter was with a rabid dog.

"Allen, our daughter is just like you. She will always do the right thing. Ethan is safe with her, and she's safe with him." Allen came to the bed and sat down knowing Alicia knew their daughter best. "I'm very certain Bethany is asleep right now in the boardinghouse in Woodville, and Ethan is as well. Each in their own bedroom. I'm more worried about our Shane bleeding in church and needing to stay in Rockhaven than I am about Bethany being alone with Ethan Tucker."

"Yeah, it's been a long day. Andrew can come out here check on you and then go and check on Shane. And you're right. Bethany is probably already asleep, and Ethan as well. They wouldn't risk riding home in the night." He felt Alicia tense next to him, and he pulled her close. "What's wrong?"

"Bethany," she spoke her daughter's name in a strained voice. "Riding home in the night, alone with Ethan in the woods. Thank you for that last thought before I go to sleep." Alicia closed her eyes and whispered to herself, "boardinghouse. Our beautiful daughter is alone in a bedroom at the boardinghouse in Woodville – asleep."

"Ethan," Bethany spoke his name as he closed the door to their room and put her on her feet. "Ethan, I don't know what to do," she laid her head on his chest, and she felt his arms around her. "Mama never talked to me, and I never talked to her. I know there's more than kissing. I'm a farm girl," Ethan put his fingers over her mouth and smiled down into her bright eyes.

"I have this, Bethany," he said tenderly as he pulled her to the bed. "We pull down the covers," which he did and she watched. "And then I do this," he lowered his head to kiss her, and she put her arms around his neck, and he kissed her long and deep and well.

"What are you doing?" she asked as her dress slid to the floor. Ethan had unbuttoned the back without her knowing. She watched as he unbuttoned his shirt before his mouth covered her mouth again. "Ethan?" she said softly as he pulled his shirt off and she touched his bare chest and lost her breath when she did as he felt so firm beneath the palms of her hands. She touched the scar where he had been shot, while he kissed her neck, running his mouth down her neck to her shoulder causing her to gasp and hold on to him tight.

"Are you all right?" Ethan asked Bethany in a gentle way as he cupped her face and kissed her mouth gently. She nodded her head as he reached down and pulled her slip up and over her head. She gasped when he touched her breast with his hand. No one had ever done this to her before. She had never dreamed anyone would touch her the way that Ethan now was touching her, and all she could do was cling to her husband feeling lightheaded and anxious as to what he might do to her next.

"You're even more beautiful without your clothes on," Ethan said as he finished undressing Bethany and he saw her shiver. He gently picked her up, and he laid her down on the bed. He saw her looking at him with huge trusting eyes, and he was thankful that she was trusting of him. "I'll try and not hurt you," he said as he eased himself over her still wearing his pants. He didn't want to shock her with his nude body all too aware that she was innocent of a man.

Ethan stretched her arms above her head, and he took her hands in his hands while he laid on her and he heard her gasp. The hardness of himself touched the softness of her, and he pressed against her gasping when her legs wrapped around his hips. "That's it," he breathed, and he felt her moving against him as he covered her breast with his mouth. "You're going to make me lose control," he breathed against her breast. Bethany went still, she did not understand his words. She was unable to think as he moved his mouth from one breast to the other causing her to shiver and cling to him wondering what might happen next between them.

"You feel so good, Ethan," she cried out, and he reached to remove his pants. He saw her watching him knowing that she had never seen a man without clothes before. Ethan heard her gasp and move up on the bed and away from him, her eyes looking from the part that made him a man to his eyes. "Are you going to?" she couldn't finish what she was going to ask him. She was too innocent despite knowing what she knew as a farm girl. She saw Ethan move gently toward her, she laid still, and she looked up at him with pleading eyes, "you won't fit," she assured him knowing something of the mating ritual.

Ethan stopped what he was about to do with his new wife. Bethany looked frightened of him, he thought as his eyes met her huge eyes in the dim light of their room. "I'll know when I will fit, darlin'," he said against her neck as he resumed kissing her.

Bethany wasn't his first time. Ethan had been with a woman before when he was in Madison. That woman had been much older than he had been and the woman had taken to him for his pretty face. When he had left the woman, Ethan knew many things, and he had only in his teen years. Sometimes he was ashamed of what he had done, other times, like right now, Ethan was thankful that the woman had taught him how to please a woman in bed.

"Don't move," he said softly to Bethany as he moved down her body kissing her stomach and lower still, hearing her cry out when his mouth moved between her legs. Within a few minutes, Ethan knew that he would fit with Bethany, no problem, and she would welcome him coming inside of her.

Bethany felt her whole body throbbing. All she could do was hold on to Ethan not knowing for sure what he was doing to her, but no longer frightened of what he meant to do to her. When he came back up and over her, she was breathing hard and shaking all over in what he had made her feel with his mouth. Then he was inside of her, and it wasn't painful, or awful as she had at first feared that it would be.

"I love you," Ethan said, and Bethany lifted up to meet him holding still while he made her tremor more than she was. "I love you, Bethany," he cried out, and she was breathing hard when he fell on her.

"I love you too," she said against his ear, her hand touching his back and feeling his bare chest against her bare chest.

An hour later, Bethany lay in her husband's arms on her side with his arms around her holding her close. His lips were on her forehead. What they had done was nothing of what she had thought would happen on her wedding night. This, with him, was more than she dared to hope for between them.

Bethany heard Ethan's deep even breathing, and she knew that he was asleep. She was glad that he was asleep so she could think. She almost laughed knowing now why her mother and her father spent so much time alone in their room. She curled up closer to Ethan, and she put her hand on his bare chest. He had told her that he loved her. She was more than in love with him. He was her gift from God.

Bethany's thoughts turned from Ethan and her parents who she was worried about, to Shane and Sarah. Shane and Sarah belonged together. They needed to be together. They both had lost Shaun, and they both had loved Shaun. Her cousin Shaun would want them together. She knew, that in time, when Sarah wasn't grieving so much, she was going to encourage Sarah and Shane to be together.

"No," Bethany heard Ethan crying softly in his sleep, and she leaned up looking down at this pretty face. The moonlight coming in through the window helped her to see him clearly. "I'm sorry," he cried softly as he moved on the bed and she saw his whole body shaking. "I can't, no more," he cried in his sleep, and she sat up, her long thick curly hair falling all around her covering her nude body as she touched Ethan's tear-soaked face. She had heard the family talking about Shane and Ethan suffering from shellshock, and she knew that was what this was, this horrible thing happening to her husband.

"Ethan," she said his name softly and then felt him move quickly. He grabbed a hold of her, and he shoved her down onto the bed. He was above her looking down and breathing hard and fast. He had her pinned to the bed, and he was hurting her. "Ethan," Bethany cried out softly, and she saw him let her go and lean back on his heels. "It's all right," she said sitting up and reaching out to touch his face.

"I didn't hurt you?" he pleaded to know, and she shook her head.

"Never," she said gently and moved closer to him. "I didn't mean to wake you as I did," she said, and she saw him start to relax. "Will you do to me again what you did to me earlier?" she asked of him, and she relaxed when she saw him relax.

"Yes," he spoke in a hoarse voice filled with passion as he pulled her close in his arms holding her for a long time before he moved to make love to her again. "I don't want to ever hurt anyone again Bethany," he said as he joined himself to her and she knew he wouldn't hurt her. Ethan was everything gentle and kind. Ethan loved her, and she loved him.

"Uncle Andrew!" Bethany waved her hand in the air as she saw in the distance her Uncle get off the train and come her way. "You can take my horse." She handed the family member that was a doctor the reins to her horse as she climbed on behind Ethan. "Hurry to my mama." Bethany saw her Uncle kick her horse hard and she felt Ethan kick the horse they were on. Soon, they would be home soon.

"I love your mother very much," Andrew Martin said to his niece as they galloped down the sandy dirt road toward Rockhaven. "If she's not lost this baby, I want to take her home to Tallahassee with me and see if we can see her keep this little one inside."

"Uncle Andrew, you won't ever get her away from Daddy," Bethany said this with certainty. "Mama and Daddy can't ever be apart. Daddy told me he had been parted from Mama years ago and he nearly died without her. He was serious in telling me that too."

"I won't try to part those two," Andrew thought of Allen knowing his brother wouldn't be without Alicia for more than a few hours as Andrew knew his siblings' history far better than anyone else. "They both can come and stay with me in town. Julie and Jenny can come as well. You too, Bethany. All of my Blackburn family can stay with me." Andrew looked over, and he saw his niece clinging to Ethan Tucker causing him to wonder about the young couple. They were acting far too intimate. Allen wouldn't be happy to see them as they were.

"Reverend Farmer married us yesterday evening," Bethany said seeing how her Uncle was looking at her. "I think if Mama and Daddy and the girls come to you in Tallahassee, I'll go home with Ethan to Cherry Lake for a while."

"Does your Daddy know you two are married?" Andrew looked at Bethany, and he saw her blush letting him know the answer to his question before she spoke.

"No, not yet. But the Reverend Farmer married us, so I know it'll be all right with Daddy. It just happened, Uncle Andrew. We neither planned to marry without Mama and Daddy there," Bethany said this truth hoping that her father wouldn't be upset with her, but knowing that he very well might be furious.

"It was my fault, sir," Ethan said meeting Andrew's eyes. "I didn't get her back home before dark, and I couldn't let her stay alone in the boardinghouse. And the Reverend Farmer was there, and he offered to marry us, and it just happened."

"No, it was me," Bethany said interrupting her husband. "I should have stayed home with Mama and let Ethan go alone to Woodville to send you the telegram."

"I just have one question," Andrew said looking at the two of them standing up for one another knowing that was a good sign for their marriage. "Are you happy?"

"Yes," they said at the same time, and he smiled at them kicking his horse harder.

"Then everything will be fine. Best to let me tell Allen and Alicia though," Bethany nodded her head just as Rockhaven came into view and she knew that soon they would be home.

Allen saw his daughter dismount the horse with Ethan holding her close. Bethany's body seemed to slide down Ethan's body, and Allen groaned out loud. He had been that way with her mother, holding Alicia's body molded to his own many many times, and all very intimate moments. He greeted Andrew at the door and told Andrew that Alicia wasn't in the agony that she had been in yesterday seeing Andrew hurrying up the stairs with the intent of checking on Alicia.

Bethany didn't see her father in the doorway watching her as Ethan helped her to the ground. Nor was she aware that her father saw Ethan bend his head and cover her mouth. She didn't see her father close his eyes and hear the older man groan.

Allen opened his eyes to see his eldest daughter was pressed so close to Ethan that the two of them might as well have been nude and making love before his eyes. Bethany did hear him groan the second time, and Allen knew that she saw him when Ethan bent her to deepen the kiss they were sharing.

"Daddy," Bethany spoke to her father as she pulled away from her husband seeing her father walk away from the door and hearing his footsteps on the stairwell seconds later.

"Our daughter spent the night with Ethan," Allen said this while coming into his bedroom not seeing his wife's face. Her brother had just examined her and told her what she didn't know.

"She's farther along than she thought," Andrew interrupted Allen's agony over Bethany and Ethan as he turned and looked down at his wife. "This baby is past the fourth month, Allen. How did you two miss this bump?" Andrew touched his sister's nightgown, and Allen looked dazed, as though he was just now seeing how rounded his wife was. He had thought that her stomach was flat just yesterday.

"It's been a stressful summer, Andrew," Allen made excuse.

"What did you say about Ethan and Bethany?" Alicia sat up straighter in the bed and leaned forward. Allen turned to her and then looked at Andrew as though Andrew might confirm what he was thinking. And Allen didn't want to think what he was thinking.

"It's not as bad as you might suspect," Andrew said in a calm way hearing Allen groan out loud before his brother did a full spin in the middle of his bedroom floor while Alicia gasped and fell back against her pillow. "The way you two carry on and have been for years," Andrew laughed looking from one to the other, "you can't honestly think you're daughter wouldn't grow up to crave the same sort of love you both have together." Allen groaned again before he sat down on the foot of his bed.

"They have to get married," Allen said seriously. "I married Alicia right away." He took his wife's hand, and their eyes met and held.

"Reverend Farmer joined the two of them in matrimony last night at the boardinghouse, so that's taken care of. Now, can we get on to a serious discussion about this baby and my little sister?" Allen nodded his head in shock that his daughter was married and only half listening to what Andrew was saying to him and to Alicia. "I want you both, along with Jenny and Julie to come to Tallahassee and stay with me and my family until this baby comes. Alicia, I think if we put you to bed and you're where I can help you, we can deliver this baby safely. I know you hate to leave your river, both of you, but this baby will be here shortly after the New Year, so you'll not spend that much time away from this place. Allen, I want Alicia in the bed round the clock until this baby comes. She has to come to Tallahassee and be with me."

Allen focused on what Andrew was saying while thinking still of his daughter. "Bethany and Ethan are married?" Allen saw Andrew nod his head.

"Bethany is going to be happy, Allen. Focus on your wife now and this little one that's on the way," Andrew said and saw Allen nod his head.

"Well, certainly I'll have the girls pack for us, and we'll come to Tallahassee for as long as we need to be there. I want Alicia well and safe. And I want our baby to be well and safe. My family comes first. You know it always has Andrew." And he thought again of Bethany married and grown. His oldest daughter had grown up too fast.

"Andrew, I can't take getting bounced in a wagon on the road all the way to Woodville to reach the train station," Alicia said in a weak voice seeing her brother agreeing with her in a single glance.

"We'll need a smoother ride than a wagon, Allen," they looked at one another, and Allen grinned.

"I was saving it for your birthday in November." Allen took Alicia's hand again and laughed. "I bought you an automobile, the latest model, and it rides as though you're floating on a cloud."

"No, you didn't," Alicia spoke on a laugh as her husband nodded his head.

"It's been down in the stables for a month. Let me go get the girls to pack, and I'll pack for us," he saw his wife frown. "All right, I'll get Lonnie to pack for us. We can be on our way tomorrow."

Alicia watched her husband leave the room before she turned to her brother. "Do you really think I can deliver this baby safely?" she saw Andrew nod his head and reach for her hand. "Don't tell Allen. He wants an even five girls in his house. But I really want this baby to be a boy."

"I just want you well and healthy. You've been through so much in your life, Alicia" Andrew said firmly. "Now, I'm going to get back on Bethany's horse and go to Rockhaven. She told me Shane is at the Cartledge house because he started bleeding in church again yesterday."

"Yes, he's not healing fast," Alicia spoke in a worried tone of voice.

"Shane had a bad wound. I'll be back." Andrew kissed his little sister on the forehead and left the room just as Allen came back into the room. Andrew turned around and looked back into the room seeing his siblings' looking at one another. "Um, not to overstep my place as your family doctor, but can you two not do anything more in the bed as husband and wife until we get this little one here safe and sound?" He almost burst out into laughter at the look on his siblings' faces. "It's just a few months," he said and shook his head, "you need to take it easy with her Allen." He saw Allen nod his head and knew that his brother would only hold his sister until after their baby came.

"I think he knows too much of what goes on between us," Allen spoke in an uncomfortable way to his Alicia.

"Andrew knows we're in love and that we've been in love with each other for years," Alicia pulled Allen by his hand onto the bed and made him lay down. "I know how to make you happy without risking my health," Allen rolled her over and looked down into her beautiful eyes knowing she was his whole world.

"No lovemaking for you. No lovemaking for me. And I can't find our daughter Bethany and her new husband," Allen groaned aware that Bethany didn't want to be found because she was with her new husband behaving like he and Alicia behaved as much as they possibly could.

"Take a nap with me and then go look at their new house," Alicia advised. "They're married Allen, so we know what they're doing. Be sure to knock on the door and wait for them to answer before you go inside." She felt Allen's chest moving and wasn't sure if he was laughing or crying. Their beautiful baby girl had grown up and was now a married woman; this was hard to believe.

Sarah slipped into the room Shane was in, and she looked down at him sleeping. His shirt had dried blood at the waistline where his wound was, she couldn't tell if he had been bleeding again. She had heard him in the night crying out for Shaun. But then, she had heard him crying out his own name as well, and she wondered why he would do that. He had called out so many times for his brother and for himself that she had almost come to him and awakened him to bring him away from his tormenting dream.

"Sarah," Shane said when he opened his eyes, and he saw her standing over him. He then looked at the window, and he knew that it was late in the day. "Any word on Aunt Alicia?" he tried to sit up, but he grabbed his side instead, and he held his breath when he did.

"She's holding her own," Andrew Martin said from the doorway, the doctor giving Sarah a smile. "Good to see you again, Sarah," the doctor said as she moved aside so that he could sit down on the edge of the bed his nephew was laying on. "Alicia and Allen and the girls are coming to Tallahassee with me until the baby comes," Andrew spoke to Shane as he changed the young man's bandage. "It'll be their first Christmas away from Riverbend and the family. But I know you'll watch out for their home while they're away." He saw his handsome nephew that greatly favored him meet his eyes and Andrew patted Shane on the shoulder. "You're slow healing Shane. You have to take it easy. Give this another month."

"Uncle Andrew, it's still happening," Shane said, and he didn't look to see Sarah, but he knew that she was still standing in the doorway. "Every night I'm dreaming the same dream."

"I can't say I know what you're going through Shane, but this will pass. You just have to give yourself time to heal. I'm keeping up with the latest reports out of England on shellshock." He saw Shane turn away from him and he knew that his nephew was having a really hard time. "Your friend Ethan is suffering from this as well, Shane. You're not alone. Well, I should say your new cousin Ethan instead of a friend since Ethan married Bethany last night."

Andrew smiled at the look on Shane's face. "Yes, they got married in Woodville by the Reverend Farmer. Your Uncle Allen and Aunt Alicia took the news better than I thought they would."

"My little cousin married," Shane said with a smile. "And to a man that is one of my best friends," Shane said. "That's wonderful news." He heard Sarah breathing hard, and he looked at her standing in the doorway near tears one second, and then the next second she was gone.

"It has to be hard on her to see you," Andrew said absently as he stood to leave his nephew.

"What do you mean, Uncle Andrew?"

"Sarah does not see you when she looks at you," he said looking back down at his nephew. "She's seeing Shaun."

"I need to go home," Shane said seriously. "Am I well enough?" Andrew nodded his head.

"I'm driving Alicia's new automobile," Andrew said to his nephew. "You can come to Riverbend with me and stay there a few days. The family is going home with me tomorrow so you'll have peace."

"Aunt Alicia has a new automobile?" Shane put on his shoes carefully, and then he followed Andrew out into the general store that was attached to the Cartledge home. "Thank you for allowing me to stay here Mrs. Cartledge," he said politely and looked around for Sarah knowing that it was for the best that he not see her. "Thank you too, Mr. Cartledge. My Uncle says it's all right for me to return home now." He moved to the door as the couple assured him he was always welcome. Shane was completely unaware that the couple that he was bidding farewell to were hoping that he would be their next son-in-law. If he had been aware of their thoughts, he would have assured them there was no hope for him and for Sarah. Sarah would always belong to Shaun.

Bethany was running to the house with Ethan beside her and laughing as he caught her in the yard and spun her around. "Hey, you two!" Allen called out to the couple from the upstairs porch of his house, and he saw his daughter and new son look up at him at the same moment. "Is there something you might need to tell your mother and me?" Bethany looked at Ethan and then back up to her father.

"Uncle Andrew said he would tell you," Bethany said with her head tilted back to better see her father.

"Get up here, both of you," Allen hollered down to them seeing his daughter, Bethany walk slowly into the house as he left the porch to meet her in the stairwell.

Allen was waiting at the top of the stairs for his daughter and saw her look of concern from the bottom of the staircase. "Daddy, it was all my fault," she started to say,

"No, sir," Ethan interrupted his new wife, "she's not to blame. It's all my doing." Ethan fell silent as Allen came down the stairs and pulled Ethan into his arms along with Bethany.

"Your mother and I wish we could have been there when you two married, and I'm sure your parents will feel the same way, Ethan." Bethany looked up at her father and sighed in relief.

"So you're not mad at us?" She felt Allen shaking while he held her.

"When have I ever been mad at you Bethany?" Allen asked this question in his most serious voice. "You're your mother made over, and I have a soft spot for you. I always have and I always will. Now enough talk of you," Allen pulled away from his children to say this. "We need to do all we can do to help your Mama and this new baby. Jenny, Julie, your mother, and I are going to Tallahassee to stay the winter with Andrew and his family. He's going to try and help us keep this little baby. Shane is going to watch out for this place since Twin River is only a little way through the woods. Now, what are you two going to do Ethan?"

"Bethany and I have already talked things over, sir. We can come back in the summer, and I can work here with you and Shane cutting the trees and planting new seedlings. Shane said he would handle all the cattle here and help his Dad and Uncle Heath when he's well. So I'm really not needed here." Ethan pulled Bethany close and looked down at her, "And I do want to show Bethany my lake." Ethan smiled down into his wife's eyes seeing her looking up at him. He was anxious to take her home to his lake. He was hopeful when they reached the home he grew up in that the nightmares would end for him, and for her.

"When things settle down for me," Allen said in a kind voice. "I'm going to make the trip and see your lake, Ethan. Until that time, I need you to swear you'll take good care of my girl. She's the best daughter a father could want."

"You have my word, sir," Ethan said seriously, and Allen knew; he had the word of a dedicated soldier, a dedicated Marine. His daughter would be fine. Now if only his wife could have their baby and be safe and the baby survive.

"I have a feeling that it'll be a long winter," Allen said more to himself than his children. "A winter spent in prayer."

PART TWO

Shane and Sarah

Chapter Six

Early March 1919
Twin River, Florida

Shane Blackburn watched the sunset while out on the river in his rowboat. He saw a water bird come in on a glide landing on the river. The majestic fowl settled down for the night. The spring was peaceful, Shane thought. More peaceful than the previous spring as he remembered the trip to Europe and the skirmishes and finally the large battle that he had been involved in, a battle that had cost him the life of his identical twin brother.

The Great War had been a violent and bloody and evil. Every battle had been different from any other war that had been fought before. Poison gases had been used and machine guns that had killed hundreds of men a day. Shane didn't like thinking of the war. He wished there'd never been a war.

In the past weeks, Shane had found that he was getting better from the shell shock that he had been suffering from since his return home. He wasn't feeling as jittery as he had been, and he was more peaceful inside of himself. Though Shane was still struggling with missing his twin brother every day, this grief, he felt certain, he would never move beyond.

The winter on the Saint Marks River had been a calm winter for Shane. Most of the family had gone to Tallahassee and other than tending to the cattle and hunting Shane's life had been solitary. He had gone to church once a month and there he had seen Sarah, and he had loved Sarah from afar.

Shane often remembered his last words to his brother. The cruelty of those words and he had only said them to make his brother mad at him so that Shaun would stay safely behind him in the battle. Shane had told Shaun that he would come home and steal Sarah from Shaun if Shaun didn't return home. He had said those words for one reason only, and that reason was to protect Shaun from the German snipers as he ran into the woods through that wheat field in France. Shane's plan hadn't worked. Shaun, the brave one, Shaun the twin willing to face everything head on and appear fearless, had run into the battle and been gunned down before his twin brother Shane's eyes.

And now here Shane was, finally healed up from the battle wounds he had suffered, alone in the split family home that he and his brother had built to grow old in together with their families. And him in love with Sarah, Shaun's wife, knowing full well that Sarah would always belong to Shaun and never to him.

He had loved her all of his life, Shane thought now watching the sun sink out on the river and wishing he could freeze this moment and make it last longer than it would. Sarah was easy to love, he thought. He started to row for shore intent on getting to the house before full dark set in on him still thinking of her, thinking of Sarah. She had a heart-shaped face and beautiful huge eyes that when she looked at you, she made you know she was only looking at you. She was attentive and caring and sweet, and tiny standing a good fourteen inches below him. And she belonged to his dead brother, a brother he missed every single day.

Shane rowed the boat to shore, and he pulled the boat up and onto the bank before taking the fish he had caught up to his house. Tomorrow was Sunday. He would go to church. This was the Sunday Reverend Farmer came and ministered to the families and the first Sunday this year that they would have dinner on the grounds. He loved dinner on the grounds at the church. Everyone brought a large blanket and spread it out, and a long table was set up where all the women brought their favorite dishes, and there were sweet tea and lemonade, and everyone sat around and talked, and he could remember way back to the days when he was little and his father and his Uncle, both men would chase him around the churchyard and toss him and his brother in the air back and forth to one another while his mother would fret that one of them would drop him.

Shane loved his family, and they would all be together tomorrow. His Aunt Alicia had been safely delivered in early February of a baby boy. At long last, his Uncle Allen had a son, and they were back home on their river. His cousin Bethany and her husband, who was his best friend, Ethan Tucker, had spent the winter in Cherry Lake, Florida with Ethan's family and they were also home. The coming week, he and Ethan would plant the fields in corn and beans and the trees were growing well. They would thin out some areas of the planted pines and ship the wood to Ethan's father in Madison County to cure in his sawmill. They would clear cut other fields of the mature trees and replant in the late springtime or early summer. They would also collect the pine tar from the longleaf pines and in the blacksmith shop Uncle Heath had, they would re-shod all their workhorses. The world was coming to life. Hard work was ahead of them. There would be no idle hands as even the women would go to work in the gardens planting vegetables they would jar for the coming winter.

Life was good on the river. There were plenty of fish, and he and his father had killed and smoked 11 deer in the winter. They had also butchered their hogs and smoked those animals and cured the meat. No one would go hungry in the coming months, and he knew they would often all meet for breakfast at his Aunt Alicia's home where the women would gather, and there would be fresh ham and bacon and venison as well as grits and eggs. Thinking of the buffet, his Aunt Alicia laid out in the mornings made Shane hungry. He was glad his mother had made her yeast rolls yesterday and sent a pan home with him. His mother's yeast rolls were well known in the community. Mary Blackburn made the best rolls of anyone and Shane knew why. His mother put in a hearty helping of sugar in the dough, and she melted some sugar in the butter she brushed on the top of the rolls after they came out of her oven hot and fresh.

Full darkness had caught him before he bounced up the steps of his house and he was thankful Shaun had insisted that they have the gas lights put in. Shaun had also had a bathroom put into the house and had bought a top of the line stove for the kitchen. Things had changed a lot since Shane was little, he thought, and he wondered if he would have enough money this year to buy himself an automobile. He really wanted an automobile.

After frying his fish and eating one of his mother's yeast rolls, Shane went to bed laying in the darkness staring at the ceiling. He had never been alone much in his life. He was a twin, one of two. Everything he did, he had his brother to do that thing with at all times. And now, for almost nine full months, he had to learn to be alone, and he didn't really like being alone. He wanted his brother with him, and that was never going to happen. And then he thought of Sarah. He would see her in the morning at church. He wondered if she would speak to him, and he hoped that she would. Sarah, was his last thought before sleep took over him.

Sarah woke early on Sunday morning. She saw Eddie bouncing around in the hallway, knowing that it was springtime and Eddie could now be out in the open and breathing in the fresh air again. No longer was the outdoors an icy cold from the winter they had just gone through.

Sarah flung open her parents' front door and looked out on the city of Rockhaven where she lived seeing that the dogwood trees were all in bloom and covered in beautiful white flowers. There were trees beyond the house and toward the church that were blooming with pink flowers and some trees were blooming with flowers that actually looked like feathers. The azaleas bushes were in bloom as well, those bushes having grown larger in the springtime and covered with white and pink, and even red flowers. The oak trees had new green leaves on them and the pine trees seemed to have grown two feet taller than they had been in the fall. Everything was awake and alive and beautiful. The birds were loud in the tree, and Sarah smiled, she was almost happy again. She wasn't thinking of Shaun all of the time now. She was aware that she had changed. She was alone and more lonely. Having been the wife of Shaun, even for that short time that they had been joined together as man and wife left Sarah now lost and afraid that forever she would be by herself. She and Shaun had clung to one another in those moments before he left for war. She had known and loved Shaun Blackburn all of her life. She would miss him forever. Had he lived, they would have been happy together, of that fact she was more than certain.

All winter long Sarah had come outside and looked down the road certain that her husband would come riding down that road, wild and out of control and laughing at her for being silly enough to think that any old bullet could stop him from coming home to her. But Shaun never came riding down that road. And finally, the cold, harsh, hurtful reality had set in on her, and she had grieved her loss, and she was now moving into accepting that the love of her life, the man meant for her and her only, was really and truly gone, and no coming back to her ever.

"Shaun," Eddie bounced to the door, and Sarah saw Shane riding up to the church. Why Eddie insisted on saying Shaun's name first when Eddie saw Shane, she would never know. But then,

Eddie always confused the twins, and she knew, eventually, Eddie would call Shane by his rightful name and say he was sorry. But the agony of hearing Shane called Shaun was always too much for Sarah to bear. Maybe this was Eddie's way of grieving, Sarah thought. Eddie wasn't like her, Sarah knew as he often got things confused. Eddie had also loved Shane and Shaun equally. He always had, whereas she had loved both of the twins as well, but she was in love with Shaun, and maybe that was why she didn't get them confused as her brother was doing even though one of the twins was gone. "Shane," he said from beside her, and she hugged Eddie, he was special, he was sweet.

The fact was, had her family lived anywhere besides here in this small town, Eddie would have probably been hidden away in the attic or out in the tool shed as her brother-in-law Clayton Nichols wanted. That's what folks did with people like Eddie. But here, everyone protected him and reached out to him. Everyone knew that Eddie was like a six-year-old boy in his mind and always would be. He was harmless, and he was sweet and loving, gentle and kind, and he just loved to clap his hands and bounce around and run along the banks of the river, and he knew never to go into the river ever. He knew to just stay on the riverbank. The river had almost kept Eddie once, Sarah thought watching her brother run to Shane and help take a basket of food inside the church, Shane ruffling his hair after giving him a quick hug. She was glad Uncle Allen had saved her brother that day long ago. Very glad.

The buggies had started arriving, Sarah saw. Church would be packed today. The Reverend Farmer was here for services, and it was Sunday dinner on the grounds. All the ladies had on their hats and shawls, and everyone had a covered dish they were taking inside the church, and Sarah knew the Reverend wouldn't have a long sermon today, the smell of good food would make everyone want to eat and not listen to the Minister. She smiled and heard her parents come up behind her and both hug her good morning before her mother handed her a dish of bean salad she had made and her father carried the fourteen layer chocolate cake that Sarah had made.

"Shane is here," Thomas Cartledge said and turned to look at his wife. They both had hoped that the winter would heal Shane and Sarah of their grief and the two would turn and find one another and grow close again. Shane wasn't Shaun, but they knew their daughter had grown up loving both brothers and Shane was a fine and good man that would provide for Sarah a good life. They both wanted Shane for their daughter.

"Hello, Sarah," Lester Billings said as he rushed to take the food she was carrying from her and take the food inside the church. Sarah didn't see her parents frown. They knew Lester wasn't right for their daughter. He was lazy, and he always showed up around dinner to get a free meal. They didn't think he was a bad sort; they just didn't want him for their daughter. The Cartledge's had their heart set on Shane Blackburn for their Sarah and looking up at Shane standing on the top step of the church entranceway they felt certain that Shane wanted their Sarah as well.

"Lester," Sarah pulled away from him, the man was too close. She hadn't told her parents, but several times Lester Billings had tried to touch her in an inappropriate way, and she was very uncomfortable around him. He was smiling at her now, and no one saw, but he pinched her bottom, and she almost cried out in horror of what he had done to her. How dare this man do that to her, Sarah thought, and she turned red in her face stepping closer to her mother with a feeling of humiliation consuming her.

Shane saw what Lester had done to Sarah, and his eyes narrowed. He came down two of the church steps, and he faced Lester without hesitation. "She's a lady," Shane growled in a low voice so no one could hear him besides Lester. He saw out of the corner of his eye that Sarah heard him as did her parents, but he kept his attention on Lester. "No man touches a lady like you just did,"

Shane balled up both fists as he looked at Lester and saw the smaller man back down the church steps half afraid of Shane and Shane wanted this man to be terrified of him in this moment. Lester would have no doubt that Shane would do whatever must be done to protect Sarah.

"Here," Lester thrust the food he had taken from Sarah at Shane hoping to fill the man's hands so Shane would not pummel him as Shane looked ready to do. Within seconds, Lester was hurrying up the steps and into the church.

"I'm sorry he did that to you," Shane said to Sarah and saw her blushing worse than she had been. She was almost in tears, but he saw that no one beyond her and her parents had heard what he said to Lester, though her parents hadn't seen what Lester had done to Sarah, and Shane felt relieved that they hadn't. No parent should see their daughter humiliated.

"Thank you for standing up for my daughter," Thomas Cartledge said turning to his wife. "If that Lester comes around again, let me know. I'm sending him on his way, away from my daughter."

"I heard he molested a woman over in Jefferson County," Sarah heard her mother Ester say this, and she saw Ester shivered physically while Sarah stood shocked and still by her mother's words. She had never heard of any woman being molested near here. Their community was small and peaceful and happy. Her brother-in-law, Sheriff Deputy Clayton Nichols rarely ever had an issue with anyone. Only on Saturday night someone in Woodville might get drunk and cause a scene. Where they lived, down here on this river, life for everyone was kind and gentle and good.

"Let's go inside so you folks can see my new cousin," Shane said with a smile and led the way into the church. "Uncle Allen really wanted another girl, but I can tell he's happy over the boy."

"What did they name the baby?" Sarah asked, and she saw Shane fall silent and pinch his lips. Aunt Alicia was holding the new baby wrapped in a beautiful bright blue blanket, and Sarah suddenly knew just why Shane had gone silent. She knew the baby's name. "His name is Shaun," she breathed and saw Shane look at her.

"Yeah. The baby is Uncle Allen's son, and everyone knows that Shaun and I look just like Uncle Allen. Shaun was wild and full of life like Uncle Allen has always been. Aunt Alicia said no other name would do. And it would keep the memory of our Shaun always alive. They're calling him Shaun Allen."

"I understand," Sarah said softly as her eyes met Alicia Blackburn's eyes, and she saw the joy of the new mother. Tears pooled in Sarah's eyes while looking at Alicia. She had wanted a baby by Shaun, but she hadn't been gifted with a baby. And now she was alone, too alone, and all alone.

"Sarah, it's so good to see you," Alicia said, and Sarah was hugged by Uncle Allen who proudly showed off his son.

"He's as pretty as my girls," Allen teased the crowd that had gathered around to see his new son. With his arms around his wife Alicia, and with her leaning into him and looking healthy and stronger than she ever had in the past, Allen showed off his new baby son knowing that having this son was a miracle from God.

"Shaun," Sarah said looking down at the baby.

"Shaun Allen," Alicia said gently. "Would you like to hold him?" Alicia saw Sarah's head nod before taking the baby into her arms and cradling the baby unaware that Shane was watching her and everyone watching Shane standing close beside Sarah as though they were a couple. "I'm so glad you gave him such a beautiful name. Now we'll never forget my husband." Sarah handed the baby back to Alicia realizing that her face was covered with tears. "If my Shaun were here, he would be pleased as punch to know you gave your baby his name." Sarah wiped her face and forced a smile onto her lips.

"Knowing Shaun, he would have expected us to name the baby for him," Allen forced a laugh. "He was on fire with life," Allen's voice lowered, and everyone knew that Shaun's light had burned fast, hard, bright, and gone out too quickly.

The Reverend entered the church, and everyone took their seats and as expected the service was shorter than usual. The Reverend loved to eat, and he said so when he ended services after only thirty minutes. No one even sang the final hymn.

"Thank goodness for these Sunday dinners on the church grounds," Shane said to his mother Mary as she set a large pan of her rolls out on the table. "I'm so tired of my own cooking. I need a real meal." Mary frowned at her son and slapped his hand as he grabbed a roll.

"Shane Blackburn," she said sternly. "With all the women and food cooked in homes all around you and you are starving. Bring yourself home every day, I'll feed you." He laughed and kissed his mother's cheek.

"I'm trying to learn to live with my own company, Mama," he looked up, and he saw Ethan Tucker coming toward him, and he quickly grabbed another roll which he threw to his best friend.

"You look better than the last time I saw you," Ethan said taking a bite of the roll. "Tomorrow let's ride out to the north field and check on those trees we planted last year."

"Sounds like a plan," Shane said going toward his cousin Bethany with Ethan by his side. "I also need to check on the longhorn cattle we have out that way. It's been a quiet winter. Are you and Bethany here for the summer?"

"Yeah, my folks are planning a visit for a couple of weeks this summer as well. It's really nice that Bethany's Mama and Daddy have grown so close to my Mama and Daddy. The friendship between our parents makes our family feel more complete." Shane nodded his head as he hugged his cousin Bethany, she was little like Sarah, he thought.

"I see Sarah all alone," Bethany said gently looking at Shaun's widow standing under a tree. "Oh no, that lazy Lester," she hissed, and Shane turned to see Lester coming up behind Sarah, and the man pinched her bottom again and then laughed as Sarah jumped forward with a horrified look on her face. "How dare he," Bethany said and made a move to go to Sarah with the intention of telling Lester how wrong he was to touch a woman that way.

Ethan grabbed his wife by the arm to stop her while he shook his head hard. When she looked up at her husband she saw him nodding toward her cousin Shane who was walking with long strides across the churchyard and within seconds, Shane had lifted Lester up off the ground by the shirt collar and shoved Lester back into the tree Sarah had been standing under only seconds before.

"You lay one more hand on her or any woman in this county again Lester," Shane hissed in the man's face, "And I'll take you down. Do you understand me?" Shane saw Lester's head nod, and he let Lester go watching Lester fall to the ground. Shane turned to Sarah, and he saw her hurrying toward the crowd at the table.

"It's not like she's pure, Shane," Lester said looking after Sarah. "She lay with your brother before he left for war. Shaun taught her how to please a man I bet. She shouldn't be alone now." Lester had stood up, but only for a second. Shane had punched Lester in the face and then lifted the man up off the ground where Lester had fallen, and Shane punched Lester in the face again.

"Hey," Deputy Nichols yelled seeing Shane punch Lester. Everyone knew Lester was a nasty person, but that didn't give Shane the right to knock Lester's head off, and Clayton Nichols said so.

"He assaulted Sarah, twice," Shane said softly so only the Deputy could hear him and he saw Clayton Nichols looking down at Lester in a stance that made Shane know that Clayton was going to knock the man down if Lester tried to get up.

"He touched my wife's sister?" the Deputy asked looking quickly at Shane.

"Twice, and he said something very ungentlemanly about her," Shane informed the Deputy who looked down at Lester.

"I have a gun," Clayton said firmly to Lester. "And I know how to use my gun. I always hit what I aim for. You touch any woman in my county again, and I'll gun you down." Shane nodded his head backing up the Sheriff.

"You lay one more dirty finger on Sarah, and the Sheriff won't have to gun you down. I'll kill you with my bare hands, and as a Marine, I know just how to do that," Shane said to Lester not seeing the crowd in the churchyard looking at them and hearing their words to Lester.

"Shane was always the quiet one," one of the ladies at the table said hearing Shane's words to Lester. "Shaun was the one that would have punched someone in the face and threatened to kill any man that touched his Sarah."

"I never liked that Lester," Ester Cartledge said to the woman. "And rumor has it he molested a girl over in Jefferson County." Several of the women gasped, and the men stood still at the table watching the scene of Shane standing over Lester and the Deputy with a hand on his holstered gun.

"Are you hurt, Sarah?" Bethany asked as she came up to Sarah, who was watching Shane. Sarah had never seen Shane like this before. Shane was like she was, calm and quiet and gentle. He would have done as she had done and walked away from someone like Lester. But there he stood, his fists clenched at his side and having hit Lester not once, but twice.

"The war changes a fellow," Ethan said thinking what Sarah was thinking. He knew Shane to be calm and quiet and easy going. Shaun would have beaten Lester half to death for having looked at Sarah.

"It's not just the war having changed him," Bethany said taking her husband's hand. "It's Sarah. Shane and Shaun always loved her. The three of them were best friends. We all were really. Shane wouldn't let anyone hurt or touch Sarah anymore than Shaun would have."

Sarah stood still looking at Shane. She knew that Bethany was right. Shane would protect her, maybe not as firmly as Shaun would have, but he would protect her with his life. She saw Eddie bounce up to where Lester lay on the ground and hug Shane and then hug Clayton Nichols. The Deputy didn't hug her brother back as Shane had done. It was no secret that Clayton felt that Eddie should be hidden away. The Deputy had suggested it to everyone, even to her own parents, but no one listened to him. Eddie was loved and accepted here, and the Deputy knew that the Blackburns took care of their own. And Eddie, though not a blood relative to the Blackburn clan, had long ago been taken in as one of their own and they liked him running around hugging everyone. The Blackburns saw Eddie as a valuable asset. He could run errands and deliver messages. Eddie never lied, and he could keep a secret – sometimes, Sarah thought. He could chop wood and fish better than anyone around, and when his father came home from hunting, Eddie would clean the squirrels so well they would have the least amount of lead to be found in them. Eddie was well loved, but not by Clayton. Given half a chance Clayton would have had Eddie locked away for good to hide what Clayton felt was the family's shame when Eddie was really and truly the family's joy.

Shane fixed a plate of food and went to sit with his family on one of several blankets that his father and mother had spread out. He saw Sarah with her family only a few yards away, and he lifted his hand and nodded his head to her, but she only looked down at her food and away from him, a slight blush staining her cheeks. He wondered if she were upset with him for making a scene in the churchyard with Lester and he hoped that she wasn't. At least Lester had left the gathering and was no longer a threat to her.

Bethany sat watching her cousin Shane. Her father sat beside her, and he caught her eye, and she saw Allen look at Shane and then to Sarah. Her father knew what she knew, Bethany thought as Allen's eyes came back to her. She was certain that Allen knew that their Shane was in love with his brother's wife, Sarah. Bethany silently wished that they would find one another. Shaun would want Shane and Sarah together, and she almost said this to her father. But she knew that she didn't have to tell her father anything. Allen was looking at her, and she could read his mind, they were that close. Her father's thoughts mirrored her own thoughts.

How could she play matchmaker? That's what she felt her father was trying to ask her with his silent questioning beautiful grass green eyes looking into her own and she shrugged her shoulders. They really couldn't interfere, all anyone could do was let nature take its course and hope for the best. She reached for her father's hand, and they both nodded seeing her mother smile. Bethany knew her mother didn't know what was passing between them, but her mother knew how Allen and Bethany could communicate with one another without words being spoken.

Bethany looked from Allen, her father, to Alicia, her mother, and she knew that she only knew a part of her parents' story. They had nearly been driven apart early in their marriage, and she had been born while her father was away. But Allen had returned to the family and the moment he saw her in her cradle, she had belonged to him forever and always. She was his special girl, born when he was gone, but born again when he returned and born into his heart.

Shane watched Sarah stand and wander down to the river. He wanted to join her but didn't dare do so. He'd embarrassed her today by fighting with Lester, and he didn't want to ever cause her any harm. He kept thinking of his final words to his brother before they went into battle and he fought not to cry. He had told Shaun that if Shaun didn't come home, if Shaun didn't stay behind him and died, then he would come home and he would take Shaun's wife as his own. He had told his brother that he would love her better than Shaun ever had. He had told Shaun the truth, that he loved Sarah. But he hadn't meant that he really would come home and marry Sarah if Shaun died. Shane had only said those words to make Shaun stay behind him so that Shaun wouldn't get shot.

And then, in the thick of the battle, Shane had seen his brother Shaun shot. Now, closing his eyes, Shane saw that scene within his mind all over again. He remembered his brother's death, and he lost his breath watching as Shaun had fallen away from him, his hand stretched out and reaching for Shaun as he too fell shot to the ground only seconds later.

"Shane," Ethan said and touched his shoulder as Shane came back to the place he was in and away from his memories of the battle. "Are you all right?" Shane nodded his head, and Ethan removed his hand from his friend's shoulder.

"Some things, you just can't ever forget," Shane said and wiped his face with his handkerchief. "Time doesn't heal all wounds," he said softly and felt his mother touch his back.

"You're not alone, son," Seth said to him, and Shane looked around at all the people surrounding him. The people that were his family. Julie and Jenny, his younger cousins, were fussing over the baby. Aunt Alicia was leaning into Uncle Allen who was holding her with a pleased look on his face. Ethan had laid down his head in Bethany's lap, and she was tracing the scar on his face with her fingertips and smiling down at him like they were completely alone. He saw Heather sitting by herself and quiet which was her way, and Heather's mother Emily, and father Heath were facing away from everyone and looking up at the fluffy white clouds overhead. His parents were looking at him with tender smiles, his handsome father holding his sweet, gentle mother's hand and Shane knew; he had a good family. He was deeply blessed.

"We're the Blackburns," Shane said seriously. "We'll always stand by one another." He saw his Uncle Allen's head nod in agreement with his words before he stood up knowing that he would find his way to the river. He would find his way to Sarah, and then he would go home and enjoy the peaceful end of the day secure in who he was, and that he was surrounded by a clan that loved him as much as he loved all of them, even though he was without his identical brother Shaun.

Sarah leaned back against a cypress tree while she looked out at the river. The breeze coming off the river was cool, almost cold in the springtime, but Sarah didn't mind. She was wearing thick clothes, and she had on her shawl. She wondered why Lester Billings had suddenly focused his attention on her. He was always around the store, and he kept trying to touch her. She was having to step away from him, and he was worrying her almost constantly. She never gave him any indication that she wanted his attention. In fact, she had shown him by her reaction toward him that she wanted him to leave her alone.

She saw Eddie off in the distance chasing a squirrel, and she thought of how Lester had treated Eddie. While he pinched and tried to touch her, he had hit Eddie in the head several times in the past. Lester was mean to her brother, and she had told him to stop, but Lester had kept on, and she just wanted Lester to away, to go back to Jefferson County and leave them alone. She wished Lester had never come here, and now today, Shane had seen how Lester had touched her and humiliated her.

"Sarah," she heard Shane say her name from behind her, and she spun around losing sight of Eddie off in the distance. "I'm sorry if I embarrassed you today," he said gently, and she nodded her head.

"I'm grateful to you, Shane," Sarah took his hand as she uses to in the days before she married Shaun and she swung his hand back and forth within her own. "Clayton knows that Lester has been mean to Eddie. Lester hit Eddie in the head, Clayton never stood up for Eddie. So today, when you stood up for me, I felt like you were helping keep Eddie safe as well." She let go of Shane's hand, and she didn't see the look on his face.

When Sarah had taken hold of his hand, a fire had shot through Shane. A fire of pure desire and he knew that he didn't want her to ever let him go. That feeling faded fast when he remembered she belonged to his brother Shaun, and that feeling was followed by shame that he desired her as he did.

"I was just standing here praying and hoping that Lester goes back to Jefferson County soon. Tomorrow wouldn't be soon enough." Sarah spoke having no idea what her brother-in-law was thinking and feeling in this moment.

"Has he bothered you that much, Sarah?" Shane stepped closer to her. "If he does anything to harm you Sarah, or to harm our Eddie, you come for me. I'll kill him for you." Sarah looked up into Shane's grass green eyes, and she knew that he was serious in his words. "The war changed me, Sarah. I'm not like I was. I'm sorry if that upsets you or shocks you. But I won't allow anyone to harm my family, and you'll always be my family. Lester touches you in any way ever again, and I'll bury him in that river so no one will ever find him."

"You almost sound a little like Shaun," Sarah said with a forced laugh.

"No, I don't." Shane looked out at the river thinking of his brother. "Lester would already be dead for having looked at you were I Shaun." He looked down at Sarah. She had taken his hand again, and he wanted nothing more than to turn and pull her into his arms and hold her forever against his body. But he knew that he would offend her. She was Shaun's wife forever. He had no right to her. And he heard in his mind the words that he had said to Shaun before they went into those woods and faced the Germans, words of betrayal and coveting his brother's wife. Shane knew he could never touch her. If he did touch Sarah, he would be following through on the horrible words that he had said to his brother all those months ago.

"Can we be friends again?" Sarah asked Shane, and she felt his hand relax in her hand. He could be her friend. He could always be her friend. He forced a smile onto his handsome face, and the more he forced the smile, the more natural the smile became. And like her, he swung her hand in his hand.

"We've always been friends," Shane said seriously. "Here comes Eddie," he laughed as Eddie slammed into him and gave him a bear hug.

"I love you, Shaun," Eddie said and then looked at his sister. "I'm sorry. I mean Shane." Shane messed up his hair and hugged him close.

"It's all right, Eddie. You can call me Shaun if you want to," Shane saw Eddie's eyes light up.

"Shaun," Eddie said and hugged Shane again this time pushing on him until the tree Sarah had been leaning against stopped him. This was probably Eddie's way of dealing with grief, Shane thought, and was overwhelmed again with regret. When the man was taking their names while he lay wounded on that cot and the man kept asking his name, had he only said Shaun's name instead of his own, right now Sarah would be his. But he wasn't Shaun, and he was certain of that in his own mind, and Sarah would have known in time that he wasn't the man that she had married. She had been intimate with Shaun. A wife would know her own husband in bed. He was Shane; he would always be Shane no matter what name Eddie called him.

Sarah's prayers weren't answered. Lester Billings didn't go back to Jefferson County. In fact, he was a fixture for the whole month of March and into April in the small community of Rockhaven. No one knew what type of work Lester was doing to support himself, or even where he was living. No one had him staying in their home or working for them because they all disliked him heartily for his treatment of Eddie. And Eddie would see Lester and run the other way afraid of Lester. Deputy Nichols, Eddie's own brother-in-law knew that Lester was hitting on Eddie and Clayton made no move to stop Lester or to protect Eddie in any way, and the whole town was furious with the Deputy for being so heartless where his own family was considered. And Eddie was the deputy's family.

Lester was leaving Sarah alone physically. He hadn't laid a finger on her, but he was saying rude things to her, asking her what Shaun had taught her in bed that she might now teach a man. She had burned inside by his disgusting questions of her. He was always around the store, and she tried to never be alone in the store for fear that he might touch her as he had in the past.

Shane had come in that morning and purchased a coke while he was on his way to Woodville, and he said he would stop back by on his way back home. Sarah had stood in the doorway of the store and watched him gallop down the road watching Eddie chase after him for a way before Eddie turned and came back to her.

"I saw Shaun," he yelled, and she hoped soon her brother would accept Shaun was gone and call Shane by his rightful name.

The sun was sinking low when Shane came back by the store and stopped thinking he would grab another coke. The drink had become all the rage, and it was better than water. "Shane," Ester said as he came into the store. "We were just fixing to lock up and have dinner, won't you stay?" He smiled at Ester and saw Tom nodding to him, and he smiled at them both

"I'm not dumb enough to turn down a meal you make, Mrs. Cartledge," Shane said and saw Tom move to lock up the store. "Not when I cook as bad as I do."

"Shane," Eddie bounced in, and he smiled, his friend finally remembered his name and didn't call him by his brother's name. "I ran after Shaun's horse this morning," Shane knew Eddie had chased after him on his way to Woodville today, and he hugged Eddie close when the man came into his arms.

"You sure did," he agreed with Eddie feeling it was best to agree with Eddie.

"Mama said she invited you to dinner," Sarah said in a shy way. "I have the table set and everything ready for dinner. I need to talk to you later Shane," she said almost in a whisper, and she saw him nod his head to her.

"It's nice to have you join us, Shane," Thomas Cartledge said after he said grace and filled Eddie's plate with food and then gently ordered his son to be still and eat. Eddie smiled at Shane across the table from him, and Shane winked back at Eddie feeling comfortable with this family despite the fact that his brother was the one that belonged here at this table.

"So, how are you liking your new stove?" Ester asked Shane to make conversation, and his eyes met Sarah's from across the table. She sat next to her brother and looked like she wanted to hear his answer as the stove had been bought with her in mind.

"Mrs. Cartledge," Shane said in a serious voice, "I don't use the thing." He looked at Sarah eating a fork full of mashed potatoes, and he smiled. "I'm not much of a cook really. I fry fish in a cast iron skillet out in the yard over an open fire, and I eat yeast rolls mama gives to me. This is the best meal I've had in a week," he said seriously.

"Sarah made dinner for me tonight," Ester said proudly. "She's a fine cook." Shane nodded his head in agreement.

"Judging by this meal," he said smiling at Sarah, "she's one of the finest cooks in the county." He saw Sarah blush and look up at him and he winked at her nodding his head, he was being honest with her about her cooking.

After the meal was over and the kitchen had been cleaned, Sarah joined her father and Shane on the porch. She took his hand and swung it as she always had when they were innocent children totally unaware of the desire that shot through him again, or of the love he held for her. Sarah had no idea of how much Shane wanted to hold her in his arms as his brother Shaun had and to make love to her, to love her forever.

"Can we go for a walk," she asked him before looking at her father. "Can you keep Eddie here, Daddy? I need to talk privately with Shane." Sarah saw her father nod his head and smile a very pleased smile and she shook her head hoping her father understood that Shane would always only be her dear friend.

"What's the matter, Sarah?" Shane wasn't hopeful that she wanted to be alone with him because she wanted only that, to be alone with him. He knew how Sarah felt about him. She only wanted him for her friend. If she wanted to talk to him, it was nothing to do with him personally.

"I want you to know that Lester Billings is still hanging around. He hit Eddie again today in the head. I hate him, Shane," she said harshly. "He's a cruel little man." Shane silently agreed with her.

"How can I help?" he asked and turned to look down at her.

"If he's in church this Sunday and you see him, can you tell him to leave Eddie alone? He's not touched me since you confronted him."

Shane saw Sarah's lips moving, and heard her words. He knew that he would do anything for Eddie. And then he had her pulled close, and his mouth was covering her mouth. This just happened. This had not been anything that Shane had planned. For so long he had wanted to kiss her. Forever, he had long been dying to hold her, and for what felt like forever, he had loved her. And he had never made a move because she was Shaun's.

She was molding her body into Shane's body. Her arms came up and around his neck, and he heard her soft cry and caught that soft cry in his mouth. He lifted her feet off the ground. She was so much smaller than him that he couldn't get her close enough without pulling her up to him and she was holding him just as tight. His mouth left her mouth and traveled up her cheek and then down her neck. Her head was thrown back, and she was crying as her hands held his head and she pulled him closer. And then he knew, she was crying. Not crying out in desire, but actually crying.

"God, forgive me, Sarah," he said as he lowered her to the ground and held her sobbing in his arms."I didn't mean to do that to you. I'm so sorry." He looked down at her and wiped the tears off of her face with his thumbs, his hands cupping her face. "I'll protect Eddie with my life. I'll face that dirty Lester on Sunday, no fear. Please, forget what just happened." He pulled her close and couldn't see her face any longer, her face was buried in his shirt, and he knew, he had brought her to tears with his selfish ways, and he shouldn't have done that. He might have harmed their tender friendship.

"I have to go home," Sarah said and pulled away from Shane. She didn't look up at him, and he felt worse for what he had done. He grabbed her hand before she left him and he pleaded to know,

"We can still be friends? You don't hate me for this?" He saw her face turn slightly toward him, her cheeks still stained with tears.

"You'll always be my best friend, Shane," she said, and he let her hand go and watched her run home knowing that he had to go back to her home to get his horse. He waited for a long time before he moved knowing she would have reached her house and gone inside by now. In a moment he would know that it was safe to go back for his horse.

Sarah ran past her father and into the house and closed herself away in her bedroom. What had just happened? Her mind screamed as she flung herself onto her bed. Shane Blackburn had just kissed her, like a husband kisses his wife, like Shaun had kissed her, no she thought, better than Shaun had ever kissed her, and she was on fire yet with the desire his kiss had caused to spread throughout her.

She lay on her back and looked at the ceiling wondering what she was going to do. She wouldn't ever look at him the same way again. Sarah knew the truth, her truth. She wanted him, and maybe she always had wanted him. She moaned out loud and rolled on her side. If Shane hadn't have kissed her she never would have known she wanted him. How could she be this way? She loved Shaun. She wanted Shaun forever as her husband. And now she wanted Shane. Shaun was gone, and with all her heart, with every ounce of her soul, Sarah wanted Shane to do to her what Shaun had done to her.

Shane went back to the house and got his horse. He saw Thomas on the porch and mounted his horse thanking the older man for dinner. "Wait," Thomas left the porch and came into the yard. "Sarah just ran past me looking upset. What happened?" Shane looked down at Thomas Cartledge, and he couldn't lie to the man.

"I'm sorry sir. I forgot myself, and I kissed her. I'm hoping that in time she'll forgive me." Shane didn't see the look of gladness on Thomas Cartledge's face, nor did he see Ester's at the door turn and run to her daughter's room. Shane was galloping out of their yard feeling a guilt consumed him. "I'm sorry Shaun," he said to his brother in the stillness of the night hoping that his brother in heaven wouldn't hate him.

Ester burst into her daughter's room and stood in the doorway looking at Sarah on the bed. "Shane," her mother said his name and Sarah sat up and faced her mother. "He just told your father that he kissed you and he hoped that you would forgive him." Her mother was smiling from ear to ear and bouncing around so like their Eddie often did. "Shane really kissed you?"

"Mama, I'm Shaun's wife," Sarah moaned, and her mother hurried to her.

"Shaun is gone. Shaun is dead Sarah, and he loved you enough to want you happy. He would want you protected and cared for. And who better to do that than his own twin brother. Shaun would sanction this budding romance. I'm certain of it." Sarah laughed out loud at her mother for being romantic at heart.

"Let us just take it one step at a time, Mama," Sarah said. "I'm not certain I want to be with any man much less marry again. And Shane has always been my friend." Her mother hugged her and smiled before Ester jumped up, again just like Eddie, and Ester ran out the door to tell her father that Sarah didn't need to forgive Shane for kissing her. Sarah had liked that Shane had kissed her.

It seemed like all of a sudden, life wasn't so hard, Sarah thought. She felt as though even in the darkness there was a light. She laid back on her bed, and she thought of Shane at her window with the catalog in his hands, and she thought of him down by the river, their hands held and swinging. All the times she had played with him in the river growing up, and that Sunday he had punched Lester in the face for coming near her. Shane, he wasn't Shaun, but she knew, she had always loved Shane dearly.

Eddie wasn't what you would call a smart man, not in the way of reading and writing and arithmetic. Eddie wasn't stupid either. Eddie knew right from wrong, good from bad. He knew you always should be nice and hold a door open for a lady. You should always put your napkin in your lap. You shouldn't gossip and say mean words, and you should be nice to everyone and give hugs. That's all Eddie wanted to do, was to give hugs. No, Eddie wasn't a smart man, but he wasn't a stupid man either.

His parents had gone to Woodville for the day and left Sarah in charge of the store. He had been helping her, and at the close of day, she had him bring in the cracker barrel and sweep the front store porch while she put things up in the storeroom and they prepared to lock up. He had heard a noise and put the broom by the door, and he had gone to see what the noise was. He saw his sister looking different than he had ever seen her before and he turned away from her leaning against the wall outside the storeroom. He put his hands over his face and rocked back and forth trying to think what he should do.

Eddie went into their home which connected to the store, and he hurried into his father's bedroom looking at the hunting rifle that was kept by the bedroom door. His father had told him never to touch that rifle ever unless there was a rabid dog in the yard or a snake in the house. Eddie knew how to shoot the gun. He knew that the gun was loaded. But he had been taught to never touch that gun unless there was danger and he knew, right now, there was danger to his sister.

Carefully he picked up the gun, took hold of it as his father had taught him too and he walked back into the store and into the storeroom where his sister was. Sarah was on the floor, and she was crying, then he heard her scream and Eddie, sweet, gentle, kind, loving and caring Eddie, fired that gun he had never touched without his father with him and Eddie killed a man.

Sarah had gone into the back storeroom while Eddie swept the front porch preparing the store to close for the night. The storeroom wasn't well lit, but she knew where everything went, and she felt all right putting things away in the room full of shadows with very little light. And then someone grabbed her. Someone shoved her to the floor, and she was fighting for all that she was worth trying to get out from under whoever had her pinned down to the floor. She had tried to scream, but the man's hand was over her mouth, and she bit down hard on the palm of his hand causing him to pull back and punch her so hard in the face that she saw stars.

Before Sarah could grab a breath, the man punched her again, this time in the side of her head. He went to punch her in the face again, but he wasn't laying full on her, and she was able to crawl out of the storeroom and into the doorway. She saw her brother, Eddie walking calmly into their home and she tried to yell his name, but the man had caught her again. Then the man had pushed up the skirt of her dress and ripped her panties, and before she could think, he shoved himself into her, and she screamed in an agony of pain. He shoved again and punched her in the breast, and she was crying out loud. The man was hurting her, and she knew that he was hurting her badly. And then the gun sounded loud in the room, and the man on top of her went deathly still.

Sarah had gotten out from under Lester Billings and was crawling across the storeroom floor to a corner pulling down her skirt and crying hysterically. Eddie had dropped the gun and had his hands on his head turning in a circle and rocking on his feet at the same time. Eddie, like his sister, was crying hysterically.

Sarah's hair was down and in her face causing her to not see who had run into the store, nor did she see them run to the door and slam and lock the thing. Sarah only knew that she and Eddie were no longer alone in the store with a dead man. Her brother's crying as loud as her own sobbing.

"Oh my Lord in Heaven," Sarah heard her mother cry out, and she saw her mother rush to Eddie and her father pick up the gun and put it in a corner of the room.

"He hurt Sarah," Eddie pointed to Lester dead on the floor and then to his sister, the young man was still rocking on his own feet and crying loud.

"Sarah," her mother passed Eddie to his father and ran to her daughter. "Oh, Sarah."

"Don't touch me," Sarah screamed and pushed herself more into the corner she was trying to hide in while holding on to her ripped and torn dress trying to hide her exposed body also.

"Your eye," her mother said seeing her daughter's torn skirt and cotton panties on the ground near Lester. "What did he do to you?" her mother's voice sounded awful. "No," Ester Cartledge screamed out, and Sarah's father had to pull her mother off of Lester's dead body as the woman was kicking him, and Sarah was glad her mother was doing so.

"Ester, stop and think," Thomas said looking with pity filled eyes at his beaten daughter. Blood was dripping from Sarah's nose, and her eye was swollen shut, the side of her head had a round knot and looked awful. "If anyone finds out that Eddie killed this man, they'll lock him away." He saw the reality dawn on his wife. "They won't care he acted in defense of his sister," Thomas was saying, and Ester was nodding her head.

"Ellen's husband Clayton has just been waiting for a reason to get rid of our Eddie," Ester said and saw her husband go into the storeroom. "What are you doing?" she didn't follow her husband but went to Sarah who still wouldn't let her mother touch her.

"Someone needs a new carpet," Thomas said in a serious voice to his wife. "Eddie," he called to his son. "Come help me." Thomas unrolled the carpet and had Eddie take Lester's feet while he took Lester's shoulders and they put Lester in the carpet. And then Thomas rolled Lester up in the rug. "Eddie, get the bucket and mop and clean up this floor real quick for me, son." He saw Eddie run to do as he had said and with his wife, he moved to sit on the floor in front of his daughter.

"Sarah," her mother kept saying her name and reaching for her hand, but Sarah wouldn't let her mother near her. "Thomas, what are we going to do?" his wife cried as she turned to see Eddie cleaning the floor. "No one must see her like this," Ester fretted. "No one must know what that man did to our baby. We have to protect her too."

"No one ever will," Thomas said firmly. "Sarah," he spoke to his daughter just as firmly. "I'm going to take you to your room. Your mother will stay with you, and I'll figure out how to fix this for you." He went to Sarah despite his daughter's objections and insistence that he not touch her, and Thomas lifted her up and into his arms hearing her cry out in pain before carrying her to her room. She didn't hold on to him, and she was limp in his arms, her hair was loose and reaching to the ground as she laid more dead than alive against her father while he placed her on her bed.

"What are we going to do?" Ester asked in a worry filled voice as she followed Thomas back into the store. Eddie had gotten the floor cleaned of the blood and was emptying out the bucket. All evidence of a murder and rape were gone from this room. Only a large carpet lay in the center of the storeroom floor, that carpet holding the dead body of a man that needed to be dead.

"Eddie," Thomas called his son over to him and put an arm around him. "You've been a good boy today. You took care of your sister like we wanted you too. Now you have to make me a promise." Thomas saw his son's head nod. "We won't ever talk about this again. You never touched my gun. You never saw Lester here. Do you understand?"

"Never saw Lester," Eddie repeated without looking at his father and rocking back and forth from his heals to his toes.

"Good boy," his father praised him. "And you never touched my gun." Thomas saw Eddie nod his head and patted his back. "Tell me. You never touched my gun."

"Never touched my gun," Eddie said and saw his father was pleased with him. "Never touched my gun," Eddie repeated again.

"Oh Thomas," his wife almost cried out as they both turned at the sound of a knock on the door and saw their son in law, Clayton Nichols looking in the window.

"Be calm Ester, if we're calm, he'll be calm," he nodded toward Eddie before Thomas went to the door and opened it to Clayton.

"Hi folks," Clayton came into the store and saw Eddie rocking on his feet and flapping his hands back and forth as he almost always did.

"Clayton," Thomas said the deputy that was his son in law's name.

"It's a beautiful night out. I heard you went to Woodville today." Clayton notice the way his mother in law was looking at him as he reached in the icebox for a coke. "I'll pay for it Mother Cartledge," he said mistaking her look of concern for one that he was getting a coke without paying.

"Oh no," Ester breathed, "please, help yourself to whatever you want." She turned her back to Clayton and went to stand by Eddie not seeing the frown on the Deputy's face.

"Who is getting the new rug?" Clayton asked not seeing Eddie bouncing more than usual or the shock on Ester's face as he pointed to the rolled up carpet on the storeroom floor.

"Shane Blackburn ordered it," Thomas quickly said and looked back at his wife with a pained look.

"Need help loading it onto your wagon?" Clayton asked casually swallowing the last of the coke. "I saw your wagon was still out front. Are you taking it out to Shane tonight? It's not so dark with that full moon. But still, if I were you, I'd wait until morning to deliver that rug." Clayton drained the last of his coke and came to grab one end of the rug. "Hey, I can't load it alone," he said to Thomas who seemed to spring into action along with Ester.

"It's very nice of you to help me like this Clayton," Thomas said and saw his wife's look of agony as she held the center of the rug.

"The rug you gave Ellen, and I wasn't nearly this heavy Father Cartledge," Clayton complained as they heaved the heavy rug into the wagon. "And our rug bent in half. Shane must have bought a top quality rug for it not to bend in the middle while rolled up. I'll have to ride out one day and see what it looks like on his floor."

"Oh my," Ester breathed and fell against her husband.

"You all right?" Clayton asked in concern and Ester nodded her head. "That rug weighed a ton. Well, I had best be going," Clayton started to walk away and then turned back to look at his in-laws. "Are you folks all right? You're awful quiet tonight."

"Long day for us," Thomas said and held his wife close, her face turned away from their deputy son-in-law. "And I still have this rug to deliver to Shane."

"I'd wait till morning were I you, Father Cartledge, but do what you want. Have a good night. I'll tell Ellen to stop by tomorrow and look at these rugs you have in that seemed better made than the one you gave to us. You know how she likes things to be of quality." He didn't hear Ester groan into her husband's shirt.

"That's the only one we have," Thomas called out in a shaky voice. "Shane special ordered that rug, Clay. I don't even think we can get another like it."

"The Blackburns have the kind of money to spend on special orders," Clayton said as he mounted his horse and waved before quickly fading off into the darkness.

"What are we going to do?" Ester cried as Thomas hurried back into the store and locked the door seeing Eddie still rocking back and for on his own two feet with his hands now over his ears.

"Shane would do anything for our Sarah," Thomas said pulling on his coat. "Shane needs a new rug, Ester. Let me get Sarah into the wagon. I'll take her out to Shane, and he and I will bury that man where no one will find him. First, we need to get a new rug from the storeroom for Shane to show our nosy son-in-law." He grabbed Eddie and pulled Eddie into the storeroom while his wife unlocked and opened the door.

"Sarah needs me, she's been hurt," Ester moaned as her husband, and Eddie quickly threw a new rug into the back of the wagon.

"We'll all go out to Shane's," Thomas said going back and seeing his wife lock the door. "Help me get Sarah in the wagon, Eddie," he gently ordered his son and then told his wife to put some clothes for Sarah in a bag and to hurry.

With a lantern lit, Ester rushed to do as her husband said. "No one will see us in the night. No one will be out and, Clayton hopefully went home to Ellen," Thomas said this with Eddie's help as he gently lifted his daughter into the wagon. She wasn't talking. Sarah wasn't looking at anyone. She was limp and silent, and Thomas was afraid for her. She had been beaten, he grieved as he saw one side of her face, her dress torn and he could see her breast was black and blue.

"Clayton went in the direction of his home," Ester said as she climbed into the wagon and she saw Eddie sitting next to his sister in the back of the wagon holding Sarah in his arms. Ester knew that she should be holding Sarah, but Eddie had saved Sarah today, Ester thought, so she let him stay where he was.

Thomas lit the lanterns he had hung to light the way to Shane's home and started the wagon down the road knowing they wouldn't get any sleep tonight and they would have to open the store tomorrow and pretend everything was all right. "Let's tell folks that Sarah went to Tallahassee to visit that friend of hers from way back when she was a girl. What was her name, the girl that moved to Tallahassee?"

"You mean Sally Collier?" Ester asked in surprise. "We don't know what happened to that girl, Thomas. I keep thinking, 'oh what a tangled web we weave when first we practice to deceive.' We need to think."

"We need to protect our children," Thomas said firmly. "Sarah will leave for Woodville and the train to Tallahassee tomorrow. I'll hide the day in the house while you tell everyone that comes into the store that I took her to the train as she got a letter today from Sally who wanted Sarah to come for a visit to Tallahassee." Thomas then looked at his son Eddie in the back of the wagon holding his sister. "Eddie won't say anything to anyone. You know how he is. He never has talked much anyway, repeats what he hears or short phrases, it's usually only with us that he really talks, thank goodness."

"What if Shane won't help us?" Ester worried, and her husband covered her hand with his own.

"Shane gets one look at Sarah right now, and he'll kill Lester Billings again himself," Thomas said firmly looking back in the wagon at his daughter. "Say some prayers while I drive us to Shane, Ester. We need to say prayers. What we're doing tonight isn't right, but it's the only thing we can do." Thomas saw his wife bow her head and he heard her praying out loud. He hoped God heard her and protected all of them through this nightmare.

Shane was sitting on the porch of his home listening to the river run nearby and slapping at mosquitoes. The moon was full and lighting up the whole world, and Shane thought it was almost like dawn. If he wanted, he could reach out and touch the moon, and he did reach out, and it felt like he was touching the large round white globe hanging in the night sky.

"Hello, the house!" Shane had been leaning back in his chair and almost fell over when he heard the yelling on the other side of his house. He ran through his home stopping to turn on the gas lights, and he looked out on the porch that was on the back of his house seeing a wagon pull up in the yard.

"Mr. Cartledge?" Shane said the older man's name as he jumped down off the porch not using the steps. "What's going on?" he got to the wagon, and he saw Eddie holding Sarah. "What happened?" he looked up as Thomas was climbing down and reaching back up to help Ester down.

"I need your help," Thomas said facing Shane who was much taller than he was. "We all need your help," Thomas nodded his head to Eddie and told his wife to stay where she was. He had to talk to Shane private. Shane was looking at Sarah and didn't want to leave her. Shane could see that she was hurt. Thomas pulled hard on Shane forcing the younger man to come with him to the side of the house. "I didn't want to speak in front of my children," Thomas said softly, and Shane kept looking back at the moonlit wagon.

"Sarah," Shane lifted his hand toward the wagon, he hadn't been able to see her because her hair was down and in her face, but he knew by the way Eddie was holding her that she was hurt.

"Lester Billings came into the store while the wife and I were gone today," Thomas said softly. "I don't know the details, but Eddie shot and killed Lester."

"Dear God," Shane said leaning against his house and feeling weak.

"Lester was hurting my daughter," Thomas's voice broke. "Shane, Lester badly hurt my daughter if you get my meaning."

"Son of a bitch," Shane growled, and Thomas nodded in agreement.

"Clayton doesn't feel about Eddie like we do. If Clayton finds out about this, he'll arrest Eddie, and it won't matter that Eddie was defending his sister. All that will matter to Clayton is he finally has an excuse to put Eddie away, so Eddie doesn't embarrass our family. You know how Clayton is, and he's the law around these parts, people will listen to him."

"So who are we going to say shot Lester?" Shane asked looking back at Ester by the wagon trying to hold her daughter's hand, and he could hear one or both of them crying.

"We're not going to tell anyone Lester is dead. I have him rolled up in a rug in the back my wagon. I thought we could bury him good and deep somewhere out here with the rug. Clayton helped me load the rug up on the wagon, and I had to tell him where I was taking it," Thomas fell silent, and Shane nodded his head.

"And you thought of me?" He again saw Thomas nod his head.

"Yes, I brought another rug in case that nosey old deputy son-in-law of mine wants to see the one I delivered to you. But I need your help getting rid of Lester and the rug he's in." Again Shane nodded and looked back at Ester.

"And Sarah?" Shane asked.

"She's beat up bad, Shane. I can't keep her at my house. Someone will see her and how do we explain her injuries?" Shane again nodded. "She'll be ruined," Thomas almost broke into tears.

"So what are you going to do with her?" Shane reached a hand to Thomas and put it on the older man's shoulder in a supportive gesture.

"We gotta leave her here with you Shane." Shane stood up straight and shook his head. "We're going to tell folks she's gone to

Tallahassee to visit her friend Sally Collier. She'll stay here hidden at Twin River until she's well enough to come home."

"Mr. Cartledge," Shane started to speak,

"After tonight you're gonna call me Tom," the older man said, and Shane knew in that moment he would do whatever he had to do to protect Eddie and help Sarah.

"Eddie might tell someone Sarah's here with me and not with that person in Tallahassee," Shane said, and Thomas shook his head.

"He won't, we're going to make him think Sarah, and I left early with you and went to Woodville to catch the train. Eddie won't ever know different. He trusts everything he's told." Shane knew that was correct and finally agreed with Thomas' plan.

"So what do we do first? Get Sarah inside or bury Lester?" Thomas went to the wagon and had Eddie lift up Sarah.

"We'll get her settled, and her Mama can get her cleaned up and looked over while we take care of the rug. Eddie," his father said his name. "You get that rug we put in the wagon for Shane into Shane's house and on the floor for me boy, do a good job." Eddie nodded his head and went to pull the rug out with Lester's body in it. "No son, the other rug," his father said, and Eddie moved over while Shane stopped Thomas from trying to get Sarah out of the wagon.

"I've got her, sir." With strong, firm arms, Shane reached into the wagon and lifted Sarah out. She looked at him and cried, the cry pathetic to hear causing Shane to hold her close. "You're safe now Sarah," Shane spoke in a low voice trying to hide the horrified look on his face when he saw the bruises made clear to see by the bright moonlight. With a glance toward her mother, Shane saw the heartsick look that the older woman had on her face, a look that he quickly mirrored.

"Shaun," Sarah cried as Shane laid her in the bed, she had shared long ago with her husband. "I need Shaun," she sobbed, and Shane backed away seeing her torn dress and exposed breast, one of her breasts was so bruised that it had already turned purple and orange.

Shane moved aside letting her mother move in to comfort her. "He beat her," Shane stated as they moved out of the room. One side of Sarah's face was black and blue, her eye was swollen shut, and dried blood was under her nose. Her lower lip was swollen and split open. "He beat her," Shane said again and pulled back his fist punching the wall in his upstairs hallway. "You're certain Eddie killed him?"

Thomas nodded his head in answer to Shane's questions. "That's not all Lester did to her, Shane," Thomas turned his face toward the wall, and leaning his forehead against the wall he broke into sobs.

"Tom," Shane said his first name for the first time, and the older man pulled himself together. "I know a place," he said and went outside with Tom Cartledge following him.

"What sort of place?" Tom asked before telling Eddie to stay in the house and not leave until he got back. Seeing Shane get into the wagon and take the reins, Thomas climbed up onto the seat as Shane started the wagon down to the river. "Good thing it's a full moon," Shane said as the trees at the river's edge cast long shadows, and where the moon shone through those trees it looked like ghosts in the night.

"My rowboat," Shane said pointing to where it sat on the bank. "We have to get Lester out of that rug and put him in my boat." He went to the back of the wagon once he stopped and secured the horses, and then Shane pulled the rug out unrolling it as it fell to the ground. He saw Lester hit the dirt and heard a loud thud.

"We could have buried him in the rug," Tom said looking away from the dead body of the man that had assaulted his beautiful child.

"Help me get him in my boat," Shane said as he grabbed hold of Lester's shoulders and saw Tom grab his feet and they carried him to the boat. "Get in Tom," Shane said and pushed the boat out into the river.

"Where are we going?" Tom asked as he saw the moon shining on the river making the water sparkle.

"There's a swampy area I know well," Shane said this as he let the current take them far down the river before he turned the boat toward shore. "No one comes here ever, too many alligators. They nest here and it being spring, they're nesting now." He saw all the alligators on the bank by the full moon and Tom went down into the bottom of the boat as the Gators swarmed the boat. "Stay calm and help me throw Lester in," Shane said and lifted Lester up with Tom's help.

"Lord have Mercy on me," Thomas all but cried out as he saw the alligators in the dark attack Lester's body and rip it apart before Shane started rowing back into the river and away from the alligators.

"I had to make sure those gators got him," Shane said firmly as he watched the alligators from a distance feast on the remains of Lester. "Now if any part of Lester is found, they won't know he was shot by Eddie. They'll think Lester fell into the swamps and got eaten by gators, which he did that too." Thomas sat in the bow of the boat with his hands over his face, and Shane knew the older man was crying. "It's going to be all right, Tom," he assured the older man. "Even by the light of the moon, I can clearly see there's almost nothing left of Lester."

"I just wish we could take care of Sarah as fast as we took care of Lester." Shane nodded his head in understanding before putting his back into rowing the boat back up river to his house and to where they had left the wagon. "What are you doing?" Tom asked Shane as he saw the younger man jump out of the boat in a hurry.

"We have to get rid of this rug now, Tom." The older man watched Shane roll the rug up and pull it to the boat knowing that Shane was right. "Come help me," Shane called out, and Tom moved to grab an end of the rug and swing it into the boat. "Go on back to the house," Shane said pushing Tom toward his wagon. "I'm going to row out to the middle of the river and throw this rug in. I'll be back up to the house in a bit. Go to Sarah and Ester and Eddie."

Thomas Cartledge watched Shane row away before he turned to go to his wife knowing their prayers were being answered. Shane was taking care of everything. No one would find Lester now, not after what Thomas had seen those alligators do to the man. The Gators had ripped Lester apart, and Thomas was glad, Eddie would be safe. Now to care for Sarah.

CHAPTER SEVEN

Shane sat by the bed Sarah was lying in. The sheets were pulled up to her chin just where her mother had placed them before Ester had left late in the night. He had slept a little, but not much. He kept having dreams of gators tearing his flesh apart and of Shaun falling dead on the battlefield. He wished he could sleep peacefully, but that didn't seem likely to happen anytime soon. He had come to accept his shellshock condition. He had come to know that he would always be troubled and nothing would take those troubles from him.

He looked down at Sarah small in the bed and he saw her horribly bruised face. He could clearly see in the daylight that her eye was swollen shut and had even turned a dark green. Her lip was cut open, and he knew that she would have a scar there that would never heal and would remind her of what had been done to her all of her life. The side of her jaw had what clearly looked like a fist print, and Shane wished Lester had been alive when he fed the man to the alligators.

He gently reached and pulled the covers down to see that Sarah's nightgown was up to her collarbone and wondered if she might be warm in all the covers. She wasn't complaining, so he lifted the covers back up and looked again at her face. The one eye that wasn't black and blue was open, the other eye, he realized, was swollen shut. Weeks would pass before she would heal, of that Shane felt certain.

"Sarah," he said her name and she made no noise, she just lay staring out of her one open eye for a long time, and he didn't touch her. Shane waited patiently for her to speak. He saw a tear slip out of her swollen shut eye, and he wondered if she were in pain. He knew she probably was and he was sorry that she was. "You'll be all right, Sarah," he said gently, and he saw her head shaking from side to side.

"Soap?" she said this word in the form of a question and turned to look at Shane, the expression on his face let her know that he didn't understand her. "Soap?" she said again and rolled onto her side crying when she did. "I need soap," she cried in a pathetic voice and Shane went to find a bar that he knew his mother had made fresh. This bar of soap would belong only to Sarah he thought as he came back to the room handing it to her. "Washcloth, I need a washcloth too," she cried in an even worse voice and he hurried for that item wondering if she meant to take a bath, and then thinking that she obviously did intend to do just that though he thought she would be better off staying in the bed as injured as she was.

Shane watched Sarah stand on shaking legs, her bare feet peeking out from under her long nightgown and he thought that she was going to his bathroom. "Sarah," he said her name as she went to the stairs and started down. "The bathroom is this way." He went to touch her, and she pulled away from him walking down the stairs ignoring him completely. Shane realized that all he could do was follow her, and he felt helpless because he was helpless to her.

Sarah made it out the door facing the river and then carefully down the steps knowing that Shane was behind her. She had no shoes on so she watched each step she took as she left the grassy yard and got closer to the river not wanting to step on a rock or stone and hurt her feet. She didn't see that Shane was also barefooted and doing as she was. She stood on the grassy bank and looked out at the river, it was clean, it was pure, and the water would make her clean and pure again as well.

Shane was speechless as he watched Sarah move on the grassy bank and then lift up her long nightgown and pull it over her head. She was completely naked when she dropped it on the bank still clinging to the soap and washcloth. She turned back and looked at Shane and said in a frightened voice, "help me." He didn't know what to do as he watched her walk into the river and then he was running in after her afraid she meant to drown herself. "Help me," she cried taking the cloth and scrubbing herself all over, and handing Shane the soap. "We have to get him off of me," she cried, and Shane shook his head. "I have to be clean again," she sobbed hysterically and up to his waist in water, Sarah up to her breast, he took the soap from her and began lathering her body. "More, scrub more and harder Shane. I can't be dirty like this." She was crying so hard, and he saw the marks on her body in the crystal clear water. Lester had hurt her hips, and then he saw lower. Shane saw her thigh, and he saw her grab the soap and clean between her legs crying the whole time and being rough as she did so, rough on her damaged and bruised thighs.

"No, Sarah." Shane took the soap from her. He wouldn't let her hurt herself like this. He saw her go limp and he pulled her into his arms, her back to him, and cradling her close, her head lying on his shoulder he moved out of the deep water.

"Shane, clean me, Shane. I can't stay dirty like this," she sobbed, and he took the soap and with gentle care put it between her legs and did as she ask, lightly cleaning the part that Lester had touched yesterday evening. And Shane could see, Lester had ripped and torn Sarah leaving her more than bruised.

Shane held her in the river for almost an hour, her lying back against him and him back against the bank as the river as gentle waves caused by the soft breeze washed Sarah clean. After a time he let go of what was left of the soap his mother had made, and he watched the soap sink to the bottom of the river. He hoped what they had just done was something positive for Sarah, but he worried that it hadn't been. At least she could be sure Lester's touch was taken from her body and replaced by his own.

Sarah felt Shane lift her into his arms and she wrapped her arms securely around his neck as he came up out of the Saint Marks River and bent to pick up her dry nightgown. He realized that his clothes were soaking wet and clinging tightly to him, he was not comfortable, he thought as he walked onto his porch dripping wet with Sarah nearly dry and still held close to him.

"Sarah," he said her name softly, and he felt her head nod against his shoulder. "I'm going to put you down for a moment and take off my shirt to hang over the porch rail to dry. Are you all right standing up for a minute?" He again felt her head nod though she still clung to him as he put her on her feet. He unbuttoned his shirt and pulled it off thankful that his mother had made him several changes of clothes so he wouldn't have to worry about laundry. Right now he could focus on Sarah. He pulled her back up into his arms and he heard her cry out making him know that he had touched her somewhere that hurt her. "I'm so sorry," he said as he went up the stairwell in his wet pants with Sarah in his arms and her nightgown draped over his shoulder. He could see her one breast was beaten badly and he lost his breath knowing she had to be in pain all over.

"I'm glad Shaun isn't here now," Shane heard Sarah's soft voice say as he laid her on the bed getting his first full view of her whole nude body. "I'm so dirty," she sobbed, and Shane shook his head hard knowing she couldn't see him, her eyes were closed.

"Give me a minute Sarah, and we'll talk." He covered her with the sheet and hurried to his own room across the hall where he pulled off his wet pants and put on dry ones throwing the wet ones into the bathtub in the bathroom down the hallway. He was almost as nude as her, he thought as he hurried back to her room with his chest bare and feet bare, but he didn't want to take time away from her to dress. He had to be with her, and he saw as he entered the room that she had her eyes closed, but she had heard him come into the room, he had seen her head turn in his direction.

"Shane," she cried for him just as he went to her. "Don't tell Shaun what happened," he took her hand, and he swore that he wouldn't knowing that he couldn't tell Shaun anything. Shaun was dead. "I think my brother Eddie might have shot and killed Lester," she said, and he wondered how much she might remember of what happened yesterday. "I remember what Lester did to me," she seemed to answer the unasked question in his mind. "All my beautiful memories of Shaun making love to me," she turned her head and looked up at the ceiling, "memories were all I had left of him. And now I can't remember what he and I did together. I'll always only remember Lester," she caught her breath on a sob and tears fell from her eyes and slid down the side of her face and into her ears.

"You'll forget in time, Sarah. You just need time, like me with the war," Shane said softly trying to reason with her. She wouldn't forget his brother. Nothing could erase Shaun from anyone's memory.

"Will you hold me? Will you keep me safe from Lester?" she asked him in a choked and broken voice and Shane, against his better judgment, climbed into the bed beside her. He laid on his back, and she put her head on his shoulder, her hand over his heart, and he held her this way while she went to sleep.

Shane woke up and saw that it was mid-afternoon. The sun was high in the sky. And then he saw Sarah, and he felt Sarah, she was laying on top of him, she had straddled him like she were on a horse she was going to ride, her head was up under his chin, her lips were against his neck, and he could feel her breathing. Shane lost his breath.

He lay perfectly still and could tell she was asleep because of her soft even breathing, her body gently moving on top of his with each breath that she took, and he closed his eyes, counted to ten trying not to think of her beautiful nude body covering his. His mind was screaming for him not to feel anything, and all he could do was feel desire throughout every inch of his being. He knew this was wrong. He had seen too much of her today. In the river this morning he had touched her places he would never have touched Sarah unless she was his wife, though this morning in the river he had been intent on helping her, and he hadn't been aroused by what he was doing. Having her lay on top of him as she was now was a completely different situation.

Taking a deep breath, Shane rolled over taking Sarah with him until she was lying on her back flat on the bed. She hadn't woken up when he moved, and he sat up looking down at her knowing he shouldn't be looking at her the way he was. He was breathing hard, like he had run a race with Shaun and had at last won a race against his faster brother when he was really lying in the bed with his brother's wife. And she didn't have anything on.

When he saw the black and blue marks on the inside of her milky white thighs and her hips he remembered what she had suffered the day before. Her eye was still swollen shut and her lip was huge. He reached down for her dry nightgown and tried to figure out how to put it on her while she was asleep. Several minutes passed before he figured out how to dress her and still, she didn't wake. He got up and went to his own bedroom where he dressed completely, even shoes and socks and he brushed his hair.

Sarah lay with her one uninjured eye open looking at the wall when Shane came back into the room, and he went to her and sat on the edge of the bed. "Are you feeling any better?" he asked her, and she laid still for a long few moments.

She finally reached out and took his hand, and Shane lay down next to her so that he was laying on the bed with her and looking at her. "I went into the storeroom while Eddie swept the porch," she said softly, her eyes locked with Shane's eyes. "I didn't see him, Shane. I didn't know he was there until he grabbed me and threw me to the floor. I kicked at him." Shane saw her eyes close. "I couldn't get loose of him. He was holding me too tight. And then he was pulling up my dress and tearing at my clothes. Everything happened so fast. I bit his hand, and he punched me, hard. He called me a dirty name. He said I should know how to please a man since I'd been with Shaun and you too."

"You've never been with me," Shane said in a shocked voice, and more tears fell from her eyes.

"He saw you kiss me," she sobbed. "He said I was going to give to him what I gave to you. I told him no, we had only kissed by accident and he called me that dirty name again. I was fighting him hard Shane, really hard. He was lying on top of me. He had me pinned down, I couldn't move. He, he, oh Shane," she was sobbing when she felt him pulling her into his arms, and he was rubbing her back in a gentle way. "He shoved himself inside of me, I was kicking and screaming and crying, and then I heard the gunshot, and he fell, and I was able to get away."

"Eddie was brave to do what he did," Shane said seriously. "Your parents are afraid that if anyone finds out what Eddie did, the law will lock him up." He felt Sarah go stiff beside him.

"Eddie protected me, Shane. We have to protect Eddie." Shane nodded his head and sat up.

"Your mother was coming out here this afternoon. I hear a wagon." Shane got out of bed, and he went to the window to see Sarah's parents both getting down from the wagon. He was thankful they hadn't come while Sarah was asleep on top of him. No one would understand this strange bond the two of them had seemed to have formed this morning in the river as he washed her clean of Lester. Shane didn't understand what was happening between them, but she needed him, and he needed her to need him.

"Sarah, while they're here, I have to do something. I'll be back within the hour." He saw her sitting up on the edge of the bed, and he told her to lie back down which she did. She was dizzy and she was weak, she told him so.

Shane met Thomas at the top of the stairs, Ester had hurried past him going to Sarah, and he heard mother and daughter talking in low voices, and then he heard Sarah crying. "Tom, I have to do something. I'll be back soon. Stay here until I get back. What I'm doing is important," Shane said seriously, and he took the stairs two at a time before hurrying out of the house. He had thought of saddling a horse. But then he thought not to. He could run faster to his Uncle's home.

Allen Blackburn was dismounting his horse in his yard when he saw his nephew running toward him through the woods near the river. He saw Shane lift his hand and Allen turned to his wife Alicia seeing her on the porch steps "I think something might be wrong with Shane," he said to her, and he saw her looking off in the distance at Shane running to their house.

"Whatever is the matter, he didn't take time to saddle his horse Allen," Alicia said as she leaned over the porch rail, "This is serious because he took to foot to get here."

"He sure did," Allen got back on his horse. "Don't wait supper on me, Alicia," he called over his shoulder and rode to meet his nephew.

"I need you, Uncle Allen," Shane said out of breath, and took his uncle's outstretched hand swinging himself up into the saddle behind Allen. "Can't talk right now, my house," he said breathing hard.

Allen turned his horse to Twin River with no idea of what he would find that had caused his nephew to run the full mile between their homes. Allen knew one thing for certain; this was his calm level headed nephew, the one that never overreacted. And this reality caused Allen to urge his horse on faster.

Shane was still breathing hard when he dismounted his Uncle's horse in his yard, and he bent forward and caught several deep breaths while Allen got down and tied the horse to his porch rail. "Can I hire you for my attorney," Allen took a step back and then gave his nephew a hard stare and seriously asked,

"Who did you kill?" Shane swallowed hard before he answered.

"Well, I need you for an attorney, but so does Eddie," Shane revised his need and Allen still stared hard at him. "So anything I might tell you, you can't tell anyone else. You told us that when we were kids if we ever did anything wrong, we could tell you and as our attorney you couldn't tell anyone else." Allen shook his head hard.

"Shane, when I said that, well it was sort of a joke son. I just meant you boys could trust me." He saw Shane needed to trust him right now by the look his nephew gave to him and he nodded his head. "But it is a fact. If you hire me for your attorney, anything you might tell me, no matter what it might be, I cannot disclose to another living soul."

"Come with me," Shane said leading Allen into the house and up the stairs. He didn't know that his Uncle was half afraid of being led up the stairs to see a dead body in one of the bedrooms.

"Sarah," Allen said her name in shock, his eyes going to where Shaun's wife lay on the bed all battered and beaten. Allen looked up from the bed at Ester's sitting in a chair, and he could see the older woman was pale and worn. Allen saw Sarah's father Thomas looking like her mother, pale and worn standing by the window. "Who did this to her?" Allen asked everyone in the room, and he saw Sarah turn her face trying to hide herself in the pillow. "Sarah, listen to me. Shane has hired me as an attorney. Anything said in this room; I cannot talk to anyone about. What we say in here, stays in here. But as an attorney, I need assurances you're safe." Slowly

Sarah turned and looked at Uncle Allen, and slowly she nodded her head in understanding.

"You want me to tell Uncle Allen what happened?" Sarah didn't ask this of her parents. She asked this of Shane.

"You know we have to protect Eddie," Shane said going to the bed, kneeling down beside her, and taking her hand. "He protected you."

Very slowly Sarah told Allen what had happened the day before. She didn't go into the details that she had gone into with Shane, but by the look on Allen's face, Sarah knew that he understood what had been done to her. Sarah let the tears fall when Allen sat down on the edge of the bed and put his head in his hands after telling her he was so sorry. Sarah fell silent from telling what she knew, and she saw Shane turn to her father, and she saw her father shaking his head hard.

"We have to tell Uncle Allen everything," Shane said firmly. "I don't want Eddie going to jail." Thomas looked at Allen and told him how they had put Lester's body in the rug, and Clayton had helped them load it into the wagon. The older man was so intent on his story that he didn't see the look on Allen and Shane's faces, but he heard his wife's sob and added to his story,

"We were almost caught right there in the store," and Allen nodded his head knowing that moment must have been terrifying for the couple. When Thomas got to the part where they came to Shane to hide what Eddie had done, Shane turned to his Uncle and finished telling what they had all done together,

"I put Lester's body in the rowboat and took him down river to the swamps. You know where all the alligators nest in the springtime?" Shane saw his Uncle nod his head and Allen knew just what Shane had done before Shane told him what he had done. "We stayed to make sure there wasn't going to be much left of Lester. If any part of him is found, no one will think Eddie shot him anyway."

"I wish you had come for me last night," Allen said to Shane then looked at Sarah. "I'm not saying what any of you did was the correct way to handle the situation. But I'm not saying you were incorrect either. As the father of three beautiful daughters," he squeezed Sarah's hand tight, "I would have done the same and I'm proud of Eddie for protecting his sister.

"I agree wholeheartedly with you, Tom," Allen turned to look at Sarah's father still standing at the window. "Clayton would love to lock Eddie away. Clayton still might try someday, the man doesn't know what unconditional love is, and he doesn't see that if you want love, go to Eddie. Eddie's love is pure, sweet love. Again, I'm not saying you did the right thing, what I'm saying is, you did the only thing as a father that you could do to protect your children and I admire you for what you've done.

"If I had shot a man harming anyone in my family, the law would have given me a medal. But Eddie," Allen said looking at Ester, "well, he deserves that medal. So we don't say anything to anyone beyond this room, none of us." Allen turned to Shane. "There's no body, Lester's gone. The law can't prove a crime. But if anything happens in connection with Lester, well don't say anything to anyone, especially not Clayton. Come get me, I'm your attorney now, and it's my job to protect all of you."

"And Eddie, we have to try and keep Eddie away from Clayton," Shane said looking at Tom and Ester seeing that they both looked frightened.

"Everyone knows that Eddie roams," Ester almost cried, and Tom nodded his head in agreement with his wife. "We can't keep him tied down to the store, that won't be natural for him."

"I understand that Ester. We can only do the best we can do," Allen touched her hand gently. "I'm representing all of you now, just remember, if anyone asks you about Lester in any way, say nothing. Do not speak to any deputy in this county or any county about Lester. Say nothing to no one. We'll just have to pray Eddie doesn't say anything." Allen saw all the heads in the room nod, and he looked at Sarah. Sarah was the victim in all of this, and around her, in this room, were her protectors. "Shane, I'm proud of you for guarding Sarah like you are. Shaun would be proud of his brother if he were alive today. No one needs to know what happened to her. Keep her here. This is rightfully her home as Shaun's wife anyway. Good job thinking to bring her here, Tom."

"There's more Allen," Thomas spoke looking at the man that saved his son years ago from drowning and now was going to help save all of his family. "You should know that I pretended to be gone today and my wife told everyone that came into the store that our Sarah was in Tallahassee visiting her friend Sally."

"I don't have a friend named Sally in Tallahassee," Sarah said from the bed.

"Your friend when you were little that use to live down near the Old Morris place," her mother gently reminded her, "Sally Collier." Sarah shook her head looking at both parents.

"No, her name was Lydia Conway, and they moved somewhere in Texas years ago. Sally Collier was Ellen's friend, and she lives over in Wakulla County now," Sarah said to her parents seeing her mother wave a hand in the air and turned to Allen.

"That doesn't matter, the point is everyone thinks Sarah is in Tallahassee, and she's out here healing from what that man did to her," Ester said, and Allen nodded his head hoping that this minor detail didn't cause a major problem later on.

Tom, Shane, and Allen went out into the hall, and Tom asked Allen honestly, away from the women, if he thought they had done the right thing. "Tom, what is the right thing to do when you've just found your daughter raped and beaten half to death? And your son that has the mind of a five-year-old, so he really is only five years old, has killed the man that raped your daughter? I think you did the only thing you could think to do. Say Eddie was a normal man and he had done this and you had gone to Clayton. By dawn, all of the counties would have known that sweet innocent Sarah was brutally violated. It's enough that she has to live and deal with what was done to her. Sure, Eddie would have been a hero for saving his sister, but she would have never been treated the same again in this town.

"There are people that would say it was Sarah's fault. That she asked for what happened to her, maybe that she egged Lester on in some way. Gossip is bad, and sadly we all know that. If I were in your shoes last night, I probably would have done the same thing.

"As of today, I can't say anything of what has happened. I'm bound by an oath I took. Leave Sarah here to heal and don't come out here every day Tom, people will notice, and they'll wonder why you're out here. I'll bring food from my house to these two and check on them every day. And I'll stop by your place and let you know how they're doing often. Go home now, go home, and live like you would be living if Sarah were visiting her friend in Tallahassee. Make good the story you've created to protect your children."

Allen had turned to go downstairs, and Tom knew Allen was right. He and Ester had to go home, and they had to leave Sarah out here with Shane to heal. After a tearful farewell between mother and daughter, Shane walked Allen outside to his horse and held his Uncle's arm to stop him from leaving.

"About what you said of gossip blaming Sarah," he said in a low voice, and his Uncle moved closer to him. "Lester saw Sarah and I kissing the other night," he confessed more to his beloved Uncle. "And Lester said that she would give to him what she gave to me, Uncle Allen. But what we shared was just an innocent kiss, it went nowhere. I swear."

Allen knew his nephew well. He had known Shane all of Shane's life. Allen knew Shane was in love with Sarah and had been for years. And Allen knew that Shane had eaten his heart out when his brother was courting Sarah and then married Sarah. But

Shane had never shown anyone his true feelings for Sarah. Shane had been a real man about the situation and shown joy for his brother's happiness.

"Shane," Allen said his name in a firm yet gentle voice. "Shaun is gone, Shaun is dead, and Sarah is alive, and you are alive. And here you are together healing over the loss of someone that both of you loved. Shaun made you and Sarah whole. Shaun was your other half, Shane. When he married Sarah, he joined to her and was the half that made her whole. Shaun is the tie that binds you two together. You might be complete again with her, and she might be complete with you as well." Allen looked at his nephew, and he hoped that Shane would find joy with Sarah, they both deserved one another. "I know you're in love with her. I hope she will someday soon return that love. But you need to understand something. The girl that married Shaun hadn't been raped. I know about rape, Shaun. I know what it can do to a woman. You're going to have to be careful of her. That son of a bitch Lester beat her badly."

"She's covered in bruises, Uncle Allen," Shane blushed at what he said as he looked into his Uncle's eyes. "I had to help her today," his voice sort of faded and he knew he couldn't explain what had happened in the river this morning. "Anyway, thank you for being my Uncle," Shane said sincerely. "All my life you've been here for me and made everything all right. Just like Dad." Allen pulled him close and patted his back. "I love you, Uncle Allen."

"I love you too, Shane. I just want you safe and happy," Allen said before letting Shane go. "I'll come by tomorrow with food, and I'll let everyone know you need to stay home for a while. Your mama will come for certain if I tell her you're sick, so I'm telling her I'm giving you a week off to fish and hunt and swim, a week of no worries. Ethan is here to help us older men." He heard Shane laugh as Allen mounted his horse. "Go take care of your girl. Her mama left supper for you both on the stove."

Shane watched his Uncle ride off into the trees down by the river before he turned and went into the house. He put the stew that Ester Cartledge had left warming on his stove in two bowls, grabbed two spoons and the dish towel and went upstairs. He saw Sarah looking out the window, and he set the bowls down on a bedside table.

"I'll be right back," he said and took the stairs two at a time to get the pan of corn cake that Ester had left in the oven warming.

"Mama makes the best stew and corn cake in the county," Sarah said watching Shane spread out a towel on the bed before he put the food on the bed as though they were having a picnic.

"Let's eat," Shane said and sat cross-legged on the bed taking up his bowl of stew. Two bites in and he saw Sarah wasn't going to eat and he stopped eating himself. "Do you want to talk?" he asked, and he saw her look at him with an uncertain look and then shake her head hard. "I'll talk," Shane said holding her eyes with his own. "I'll tell you something," he spoke on in a low and soft voice to Sarah, "In the field hospital with Ethan," Shane said, "over in France. When I came awake, I couldn't talk at first. There was this man standing over me asking me my name over and over and over again. And I finally yelled at him 'Shane.' I could have said Shaun," he confessed now to Sarah. "I was supposed to bring Shaun home to you, and I knew, I had seen him shot. I knew he wasn't coming home. But I said Shane because that's who I am. And then Ethan found me. He was all torn up over his face and not being pretty enough for Bethany anymore," Shane saw Sarah listening intently to what he was saying. "Ethan and I started talking. We talked about everything that happened, and it helped a lot. Keeping things inside, not talking about them, it doesn't help, Sarah."

Sarah watched Shane take another bite of her mother's delicious stew and look at her when he did. He looked just like Shaun. He sounded just like Shaun. He really could have said he was

Shaun, and no one would have known the difference, not even her, and she was Shaun's wife.

"This morning, in the river," Sarah said, and Shane stopped eating. "Thank you for helping me to get clean," her voice was weak, yet Shane heard no tears now. She was much more steady than she had been this morning.

"I was uncertain about touching you," he said softly, and he looked down at the stew left in the bowl and away from her. "I didn't want you to hurt yourself."

"I was hurting myself, and you didn't hurt me. I don't know why I behaved that way," she looked out the window. "I just had to get him off of me." Shane heard her voice break again. "Shane," she looked back at him, and he saw the look of agony on her face, and he hated that look of agony that was on her face. "Do you think I might be with child?" She started to cry, and Shane set up straighter shaking his head hard knowing that he could ease her worries over that. She had told him that Lester had just started to hurt her when she heard the gunshot and Eddie had killed Lester.

"You told me," he swallowed hard and almost choked on his words, but he knew he had to continue. "You said that Eddie shot Lester right when Lester forced himself into you." Shane saw Sarah nod her head; tears fell onto her cheeks when she did nod her head. "Then no, you won't have his child. A man has to – well it takes a minute for a man to put his seed inside a woman." Shane put his bowl down and picked it up and shook his head, "Just take my word for it, Sarah. There wasn't enough time for Lester to do that to you."

"Thank you, Shane." He saw her reach for her bowl and spoon and take a bite flinching as the salty stew hurt her lip. He felt bad for her, though he encouraged her to eat as eating would make her feel better and him as well. Mrs. Cartledge was good at making stew, he thought after going down for a second bowl for himself and a little more for Sarah too.

The world outdoors was dark, the light of the moon shone down again tonight, but the moon wasn't full, and that moonlight was dim. Shane stood from the chair where he had sat by Sarah's bed, and he put down the book that he had been reading to her from. "My bedroom is just across the hall, Sarah. If you need me, all you have to do call out. I'll leave the doors open."

"I don't know what Mama and Daddy were thinking bringing me here," Sarah said softly. "If anyone were to find out I was here alone with you,"

"No one will find out," Shane's words stopped Sarah from saying more, and his tone was very reassuring. "Don't worry about anything but getting well. I'll see you in the morning, Sarah."

Sarah watched Shane fade into the shadows of the hallway beyond her room, and she knew that she was now alone in the room. She was alone in the dark, and with memories she didn't want to have. She lay still on the bed thinking of the river which she could hear flowing by in the distance. She tried not to think of anything, and then she tried to think of Shaun. She tried to remember what they had done in this bed, what he had told her about the book, and all he had taught her. She tried to think of anything that could help keep her from thinking of what had happened in the storeroom. She rolled onto her side and looked at the moon out the window, and the stars beyond, they seemed so bright, and she tried to focus on those stars, but she kept thinking of Lester Billings. And then she thought of Shane, of how they had been talking one minute and the next he was pulling her into his arms and kissing her, kissing her almost like Shaun use to kiss her, and yet nothing like Shaun ever had.

The moon was moving away from her window as she lay still on the bed thinking of Shane. This morning she had lost her mind and walked into the river with no clothes on and scrubbed herself raw everywhere that Lester had touched her. And then Shane had taken the soap and gently he had run that soap over her body, where

Lester had touched her, and he made everything better. Shane wasn't her lover. Shane wasn't her husband. Shane was her best friend, and what he had done, holding her in the crystal clear, clean water of the Saint Mark's River had made her feel less dirty than she had. He had made her feel less shame when she should have felt more shame. She had been in the river without her clothes on, allowing him to touch her only hours after she had been violated by a very bad man.

"Sarah," Shane said her name from her open doorway, and she looked toward him only then realizing that she was crying and she had very likely woken him up. "Don't cry, Sarah," he said as he came into the room and by her bed. "I don't want you to hurt," he said, and she reached up for him, and he came to her feeling her pull him into her arms and he wanted to only be in Sarah's arms right now.

"You're so different from Shaun," Sarah said as she snuggled close to Shane. "I love how caring you are Shane. You were always; always my very best friend." She had no idea how her words affected him. Sarah found something to love about him. Maybe Uncle Allen was right, and they had a common ground to build a relationship on. He hoped so in this moment with all of his heart because he loved her. He just wanted to hold her, to love her, to have her beside him, and he wanted her to love him and want him back, to have him with her as well.

"I'm safe with you Shane," Sarah whispered. "I always was."

Sarah woke up and she found herself in Shane's arms, her leg bent and draped over his stomach, her hand on his heart, and his hand was on her shoulder holding her close to him. She saw him sleeping, he looked so peaceful, and she saw how he really wasn't just Shaun's twin, he was his Uncle Allen's as well. There would be no surprise what Shane would look like in twenty more years.

Once, Sarah thought as she looked at his profile and knew him to be a pretty man, she had thought that she was in love with both him and Shaun. And maybe she had been, Sarah thought now. The two brothers were so much alike, even in their differences they favored one another. And they were easy to love. Shane and Shaun were good men. Any woman to win either one of them would have been blessed.

Slowly, and with care, Sarah lifted up and touched Shane's hair. She ran her hands through his bangs, and she saw them fall forward, and she smiled. Yesterday in the river, his hands had been so gentle on her. He had touched her in her most private places as though that were natural for him to do. She would never understand why she had behaved the way that she had with him, but she was forever grateful he was there to keep her from drowning herself. And she really had felt like dying yesterday; she was so ashamed. She saw no future for herself, no tomorrow, just day after endless day of feeling ashamed and disgusting.

Sarah looked at Shane still. She remembered how he had kissed her that night not long ago and how he had made her feel. And she remembered Lester on her, tearing at her clothes and punching her in the face and breast. She remembered how Lester had entered her body, and the pain was the worst she had known. She closed her eyes and fought to forget. She ordered herself to never think of that moment again. She was here with Shane, in Shane's arms, and he was keeping her safe and protecting her. She could forget what Lester did to her as long as Shane was here.

"Thank you," she said softly, and she snuggled up to him and felt him tighten his hold on her, and she knew in this moment they were more than best friends.

Shane rolled Sarah over onto her back, and he looked down at her. The morning sun was flooding the room, and he knew that the hour was well past dawn. "Well, what were you thanking me for?" he asked her in a sleepy husky voice looking into her sky blue eyes with a playful smile on his face.

"You made everything wrong all right," she said and put her arms around his neck thinking he had the most beautiful eyes in the world. Shane's eyes were the color of Shaun's eyes, a bright yellow-green, reminding her of grass in the springtime. She had gotten lost in Shaun's eyes when she had stared up into them, and she knew that she could get lost in Shane's eyes now.

"Actually, it was your father that made everything all right for you Sarah. Tom thought of what to do to protect his children, and he did what needed to be done." Shane knew he shouldn't touch her. She wasn't his to touch, but he couldn't help himself, and he pressed his lips to her forehead. He didn't want to be any more intimate with her than this simple kiss, not after what she had been through. But Sarah felt so right in his arms. She belonged here with him, and he didn't want to let her go.

"I feel safe here, Shane. I feel like I belong here." Sarah said what he was thinking and clung tightly to him, and he held her back gently in his loving embrace wishing that she would fall in love with him, and yet knowing when she looked at him, she saw his brother and not him.

"This is your home too, Sarah. I should actually buy your half of the house. I should have already done that. I never thought of you, forgive me. As Shaun's widow, you are entitled to half of his estate."

"Shane, your Uncle Allen, and Father took care of me months ago. Shaun actually did leave a will, and I know your Uncle and Father were more than generous. I've put the money in the bank, and I've not touched a cent of it. Uncle Allen told me that I should wait a full year after I learned Shaun was dead before I make any major moves with my life."

"Don't leave Rockhaven, Sarah," Shane said as the fear came over him that he might lose her if she had means in which to go away and start a new life. A life without him in her life.

"This is my home. My family is here. I don't even want to go to Tallahassee." Sarah almost laughed, and he thought the sound was lovely. He couldn't stop himself, and his lips found her cheek that wasn't bruised, and he pulled her close wishing that she was his to make love to. "Shane," she said his name and felt his wanting her. "No," she begged softly, and he pulled away from her and brushed her hair from her face. "No," she cried thinking of Lester.

"I'm sorry," he said gently. "You're right, and I don't belong here." Sarah watched him sit up on the edge of the bed and push himself up. "We can go out in my boat, and I'll row you upstream where no one lives. We could at least get you out of the house." He saw her sitting up out of the corner of his eye, and he turned to leave.

"I would love that, Shane. Sunshine and fresh air might help these bruises heal too." She saw him turn back to her and she thought again how handsome he was, and how kind. He was so like Shaun and yet, he was nothing like Shaun. Shane had always been much more sensitive than Shaun had been. Shane had a gentle soul. "I'll be dressed and ready in a few minutes," she said as he left the room they had shared for the night, and she closed the door knowing the pain in her body kept pulling her mind back to what had happened to her. "Oh God," Sarah cried as she clearly remembered what she feared that she would never, in this lifetime, forget.

Sarah stood looking at her eye and her lip in the mirror. She looked awful. One half of her face was swollen and black and blue. And she was now red from a day in the sun out on the river. When she had seen Uncle Allen bringing in food he had caught her hand and offered her a kind smile saying to her that he was glad she was getting out on the river. Allen Blackburn had told Sarah that the river had healed him and his wife many times. He knew the river could heal her as well.

"Whatcha doing?!" Shane hollered up the stairwell, and Sarah came out of the bathroom.

"My face," she said on a choked sob. "The least you might have done was told me how awful I look now," she called out as she started down the stairs to go to him.

"Aunt Alicia made chicken and dumplings," Shane said to her as she lifted the lid off of the pot on the stove and she saw the thick and hearty chicken stew.

"Just smelling Aunt Alicia's cooking and I gain ten pounds," Shane said coming to where she was and bending over her shoulder to smell their dinner. "I'm glad you're here. I didn't realize how dull my life was without your good company, Sarah."

"I feel the same way, Shane," Sarah turned her face and looked up into his eyes. He looked just as Shaun had looked and she knew, given half a chance, she could live with him forever as though he were her husband, Shaun. "Can we eat?" Sarah watched him turn away from her and pull clean bowls off of a shelf and two spoons from a drawer. "The few days I was here with Shaun," she said to Shane as she moved to sit down at the dining table, "we didn't really eat." Shane saw her blush and look up at him quickly as he put a bowl of the chicken stew in front of her.

"It's okay to talk about him and share our memories of him," Shane said. "I loved him too. Shaun was something special. Mama said he never slowed down. He lived in twenty years what most folks don't live in forty."

"He didn't let grass grow under his feet," Sarah said and kept looking at Shane thinking how much he was like Shaun and she hadn't known.

"He was the hero," Shane said.

"Yes, he was," Sarah said and looked back up at Shane. "But you were the real hero the day Shaun died." She saw him looking at her with an expression that told her he didn't know what she was saying. "I know that you told Shaun that you loved me and if he died you would come home and take me for yourself, or something like that. I just know you were trying to make Shaun mad so he would stay behind you when you both ran into the gunfire."

Shane got up from the table and went to the window looking out at the nighttime sky. He didn't want to remember that day. The last words between brothers hadn't been good. "Go to hell," he said and grabbed a deep breath before he doubled over.

"Shane," Sarah left the table and hurried to him.

"One of us told the other to go to hell," Shane said shaking his head. "And one of us called the other one a son of a bitch." Sarah saw him put his hand over his face. "Our last words were awful to one another because of what I tried to do, Sarah. I don't even remember anything clear. I just remember being hit." He turned and looked down at her, her hand on his shoulder. "How do you know about that day? How do you know, more clearly what I did that day than I do?"

"Ethan," Sarah said softly, and he still looked confused. "Ethan told everyone before dinner the night that you first came home. The night that I was cruel to you." Sarah went quiet, and she looked away from him feeling awful for how she had been toward him, and what she had said to him.

"You weren't cruel." Without thought he reached down and pulled her into his arms. "You were hurting and so was I." Sarah found herself drawn to him and she laid her head on his chest. "We're all right now Sarah. We're friends again just as we were when we were children."

"Yes Shane, we're friends again," she took hold of his hand, and she pulled him back to the table. "Let's finish eating, and thank you for keeping me so busy I haven't had time to think. I don't want to think."

"I understand," Shane said thinking of his suffering from shell-shock and her living with the memory of Lester hurting her. "I'm glad I have you around," he spoke these words in a teasing manner, and she looked at him with a questioning smile on her face. "You can do the dishes," he laughed.

"I will," Sarah said quickly. "Anything to keep busy and not think. I never want to think again." She saw Shaun giving her a concerned look, and she looked down at him holding her hand.

"I'll make you forget him, Sarah. We'll keep busy, and soon you'll forget what he did to you."

Sarah heard the cry, and she sat up in bed shaking all over in fear not knowing where that cry had come from. Maybe it came from her she thought, her heart pounding fast and hard within her chest. And then she heard the noise again. "No, get down!" and she knew the noise was from Shane. "Don't go that way! Get behind me. Stop playing hero!" Carefully Sarah left her bed and went to his bedroom doorway hearing every word that he spoke and seeing that he was sitting on the floor under his bedroom window. The moon was casting shadows everywhere, but she could see Shane. "Sarah," he said her name in a way that was harsh and not like she had ever heard him say her name before. "I have to get home, get home to Sarah." He was crouched, and she saw him moving slowly on the floor. "Ethan, use your bayonet," and then he was up and he seem to have something in his hands he was using as a weapon. "Damn Germans," he yelled and turned looking at her. "Shane? Shaun? Ethan?" he said all three names like he was calling for them, like he had become separated from them and couldn't find them, yet he was looking right at her, right now in his bedroom.

"Shane?" she said his name, and he ran at her pushing her down hard onto the floor, knocking the breath out of her and falling hard on top of her keeping the breath from her body.

"I told you to keep down, we won't get home to Sarah if you don't keep down." He was squashing her, and she couldn't push him off. "We have to get home to Sarah," he insisted, and she held still when he covered her head with his arms and screamed and then he was up off of her and back to his invisible weapon battling some unseen force. Sarah didn't move. She was half afraid he would hit her if she did move. Or he might tackle her to the floor again. After a few moments she moved slightly to see what he might do to her next, but he had seemed to have forgotten all about her presence.

"Sarah," she heard him crying. "Oh, Sarah. Sarah. I'm so sorry. Please, forgive me."

And then as quickly as the noise had first come and woke her up, Shane went back to the bed, and he lay down as though nothing had happened and he was asleep within seconds. Sarah lay still for a few minutes to wait and see if he would stay where he was or come after her again, when he didn't come after her again she carefully stood up and moved to his bed. The covers were kicked off of him, and at the end of the bed, she pulled those covers back up and over him and then she went back to her own room and got her pillow. She was safe with Shane. They had been together for days, and he hadn't done anything to her, even at the river when he cleaned Lester from her, he had been only kind and gentle.

Sarah put her pillow next to Shane's and laid down thinking about what had just happened. It was as if he were back on the battlefield she thought, and she remembered the pictures and drawings in the newspaper showing how men fought. They called this a dirty war, and thousands of men had died, not just her husband. The ones that came home weren't the same, she remembered reading that in the newspapers, and she knew now that Shane had changed. He wasn't the sweet, innocent boy that she had grown up with. He was a man that had survived terrible things, and he was hurting inside, and yes, there were times she now knew that he was back in the battle and fighting all over again in his dreams.

As she was struggling with Lester having shoved himself inside of her and the pain he had caused her, Shane was still struggling with his own pain. He had grown up with Shaun, been born with Shaun and never a minute without his brother. If she was grieving for Shaun, might Shane be grieving more? It would make sense he would be. She realized in that moment that they both were hurting a lot, both had gone to battle, and both had lost Shaun. They were alike, very much alike.

Sarah rolled over and put her head on Shane's chest seeing him in a whole new light. She was comfortable with him. He was comfortable with her. They were like brother and sister, caring about one another. She hoped that he would miss her when she was gone from here and back with her parents. Sarah knew that she would miss him very much.

Shane woke up to find Sarah in his bed, she was facing away from him with her back to his chest, and she was curled up into him. He was breathing in and out her hair, and that hair was tickling him, that hair is also what had awakened him. How had she come to be here? He wondered. And had he done something to her? Her nightgown was up to her hips, and he was only in his boxer shorts. He was also aroused, and if she woke up now she would know for certain that he wanted her and it would embarrass her and would embarrass him.

Sarah felt Shane awake, and she turned in his arms forcing her eyes to open. "Morning," she said looking at him looking at her. "How did you sleep?" she asked as she went to sit up and then cried out grabbing a hold of her shoulder.

"What's wrong?" Shane asked Sarah as she tried to look at the back of her shoulder and she saw him looking for her. "Oh wow, I didn't see this bruise the other day," he ran his hand softly down her shoulder blade, and Sarah knew, this bruise hadn't been there the other day. This bruise was from him having slammed her into the floor in the middle of the night.

"You saved me from a German soldier," She said while looking up at him and then unable to stop herself, she reached up and messed up his bangs causing them to fall onto his face.

"What are you talking about?" Shane asked pushing his hair back out of his eyes only for it to fall forward again.

"Last night, I heard a noise and came in here, and you thought I was Ethan or Shaun, and you tackled me to the floor. You were in a battle." She saw him sit up with a look of shock on his face.

"I did this to you, Sarah?" he touched her shoulder shaking his head hard in disbelief.

"In a nightmare," she said and sat up next to him. "Don't be so upset Shane. I'm having dreams of Lester," her voice lowered, and she looked down at her bare legs, and she saw the bruises Lester had caused. "I keep dreaming that Eddie didn't shoot him and he," she stopped and shook her head hard and felt Shane touch her shoulder again. "It's all right."

"But I hurt you," he said, and she put her fingers over his lips.

"At least you didn't pull me down to the river and make me scrub you all over," she forced a smile and then it happened again. She was pulled into his arms, and he was kissing her. She was dying for him to kiss her, and he was pushing her back on to his bed, and she was begging him to kiss her more, and there was no remembering Lester in Shane's kiss. Nor was there a memory of Shaun.

"I have to stop," Shane said before his mouth covered her mouth again and he plunged his tongue inside of her mouth, and she was doing the same. "I have to stop," he said again pulling away from her. "We can't do this." He got up off of the bed, and he heard her cry when he did. "I'm so sorry, Sarah. I mean to treat you like the angel you are, I just lost my head."

"I needed your kiss," she cried. "I needed you to make me forget that man hurting me. Oh God, Shane. I can't remember Shaun. I only remember that bad man!" She jumped up off of his bed, and she ran to her room closing the door thinking how hard she had fought to keep Lester from taking her. And she had loved Shaun. And now, she couldn't even remember her husband.

Sarah sat down on the edge of the bed thinking of Shane kissing her. Was she falling in love with Shane? Or was she confusing him with his brother? "He's not Shaun," she said in a firm voice. "And if he were Shaun, I would love him." She sat down on her bed feeling confused and lost, and she didn't know what she wanted. But she knew that she needed more time here, she needed more time with Shane, she wanted to be with him because Shane wasn't Lester. Shane was making her forget Lester.

"Bethany, I don't have time for a visit," Shane said meeting his cousin on the porch and trying to keep her away from the house.

"You've been gone all week, and Daddy's nearly worked Ethan to death. What are you hiding in the house?" Bethany tried to push past him, but Shane held her firmly away from his front door and on the side of the porch.

"Shane!" Sarah said running down the stairs and into the long hallway not seeing Shane. Where was he? She did a full turn in the hallway and ran out to the porch facing the river. He wasn't here and then she ran to the other porch, and she saw him in the doorway. "Shane! Oh, Shane!" he turned to see her beautiful and bruised face, and she flung herself in his arms on the porch. "You were right. I'm not with child," she was crying in relief as she clung to him tightly.

And Shane was quiet. He should be happy for her. Or at the very least, he should be relieved for her. He knew how worried she was that Lester might have done more to her than what she knew he had done to her. Sarah pulled away from him, and she saw, standing beyond where Shane was standing and beyond where she was standing, was Bethany.

As though he were on fire, Sarah pushed herself away from Shane, and yet his hand reached out and held her still. "It's not what you think," Shane was saying to Bethany. Sarah saw that Shane was holding Bethany's hand in a death grip and Bethany's face held an expression of shock. "Come in here," Shane pulled his cousin into the house and pushed Sarah when she didn't move.

"This is not what you're thinking," he said again, and Bethany sat down on his sofa next to Sarah who Shane had forced to sit down next to his cousin."

"Please, tell me you didn't beat her face while in one of your shellshock fits?" Bethany said this in a not so nice voice, and Sarah looked at her wondering why she was so mad.

"I didn't hurt Sarah," Shane said firmly then looked at Sarah knowing that he had hurt her when he pushed her to the floor that night.

"Why would you tell him you're not with child and be so happy over that?" Bethany stopped speaking and blushed, "well you know what you told him."

"Because last Tuesday night Lester Billings raped me in my father's storeroom," Sarah said looking from Bethany to Shane seconds before she burst into tears. "Lester hurt me. And your father told us not to say anything to anyone, and now you know."

Shane pulled Sarah to him while Bethany leaned back into the sofa looking confused and shocked. "Her parents didn't want anyone to know, neither did I or Uncle Allen. So Sarah's been staying here with me so that I can keep her safe while she heals."

"So that's why you were trying to keep me outside?" Bethany asked looking from Shane to Sarah. "Don't cry Sarah, you know I won't tell anyone." Bethany leaned forward, and she hugged her friend who was in Shane's arms. Lester had raped Sarah, Bethany thought in a moment of horror. And Sarah had run out onto the porch to tell Shane that she wasn't in a family way.

Bethany leaned back on the sofa, and she looked up at Shane's face. Her cousin was holding Sarah in his arms with his cheek resting on the top of Sarah's head. What Bethany was seeing between Shane and Sarah, was a tender scene. Sarah was clinging to him for dear life, and Bethany knew in this moment that these two were falling in love.

Bethany pulled farther away from them in surprise, yet she was not really surprised. Why shouldn't Shane and Sarah be drawn to one another? Sarah was young and beautiful, and they had grown up together. Shane was an exact duplicate of Shaun in almost every way. Though Shane was more calm and easier to get along with because he wasn't always competing with everyone he knew. Shane had a tender heart. And Bethany had wanted this for Shane and for Sarah. This was wonderful to see them falling in love.

Bethany saw Shane look down at Sarah when Sarah looked up at him, and she gasped. There could be no doubt in her mind. These two were not just falling in love. They were in love. They were more meant to be together than Shaun and Sarah had been meant to be together.

"I should go," Bethany said suddenly in a hurry to leave this couple alone. "I'm sorry you were hurt, Sarah. And I'm glad Shane is here taking care of you."

"Please, don't leave," Sarah pulled away from Shane and reached for Bethany seeing her friend walking backward toward the front door.

"I love you both," Bethany said with a smile. "And I'm going because Mama probably needs help with the baby. I just wanted to make sure Shane was all right. He's not been around, and Ethan's been working hard. But I now understand the situation." Bethany stopped at the door and looked at her cousin Shane. "You punched Lester for touching her at church that Sunday. I just want to know, does any other woman ever have to worry about Lester Billings again?" She saw Shane's head shaking, and she understood. "Good. And forget I was here."

"What's a shellshock fit, Shane?" Sarah asked as they went into the kitchen and he started frying some eggs. "Let me do that. You're going to burn them."

"A shellshock fit is what happened when I tackled you to the floor and hurt your shoulder," he touched her arm and Sarah looked up at him seeing his guilt.

"It doesn't hurt," she lied as she put the fried eggs on a plate for him before pouring them both a cup of coffee.

"Shellshock is what they're calling the condition some of the soldiers are suffering from. We came home from the war and are suffering from very real dreams of the war where we actually are relieving the battle. Some of the men are like me in that they get confused or have trouble remembering things clearly. Every man seems to be a little different. Ethan's been like me, night dreams and screaming out and Bethany's been dealing with it as best as she can."

"Poor Bethany," Sarah said gently remembering Shane's plowing into her and shoving her to the floor. "Poor Ethan. To nightly revisit the horror you both survived, I'm really sorry Shane." She looked up at Shane and saw him looking down at her, "I can only identify because of my dreams of Lester," she said softly, her voice choked up when she said the name of the man that had hurt her. She was sleeping in Shane's arms at night to feel safe, and she wished that she had some way to help him. "Lester is gone, he's not coming back," she said firmly to herself and shook her head. "I'm safe here. I'm safe now with you."

"I'll always keep you safe, Sarah," Shane said seriously. "Uncle Andrew is following all the research being done on shellshock so he might can help Ethan and me when there's a treatment found. I can only tell you it's pretty hard. There are things from before the war I can't remember or that are confused in my mind. And then there's that last moment with Shaun." Sarah saw the hurt on his face. "Shaun," he said his brother's name again. "He was the real hero. He wouldn't have been suffering like I have had he come home. But then, I wouldn't have thought Ethan would have this happening to him either. Ethan is all man. Sometimes I think I'm a coward."

"You're not a coward," Sarah said and reached for his hand. "Let's take a walk upriver, maybe go fishing." She saw him smile and quickly washed the breakfast dishes so they could go. "It might be too late to fish," she said seeing the sun was up in the mid-morning sky.

"No, it's never too late to fish," Shane said grabbing two poles and a tackle box. "I'll even dig the worms for you."

"Thanks, Shane. You're such a gentleman," she teased, and he laughed taking a hold of her hand pulling her out the door of a house that belonged to them both. They were becoming more and more a part of each other and a part of this river country.

Life was changed for Sarah and for Shane. She had been alone and missing Shaun. He had been alone and missing Shaun. And now they were together. Her in hiding trying to heal from the beating that Lester Billings had given to her, and him from a war that he had somehow survived, yet the battles went on inside of him nightly. They were two people with everything in common. They had a long-standing friendship, a firm foundation to build a relationship on, and they had found one another in the pain that Sarah had suffered at the hands of a man that was evil. The time was right for Shane and Sarah. They were finding themselves in one another. He was healing her. And she was healing him.

Sarah wasn't trying to be any way other than the way that she was, and the same thing could be said of Shane. They were together now, and they belonged together now. No questions nagged them. No worries or cares. They were natural with one another, and they were together. Every morning Sarah woke in Shane's bed tangled up in him and in his covers. Every night Shane pulled her into his bed. There were no kisses, there was no touching, and there was no intimacy between them beyond their need to be together. They were comforting one another. Two lonely people no longer alone because they had each other.

"Are you telling me that Mama told you that Sarah's gone to visit Sally Collier in Tallahassee?" Ellen asked her husband, Deputy Clayton Nichols, while he sat at the dinner table.

"Your folks have been acting odd Ellen. Ever since the night, they took that carpet out to Shane Blackburn's house. And why take him a carpet he ordered out to his house in the dark? Why not wait until the next day? That's bothered me a lot too. Something feels wrong over at their house. And today I went into the store, and I realized your sister Sarah hasn't been around at all in days. So I asked your Mama where she was, and she said in Tallahassee with her old friend, Sally Collier."

"Clayton, that's not possible. You misunderstood my Mama. Sally Collier was my childhood friend, and Sally moved down to Wakulla County years ago. She wouldn't have anything to do with Sarah. I don't even think Sarah knew her." Clayton frowned and went to the window looking out as though an answer to what was going on with his in-laws would appear beyond the window.

"There goes Eddie," Clayton said seeing Eddie run across the yard. Clayton quickly pulled open his front door, and he stepped out onto his front porch. "Eddie," he called his brother in law's name and saw the man turn and see him, and Clayton saw Eddie stop and stand still. Clayton knew that Eddie didn't like him, and Clayton knew he didn't like Eddie.

"Eddie Cartledge," Ellen said her brother's name in a tone that left no doubt for anyone listening that she didn't care for her brother in any way. She came out her front door, and she saw her brother wave at her, and she frowned severely. "Get over here right now," she ordered him in a shrill tone of voice seeing that Eddie slowly come toward her. "We'll know where Sarah is in just a minute," Ellen said confidently to her husband Clayton as Eddie stopped in their yard. "Where's Sarah, Eddie Cartledge? And don't you dare think of lying to me young man or I'll hit you hard right upside your head." Ellen looked at her brother speaking in a demanding way, and she knew, Eddie was going to tell her where Sarah was.

"Tallahassee," Eddie spoke to Ellen while looking up at his sister standing on her front porch, and he rocked from the heels of his feet to his toes, back and forth while fighting the urge to run home.

"Why is Sarah in Tallahassee?" Ellen looked closely at her brother. She couldn't stand him; she thought as she saw him rocking on his own two feet and wringing his hands in a nervous manner. Eddie should have drowned in that river years ago rather than be left as he was, and an embarrassment to her, Ellen thought as she waited impatiently for him to answer her question.

"I don't know," Eddie spoke honestly while looking up and beyond Ellen and not at her. Eddie was afraid of Ellen.

"Eddie, you tell me right now your secret. And I know you and mama and daddy have a secret." Ellen saw her brother cover his head with his hands and shake his head and she knew, something was wrong at her parents' home.

"I never touched that gun," Eddie said this while looking away from Ellen.

"He touched Daddy's gun," Ellen turned to her husband to say with confidence, and then she cried out, "Oh God, Eddie, you shot Sarah!"

"No!" Eddie cried out in return and began hitting himself in the head while rocking back and forth faster on his feet. "Sarah," he called for his sister and Ellen knew what was going on at home.

"Eddie has killed Sarah," she said in near hysteria to Clayton.

"No," Eddie said this word several times followed by the name "Lester." Every time Eddie said Lester's name he cried and Ellen stood very still while her husband took Eddie by the shoulders and shook her brother hard.

"Did Sarah kill Lester?" Clayton asked what he believed had happened at his in-laws house seeing that Eddie was shaking all over, almost violently.

"I killed Lester," Eddie said and spun around in a circle in the yard. "Shane, he helped Sarah and me," Eddie said innocently when he came to a standstill.

Clayton turned to his wife, and he saw her wave, Eddie, away, and Eddie ran away fast. Ellen knew that Eddie didn't like her, and she was all right that he didn't. "I'm going straight to Mama and have her tell me what in the world is going on. And where is Sarah? And why did Eddie say Shane is helping Sarah and him? What kind of help does Sarah need?"

"Wait, Ellen," Clayton turned to his wife. "I think I've just found a way to get rid of Eddie, once and for all. Don't alert your parents that we suspect anything has happened over at their place. Give me a chance to look around and to get the County Sheriff out here. I think I have this whole thing figured out clear in my mind." He narrowed his eyes, and he smiled realizing that Eddie had just confessed to him of killing Lester Billings and Shane Blackburn had helped Eddie in the killing.

Ellen looked at her husband and frowned hard. "If you can find some way to get my parents to get Eddie out of this community, I'll keep silent for as long as you say. So go ahead and do whatever you're thinking. I'm tired of him running wild making my family look like fools. The way everyone carries on about him makes me sick," Ellen said and went into the house. "Just tell me when I won't have to see him bouncing with his hand clapping anymore. I don't want to know where you have him locked away at either. I really don't care if I ever hear his name again."

Clayton watched his wife go into the house feeling confident that he could get Sheriff Tate to see things his way, that Eddie Cartledge is really a danger to the community. At long last, Eddie Cartledge was going to be right where Eddie Cartledge needed to be. And no Blackburn was going to save Eddie because Clayton was going to see a Blackburn went down and went down hard. "Damn Blackburns think they own this end of the county. Well, I'm fixing to show them just how wrong they are."

"I have to go home," Sarah said one morning sitting up in Shane's bed. "It's been almost two weeks, and I'm better." Shane turned and shook his head not wanting her to go. Sarah still had obvious bruising on her face. She wasn't completely healed.

"This is your home too," Shane said innocently. "And your face, it's better, but Sarah, you look like someone punched you in the face still. Stay a few more days. This is really your house as much as it is mine."

"You know I can't stay here with you openly Shane Blackburn," Sarah almost laughed, but the laugh sounded like a cry. "Even if this house is half mine, the gossips in this end of the county would tear me apart were they to find out that I was here with you and as we have been."

A knock sounded at the door Shane hurriedly pulled on this shirt. "Stay here," he said seriously before he left his bedroom and bounced down the stairwell with his shoes and socks in his hand.

Sarah moved to the stairwell, but she stayed hidden as Shane had told her too. She wanted to know what who was at the door and to hear was being said. The voice that Sarah heard sounded like Clayton, her brother in law. But why would he be here? Sarah wondered, and she leaned closer to the open hallway to hear what was being said.

"I need you to come with me to talk to the County Sheriff, Shane," Deputy Clayton Nichols said to him, and Shane sat down on the sofa to put on his socks and shoes not seeing Sarah with her hand over her mouth standing in the hallway and hidden by the staircase.

"What do I need to see the County Sheriff about?" Shane asked in a calm voice seeing Sarah out of the corner of his eye.

"Do you remember Lester Billings?" Clayton watched Shane closely as he asked this and Shane knew Clayton was watching him closely. All Shane could think about was what his Uncle Allen had told him, and that was to say nothing about Lester to anyone.

"Why do I want to remember Lester?" Shane tried to laugh in an attempt to make light of his question as he saw Sarah again, and now she had her clothes on. He felt certain that she was fixing to slip out the back door, and he knew she was going to get his Uncle Allen. Shane was certain of where Sarah was going, and he knew that she was little, but she could run fast. In his mind he was urging her on, he needed his Uncle now.

"Look here, Shane," Clayton spoke in a hard way. "Lester is missing, and I know you had a run-in with him at the church," Clayton said, and Shane looked at Clayton thinking that a lot of men probably had run-ins with Lester.

"If I remember right Clayton, you told Lester that day in the churchyard that you had a gun and threatened him over his having touched Sarah, and I backed you up. I'll go to the sheriff with you, but not without my Uncle Allen. He is an attorney, and he told me to never answer a question by a lawman unless he was with me," Shane said this in an almost casual way trying to make his words come out in a teasing manner. "So I'll wait for my Uncle to come and go with me to talk to the Sheriff about old Lester."

"Why don't we just go and get your Uncle?" Clayton pulled Shane to his feet, and Shane wondered why Clayton cared about Lester, the man had touched Sarah, so what if Lester was missing? They should have the attitude of good riddance.

Shane went to the stables with Clayton hot on his heels, and he saddled his horse hoping Sarah was at Riverbend by now and that his Uncle Allen was on the way to him. He was slow saddling his horse spending time brushing the animal down well before putting the saddle on. He took a deep breath when he saw his Uncle ride up in the yard hard and fast with Sarah holding on behind him and Shane knew now things would be all right. Uncle Allen was here.

"What are you doing here?" Clayton demanded to know of Sarah when he saw her clinging tightly to Allen Blackburn.

"I'm a Blackburn," Sarah said this while looking at Shane. "I'm supposed to be here. What are you doing here?"

"Doesn't matter what I'm doing here, Sarah. Your Mama and Daddy think you're in Tallahassee with your sister's friend Sally Collier, who by the way, doesn't live in Tallahassee, she lives in Wakulla County now," the deputy said looking up at Sarah closely. "Who beat you?" Sarah shook her head hard.

"She doesn't have to answer your question, Deputy," Allen said in a firm tone of voice with his eyes narrowed looking at Clayton hard. "And it's none of your business, but Shane and Sarah are engaged to be married making this the place she needs to be. Not in Tallahassee with your wife's friend." Allen saw Shane give him a look and he gave Shane a look back that made Shane know he just needed to be quiet and listen to his Uncle. Shane then looked at Sarah, and he saw that she looked frightened, more frightened than he had seen her since that night when she had been raped by Lester, and her parents had brought her to his house.

"I've not asked her daddy's permission yet, Clayton. So don't say anything yet," Shane said, and he still saw Sarah looking scared. "I'm ready to go," he mounted his horse and saw his Uncle riding next to him with Sarah looking at him with huge terrified eyes. Shane wondered what she was more afraid of, Eddie being arrested for murdering Lester, or that everyone would find out Lester had raped her. Shane knew he was highly concerned about both things being revealed because both Eddie and Sarah were Lester's victims. He looked away from Sarah and at the deputy and Shane wondered again, why did this man care about Lester? Lester was a mooch and a wanderer, for all any of them knew, Lester could be upriver in Jefferson County or across the river in Wakulla County.

Shane thought to himself that those Alligators could have taken Lester anywhere.

"Why did your folks tell people you were in Tallahassee," Clayton asked Sarah, and she tightened her grip on Shane's Uncle Allen not saying anything as Allen had told her the day Shane went for him to not talk to anyone. "I know that Lester has a history of molesting innocent women. Did he hurt you?"

"Sarah doesn't have to answer your questions, Deputy. So stop bothering her," Allen said this, and he looked at Shane. Allen couldn't look at Sarah as she sat on his horse behind him, but he patted her hand in reassurance.

"Why would her parents say she was in Tallahassee when she wasn't?" Allen looked at Clayton and said honestly,

"This is a personal family matter. Her parents didn't want to tell anyone where she was so they told what they wanted people to believe. Sarah has been with us on the River because we needed time with her. She lost her husband that was our son and nephew and brother."Allen knew that he was saying was the truth. Sarah did need to be with Shane, Shaun's brother. She was hurt, and she could heal, protected by Shane. She might not have been hurt by Shaun's death these last weeks, it might have been Lester's raping her that hurt her, but she needed Shane and Shane needed her.

"So you married the one brother, and now you're going for his identical twin. Only the first name of the husband changes and of that name only a couple of letters," Clayton said to Sarah and realized what he was saying wasn't funny to anyone but him. Allen Blackburn was looking at him in a way that told him clearly that he needed to shut up. Clayton remembered Allen throwing that ax at him months ago, and he wondered if what he had in mind today would go off as easy as he had hoped it would. Clayton had been so certain of what he was doing that he never stopped to consider that in his plan to take Eddie down, he would wind up having to face Allen Blackburn.

Come Save Someone Like Me

"Stay right here Sarah," Allen said firmly and left her standing on the steps of the church. "Do not come inside until I come for you," he said in a low voice knowing Clayton was busy getting Shane into the church and not listening to his words to Sarah.

Allen saw Eddie running around nearby, and he looked at Clayton who had turned to see Eddie running as well. Clayton had a satisfied look on his face, a look that Allen Blackburn couldn't like. There was no doubt in Allen's mind that whatever Clayton was up too by dragging Shane before the Sheriff, it had something to do with Eddie being locked in a tool shed and hidden away from society.

"Not today, not ever," Allen said firmly to himself and he followed Shane into the church along with Clayton.

Sheriff Tate looked worn out and put out when Allen, Shane, and Clayton walked into the church and sat down in front of him. He looked at his deputy and felt confused as to why the man had dragged him out to this quiet part of the county to come way down here, to the middle of nowhere. Hell, the Sheriff thought, it's so dull out here; they didn't even need a deputy on this end of the county.

"So let me see if I understand things right," the Sheriff turned and spoke to Clayton. "You have a missing man by the name of Lester Billings, a man who by all accounts is a molester of women, a man very well known to be a lazy mooch." Allen saw Clayton turn red in the face and decided to speak for him,

"That about sums up old Lester," Allen said with a laugh.

"His folks say he comes home at least two days a week and they've not seen him in almost three weeks," Clayton spoke up.

"And you found this Lester fellow dead, son?" The Sheriff saw Clayton shake his head and the Sheriff looked even more worn down. "I came all the way out here in the middle of nowhere because you telegraphed me that you had a murder and now you're saying you just have some missing man? A grown man that hasn't gone home to his mama for a couple of weeks?"

"Lester is missing Sheriff," Clayton was quick to say, "and Shane Blackburn had a run in with him at church one Sunday a few weeks back," Clayton started to look nervous, but still attempted to speak with an air of confidence.

"So because this young fellow had a run in with this Lester fellow, you think he killed him?" The Sheriff pinched his lips and shook his head.

"My nephew Shane is a wounded combat trained Marine not long home from the war," Allen said. "This Lester Billings put his hands on Shane's brother's wife, and yes, he had an altercation with him. That's the end of that."

"You've wasted my time, Deputy. There's no murder here, just some missing lazy no good son of a gun." the Sheriff went to stand, and Clayton held out a hand for him to stop.

"I never said Shane Blackburn killed Lester Billings," Clayton said. "But I know he knows who did." Shane looked at his Uncle Allen and then saw Clayton hurry to the door. "Come in here Eddie," Clayton yelled out into the churchyard at the same time Allen put his hand on Shane's shoulder to hold his nephew still while whispering for Shane to stay silent. "Eddie, tell the Sheriff what you told me," Clayton ordered Eddie to talk. Eddie broke free of Clayton and ran to Shane giving Shane a hug then Eddie reached for Allen who gently patted the young man on the back before pulling Eddie down on the seat beside Shane.

"Eddie," Allen said calmly, "what did you tell your brother in law Clayton?" Eddie was rocking in his seat and flapping his hands as was Eddie's way.

"He told me he killed Lester," Clayton interrupted Eddie's silence at the same moment that Sarah came into the church and yelled "no" in a frantic voice.

Allen stood up and rushed to Sarah taking her by the hand and mouthing for her to be quiet. Allen then pulled her with him and sat her down next to her brother. "Eddie," Allen spoke the young man's name calmly not seeing Shane had reached for Sarah's hand and was holding her hand securely. "Eddie," Allen spoke the younger man's name again to gain his attention. "Did you kill Lester Billings?" Eddie was rocking hard and fast on the church pew and nodded his head at the same time.

The Sheriff looked from Eddie to Allen and then back to Eddie. Allen Blackburn was smiling from ear to ear as though this situation were funny. "So what does my nephew Shane have to do with Eddie telling you he killed Lester?" Allen asked Clayton.

"Eddie talked about Shane after he told me he killed Lester. There's something going on here. I know is because in the dark of night her parents," Clayton pointed to Sarah, "delivered a rug out to Shane's house and then Sarah went missing. Her folks told people she was with her friend Sally in Tallahassee. The only thing is, Sally isn't Sarah's friend and Sally doesn't live in Tallahassee."

"Are you kidding me?" The Sheriff interrupted Clayton in a booming voice. "You had me come all the way out here to tell me that the town dimwit confessed to killing a molester of women? And a decorated war hero has something to do with this Lester's death or disappearance or whatever happened to the lazy no good because her mama and daddy delivered a rug to him?" The Sheriff looked at Sarah long and hard for a moment causing her to squirm in her seat next to Eddie. "Young lady, don't your folks own the general store here?" the Sheriff asked Sarah, and she slowly nodded her head looking from the Sheriff to Allen Blackburn. "Then it would make sense that her folks deliver rugs to folks that buy rugs. Ain't my business if they deliver after dark. And we don't even know if this Lester is dead. All we know is the shiftless no good hasn't come home for a week or so? How in the Sam Hill did you become a deputy?" The Sheriff demanded to know from Clayton as Allen Blackburn sat laughing so hard he couldn't sit up straight.

"Eddie would confess to anything, Sheriff. He's a sweet, innocent young man. He would say anything to please you, that's his way. Look at him. He's not capable of hurting anyone." The Sheriff nodded in full agreement with what Allen was saying.

"I still don't see what any of this has to do with this combat war hero being here in front of me," the Sheriff said and looked at Clayton. "What's this really about, deputy?"

"I believe Eddie," Clayton said firmly. "He's a menace to society. He runs around loose and wild acting insane. He told me he shot Lester and I believe him, and he told me that this man," he pointed to Shane, "helped him and his sister. And now today I go out to bring Shane Blackburn in to discuss this situation with you, and there's Eddie's sister shacked up with him with her face healing from some sort of beating." The Sheriff sat back down and looked from Eddie to Allen to Shane and then finally to Sarah.

"I'm real sorry someone hurt you, young lady," the Sheriff said with his eyes full of sympathy. "Get out of here," he said to Clayton who looked both shocked and confused. "Now!" the Sheriff ordered, and Clayton picked up his hat and walked slowly backwards to the door seeing that Sheriff Tate was furious with him. "You," Sheriff Tate pointed to Allen, "I know you're one of the richest men in this state and I know you're an attorney to boot, don't think I don't know who I'm dealing with. I didn't get elected to this county without having a clue who folks are." Allen nodded his head, and the Sheriff did too. "So talk to me, Mr. Blackburn."

"Everyone in this room is my client, Sheriff. I can't talk and I advice them to not talk." The Sheriff shook his head and looked at Shane then Sarah and finally Allen.

"Fine, don't none of you talk. I'll talk," the Sheriff said looking at Sarah. "I think my idiot deputy wanted to make some sort of name for himself and dragged me out here not having his facts straight. That young man over there," he pointed to Eddie who wasn't looking at anyone in the room and had his hands over his ears, "told my deputy something my deputy wanted to hear. But looking at that young man, I'm certain as certain can be he couldn't shoot a gun. Now did this Lester the molester of women hurt you?" he pointed to Sarah, "I don't know the answer for certain to that question, but if you were my woman and he hurt you, he'd be six feet under and not in the county jail. I don't know where this Lester is, neither does my idiot deputy and quite frankly, I don't care where he is." The Sheriff turned to Shane, "if you killed him, well you're more a hero sir. No woman should be beat like this pretty gal has been." The Sheriff looked again at Sarah. "Looks to be healing up nicely Miss."

"I didn't kill him," Shane said honestly and earnestly. "I wish I had killed him, but I didn't."

"I believe you, son. You have an honest face," the Sheriff said to Shane sincerely. "It's real nice to finally meet you, Mr. Blackburn. I'd be more inclined to think you killed the man than anyone else in this room," he said this to Allen.

"Thank you, Sheriff. I wish I could take credit, but like my nephew, I can honestly tell you that I didn't kill Lester Billings if Lester Billings is even dead. Your idiot deputy never established that fact." Allen stood and shook the sheriff's hand in a firm shake, "And it was a pleasure to meet you as well. I hope you never have reason to come out this way again." Allen looked at Eddie who had bounced near him and gave him a hug.

"Sheriff," Allen continued to speak, "there are some people that feel Eddie shouldn't be seen, that he should be kept hidden away. People like that idiot deputy of yours. I just want you to know, if that man, or any man tries to put this young man away in an attic or tool shed or anywhere else, they're going to deal with me, and I can assure you, no one wants to deal with me. So, before anything happens, maybe you could find a new part of the county for your idiot deputy to work in. After today, a transfer should be called for." Allen saw the Sheriff look at Eddie and nod his head.

"Message received loud and clear, Mr. Blackburn. Damn fool deputy should have known better than to fool with one of the richest men in the whole state of Florida. I know you know people in high places, Blackburn, and I don't want to ever find myself having to deal with you. This part of the county is so quiet; you folks don't even need a deputy."

Allen watched the Sheriff leave the church and sat down in the front pew pulling Eddie with him and taking a deep breath and then letting that breath go. "Your parents were right in what they chose to do in this situation," Allen said to Sarah seconds before she burst into tears and covered her face with her hands. "You'll be all right now, Sarah," Allen said gently. "I'll take Eddie home to your folks. Shane, you can take care of her." Allen stood and took Eddie's hand walking to the door. "How about we get a coke, Eddie?"

"Coke," Eddie bounced ahead of Allen and across the street to his Mama standing in the doorway of her store wringing her hands in worry.

"It's all right Sarah," Shane said and put his arms around her. "Let's go back to the house. Uncle Allen knows his own way home."

"I can't go with you, Shane. I've loved every minute out on the river with you, but I need to stay here now. I'll stay at home hidden until I'm all healed. I won't let anyone see me." Sarah wiped her face with the handkerchief that Shane handed her and saw Shane shaking his head.

"I don't want to go home without you," he said holding tightly to her hand. "I've made no secret of the fact that I'm in love with you," Shane suddenly said having no intention of saying this to Sarah. "Will you marry me?" he was in the church and had gone down on one knee, and Sarah felt he was more than sweet, so like Shane and nothing like Shaun.

"I know I care deeply about you," Sarah said softly, her hand coming to rest on his cheek. "I know I love you, Shane. But I don't know if I'm in love with you. And I need to be sure. Am I marrying you for you, for Shane? Or because you remind me of Shaun? I never want to hurt you, Shane. I need time to think." Shane saw her stand up and start to leave and he couldn't let her go. He couldn't let her go until she knew who he was. He sat down again in the front pew and looked up at her holding her hand still.

Sarah was looking down at him one moment and the next moment he had her wrapped up in his arms holding her close and kissing her, his mouth moving over her mouth slowly and then he was plunging his tongue deep into her mouth while his hands were pulling her closer to him. He finally had her straddling him while he sat still on the front pew. Shane was having his way with her mouth as he kissed her deep and long, over and over again. He felt Sarah push against him and he groaned so loud that he thought he was going to pass out. She moved again, and he knew he was going to lose himself if he didn't stop now. He was inside the church Shane thought and he pulled away from her trying to think.

"I am not Shaun," he said in a gentle yet firm voice. "I don't know what Shaun did with you, but I know what I want to do with you." He put his forehead against hers and looked into her eyes. They were so close her eyelashes were touching his. "I want to lay you in my bed every night and spend an hour undressing you, touching you, kissing you from head to foot, I want to make love to you until you're so tired and limp you can't move off of me. I want to fry eggs and bacon with you every morning and swim in the river with you every afternoon. I want to take you fishing, get sunburned with you," he heard her laughing, and he laughed too. "I want to climb the tallest tree on the river and pull you up in that tree and see if we can see the Gulf of Mexico together. I want to go to church on Sunday with you and eat your Mama's stew and my Mama's yeast rolls together and have Uncle Allen as my best man.

I want you for a lifetime, Sarah. For always, and I don't care how many children we have, as long as they're all happy. I'm Shane, I'll always be Shane, the good son," he laughed. "And I want you for my wife." He put her down off of his lap, but not before he kissed her again. "With me, you'll forget Lester the first night I make you my own in every way possible. You'll only know and want me, Sarah, just as I can say right now, that I'll only know and want you for the rest of my life. You know where to find me if you want to talk about this some more. And Sarah, I'll wait for you to figure things out. I'll wait a lifetime for you cause you're worth that wait."

Sarah watched Shane tip his hat to her and turn for the church doors. She had never known him to be confident like Shaun, but he was being confident now. She watched him leave, and Sarah knew, there wasn't that much difference between Shane and Shaun, but Shane was more gentle, more loving, and calm. Maybe she had always been meant to belong to Shane.

Sarah turned and looked at the cross behind the pulpit where the Reverend stood on Sundays, and wondered if God had meant for this to be. She loved them both. She had to choose between them, and she had chosen the one that was the least like herself. She let the one that was like her, the calm and patient and laid back twin go and she loved her wild twin. And he was gone now, and every day for all of her life she would miss Shaun. And yet here she stood with the one like her, and he wanted her still. And they would fit together well, and she knew, there was no doubt in her mine, Sarah had fallen in love with Shane too.

"He tried to bring Shaun home," Sarah said when she turned and saw Uncle Allen standing in the doorway of the church. "He told Shaun he loved me. He said he would marry me if Shaun died. He told Shaun that so Shaun would stay behind him and get to come home to me. Shane loved Shaun too." She moved to his Uncle, and Allen looked down at her when she stood in front of him and nodded his head. "He made a threat to come home and steal me if Shaun didn't return. But he didn't mean that threat. He was just saying that to keep Shaun safe. And now it's come true." Sarah was searching Allen's eyes for an answer that she couldn't find within herself.

"Would Shaun approve of you and Shane being in love?" Allen asked her, and she nodded her head. "What do you think? You knew Shaun as well as I did. Do you think he would want you to never marry again? To never know love? To grow old alone and lonely?" He saw her head shake and he smiled. "Do you think that Shaun, who loved Shane so much he died reaching out for him, would be unhappy to see the two people he loved most in the world happy and in love and together?" Allen saw the emotions cross Sarah's face and knew she wasn't as conflicted as she had thought she was. This young woman knew what she wanted. "Shaun knew Shane was in love with you in that battle from hell, and he still loved his brother, he died loving his brother. And he died loving you. And Sarah, ask yourself how you feel about Shane, really feel. I don't mean to embarrass you, but I came by the house yesterday morning, there was no answer to my knock," Allen saw her turning red, the stain of red on her face spread quickly. "Yes, I came upstairs, and I saw you two."

"It was innocent," Sarah rushed to say. "He has bad dreams. Sometimes he's even up out of the bed reliving the battle trying to kill the Germans again. But when I'm with him, he stays in the bed. He doesn't let me go," her voice faded off as she realized her situation wasn't just about being in love with Shane. She wanted him, and she needed him.

"I know Bethany is dealing with Ethan having the same sort of thing happen. I'm glad to hear you're able to keep Shane calm." Allen saw Sarah was only half listening to him and then she left him. Sarah ran out the door of the church, and he saw her going down the road toward his home. "Silly girl could have asked me for a ride," Allen said as he mounted his horse and galloped toward home. Within a couple of minutes, he overtook Sarah and reached an arm down for her and swung her up into his saddle behind him with ease.

"Can you catch Shane?" Allen shook his head,

"I doubt the boy is riding hell bent for home. Hang on," Sarah did as she was told right when Allen kicked his stallion and bent low urging his horse onward and seeing Shane ahead of him, the gap between them was closing fast.

Sarah laughed when Allen pulled hard on his reins and sat up straight stopping his horse. "Shane," he called out to his nephew who turned and saw him. "I have something that belongs to you," Allen held out his arm and Sarah grabbed a hold as he lowered her to the ground, but only for a second. She was being swung up into Shane's saddle within the second. "Yeeehiii!!!" Allen called out as he kicked the horse and disappeared down the road leading home.

"You're gonna be my best man!" Shane called out and knew his Uncle heard him because he saw Allen's hand go up in the air and give a wave.

"Shane, we can't go back to your house," Sarah said as she laid her cheek against his back and held on to him with her arms wrapped around him from behind. "We can't sleep together again until after we're married even though all we've done is sleep together."

"I can't wait long," Shane said seriously, his voice sounding deep and husky, so much like Shaun's voice and yet not like Shaun's voice, Sarah thought.

"Reverend Farmer comes out next Sunday," Sarah said. We could plan on marrying after services. She felt Shane put his hand over her hand and turned his horse back toward her parents' house.

"I have to ask your father for permission." Shane closed his eyes and grabbed his breath as he heard the words in his head, words that had come true that weren't supposed to ever come true;

"If you die, I'll marry Sarah, I'll love her better than you ever would have." Sarah felt Shane tense and held him tighter. "I want you to know," Shane said in a very serious voice, "I'd rather be dead and Shaun here holding you and loving you than the way things are right now, Sarah. But Shaun is gone," Sarah heard Shane's voice break, and she knew without seeing his face or his eyes that he was crying. "I tried to protect him. I'm sorry I failed. I have to believe he would be all right with us being together."

"Uncle Allen said that Shaun was reaching for you even when he was dying. Shaun loved you, and he loved me. He would want us to be together. I think Shaun is the reason we are together right now, Shane. Let's not feel guilty about Shaun. Let's love Shaun like he loved us, and love one another." Shane brushed the tears from his face as he dismounted the horse in front of the general store.

"Tom," he said when Sarah's father stepped outside with her mother who rushed to check her over and make sure she was healing. "I need to ask your permission to marry Sarah," he felt her hand slip into his hand when he said this, and he heard her mother give thanks to God.

"You have it, Shane." Tom shook his head as Eddie came from beyond the door and hugged him.

"Marry Shaun again," Eddie said, and both Shane and Sarah laughed. "Shane," Eddie said and laughed with them. "You're not Shaun. Sarah's marrying Shane this time."

"It's all right for you to call me Shaun, Eddie," Shane said looking into Sarah's eyes, "as long as Sarah remembers which brother I am." He kissed her cheek and Shane knew that his life was incomplete and always would be without his brother. He was standing in the place that Shaun should be standing, but Shaun had fallen on the field of battle and left Shane behind. And Sarah was left behind as well.

Bethany went into her father's study, and she found him staring off into the distance with a satisfied look on his face. Her mother had just come out of the room, so she knew that her father was lost in thought of her mother, Alicia. Bethany didn't want to disturb him, but she needed him. She needed his help.

"Daddy," she said softly, and her father met her eyes with his own.

"Bethany," he said her name as he stood coming around his desk to pull his daughter into his arms. "What's the matter?"

"I need your help," she spoke on in her soft way. She knew that her father was very aware of what they were going to talk about. Her parents were her best friends. She had no secrets from her parents, and Bethany believed that her parents had no secrets from her. She trusted her parents with everything.

"Ethan?" Allen spoke his son in law's name as he pulled away from his daughter motioning for her to sit down in one of the overstuffed chairs in his office.

"I know you've helped Shane and Sarah a lot," Bethany began to talk, and her father nodded his head in agreement with her words. "I want you to make Ethan go to Tallahassee and talk to Uncle Andrew about what's happening to him. Daddy, he's not sleeping. He's not eating. You can see the change in him. I thought our being married and happy together would have settled him down. But he's still going into battle every single night of the week."

Allen leaned back in his chair and looked at his daughter wanting to advice her and support her in any way that he could. But the truth was, Allen knew almost nothing about shellshock, and he knew that's what the boys coming home had. He also didn't think that a trip to Tallahassee to see the Doctor was going to make much of a difference for Ethan Tucker.

"What's happening to Ethan isn't something any Doctor can put a bandage on or sew up and fix, sweetheart." Allen saw the defeated look on his daughter's face at his words. "Something's just take time," Allen counseled her gently.

"Daddy, you didn't see Ethan in the yard yesterday when you were cutting up firewood. Every swing of the ax that you made the noise Ethan jerked. He flinched Daddy, and one time, the ax was so loud that he ducked down low as though the ax was going to hit him or something. Daddy, he was afraid, and I'm afraid for him." Bethany leaned forward appealing to her father for help that she knew her father, nor any man could give help to her husband.

"He went into hell," Allen said gently as he stood up going to his desk. "Here's the article in the New York Times of the Battle of Belleau Wood in France. The battle where Shaun died, and Ethan and Shane were wounded. I've kept this newspaper hidden because it's too horrible to read. I didn't want my girls to see what our Ethan and Shane survived and what cost us our Shaun." Allen handed the newspaper to his eldest child. "Bethany, that battle lasted twenty days. Our boys were in the front lines. Well, read for yourself, and it'll help you understand why Ethan's still struggling a year on. And I talked to Sarah. She told me that Shane's asleep at night, but he's out of the bed in his sleep reliving the battle."

Bethany sat still for a long while reading the newspaper that her father had handed to her, and she was thankful to have him here beside her and supporting her while she read.

The day that her cousin Shaun had died, Bethany now knew that the Marines suffered a huge loss of men. More Marines were lost in this battle than in any other battle they had fought. Those Marines had gone across an open wheat field toward the Germans, and the Germans had machine guns firing into those men. The Marines stood almost no chance of survival as hundreds were shot down before they could even reach the woods where the battle would take place. Bethany also knew now that the battle took place while it was still dark out, more night than day when Shane and Shaun and Ethan had crossed that field with wild shots going past them, killing the men with them and around them. They had somehow made it to the woods where they had to fight for their lives. Hand to hand combat, using their bayonets and Bethany closed her eyes seeing her husband's scarred face.

"They were fighting to come home to us," Bethany said softly. "Ethan was fighting to live to come home to me." Allen reached over and patted her hand.

"And he did come, home sweetheart. But he's scarred, and more than just his face. We have to give him time to heal, Bethany. We have to keep supporting him and Shane. Thanks for telling me his reaction to my chopping wood, maybe having him chop the wood will help him get use to the sound, and he'll be all right with it. I don't know what more to do than that for him." Allen stood, and he saw his wife standing at the door of his study looking in at him, and he smiled at his quiet and sweet beautiful wife that he adored more than anything in this life.

"I think having Ethan chop the wood is a good idea," Alicia said in her kind and gentle way. "May I please talk to Ethan?" she asked both Bethany and Allen, her eyes looking into her husband's eyes. He knew her. He knew that she had dealt with the horrors of her own past and that she had overcome a great sorrow and a worse loss.

"Mama, if you have any idea of how to help my husband," Bethany broke down in tears, and her mother came to her quickly as a mother would, and Alicia pulled her daughter close.

"She's old enough now to know," Alicia looked up at Allen with tear-filled eyes, and she saw him nod his head. "We need to tell her." Again Alicia saw her husband nod his head and she was thankful that she had him here with her. Allen had always been here with her.

"Alicia, we'll tell them together. Let me go find Ethan and make sure Lonnie can watch the baby for us." Bethany watched her father hurry from the room, and she looked up at her mother with questioning eyes, eyes that were just like her mothers.

"Before you were born, your father and I went through something terrible together," Alicia saw her daughter was listening closely to what she was saying. "We never told you what happened to us. We never would have even thought of telling you as it's in the past. But it might help you and Ethan both go through what you are having to go through. Sweetie, the bad doesn't last forever. Eventually, we get past the difficult time and then we face a new difficulty, a new uncertainty. I never wanted you to know what I lived through, what your father saved me from, but you need to know what love is capable of doing."

Bethany looked at her mother feeling confused. Her mother was sweet, often quiet and when Alicia spoke, the words were softly spoken and gentle, always kind. She never even heard her mother's raised voice. For Bethany and her sisters, even if they did something wrong, their mother was always kind and gentle with them making them want to be gentle and kind to their mother. In a way, Bethany had never seen her mother as a person. She viewed Alicia as a caregiver, a helpmate, a partner, seated at the foot of the table smiling and appearing strong and always in love with Bethany's Daddy.

Allen came into the room with Ethan and Alicia knew the time had come to tell what she had been through, and in the telling, there might be healing and understanding for the younger couple in the room with her now. Ethan sat down, and she saw him sit with a questioning look on his beautiful face. Gathering courage on the taking of a deep breath, Alicia swallowed hard and walked to the window looking out at the river nearby, a river that can take the pain of the past away if you let the pain go. She knew there were many times in the years since she had married Allen that the pain crept back onto her and stole her breath and hurt her heart, but only for a moment. The pain was distant now, with love and care she had been able to let that pain go.

"I don't know how to start," Alicia almost sobbed when she turned around and saw her big, strong, brave, good husband come to her and take her hand. "Would you help me?" she asked him in her sweet way, and he touched her cheek with the tips of his fingers.

"Always,' he said in his firm voice and Bethany thought that her parents were as in love today as they had been nearly twenty years ago. "Bethany, I didn't want to marry your mother. I didn't even know her," Allen started to talk with his arm around his wife, and he went to one of the overstuffed chairs and pulled Alicia down onto his lap.

"You didn't know her when you married her?" Bethany looked at her parents and then at Ethan, and she heard her father laugh softly.

"My father, your grandfather, left in his Will that I was to marry Alicia or lose this place." Allen waved his hand toward the window. "I would have to leave here, everything that we own would have passed to Shane and Shaun unless I married your mother." Allen saw Ethan sit forward on his chair and Bethany took Ethan's hand. "And I was leaving here. I was going to Charleston, South Carolina and starting a whole new life." Allen turned his head and met Alicia's eyes, aqua he thought to himself, the most beautiful and unique color eyes could be. "But before I left here, before I gave up everything I'd ever wanted in my life, I had to meet this woman my father was demanding I marry." His wife leaned her head onto his, and they looked together at their daughter.

"He came and found me, Bethany," Alicia almost sobbed. "I was living in a hell, not of my own making. Your Daddy came, and he found me, he saved me, and loved me." Alicia felt her husband hold her closer and she let him. "I can't tell them how you found me, Allen."

"It's all right, Alicia," Allen said softly, and he turned to his child and her husband, and he told them everything, from the start of when and how he found Alicia, what she had been through and suffered. The actual hell that she had survived and how she had blocked things out of her memory to just be all right when things had not ever been all right for her. "We all suffer just from living life," Allen said, "and others suffer far more than just life. Alicia was in a war battling to survive, and she did, but she didn't come out of that war without being changed. Had she not gone through all that she went through Ethan," Allen looked at his son in law, "she might very well be different than she is today. I love my wife. I know, I was there and saw what happened to her and what was done to her. Bethany, you weren't there with Ethan, you didn't see all that he went through just to get home to you. But you can hear from me because the battle your mother won is very similar to the battle Ethan won. Alicia doesn't laugh spontaneously. She isn't carefree and like the rest of us. She tends to worry over things the rest of us don't give a second thought too. Ethan is very much like Alicia. In the crowd of our family, he's there, but he's not really a part of the crowd. That's what a war does. War takes away a piece of you that you never get back." Allen saw his daughter had been crying in his telling of what happened to her mother when her mother had been young, younger than Bethany was now.

"I'm sorry, Mama," Bethany left her chair, and Allen saw his wife stand and hold her child close. "I never knew."

"I never wanted any of my children to know what happened to me," Alicia said softly.

"So now you understand Bethany, what real love is," Allen held his wife's hand as his daughter looked from over Alicia's shoulder and into his eyes. "We Blackburns are sturdy stock, and you're like me. Love isn't always easy to give. And there are times that are not good in all relationships. But real love is sticking together in the worst of times. Clinging to someone for dear life because they need you to cling to them for dear life, and to have complete understanding for what they're going through, even when you've no idea just what they are going through."

"You're the best Daddy ever," Bethany said, and Allen gave a bitter laugh.

"Bethany, I am what your mother made me. She taught me to love unconditionally. To never ever judge anyone, to be patient and kind to others. I was awful at the start of our marriage," he saw Alicia shake her head and turn toward him. "You know I was awful," he said to his wife as he pulled her back down onto his lap. "I had no understanding of what she was going through and had already gone through. I was a selfish bastard."

"He wasn't that bad," Alicia interrupted her husband and quickly defended him before she placed a kiss his cheek.

"Yes, I was bad," Allen said firmly. "Despite all that your mother had gone through, all I had put her through, she forgave me. I'll never forget," a smile touched Allen's face as he looked up, but it was as though he were seeing not the ceiling, but a memory from his past. "I was sitting on the porch, and I turned, and she was there," Allen looked down, and his eyes met Alicia's eyes, and he saw that she was smiling.

"And he was there." Alicia leaned into her husband and felt his lips touch hers. Neither of them saw their daughter take her husband Ethan by the hand and leave them alone in the room.

"It was very brave of your parents to tell us what they just told us," Ethan said as he walked out onto the porch. "Your mother is a hero. I'll never look at her the same way again. And I'll protect her just as I will protect you, Bethany."

"Ethan," Bethany turned to her husband and looked up at him. "I've been like Daddy," she said softly. "I've been selfish and had no patience with you." She knew that he knew that she had been hard on him for his flinching over the slightest noise, and for his night terrors. The screaming in the night was hard on them both.

Without any warning that he was going to fall down on the step, Ethan fell, and Bethany cried his name and went down with him trying to hold him in her arms.

"I'm not weak," he sobbed, and his wife held him.

"Not in any way," Bethany agreed smoothing his hair as he laid his head on her shoulder.

"I've been afraid I would fail you,"

"Never," Bethany pulled him closer. Neither Ethan nor Bethany saw their Uncle Heath standing at the end of the porch watching the tender scene of this hurting young couple.

"I don't know how to start over, Bethany. I love you so much, I just wanted to come home to you, and I don't know how to put everything behind me and start over."

"Maybe you need to stop trying to put everything that happened behind you," Bethany touched Ethan's face when he pulled away from her and their eyes met. "I read about that battle near France," she said softly, "the one where you were hurt," she touched his scar, kissed his scar, "and we lost Shaun."

"We lost Shaun," Ethan repeated, and Bethany heard his voice, he sounded like his heart was breaking.

"Daddy let me read the story in the newspaper of what happened in that battle," she said gently and saw her Uncle Heath listening to them. "I know it was one of the worst battles of the war, Ethan."

"There was this man, no, he was really only a boy. He couldn't have been nineteen years old. He was walking next to me," Ethan said to his wife. "We were in the field and fellows were dropping like flies all around us. I was trying to watch out for Shaun and Shane with this boy next to me, and I turned, and the boy was gone. I looked all around for him before I looked back to where he had been and I looked down, and I saw him lying on the ground. He was reaching for me. He looked gut shot. I didn't stop and help him. I kept going with the twins toward the woods. I left him alone and scared. For weeks in the hospital, I searched for that boy, Bethany. I couldn't find him anywhere. I never even knew his name."

"Ethan," Bethany saw her Uncle Heath come to the steps of the porch where they sat. "If you had stayed with that boy, what would you have done for him?" Heath watched as Ethan sat up straight looking at Bethany.

"I don't know what I would have done for him," Ethan said, and his shoulders seem to relax some as Heath put his foot on the bottom step and leaned in closer to the couple.

"If you had stayed with the boy, not left him alone, you might have been shot too, Ethan. You said the fellows around you were dropping like flies. And you had orders to march across that field and into those woods. You had a job to do," Heath continued and saw Ethan nodding. Bethany heard in her Uncle Heath words that the old man was giving Ethan a new way to think about having left that boy behind. Instead of feeling guilty, Ethan would feel he had done the only thing that he could have done. "You did what you had to do, what was right for our country and the other countries being harmed by that war. You went into those woods, you fought the bad men that were harming others, and together, as a team, you and Shane and Shaun did what had to be done to keep all of us safe. You just didn't come home alive to Bethany and your family Ethan. You made us safe here at home from invaders that had nothing but a harmful intent. You did good, son."

"I never stopped and thought about what happened in that way," Ethan was still looking at Bethany's Uncle.

"When we're close to something, we don't see it as clearly as others who are farther away," Heath said as though he were talking to himself. "We also tend to be harder on ourselves than we are on others, Ethan. I'm not saying change the way you think and feel. You can't do that, none of us can. What I'm saying is maybe look at things another way like Shaun's death. I was talking to Shane about his marrying Sarah the other day. And I know you know because Shane told me you were there and heard him tell his brother that if Shaun didn't stay behind him and Shaun were killed, Shane would come home and marry Sarah. And that's what happened. Shaun died, and the words Shane used to try and get Shaun safely behind him in that battle are coming true. Shane's struggling with what happened. But like I told him, Shaun would want Shane to be happy and Sarah too. Just try and look at things in a different light, Ethan. And don't be so hard on yourself."

"And I won't be so hard on you either," Bethany said reaching out to her Uncle and taking a hold of Heath Ferrell's hand. "Thank you, Uncle Heath. Daddy is right; it's better to talk things out."

"My father has a saying," Ethan said, "the silence makes no sound, and in marriage, silence isn't good."

"Your Daddy is a smart man," Heath smiled before he walked away from the young couple feeling today would be better than yesterday.

Chapter Eight

"Heather," Sarah called out to her friend before Heather could mount her horse out in front of the general store. "I need to talk to you." Sarah saw Heather looking away from her and took a hold of her friend's arm. She and Heather had always been close. The two girls had run wild on the river banks with Shane and Shaun. There had been the four of them growing up. But in the past few years, Heather had changed. Heather had pulled away from Sarah, the bond they had as children had started to unravel and now they had grown distant from one another. "What's wrong, Heather? I've not seen you in the longest time, can't we talk for a while," Sarah pleaded.

"I have nothing to say to you, Sarah," Heather spoke in her soft way, and Sarah let go of her arm.

"We use to be best friends Heather, but the past few years, you've changed. I feel like you don't like me any longer. Did I do something wrong?" Sarah watched Heather mount her horse. Her eyes averted from Sarah's face. "Heather please, Shane and I are getting married on Sunday after church services. I want you to stand with me."

"Don't ask me to do that, Sarah." Heather Ferrell, the daughter of Allen's sister, Emily Blackburn and Heath Ferrell, turned grass green eyes onto her friend. "There's something you don't know about me," Heather said, and Sarah saw what looked to be anger in Heather's eyes.

"Whatever it is can't be that bad Heather," Sarah said and reached up for Heather's hand. "I want you there with me when I marry your cousin."

"I won't stand with you, Sarah. Not while you marry Shane," Heather spoke in a harsh and firm voice. "You don't know how I feel about him. You don't know anything."

"Oh," Sarah gasped and took a step back and away from Heather. "You're in love with Shane?" Sarah guessed.

"In love with that coward?" Heather laughed out loud, and it wasn't a nice sounding laugh. "I hate Shane more than I ever loved him." Heather saw Sarah's hand go over her mouth and then Heather saw Sarah physically back away to the front doorway of her home as though Sarah couldn't get far enough away from Heather. "I know what Ethan said about how Shaun died and of Shane telling Shaun to stay behind him so he could come home to you. I was with you when Ethan told everyone how Shaun died, but I don't believe one word of Ethan's story. I know Shane. I grew up with those two, and Shane was always the coward. Shaun was always the hero. Ethan had it wrong. Shaun told Shane to get behind him, Sarah. And now Shaun is dead, and Shane is stealing Shaun's wife from him. No, I won't stand up with you while you marry that coward. I won't watch you betray Shaun! And not with Shane, who has always been a loser." Heather turned away from the stricken look on Sarah's face and kicked her horse hard for home; dust flying up from the road was all that could be seen of horse and rider within seconds.

"Shaun," Eddie said from beside her and Sarah shook her head.

"I'm marrying Shane," she reminded her brother Eddie and turned to see him smiling. Eddie hadn't understood what Heather had just said to her, and she was thankful for that reality. She was also thankful that Heather was quiet and kept to herself. Shane didn't need to hear what Heather thought of him. "Let's go inside Eddie," Sarah said and pulled her brother into their house.

Allen Blackburn stood in the general store doorway looking at his only sister Emily who stood with her hand over her mouth looking ready to cry. Her daughter Heather had just called Shane a coward, Shane had come back from the war shot in two places, and he had fought to live. Shane was anything but a coward. And Sarah couldn't betray Shaun because Shaun was dead and everyone in the family honestly felt that Shaun would want Sarah safe and happy in life and who better to make her safe and happy than his brother Shane?

"Your daughter grew up to be just like me," Allen said seriously to his sister and he saw her pain filled eyes look into his. "Do you have room on your horse to take these few things by my house?" he asked as he handed Emily a sack of sugar and some lemons.

"You tell her I'm disappointed in her Allen," Emily said as he mounted his horse and looked down at her touching her cheek.

"I remember a time I was cruel to Heath," he said softly. "And I was forgiven, and Heath is now my very best friend in the whole world. He always was. You weren't disappointed in me Em, you were understanding and showed me how wrong I was." Allen saw his sister nod her head and touch his hand.

"You've become the leader and moral fiber for our family, Allen. I trust you to handle this. Knowing Heather as I do, she didn't go home first. She's down on the river where the pool is beyond the family cemetery." Emily saw Allen nod his head as he turned his horse for the road.

"I'll find her even if I have to come to your house," he said gently to his beautiful sister, a sister that had stood by him and Alicia through the nightmare they had survived. He would do anything for Emily because he knew that Emily would do anything for him.

Heather Ferrell was a beauty, and she knew it. Her hair was a light brown with gold in several places and very heavy and thick with a slight wave. Her eyes were the Blackburn grass green in color. She was taller than any of the other women in the family with a tiny waist that she could wrap her own hands around. Heather was also very smart, and she managed the accounting books with her Uncle Allen for the tree farm and their own small mill.

"We need to talk," Allen said from behind his niece where she waded in the pool at the river's edge, and he saw her surprised face as she turned around and watched him dismount his horse. He pointed to a large limestone under the huge oak tree only a few feet from where he stood, and he went to sit on the stone seeing Heather come to him.

"My figures were right on that last load of cut timber," Heather said as she went to her Uncle who was as much like her father as Heath was with her, and she knew Allen adored her. But right now he looked very upset with her, and she didn't understand why.

"I'm fixing to tell you something that I don't want to leave from right here at this river's edge," Allen said seriously. He was so serious that he pointed his finger at her and held her eyes with his own. Heather couldn't look away if she had tried too. Allen's stare was that intense.

"I won't tell anyone, Uncle Allen," Heather said softly worried over why he was looking so mad with her. All she could do was breathe deeply and wait for him to tell her what she had done wrong.

"Your father and I grew up together on this river," Allen said without looking away from her, grass green eyes looking into grass green eyes. "He was as much a brother to me as Seth, and I love him, but his daddy worked for my daddy, they weren't wealthy and owners of a lot of land as we were." Allen narrowed his eyes as he spoke the truth. "I looked down on your Daddy, Heather. I didn't think he was good enough for my sister and I told him so too. I was mean and cruel to my best friend, and I treated him like he wasn't worthy of being the dirt under my feet."

"Uncle Allen," Heather took a step toward him not believing what he was telling her. Her good and loving Uncle would not treat her father the way that he was telling her that he had. "Do you still feel that way about Daddy?"

"No, I do not. And I hated that I ever felt the way I did about Heath Ferrell. I'm not worth ten of him. And right now I'm looking at you and knowing that you're more like me than you need to be. I didn't want any of you children to be like me. I'm ashamed of you Heather," he said these last words with a heavy heart and Heather heard the sorrow in his tone.

"What did I do wrong?" she cried out and saw him, for the first time look away from her and out at the clear river, a river that seems to flow on forever and for always and was clean, innocent and perfect.

"Shane was shot twice. He's fought to get well. He went into battles, and we won't ever have any idea how he had to fight and what he had to do to survive. And you just told Sarah he was a coward." Allen shifted his hard gaze back to Heather. "That man is a hero. He tried to save his brother. No one, and Heather, I mean no one, loved Shaun like Shane did and does. That's his twin brother. He has far more memories of Shaun than you or I ever will. They were born together. You would honor Shaun by standing up with Sarah when she marries Shane." Allen saw the tears fall from Heather's eyes and fell silent as she looked ready to speak, and he wanted her to explain what made her feel as she did.

"I love you Uncle Allen, but I don't agree with you on this. All my life, I've watched Shane let Shaun win in everything they did together, skipping rocks on the river, swimming against the current, climbing trees, racing their horses. No matter what they did, Shane never even tried to win. He just let Shaun win because he's weak; he won't even try." Allen was shocked. Heather didn't know Shane at all. Heather was completely blind to the good person Shane was.

It was Shane's way to be thoughtful. Allen grieved that he hadn't been more like Shane in his younger years.

"Well young lady," he spoke firmly and stood up walking to her pointing his finger in her face, "you don't know what good, and kind, and generous, means." Allen was in her face, and she wasn't backing down from how she felt, Allen could see that she wasn't. "Shane knew early on that Shaun loved to win, and Shane loved Shaun enough to want his brother happy. Shane was always giving of himself. Selfless, something you wouldn't know or understand." Allen turned away from Heather thinking of Emily saying she was disappointed in her daughter. "Shaun knew," Allen's voice was filled with grief for his lost nephew. "Shaun knew Shane was letting him win." Allen turned back around and faced Heather. "You're entitled to your own feelings," Allen all but spat these words at his niece before he turned and went to his horse. "I saw my mistake with your father and I was ashamed of myself. That shame made me change. If the truth be told Heather, I'm still ashamed of myself for what I did to your father." Heather watched her Uncle turn his horse away from her, but not before he said one last thing, "Shaun would hate you for not being good to Shane. And right now I know one thing for certain. As you are, I don't like you." He kicked his horse and rode away from his niece. He loved Heather, she was like one of his own children, but in this, she was wrong, and he wouldn't let her believe for one second that he thought she was right in what she was doing.

Heather went to the stone her Uncle had been sitting on, and she pulled on her stockings and her shoes before going to her horse. She thought of what he said for a few minutes, and she felt a little bad that she wasn't being nice to Shane, but she felt she was right in not betraying Shaun by supporting this marriage. Sarah belonged to Shaun, and as far as Heather was concerned, Sarah would always belong to Shaun.

"Allen," Emily chased after him as he stormed into the house, his face was red, and he looked like he wanted to punch something. "Allen, please tell me that Heather is going to stand by Sarah on Sunday." Allen shook his head, and Emily frowned as he drew back his fist and punched the wall in the entrance hallway, and then he said a very ugly word, not seeing Alicia running into the hallway at the noise his fist made when it connected to the wall, but he heard his sister cry out.

"I hope you can talk sense to your daughter Emily," he said and looked down at his sister. "Do you remember the day Alicia fell down the stairs?" Allen saw his sister nod her head. "That day changed the man that I was then to the man that I am now. I was a bastard until the minute I saw the woman I loved more than life itself hurt like I had hurt her." Allen wiped his face with his hand and turned away from his sister with the intent of finding his wife.

"Allen," she was there behind him, only a foot away was his Alicia.

"I'll always be sorry for what I did to you that day," Allen grabbed his wife, and she wrapped her arms around his neck, her feet leaving the floor as she clung to him. Emily backed away from the couple and saw Ethan and Bethany looking down the long hallway as Alicia's lips met her husband's lips, and Allen lifted her into his arm.

"I love you so much," Alicia said as her husband carried her up the stairs.

"Thank God that you do," Allen spoke to his wife only.

"He'll never forgive himself that day," Emily almost cried as she sat down on the bottom stair. Ethan and Bethany came to her, the young couple looking up the stairs where Allen and Alicia had disappeared only a few seconds before.

"Mama and Daddy told us their story," Bethany said while looking down at her Aunt Emily.

"They did not," Emily insisted on a gasp.

"Mama started to tell us, but she couldn't. Daddy told us. He even told us about how he was toward Uncle Heath and everything he did wrong to mama. He told us about going to his Grandmother in Charleston." Bethany leaned back into Ethan's arms. "I know Mama has bad times because of what was done to her. That was awful to have happened to my sweet Mama, and I'm so sad she suffered as she did. But in the telling of their story, Ethan and I both heard how sorry Daddy was that he had hurt Mama. They both are like Ethan and have shellshock from the past." Bethany could hear her father's soft voice drifting down the stairwell as he was right now telling her mother he was sorry and he loved her over and over again, and her mama was telling him that she loved him over and over again. "Daddy says we all suffer from life in some way."

"My brother's marriage didn't start out well. That was a bad time," Emily said as she looked up at Bethany and realized that her niece had grown into a beautiful and loving young woman very unlike Heather. "But we got through it as a family, and then you came to us, Bethany. You were the creation of not just their love, but your mother's forgiveness of your father." Emily said softly and wished that she could say something this nice of her own daughter as she reached out for Bethany's hand.

"I didn't know that," Bethany said softly looking back up the stairs. Her parents were now silent, and the house was calm and still. "My mother has always meant the world to me. Daddy too, but I feel like I really didn't know them until just these past few days. I knew they have a rare love for one another, but I really didn't know how deep that love goes for the two of them."

"Deeper than our river," Emily said and looked at Bethany and Ethan. "You two go somewhere and be together. Jenny and Julie can listen out for the baby." Emily watched Bethany pull Ethan to the door of the house and disappear out onto the porch, and she smiled for them and tried not to think of Heather, her only child that she loved, but she was not happy with right now. At least she wasn't punching the wall as her brother had, and Emily looked at the place he had hit, and she saw a hole. There was more than one hole in the hallway of Riverbend, and Emily smiled. Allen had his own unique way of dealing with frustration, and seeing these holes in the wall made her forget her worry over her daughter. She had a good brother, a brother that had learned from his wife Alicia how to love.

The Reverend Farmer arrived in Rockhaven early on Saturday and looked around at how quiet the town was. This was a nice place to settle, he thought, and Tom Farmer knew that when he retired in the coming months, this is where he was going to retire too and live out the rest of his days. He knew the Blackburn clan would welcome him as one of their own and he would find a nice comfortable rocking chair to put on his front porch. And here he would sit and watch that lazy river flow down to the Gulf of Mexico for the rest of his days thanking God for his full life.

Sarah saw the Reverend pull into the churchyard in his buggy and with Eddie, she went to help him unhitch and stable the horses. He was a fine man and had been a part of her life all of her life. "Hello," she spoke to him and reached to help with the horses seeing the Reverend smile at her.

"Sarah," Tom Farmer said her name before he hugged Eddie. "I heard that Clayton caused a fuss out here,' the Reverend said, and Sarah nodded her head.

"Sheriff Tate has assigned Clayton to another part of the county," Sarah said. "Eddie will be safe." She saw the Reverend nod his head in understanding.

"It's a shame people don't see Eddie for what he truly is," the Reverend started for the stable and Sarah came with him.

"What is he truly, Reverend Farmer?" Sarah asked. "I see him as sweet and loving, gentle and good. Not everyone does though. Some people are actually afraid of him."

"Eddie is what we all should all want to be," the Reverend spoke and hugged Eddie again. "A child at heart, and innocent of so much of the evil in this world. When Christ returns for us, and someday Christ will return for us, it will be people like Eddie that will be walking closest to our Lord." Sarah nodded her head and smiled. She was happy that Eddie was seen in this way by their Minister.

"I just love him and thankfully so does Shane," Sarah said, and she saw the Reverend turn and look at her with raised eyebrows.

"So I'm joining you to Shane tomorrow?" the Reverend saw Sarah nod her head. "I pray you'll be happy and safe always. I'm sure with Shane you will be. And Shaun would want this union," the Reverend added seriously.

"I don't have anyone to stand with me tomorrow," Sarah said as she hung the tackle on a nail before turning back to the Reverend. "Shane has his Uncle Allen standing with him, I wanted Heather," she paused and looked away from the Reverend before she blurted out what Heather had said to her, "Heather says I'm betraying Shaun by marrying Shane. And she said Shane is a coward that didn't bring Shaun home."

"Sarah," the Reverend saying her name stopped her from speaking and made her feel a calm that she hadn't felt since Heather had called Shane a coward. "First, Shane is not a coward, we all know that. Shane is different from Shaun. He always has been. He has a gentleness Shaun never had, and I think I admire his gentle nature greatly. Second, no one wanted Shaun to come home more than Shane did, not even you or his mama and daddy. That boy loves his brother more than himself. They were two halves that weren't whole unless they were together, that's why they built Twin River together. As for betraying Shaun, well that's just wrong. You could only betray him by doing him a wrong, and marrying his brother that he loved so much and being happy with his brother is no betrayal, it's pleasing."

"Thank you for these words, Reverend," Sarah said and almost sagged in relief. "I still don't have anyone to stand with me tomorrow."

"Yes, you do," the Reverend assured her as they went back into the yard and Eddie ran up to them with a smile. "Allen Blackburn. He's the one that wrote and told me I would be marrying you to Shane tomorrow. He loves you both, and he wants you happy. So ask him in the morning to stand with both of you. And anyone that doesn't approve of your marriage has no right to judge Sarah. We shouldn't judge one another for any reason."

"Thank you," Sarah said while she turned and ran toward her home. "See you in the morning," she called back over her shoulder to the Reverend right before she caught Eddie's hand pulling him to the house with her. Everything was going to be good. Life was going to be happy. Eddie was safe, and Shane loved her, and she loved Shane. And tomorrow she would be married.

"I love this dress," Sarah's mother Ester said as she helped Sarah do up the buttons in the front of her cream-colored dress that was fitted and covered in lace. The buttons were covered with material that matched her dress. Her mother had lovingly made each button on this dress and then she had sewed them on herself.

"It really is pretty, Mama," Sarah said as she smoothed the dress of any wrinkles. The sleeves were lace and long. Like the front of her dress, the sleeves buttoned from the elbow to the wrist and the skirt of the dress clung to her legs. Each step that she took, the dress swirled around her feet and wearing this dress made Sarah feel beautiful. Closing her eyes, Sarah wished that she had worn a dress like this when she married Shaun and thinking of him now, her lost husband, Sarah fought not to cry.

"We have something for you," Bethany came into the room with her younger sisters Julie and Jenny. "When Mama married Daddy she wore a ring of flowers in her hair. She told me yesterday those flowers made her feel special. So the three of us went and picked these flowers and made this for you," Bethany laughed as she put the flowers on Sarah's head, the wreath slipped on to Sarah's curls like a crown that a Princess would have worn.

"Sarah, you're beyond beautiful with your hair up like that," Jenny said, and Julie agreed as Sarah went to her mirror and looked at her reflection.

"I look so different," Sarah said, and her mother came up behind her and hugged her.

"I need to go get my food to the church. Don't be late; services start soon," Sarah heard her mother say leaving the girls in the room.

"I look so young," Sarah laughed still while looking at herself in the mirror as she touched the flowers.

"You're beautiful," Bethany said and reached to pinch Sarah's cheeks.

"I know it sounds silly," Sarah looked at Julie and Jenny and then closed her eyes. "I'm just so afraid." Bethany took her younger sisters by the hand and told them to get to church, that she would be there in a minute. Bethany then turned back to Sarah.

"You were married to Shaun," Bethany said taking Sarah's hand. "You will be all right," she assured Sarah. "Shane is a good man."

"I'm still afraid," Sarah said moving from the mirror to look out the window. "I keep thinking of what that man did to me." Sarah couldn't say Lester's name. Instead, she closed her eyes and almost cried. "What if it was painful with Shaun and I just forgot that it was and now," she stopped talking and turned to look at Bethany. "I trust Shane. Please, don't think I don't trust Shane." She grabbed a deep breath and saw Bethany blushing seconds before Bethany took Sarah's hands and held them tightly.

"Sarah," Bethany felt herself blushing worse than she had been. "The act is not painful with your husband." Sarah fell forward and hugged Bethany fighting to draw a deep breath. "With Ethan," Bethany spoke on and closed her eyes when she did. "Well, with

Ethan it's lovely. I'm certain with Shane tonight you'll be as happy as I am."

"You're right," Sarah said and stood up straight taking Bethany's hand and pulling Bethany with her out of her room. "We don't want to be late for church today."

"No," Bethany agreed as they hurried out of the house and across the street. "Today is going to be a good day Sarah. I promise."

Shane stood leaning against the wall in the back of the church. His foot against the wall and his leg was bent. He looked comfortable, and he looked confident, and he was. Today he was marrying Sarah, and he was happy. Today he wasn't going to let the past harm his future. "I feel like Shaun is with me, Mama," he spoke to Mary Blackburn, and she reached for his hand and squeezed it hard while nodding her head in understanding and agreement.

"Shaun is always here with us," she looked out as the church filled up with people. "I hope my rolls are good today. I was so nervous I can't remember if I put enough sugar in them or not."

"I'm getting married, and my mother is worrying over her rolls," Shane laughed and hugged his mother close. "I know you're nervous Mama," he said as his mother hugged him back. "Let's go sit down." As he stood up to move to the family pew, he saw the Reverend motioning for him to come forward and he settled his mother before going to the front of the church.

"I want to marry you and Sarah before I begin my sermon," the Reverend whispered into Shane's ear. "Her daddy is out front with her now keeping her from coming in here. I need you to stand right here with me." The Reverend put Shane in front of him and to the side and motioned for Allen to join them.

"I thought Heather was standing with Sarah," Shane said, and he looked out to the congregation seeing his cousin Heather was sitting in the family pew looking at him. Shane didn't like the way Heather was looking at him. Heather looked as though she was mad at him. He could almost feel her hatred for him just by the look she was giving to him. He didn't understand, and right now, about to be married; he didn't want to understand.

"Sarah asked me to stand with both of you," Allen said with a smile.

Shane saw the Reverend smiling out at everyone. And then Shane turned and he saw Tom coming inside the church with Sarah holding on to her father's arm. She looked more beautiful than Shane had ever known her to look in all their lives together. The crown of flowers in her hair made her look like a fairy from one of the children's stories he had read as a child. She was so small. Her dress showed how tiny her waist was. Sarah was perfect in every way, and for a moment he thought he didn't deserve her. For a moment, he remembered that she had loved Shaun first.

Shane felt Allen put a steady hand on his shoulder and he turned and looked at his Uncle who gave him a reassuring smile that made his heart stop beating so hard in his chest. Shaun would be happy for him, Shane thought to himself. Shaun was gone, and his brother would want Sarah cared for and loved. Shaun would understand this marriage and this love that Shane had for Shaun's wife.

"We are gathered here today to join together this man and this woman," the Reverend spoke, and Shane took Sarah from her father and looked down at her.

"You're too beautiful for me," he whispered, and she smiled.

"I was going to say the same thing to you," Sarah whispered back, and before the Reverend could say anything more, Shane bent his head and pulled Sarah close, and their lips met in an intimate kiss. They were so in love. They were so thankful to be together that they didn't notice anything other than one another in this moment.

Laughter rang out around them, and Shane lifted his head smiling down at Sarah. "You're supposed to kiss her after I marry you to her, Shane. Not before," the Reverend Farmer said loud and clear, and Shane turned with Sarah to face Tom Farmer holding Sarah's hand.

"Well hurry up and marry us so I can kiss her again," Shane said just as loud and saw his Uncle beside him laughing so hard that Allen almost fell down.

Sarah fell against Shane, and he knew that she was laughing as well. He turned and saw his mother smiling, and he knew no matter what, they were off to a good start in this marriage. His father winked at him, and he nodded to his Dad with a huge smile. Today couldn't get any better than it was right this moment, Shane thought, only his night would be better than this day, his night in Sarah's arms.

Shane slipped a simple gold band onto Sarah's finger. He repeated his vows and heard her saying her vows, and then the Reverend pronounced them man and wife. "Now you may kiss her," Allen leaned over to say to Shane and saw the younger man smile before pulling Sarah close, his mouth an inch from her mouth.

"I also want you to know, every single day for the rest of my life, I'm going to thank God I'm married to you," Shane vowed, and then he kissed her, his new bride, and she melted into him. She was more thankful for him than he would ever be for her, Sarah thought as he moaned into her mouth in front of God and everyone. She would always love Shaun. Forever she would love Shaun, but she had loved Shane too. And now, with Shaun gone, Shane would make her happy forever.

Alicia leaned back into her husband's arms as they had finished the picnic dinner on the church grounds and she knew that he was eating one of Mary's rolls as he held her. Everyone loved Mary's rolls. "Someone needs to tell Shane to take Sarah home," Alicia spoke softly to Allen seeing that both Emily and Heath had heard her.

"He's getting around to it," Heath laughed watching Shane sitting under a nearby tree putting food into Sarah's mouth from a plate the newly wedded couple were sharing from, that plate was in Sarah's lap. The family watched as Shane took a bite of fried chicken and stared down at his new wife, his look one of devotion.

"He always loved her," Heath spoke on while standing up from the picnic blanket. He then reached down for Emily's hand and pulled her to stand up beside him. "Like I always loved you," Heath said these words while looking into his wife's beautiful Blackburn grass green eyes.

"Did we ever behave like that?" Emily asked her husband as his eyes stared down into her eyes and he nodded his head.

"We still do," he said softly, and the two seemed to be lost in one another.

Allen saw Heather watching Shane and Sarah, and he frowned thinking of her and what she had said to him that day by the river. He was proud of Shane. He always had been. His nephew wasn't a vain man. Shane was a humble man, and he was not competitive. Shane was someone to admire, and Allen did so as did many in their family. Heather stood alone in her thoughts of Shane.

"I'm going home," Heather said and stood up not seeing the look of concern Bethany gave to her. "He coveted his brother's wife," Heather said in an angry tone. "Reverend Farmer should have preached on that today since he married those two."

"Heather," her mother said her name sharply, and Bethany sat up not believing what Heather had just said. And Heather had spoken loud enough for both Shane and Sarah to hear.

Alicia sat up, and she looked at Shane knowing that her husband was looking at Shane as well. "That was a mean and hateful thing to say, Heather," Alicia said these words seconds before she burst into tears because Alicia never ever spoke harshly to anyone ever. Alicia knew firsthand the hurt that words could do. For Alicia Blackburn, words had once hurt her worse than a punch in the face.

"Oh mama," Bethany left her husband Ethan and came to her mother seeing that her father was looking at Heather with a look that Bethany never wanted Allen to give to her.

Shane leaned Sarah forward and out of his lap as he stood. His eyes kept looking at Heather seeing that she wasn't looking at him. Heather was looking at their Uncle Allen. The family was angry. Shane could see that Heather's words had upset everyone. His Uncle Heath was blood red in the face. His father, Seth, Shane saw and his mother Mary, both looked ready to cry.

Shane came to stand in front of Heather, and she had no choice but to look up at him. "I've always loved Sarah," Shane confessed. "But I never coveted her. I never wanted to have her for my own. She was always Shaun's, and I respected that and kept my feelings to myself." He hadn't known it was coming. Shane hadn't seen Heather's hand raise. The slap that she gave to him was so hard that he nearly fell down. One side of his face stinging and on fire.

"You're a liar," Heather nearly hissed this in his face. "You let Shaun die so you could have her. I bet you even shot your own brother and made everyone think a German shot, Shaun. You can lie to everyone in this family. But I know the truth about you, Shane. You wanted Shaun dead, and you saw him dead for one reason. And that reason is and was Sarah."

"Oh, Heather!" Mary cried out before falling against her husband Seth who was trying to stand and go to his son."

"Stop it now, Heather," Allen warned as he stood up helping Emily to her feet.

The war had changed Shane. He wasn't the same man as he used to be. He felt things much deeper now. Shane wore his heart on his sleeve, and he knew what the word heartache meant because his heart was easy to ache in missing his brother. He wasn't less of a man. Shane felt he was more of a man. He felt things deeply, and he felt love deeply and sorrow as well, with all of his heart.

"The war turned you into a sissy," Heather said in a worse than cruel way. "The war made you a murderer and a sissy."

Alicia saw Shane drop to his knees in front of Heather and cover his face. She saw everyone become more than still as though everyone had all gone to stone, except for herself and Shane, Shane who was sobbing and she moved toward him and pulled him close, only then did Alicia see Sarah crying under the tree where Shane had left his young bride.

"I didn't want him to die," Shane sobbed and clung to his small Aunt as she cradled him in her arms, and then Mary was beside Alicia and rubbing Shane's back, and Heath and Emily were pulling Heather to their buggy, both speechless by their daughter's behavior, and Allen was watching unable to move or to speak.

"Mary," Emily cried out, and she saw Alicia nod at her indicating no one blamed her for what Heather had said. "I'm so sorry, Mary!" she said in a broken voice.

"Take her away," Seth said to his sister waving a hand at Heather as Heath put the girl into their buggy and then helped Emily climb into the buggy before driving away.

"It was their wedding day," Heath said in a broken voice to his daughter. He couldn't look at her. He had never expected anything like this from his only child.

"Sarah," Allen said to Alicia as they saw that the young woman was alone under the tree. Sarah's parents were across the churchyard sitting on a blanket with the Reverend and hadn't seen or heard what had just happened, but others in the churchyard had seen, and they were staring in shock and disbelief.

"I have her," Alicia stood and went to Sarah with Bethany beside her.

"I need to be with Shane," Sarah said to Alicia who was wiping Sarah's face with a handkerchief and nodding her head in understanding of where Sarah needed to be.

Bethany and Alicia helped Sarah up from the blanket that she and Shane had been sitting on. Sarah went to Shane. Kneeling before him she pulled his hands from his face and leaned her forehead against his forehead.

"Shane, let's go home. I want you to take me home now Shane," Sarah pleaded, and she saw her husband look into her eyes. "Heather doesn't know you, she doesn't know me, and she has no right to judge us. I need for us to go home now Shane. Please, take me home with you now." Shane stood up, and he pulled his wife up with him not looking at his family. His eyes looked at Sarah, and she was leading him to his horse.

"Do you need any help?" Allen asked, and he saw Sarah shake her head.

"Daddy took all my things out to the house yesterday," Sarah called back to Allen. "We'll be fine Uncle Allen."

"You'll take care of him?" Mary called out, and Sarah turned to her mother in law.

"And he'll take care of me," she called back while trying to smile. Shane was looking at her; his face was red where Heather had hit him, a palm print was clearly seen on his cheek.

"How are you going to get on my horse in that dress?" he asked her and Sarah looked up at him with trusting eyes.

"You'll have to lift me up to sit sideways on your horse, I can't straddle the animal in this," she smoothed her beautiful dress.

"I can do that," Shane said, and with ease, he lifted his wife into the saddle and then climbed on behind her. "You're so close," he breathed these words into her ear, and she moved closer to him, and he put an arm around her feeling both of her arms around his neck.

"Take me home, Shane," Sarah said looking up at her husband and not seeing her Blackburn family all watching them leave. Julie and Jenny ran alongside the horse for a ways laughing and blowing kisses and Shane actually smiled, though the smile was a forced smile. He wished he could forget what his cousin had said. He wished she hadn't slapped him. He didn't know Heather hated him as much as she did until today. He could have lived a lifetime not knowing that Heather hated him.

The front door of the house was really the back door, Shane thought as he lifted Sarah up into his arms and carried her inside. The real front door was facing the river. Their house was an exact replica of Riverbend, his Uncle Allen, and Aunt Alicia's home. The breezeway ran through from the front to the back of the house. The screen door and screen windows opened from spring to fall allowing the river breeze into the house.

Shane put Sarah down and then stood awkwardly before her. "I have to go stable my horse," he said softly, and as he said this, Shane saw her nod her head. He moved to the door walking backward looking at her. His eyes were locked with Sarah's eyes as he wished again that Heather hadn't slapped him and that his cousin hadn't said the words that had been said. He felt Heather's words hurt his soul.

"Shane." Sarah rushed to the door he had just backed out of and before he turned to take the steps her saying his name made him stand still. "Meet me down at the river," she said, and he nodded his head watching her go back inside the house.

Sarah leaned against the wall and fought not to cry. Heather's words had been so cruel, so harsh, full of judgment. Shane had loved her always, she had also loved him, but she had never coveted him. She honestly believed that he loved his brother so much that he would never covet her. Shane was a good soul, she knew him, Heather didn't know him. Shane had wanted Shaun to survive the war and come home to her. But Shaun hadn't survived the war. And for her and Shane, they had known one another forever. They had always been best friends. Their marriage today would be and should be considered natural as Shaun was gone, and in death, Shaun couldn't come back. Neither Shane nor Sarah wanted Shaun dead, and they both lost him, and in the losing of Shaun, they had found one another.

Sarah pulled the pins from her long hair and let it fall loose and to her waist. The flowers she left in her hair as a crown, and she slipped off her shoes before going out the front door, what some might call the river door as it faced the river. She started undoing the buttons at her sleeves and had them undone before she reached the grassy bank and looked up at the afternoon sun shining down on her. It was so peaceful here; she thought as she undid the buttons down the front of her dress and slipped it from her shoulders following it with her slip. She entered the river and took a deep breath seeing her hair float around her and then she burst into tears, and that's how Shane found her.

"Sarah," he said her name while taking off his shoes. "I'm sorry. If you don't want to be married to me, I can talk to the Reverend about not filing our marriage license; then our marriage won't be legal." He put his feet in the water ready to grab her if she were to get caught in the current. She was too far out in the water.

Sarah looked up at the man that she was married too, and she shook her head. "I'm afraid," she said honestly, and he shook his head as he didn't understand her words. "I keep thinking all the time about what that man did." Shane stood up straight with his feet in the water as he realized what she meant by being afraid. She had been so brave, so carefree about crawling into bed with him, but beyond kisses, there had been nothing further between them.

"Sarah, can I come in with you?" he asked her, and he saw that she was going deeper into the river. He pulled off his Sunday coat and shirt and tie and laid them on the bank with his shoes. He left on his pants and waded out to her, but he didn't touch her. "We're too far out. The current," he said and reached underwater for her hand.

"I want you," she said on a sob, and he pulled her closer to him and out of the current of the river and into the mild waves at the side. "But I'm afraid."

"Why don't we just take this slow," Shane said in the form of a statement and not in the form of a question. He saw that Sarah had all of her clothes off and he almost lost his breath when he did. "You're so beautiful," he gasped and saw her looking up at him.

"I've felt so dirty since," her voice faded away and he pulled her close to his body thankful that his pants were still on so she wouldn't see what just holding her like this was doing to him.

"The river washed all the hurt and bad and dirt away from you and away from me. This river, it's a part of us, Sarah, it can heal our wounds, it can make us new. It's in our blood like Uncle Allen says. We're a part of this body of water, and it's a part of us. We grew up out here swimming and fishing and rowing in the boat. We drank most of the day from this place. This river really has been a part of us our whole life. We know almost every inch of this place by heart, which bank grows flowers and which grows grass and where all the largest limestones are. Whenever you and I have a problem, we're going to come down here and start fresh and clean. Whenever life gets too hard, we're coming into our river, Sarah. We belong here, together, and as long as we're here together, we're going to be all right, we can withstand anything."

Shane pulled his new wife to the bank of the river and leaned back against the grassy knoll feeling the minnows swimming around him and Sarah, those tiny fish were almost tickling him, and he could see them as the water was crystal clear. Sarah was facing away from him as he held her in his arms with her head leaned back against his shoulder, and Shane knew, a part of Shaun was here with them in this moment.

"You don't think less of me for Lester having done that to me?" Sarah almost choked on the words and Shane whispered in her ear,

"I adore you with all my heart. You live on a mile high pedestal." He felt her press against him, and his hands covered her nude breasts. He could see them, small and round and beautiful in the full light of day. "I could get lost looking at you," he breathed, and his mouth went over her ear teasing her there with his lips and tongue. Shane heard his wife gasp as he touched her with his mouth and he turned her in his arms to better reach her, his mouth moving to her mouth.

"I don't want it to hurt like he hurt me," Sarah cried softly into Shane's mouth.

"Trust me, Sarah," he said before he covered her mouth with his own. He would never hurt her Shane thought as he gently moved his hand between her legs and touched her softly. He would always be careful with her. He kept his mouth on her mouth, his tongue plunging into her mouth as he moaned and stroked her over and over and over again. "Am I hurting you?" he asked as he looked down at her and he saw her breathing fast and hard, her face flushed.

"No, no," she said twice, and he covered her mouth again, he couldn't get enough of her, and he knew that he had to be slow and careful with her, she had been hurt. He had been hurt as well, Shane thought, and in his memory, he saw his brother falling on the battlefield, this time he saw the hat Shaun wear bounce off of his brother's head and roll away, and he felt himself screaming inside for Shaun. Heather's words were echoing in his head, and he felt Sarah pulling him down to her.

"Oh God," he cried as he looked down at her beautiful body in his arms, his fingers touching her softest area and her looking up at him with all the trust in the world in her eyes. Gently and while looking in her eyes, Shane let his finger go up into her, he saw her eyes grow large, and he heard her gasp and then she pushed down on his hand, and he knew she was going to be all right. "I love you,

Sarah," he almost cried as she reached for him and pulled him back down to kiss her.

"Make us married," she said into his mouth, and Shane reached and pulled off his trousers throwing them up onto the bank with the rest of his clothes. He turned Sarah on his lap, and he sat her down on him, her knees on the bottom of the shallow river. His mouth covered her breast, and he heard her gasp and move, and he almost lost himself inside her.

"Slow and steady," he said as he covered her other breast with his mouth and felt her move again and again and he knew he wasn't going to make this slow and steady, he wanted her too badly.

Sarah fell forward on Shane and into his arms before he shattered inside of her, she was throbbing on him, and he wanted her more. "I love you," she said as she clung to him, her legs around his waist and her arms around his neck. She felt him laugh and pulled back to look at him with wide, huge eyes.

"You look like a fairy with the flowers in your hair and naked in my river," Shane said, and Sarah smiled at him.

"This is my river, Shane. And can we do that again?" she saw him nodding yes in answer to her question. "Now?" Shane swam out into the water but not into the current with her wrapped around him, their bodies still joined.

"It's a good thing I'm young and viral," he said before his mouth was full of her breast again and she gasped as he took them both under the water and then back up, her laughing as he stayed joined to her with his body and with his mouth.

"I never thought I would be doing this with anyone," Sarah said as Shane took them under again and then finally closer to the shore where he made love to her and finally onto the grassy bank where he touched her more. "May I touch it?" Sarah asked as he lay next to her catching his breath and he saw her reach down and touched that which made him so different from her.

"Sarah," he breathed her name as she held him in her small hand and she felt him grow to want her. "You make me lose my mind," he said and rolled her over "Have I hurt you?" he gently asked, and she shook her head. "I need you again," he begged of her, and she nodded her head feeling him come inside her again.

"I'll love you forever Shane, forever."

"You'll always be mine Sarah," Shane gasped as he held her close and then closer still. Shaun wasn't here, he thought. Shaun was in heaven. And Shaun wouldn't hate him for what he was doing now with Sarah. Shaun would want Sarah to live and him to live. "Shaun," he breathed his brother's name on a sob as he fell onto his wife and he heard her sob his brother's name. They both loved and missed Shaun; they always would.

PART THREE

SHAUN
AND
CHARLOTTE

CHAPTER NINE

August 1918
London, England

She saw him lying on the bed in the large hospital ward for wounded soldiers. She couldn't have missed seeing him if she had tried too because he was the most heavily bandaged man in the place. He was lying still, and she had no idea if he was alive or dead and she was half afraid to find out.

He was the most famous wounded soldier in the hospital. Everyone knew his story, but no one knew who he was. Charlotte went to him, she had to change his bandages, it was past time for her to have done so, but she hesitated. Her heart broke for this man with no name that would probably not live to tell anyone who he was. His mother would never know that he had died alone and suffered for months until the end of his life came.

She was like so many others, weary of this war, weary of watching handsome young men die when they had their whole life ahead of them. Grieving for the mothers and brothers, fathers and sisters that didn't know what happened to their son because he died on some battlefield and was pushed into a mass grave without even a tombstone or any marker with his name placed on it to remember that he had even been born and that he had mattered to someone, that he had been loved.

"I'm here Charlotte," she heard her father say from behind her, and she turned at the sound of his voice. Their American accent set her and her father apart from everyone else that worked in the hospital, and she was glad she wasn't here alone. She was thankful to be with her father. As he watched over her and protected her as best as he could here, she did the same thing for him often guarding him to make sure that he got some little sleep each night.

Doctor Langston Taylor went to his daughter Charlotte, and he smiled down into her dark brown eyes, eyes so like her mother's. She was only seventeen years old, and he probably shouldn't have allowed her to come to England with him when he volunteered as a Doctor six months ago to help out with the wounded. But she had begged and pleaded with him, and he had given in to her as he often gave in to Charlotte, and here she was with him. He wasn't sorry that he had allowed her to come because she had turned into one of the best nurses he had ever worked alongside. But now his daughter was looking tired. He knew in his heart that this job was too much for her; it was time for him to send her home safe with her mother and for him to carry on alone.

"I heard they had sent you to tend our unknown soldier," Lang said to his daughter, and he didn't mistake the look of concern on her face. He knew she was getting weary of seeing men die, and this one man was certain to do so soon. Lang looked down at the man on the bed and felt bad. No one even knew this soldier's name and the young man had been battling for months to live without getting any better.

"The nurses say he has a story Daddy, but they wouldn't tell me what that story is." Charlotte put the pan of hot water next to the bed and started removing the heavily bloodstained bandages and cleaning the man's wounds which were very slow to heal.

"He does have a story," Lang said and began to help his daughter. "They don't know if he's a Yank or a Brit here at this hospital. He's not spoken a word and he probably never will. But the story goes that he was found when they were burying the dead, he was among the dead and alive. They almost mistook him for dead and buried him." Lang looked up and saw his daughter watching him. "That was in France not far from Paris where a major battle had been fought. The story goes he'd been laying there shot for three full days before he was finally found." Lang came and examined the wound that his daughter had exposed and he nodded his head, "that wound is healing finally, Charlotte, it looks much better than the last time I saw him. He's certainly been slow healing."

"Go on with the story of this man, Daddy," Charlotte pleaded as she started putting on a clean bandage. "He was left three full days injured before anyone even found him alive." Lang smiled at his child thinking he wasn't that old yet that he would forget where he was in the telling of this man's story.

"So he was found and taken to a field hospital where they learned he had been shot eleven times, that's why he's the most heavily bandaged man here." Lang saw Charlotte nod her head as she removed another bandage for her father to check the wound. "Clean that good Charlotte, it's looking a little angry to me," Lang instructed and saw his daughter reach for the alcohol. "Wait," he said and came around moving Charlotte aside. "This might cause him pain, and you've done enough of this kind of thing. Go sit down, and I'll finish here."

"Daddy, I am here working beside you because I want to be a nurse. I want to help others. I want to be like you. You're a hero Daddy." Lang looked back at his daughter before he moved and allowed her to clean the wound. He thought that she was the hero.

"The real hero is the man on this bed," Lang said. "The story goes that when they got a stretcher to him to carry him to a hospital, that he stood up on his own and walked to the stretcher, they didn't have to bring it to him. The Doctors call him a miracle."

"But he has no name?" Charlotte said as she bandaged the wound. The man on the bed had barely flinched when she had cleaned the wound, and she knew that what she had done hurt this man with no name.

"Charlotte," Lang looked up at his daughter and he saw her staring down at the soldier's arm. "What's wrong sweetie?" her father stopped what he was doing, and he came around to her side of the bed. The soldier had a grip on her arm. Charlotte couldn't move if she had wanted too. She had tried to pry his fingers loose, but it did no good.

"Daddy, I think he's trying to tell us something," Charlotte saw the wounded soldier's other hand fisted and hitting his thigh. "Daddy look," she pointed to his hand and the way he held it. "You want paper and pencil?" she asked the wounded soldier, and the man nodded his head. Lang ran to his bag and pulled out the pencil, and Charlotte held the paper still on the man's thigh. "Maybe he's going to tell us who he is," she watched the word he wrote on the paper with a horribly shaking hand. He was shaking so badly that he dropped the pencil three times and had written nothing yet. Her father finally held the pencil in his hand for him. He wasn't looking at the paper; his face was bandaged so he couldn't see the paper if he had wanted too. Lang held the paper against the man's thigh seeing the man's tremoring hand as he wrote the letters where the pencil fell on the paper.

"Y," Lang said wondering what sort of name started with a y and then the man wrote an "A" and by the time he put the "N" down Lang took the pencil and patted his hand. "We know you're a Yank," he let his smile fill his voice. "Can you write your name? I'll help you." Lang reached for the pencil as it hit the floor, the man's hand was shaking too badly, and Lang shook his head for Charlotte to see. "We'll see if he can write his name tomorrow." He patted the soldier gently on the arm and leaned close to him. "Good job, sir. We'll figure out your name and get you home to the United States." Lang looked again and saw the soldier's hand shaking worse than it had been and he lowered his head knowing this was one of the main presenting features of battle fatigue. This man had gone through too much, battle fatigue was expected, and it was much more difficult to recover from than the bandaged wounds.

"I hope he lives, Daddy," Charlotte said in her soft sweet voic, and Lang hugged her before she went back to the task at hand of changing the man's bandages and cleaning his wounds.

"He's a fighter sweetie, and he's made of the stuff they use to make heroes," Lang said to his daughter as she changed more bandages on this man. "He's made it this far. I think he'll survive. We'll pray for him together tonight."

"I'll pray for him now Daddy," Charlotte said, and she closed her eyes, bowed her head with her hands clasped together. Lang stood looking at his child, so like her mother, a woman he had adored for nearly twenty years. Charlotte's hair was the color of his own hair; only she had brown curls whereas his hair had always been straight. Her eyes were a beautiful deep dark brown. Her lashes were thick and lined her eyes making them appear huge in her slender face. She was beautiful with her high cheekbone, and her heart-shaped face. As her father, he knew that everywhere she went, men stared at her. She was a rare beauty. She was like his wife Holly with his dark hair, and he was so thankful that she had come to them so quickly in their marriage, they had needed her desperately.

Lang looked down at the wounded soldier and wondered what would become of the man. It had been months since the young man had been wounded in battle and the soldier was far from well. This man needed the support and love of his family. Having a family might help this wounded veteran get better. But the man never responded to anyone or anything until today. And they had learned today that he was an American soldier, and that was a lot to have learned from a man that had remained silent for as long as this man had. And then Lang saw the tremor in his hands and knew that the road to recovery for this soldier wouldn't end with the physical healing. He was suffering from the battle scars of the mind. Lang wanted to help this man. Lang wanted to help him become whole and have his life back. Looking at Charlotte with her head bowed, Lang knew she wanted to help him as well. They would become a supportive team from now on. Daily visiting with this young man and trying to reach him with kindness and care. This soldier wouldn't lie alone in this bed all the time. He would have Lang and Charlotte.

"Charlotte," Lang spoke to his daughter and he saw her look up at him with her huge doe-like eyes, eyes that were so large and lovely in her face. "Let's you and I adopt this man. For the rest of the time that we're here, we'll visit him and cheer him on to healing." He touched the soldier's arm and smiled at his child. "We'll give him our courage and our strength."

Charlotte reached to the man's shaking hand and held it steady while she leaned close to his ear. "You're not alone Yank." She looked up at her father and smiled. "Not any longer."

"I should send you home to your mother," Lang said holding his daughter's eyes with his own. "You're tired, and this is just too much for a seventeen-year-old girl. But I need you Charlotte. I don't want to send you home alone. And now, he needs us." Lang looked to the soldier and heard his daughter give a deep sigh.

"Daddy, I wouldn't go home if you made me. My place is with you until I deliver you home to Mama safe and sound. And I don't want to leave him now that I've found him," she looked at the man on the bed. "We're going to help him get well." Lang looked at his daughter he and knew that he was blessed to have her, so was this soldier, he thought before he went back to work examining the man's wounds.

November 11, 1918

The eleventh hour, of the eleventh day, of the eleventh month, of nineteen hundred and eighteen the Great War which would become known as World War One finally ended. The battle of Belleau Woods lasted for more than twenty days. For three weeks the United States Marines had launched attacks on the wooded area. The Germans had attacked the Americans with machine guns, poisonous gas, artillery fire and then there had been hand to hand combat with bayonets as well as flame throwers. The Marines finally prevailed on the twenty-sixth of June, and this battle had turned the tide of the war.

"With the war over," Lang said to his daughter Charlotte, "It's time for us to go home. Your mother has been without us for almost seven months." Lang put his arm around his daughter's shoulders as they moved to the bed of the unknown soldier that they knew to be an American.

"What about him?" Charlotte asked her father while pointing to the man she and her father referred to as their patient. "I don't want to leave him here daddy. He should go home to America, to his family," she said, and she put the basin of warm water next to his bed preparing to change his bandages.

Charlotte had been sitting with this soldier, her soldier as she called him, reading to him daily and telling him of her home on the Atlantic Ocean and when they returned to the United States how she would stay in touch with him once they got him home to his family. She loved talking to him. She felt certain that he could hear her and she had spent hours assuring him that he would get well, and she would help him always in every way that she could and in every way that he needed her help.

"We know nothing about him, Charlotte. We don't even know his name much less where his family is." Lang looked at his daughter and then went to remove the bandages from their patient. "He's looking a lot better at last," Lang said. "I think we can leave the bandages off of him. He's really healed up, and I think the other nurses just want him bandaged, so everyone will know his story as the most wounded man in this place and possibly in the whole war.

"Hello," Lang recognized the Army officer that came to the foot of the bed and nodded in greeting toward Lang. "How's he doing today?" The officer pointed to their patien, and Lang stopped what he was doing to talk to the man.

"Physically he's doing better, sir," Lang spoke as he removed the bandage on the man's hip and nodded to his daughter. "Just clean his wounds today Charlotte, we don't need to bandage him any longer. He's almost fully healed," these last words he directed to the Army officer.

"The Doctors here say he's not come too once since he has been here," the officer looked at the man on the bed and frowned.

"He has responded to my daughter and me," Lang said. "He wrote on paper for us that he's a Yank. An American."

"Do you have a name for him?" the officer asked and Lang shook his head. "As long as he has no name, we are going to have to house him here."

"Why can't you send him back to the States to get well?" Charlotte asked and saw her father shaking his head at her causing her to frown.

"With a name, even a first name, we could start searching who he is," the officer said, "but we don't even have that for this soldier."

"Yes, we do." Charlotte looked at her father with her huge brown eyes.

"Charlotte, we don't know this man's name," Lang said in a serious voice and saw his daughter shaking her head hard at her father.

"He told me yesterday when I was reading to him," Charlotte insisted to her father.

"Why didn't you tell me?" Lang asked knowing his daughter would never lie to him. He could trust her in everything and in every way.

"I don't know, Daddy. It was like a secret that was all mine. I was going to tell you eventually." Charlotte looked down at the man on the bed, and she pushed his bangs off of his forehead. "His name is Malachi," Charlotte said from her place beside the wounded man, one of his bandages in her hand the other hand holding a clean rag. "His name is Malachi," she said with certainty.

"He's spoken to you?" Lang asked and saw his daughter nod her head.

"We're having a meeting in an hour to try and decide what to do with the man," the officer said. "The Doctors feel he'll always need care. He's a Yank with the name of Malachi; that's a start."

"I'd like to attend this meeting, if I may." Lang looked at his daughter when the officer nodded.

"Certainly," the officer turned toward Lang. "Come with me Doctor, and we'll search the records of the battle of Belleau Woods and see if there is a Malachi missing or believed dead."

Lang hurried behind the officer and left his daughter to tend to their special patient seeing Charlotte watching him leave her. She looked almost frightened, Lang thought, and he knew that he needed to pay closer attention to her. The soldier had told her his name, and she hadn't said one word to him about that, very unlike Charlotte because he and his daughter were so close he never knew them to have a secret.

Within the hour, Lang sat at a long table and listened to the men around that table as they talked of what to do with the soldier named Malachi. They all agreed he would likely never get any better than he was right now and that was about all they could agree upon. Lang didn't believe that the man wouldn't get better, the man had told Charlotte his name, and he had told them he was an American.

Lang held his tongue and listened closely to what they intended to do with this soldier. He felt like this meeting shouldn't have taken but a few minutes to decide the man's fate and it was dragging on for more than an hour as no one seemed to have a clue what to do with the wounded man.

"We should just send him back to the United States and let them decide his fate, he's not one of ours," a British Doctor asserted, and Lang thought of how we didn't want to get in this war, but we had done so to help others. That wounded soldier deserved better than to just be shoved off on a ship and left in any port to heal or die. After all, the man had been through, and the thanks they were going to show was to throw the young man out with no value.

"We can house him here," an officer with a medical insignia stated, and Lang thought the wounded man needed to be home in the United States, not just housed here with impersonal care. The soldier was a hero, he was a survivor, he might never recover from what he had been through, but he deserved better than what was being offered to him by these men.

"May I speak?" Lang had had enough and finally interrupted the meeting. He saw all eyes turn his way, many of the looks were hostile, and he realized he didn't feel very comfortable sitting in this room with these indecisive men.

"Who is he?" The British Doctor asked, and the Army officer spoke up,

"An American volunteer, he's been helping in the care of the man in question." Lang squirmed in his seat feeling the introduction of him was an understatement, and he spoke for himself,

"My name is Doctor Langston Taylor. I'm from Florida in the United States of America. In my home, I have a small infirmary where I treat people that don't need to be in a hospital but can't yet return home as they need more care than their families can provide for them. Since the man is an America, I would like to take him home with me and hopefully help him to recover." Lang saw the relief on all the faces around him, and he knew that no one in this room had any idea what to do with the soldier now known as Malachi.

The young soldier needed a voice. The young man needed someone that would be on his side. Malachi needed someone that believed that he would get well and was willing to help him get well. These men had given up on him and were ready to throw him out until Lang had spoken up and offered them a solution.

"I don't see why he shouldn't take the man with him," the Army officer spoke up and saw all the heads in the room nod in agreement.

"This Doctor has volunteered his services to the war, and now he's volunteering to help further." The officer that was speaking looked at Lang and nodded his head. "It has been an honor to meet you, Doctor Taylor. I hope this man survives and thrives under your care. In fact, I'm sure he will. And we'll get the paperwork in order to transfer him into your care. Do you know when you leave for your home?"

"My daughter and I are leaving in about two weeks. I'm trying to make arrangements now for a ship home. I'm anxious to get back to my family and my practice now that this war has ended." Lang looked at the officer that had allowed him to attend this meeting.

"I'll make all the arrangements for you and your daughter as well as the soldier, Doctor Taylor," the officer said and stood. "I'll be back on the ward in a few hours with the paperwork in hand. Thank you for what you're doing for this man. I've heard he's a real hero and he's survived more than what ten men would have. I really hope he recovers." The officer shook Lang's hand, and Lang thought that it was the soldier they should all be thanking. That young man had given up everything for his country, he wasn't dead, but he certainly wasn't alive either. Lang was glad to be taking him home, between himself and Charlotte and Holly and even his little girl Hannah, they would get this man better.

Charlotte Taylor stood on the deck of the ship and looked out at the Atlantic Ocean. The wind was cold, and she turned to be certain her patient was fully covered and not catching a chill. He's beautiful, she thought of the man they were taking home to Fernandina Beach and her mother. He had dark hair and eyes that were a pale bright green which rarely blinked when he was awake. He was a tall man with a pretty face, and she wanted to touch him, and as his nurse, she could touch him. She saw her father watching her tuck the blanket around their patient and pushed him in his chair around the deck to where her father stood.

"How's he doing?" Lang asked, and he saw Malachi's eyes looking past him and not at him. Lang felt certain the man would be healed from his wounds when they reached home. But Lang was aware that the man was far from well right now.

"I think he looked at me, Daddy. I think he really looked at me and saw me," Charlotte said and knelt before their patient Malachi.

"He might have," Lang said with doubt in his voice. Their soldier wasn't responding to them at all as far as Lang could tell. "Charlotte, can you see him to my cabin?" her father asked, and she nodded her head. Lang and Malachi were sharing one room, and she was in an adjoining room. "I have a new medical paper I was given right before we left the hospital and I'd like to take some time and read it this afternoon If you're all right alone with our patient?" His daughter saw the cover of the article and knew that her father was back to trying to learn all he could about how the emotions influence healing. She knew her father; he saw more than most Doctors. He saw more than the bloody open wound. He saw what the wound did to the soul; that's what her mother said.

"You're reading about the effects of the war on the brain," Charlotte said to her father. "I saw the study they were doing on this condition called shellshock." She saw her father nod his head. "I knew it would interest you," she said and hugged her father.

"You're my daughter," Lang gave a small laugh and hugged her close. "So like your mother, and yet so much more like me."

"Mama says you came into her life and saved her," Charlotte said, and her father hugged her closer and kissed the top of her head.

"Your mother is part angel. It was actually her doing the saving of me." Lang looked out across the ocean and thought of his wife. Holly was everything he had ever wanted in his life. He wanted only to love her and protect her and be with her. Volunteering for the war and leaving her behind at home had been the most difficult thing he had ever done in his whole life and he made a vow to never leave her ever again. "I can only hope with all my heart that you and your brother and sister find the same kind of love I have with your mother."

"We will Daddy. Love runs in our family," Charlotte said with a laugh and she looked back up at her good and strong and wonderful father. "Oh," she cried out and pulled away from her father to look at her wrist. The man in the wheelchair next to them, their patient, Malachi, had a death grip hold of her arm again and she saw tears falling down his face. "Daddy," she cried out as she bent before the man she thought of as pretty. "Daddy."

"It's all right, Charlotte," Lang said as she wiped their patient's face with her delicate handkerchief. "I think he heard us talking of love and family. I think he's remembering his own family. Tears can be a good sign." Charlotte assured their soldier that he was going to be all right before she made sure the blankets were covering him well and he wasn't upset any longer.

"I'll take him inside and read to him for a while, Daddy. You study your medical papers all you want. Malachi will be fine with me." Lang watched his small daughter push their patient down the long hall toward their cabin before he went to sit on the deck. He was reading everything he could on the study of shellshock and battle fatigue. He had to have all the up to date information on this condition in order to do what was best for Malachi.

"The condition is known as the thousand-yard stares," Lang read and thought of Malachi and how he had the dazed look in his eyes. The thousand-yard stare was considered a frequent manifestation of shellshock. The men suffering from thousand-yard stare would often be found with wide eyes appearing to be looking at nothing and rarely seen to blink. That was what he had been seeing in Malachi. Many men suffering from shellshock were considered to be cowards, but research was showing that was not the case, certainly not with this young man that Lang was taking home.

The man had been shot eleven times. He had then walked off the battlefield three days later under his own power and over many dead bodies. Word had come to Lang that the man had on a gas mask when he was found and when they took that mask off they saw that he had been beaten in the face with probably the butt of a German soldier's gun. No, that man was no coward, and he certainly had all the signs of shellshock. He was this way because he had had to fight his heart out to survive and he had survived. He would need time to recover. No one could help him through this process quickly, not even Lang Taylor who had devoted his life to helping people.

Lang looked at the article he had on shellshock that was the most up to date research by the British Expeditionary Force. Many of the men were reliving the battle, most in their sleep, some when awake and it was as though they weren't home with their families, but actually still on the battlefield. Other men were suffering from tremors, dizziness, ringing in the ears, headaches and even a form amnesia known as fugue where the soldier takes on a new personal identity including memories. These men often would return to themselves remembering their past and the time they were lost in this rare form of amnesia. A low number of men were also suffering from mutism, and Lang wondered if that was what was happening to Malachi. He wasn't even attempting to speak. The article said that almost every man was suffering from fatigue that had this new syndrome known as shellshock. It was a wide spectrum where the soldier could have one sign or have many signs and Lang realized it would be his lifetime before there was complete understanding of this battle illness.

Lang sat still and thought of Malachi, and how the man would help Lang dress him in his clothes and help Lang get him into bed. He would sit still while Lang bathed him and he would open his mouth when Lang brushed his teeth. It was as though the man were here with Lang and yet, not here with Lang. Today, seeing him cry when they talked of home and family was another example of how the young man was a part of their world and yet, not a part of their world. Lang wondered if the man might have suffered a brain injury when the German used the butt of his gun to beat him in the face. He knew the young man wouldn't be telling anyone today anything of his past. He was locked up inside of himself. Such a shame, he looked like he was a fine young man and his family probably missed him in the worst way. Lang bowed his head and prayed that someday soon they might get this young man home, home to the family he was crying for today and that he obviously loved.

"What we need to do is not have wars," Lang said out loud to no one other than himself. "Then men wouldn't have this sort of thing happening to them." If only there were never another war, Lang Taylor thought before returning to his reading.

Charlotte had Malachi in his bed in her father's cabin. His shoes were off, and a blanket was tucked around him. He was still, and he was only staring straight ahead and apparently seeing nothing. She wished she could get him out of this daze, but he seemed lost in the star, and he never saw or heard her, or if he did, he gave no sign that he did.

"I can read to you if you like," Charlotte said in her gentle voice. Her father always spoke in a gentle voice to his patients, and she wanted to be like her father. "I know it's not a boy book," she said as she pulled a chair up to the bed. "But it's a very good book. I read it as a little girl," she said softly and opened up one of her favorite stories of all time, Heidi.

The man on the bed lay still. He wanted to move. He wanted to talk. He wanted a drink of water, but he had to wait until they gave him a drink of water. No words would come out of his mouth even when he tried. He lay still remembering how he had screamed. He had screamed over and over and over again for help, but no help came. And he alone had survived the battle that had helped to win the war. He alone was here, and he wasn't sure where here was. He wasn't sure who this angel was that was reading to him a story that he never would have chosen for himself to read.

The ship rocked hard on a wave and Charlotte grabbed a hold of the bed and tried to breathe. She saw Malachi looking like he was going to be sick and she hurried for the basin before he vomited. He was having seasickness she knew, and she felt bad for him. All he had been through and now he was fighting this horror on his voyage home.

"You'll be all right. Take deep breaths, and the ship should settle down soon." Charlotte held a glass of water up to his mouth and told him to rinse and spit into the basin, and he did so with her help three times. "Better?" she asked him, and her patient didn't nod his head. He didn't move at all. She wiped his face and lay him on his back from his side and then cleaned up the basin and quietly sat back down in her chair seeing him stare without blinking.

"I can tell you a story of my own if you like," she said to him, and she knew that her patient wasn't going to indicate that he had heard her. "Once upon a time there was a handsome young man. He had been injured in the war." She went and got the comb from off of the dresser and bent over Malachi before continuing her story. She began to comb his hair hoping to soothe him while she spoke in her calm and gentle voice. "All the man wanted to do was get home to his family, to his friends, to the woman he loved." Charlotte stopped combing his hair and backed away from him. The man was having tears come out of his eyes again. "There's a woman, and you love her?" Charlotte asked gently and touched his cheek. "You'll get home to her. My father will help you. I know he will. Don't cry." She wiped his face and went back to combing his hair. "You have nice hair, pretty the way your bangs grow." She wished he would smile. She wanted to see how he looked when he smiled. He was so pretty.

Suddenly and without warning, Charlotte's hand was again caught in a death grip by the man, and he was pulling her down to him with his other arm, and she didn't fight him. She wasn't afraid. She honestly felt that he wouldn't hurt her. He wasn't seeing her, it was as though he were staring past her, and she knew he was hurting somewhere inside of himself; from a wound; not likely. Probably from a heartache.

"You're all right," she said soothingly as he pulled her closer. Now his hand was on the back of her head, and he closed his eyes and then his mouth was attached to her mouth. He was kissing her, and at first, Charlotte pushed against him, or she tried too, but it did no good, he wasn't going to let her go. She finally stopped fighting him. He held her in his arms the way her father held her mother when she walked in on them in her father's office one time and saw her parents kissing. He rolled her over so that she was under him and for a moment she was terrified. Then his mouth forced her mouth open and his tongue dove into her mouth. He was circling her tongue and moaning in her mouth. Her patient was making noise, she thought and might have rejoiced in the noise had she not been pinned down beneath him.

He didn't know who she was. He couldn't remember if he knew her. He only knew that she was warm and soft and he had to kiss her. He didn't want to smash her. He was much larger than she was and he found himself pulling off of her and yet, still holding her in his arms. His lips went to her cheek, and he heard her breathing hard. Then his mouth covered her ear, and he held her closer, in a lovers embrace, and she didn't fight him. In fact, she was kissing him back. As he kissed her ear, she had her mouth on his cheek and was moaning for more of him; he felt certain.

Charlotte couldn't believe what was happening to her. This man that was her patient was kissing her senseless, and she didn't want to stop him. She wanted more. He felt so right holding her in his arms. He felt so warm and firm and every dream of what she had ever had of a lover, just like her parents love. And then he rolled off of her, he stopped kissing her, and she lifted herself up off of the bed and looked down to see that he again held the empty stare, the stare of a man who might be blind because he saw nothing. Yet he was breathing hard, and she came up over him, looked down into his face and saw him lift his hand and take a ringlet of her hair in his hand and hold it gently, as though he wanted to touch her hair forever.

"My father must not find us this way," she said in her gentle voice and climbed over the handsome man that had just kissed her, her very first kiss with a man ever. "Don't tell him I let you kiss me," she teased wishing he would respond, but knowing that he would not.

Charlotte smoothed out her dress and then her hair and went to the mirror to look at herself. She felt changed somehow. This beautiful wounded man had touched her ear in a way she never dreamed anyone would ever touch her ear. And her mouth, she put her hand over her mouth and felt him pushing past her lips again with his tongue. If nothing else, what he had done with her had taken his mind off of his being seasick, she thought, and she went back to the bed and her chair and saw him still staring at the ceiling. She wished with all of her heart that she might make him well again.

"Charlotte," her father called her from the door. "I think he'll be all right to leave for a little while. Let's go get some dinner while we can." Lang saw his daughter stand and with uncertain eyes look back at the man on the bed.

"He was seasick earlier, Daddy," she said this, and she saw her father come into the room and look down at the young man, his eyes staring blankly as usual and he wasn't moving.

"You and I need to eat. I'll ask the maid to come in and sit with him for a while." Lang left the room and within a few minutes came back with a maid that was willing to sit with Malachi for a private fee. Lang took his daughter by the arm, and they left the room, her still looking back at the man on the bed as her father closed the door.

"Can we talk, Daddy?" Charlotte asked as she put a fork full of mashed potatoes into her mouth and saw her father put down his papers that he had been studying.

"What's on your mind?" Lang gave his beautiful daughter his undivided attention.

"Malachi," she answered simply and saw his head nod. "I know he can hear us. He cried today when we were talking about home and family. Do you think he is aware we're here to help him? That we're caring for him? Or even who we are?"

Lang Taylor shook his head and knew he really couldn't answer any of his daughter's questions. "Sweetie, I don't know if he's aware of us really. He goes through all the motions of getting dressed and allows me to shave him. He'll even sometimes help brush his teeth. But for the most part, I fear he's locked inside of himself, lost somewhere in his past or in a battle and he doesn't know how to get out and back home — poor fellow. And there's no real treatment for what is wrong with him other than time and good care. And we're giving him each of those things Charlotte. We're going to do everything right by that young man. You're a wonderful nurse for him, and if I've not told you how grateful I am that you came with me to England, I'm telling you now." Lang covered his daughter's hand with his own and saw her smile at him.

"I'm glad I came, I'm glad Mama allowed me to come," Lang made a face as he remembered his wife's insistence that Charlotte not go anywhere without her, that their daughter was too young. Their son Aaron was fifteen and had finished his studies in Jacksonville at the boy's academy and was ready to further his education. Aaron had decided long ago to go to Medical school like his father, and Lang was proud of his son. But Lang missed Aaron and so Lang had turned to Charlotte to fill the void while her brother went off to school, and she had filled the void. All of his children were devoted to him and to their mother, and he was a proud father, and he wasn't ashamed to admit how he felt.

"Your mother only allowed you to come because I begged her," Lang laughed. "She has Hannah at home," he spoke of Charlotte's nine-year-old sister who was named for Lang's little sister that had died in childhood. "I wanted to help with the war efforts. I wanted to help in a way I was trained to help, as a Doctor, but Charlotte, I'm starting to feel my age. I'm forty-five years old now, not so much a young man but not too old yet. And I needed you to comfort me. Truth to be told, the hardest thing I've ever done in this life besides deal with the death of loved ones is to leave your mother. She's everything to me, Charlotte. I fell in love with her the first second I saw her and I've carried this flaming torch for her ever since."

Charlotte reached out and took her father's hand and offered him understanding. She had seen her parents together countless times in her life. Lang and Holly Taylor were as in love today as they had been almost twenty years ago.

"I'm blessed to have parents that are still in love after all these years," she said with a smile. "I hope I have this kind of relationship someday, Daddy." Charlotte touched her lips and remembered the kiss their patient had given to her, and she felt on fire all over as she had when he had been kissing her.

"Your mother adores you, children. We had you almost right away, and a year and a half later your brother came to us. And then Hannah. We leave a good legacy behind us in our children. You three make us so proud. Your mother and I have talked about it many times in the past. The best of us is in our children."

"So about the man in your cabin," Charlotte spoke again. "When I was combing his hair tonight, he reached for me again and held on to me. Do you think he might be capable of harming me?"

"Did you feel threatened by him, Charlotte?" her father asked in an alarmed voice.

"Not in any way at all Daddy. In fact, I felt I was a comfort to him. I just wanted to know what you thought of his grabbing my arm like he does. This is the third time he's done so."

Lang took a stab at the food on his plate, and he worried about their patient. They had been together for weeks in the hospital and now on this voyage home. The young man had shown no signs of aggression beyond a death grip of Charlotte's arm a few times. The fact was, the man was very calm, laid back, and Lang felt that the wounded soldier was no threat at all to anyone.

"I think he might be aware to some degree that a very beautiful young woman is tending to him, and he wants you to stay with him. Maybe he's afraid you'll leave him." Lang saw his daughter nodding her head. "He has no one else in the world, and I think we're familiar to him. Until he gets out of this place he's in, this amnesia or mutism, or both, we're just going to have to support him in any way we can and take care of him."

"I'll take care of him, Daddy. I don't mind and I'm not afraid of him in the least, honest I'm not. I think he needs me and in a way, I need him. I've had no purpose in my life; at least I feel that way. I feel like I've been lost forever and I'm just now finding my way home. And I want to care for others. I want to care for this man with all my heart and help him heal, help him find his way home to his family and be safe. We should all be safe."

"You look just like your mother, but you're really so much my child. I love you Charlotte. I'm so thankful you came into my life. You have no idea how much I needed you. The day I delivered you I went to my knees in tears. You have no idea what your mother and I lost before you." Charlotte left her chair and came to kiss her father gently on the forehead. He didn't know because her mother and he never talked about their past to their children, but she and Aaron had gone to the cemetery many times and seen the headstone. They knew just what their parents had lost.

"I know what you lost Daddy," she confessed her knowledge to her father with her eyes full of tears. "Aaron and I found the grave years ago."

"You never get over the loss of a child. But having you helped ease your mother and my pain." His daughter hugged him close, and he was grateful her heart was so large, and she was so full of giving of herself.

"I'll go back to our patient, Daddy. You rest and eat more. Mama will be mad at me when she sees how thin you are." Lang laughed and nodded his head. He had a good daughter; he thought as he watched her walk away.

"You have a beautiful wife," the woman at the table next to Lang's said, and he laughed shaking his head.

"She is my daughter, ma'am, but yes, I do have a beautiful wife, and in a few days time, I'll be with my wife, and I'm never leaving her again." The woman at the other table looked Lang up and down and knew, this handsome man's wife was very blessed to have him.

Charlotte went back into her father's cabin and relieved the maid. She picked up the book Heidi again and started to read. The man in the bed reached over and took a hold of her hand, not the death grip hold that he had taken of her in the past, but a gentle hold. His fingers entwined with her own, his palm lost in her palm as the two hands met. Charlotte looked down at his hand holding hers, and she smiled, Malachi was going to be all right in time. And before she resumed reading the book, she looked at his face. He looked at peace. The stare was still there, but maybe now he was seeing what he was looking at. Maybe now, he might be seeing her.

Lang had several men come and help him get Malachi off of the ship. Everyone was kind and wanted to help as Malachi was a returning war hero and injured as well. Charlotte saw to the luggage and Lang was thankful that she did as she saw everything had been transferred onto the ferry that would take them across the river and home.

"I wired ahead to your mother that we would be at the ferry today. I told her to have Michael meet us with a wagon. I hope he's there," Lang worried his wife hadn't received his wire as they arrived at the ferry to make their way across the river. Malachi was loaded sitting in the wheelchair along with all their belongings onto the ferry within a few short moments. "He looks worse today," Lang said of their wounded hero and watched Charlotte touch their young man's forehead.

"He feels like he has a fever," Charlotte said and looked at her father with worried eyes. "And now we're on this ferry and its freezing cold out on this river. But we'll be home by Christmas, and I'll nurse him back to health if he gets sick."

"I don't want him sick," Lang said seriously and covered the man with another blanket. "He's weak. I don't think he'll be able to fight off a fever or worse. He's just been through so much."

"Should we leave the ferry Daddy and stay the night in Jacksonville until we're certain he's not coming down ill?" Charlotte asked and felt Malachi take her hand under the blanket her father had placed over him. She looked down at him, he was still staring ahead at nothing, but he gently held her hand as though that gave him comfort. "Daddy," she lifted the blanket and showed her father his holding of her hand. "I think he wants us to stay on the ferry. I think he wants us to take him home with us."

Lang looked at his beautiful daughter's hand held by this man who was trapped in a war. Still, the battle raging on and yet, his fingers were entwined with Charlotte's. Lang thought of himself and his wife Holly, how once Holly had been trapped away inside of herself all those years ago, how his wife had climbed out of the war within herself that she was trapped in and into his arms. Lang looked at Charlotte, then back at the man holding his daughter's hand then back to Charlotte.

"He is your patient Charlotte," Lang said seriously to his daughter. "He's your patient. Do not become more involved with him than that of a caregiver," even as he said this, Lang knew that he couldn't stop love if it were meant to happen. The man was a handsome fellow, and their soldier wasn't much older than his daughter. Charlotte was a beauty. Lang wondered if Malachi were aware of how beautiful his child was and he might have thought not, but seeing the man holding his daughter's hand gave him pause to wonder.

"Don't worry so much Daddy. I know what I'm doing. He needs me, and I'm caring for him, nothing more." She felt her patient hold tighter to her hand and she looked down at his empty eyes and wondered, had he kissed her physically while thinking of some other woman back home that he was in love with? She might never know the answer. All Charlotte could do with this man was live in the right here and the right now and pray that he became well and strong and when he did become well and strong, she would let him go and carry on with nursing another patient.

From where he stood on the ferry, off in the distance, Lang Taylor saw her, his wife, and he lost his breath like he did the first time he had seen her. She was small and pretty. Her light-colored hair blowing in the wind as no pins could hold in place on a windy day like today. She was pale, she had always been pale, and she was beautiful. Even from a distance, he could see her beauty was like none other. The ferry got closer, and he held out his hand to her, and she knew he was reaching for her, she knew that he loved her. Lang saw his youngest daughter standing next to her, and he smiled at Hannah, but his eyes went back to his wife. Holly was his world, she was everything to him, he was a part of her, and she was a part of him. He wasn't whole or complete unless he had her in his arms and in his bed. He lost his breath when she smiled, the deep dimples in her cheeks were so lovely, and there was always a twinkle in her eyes when she looked just at him.

Charlotte tended to their patient. Her father's best friend Mike helped with the luggage, her little sister Hannah had run to her and hugged her and then for a long few moments they stood watching their parents. Her father had leaped off of the ferry before it was tied to the dock, one hand holding on to his hat and he grabbed her mother with his free arm even before his feet were planted on firm ground.

"Lang," Charlotte heard her mother cry his name and then her father had her mother held tightly to him, so tightly that no one could see where her father ended, and her mother began. Her handsome father was kissing her mother on the dock, he had Holly bent back, and he was kissing his wife the way their patient had kissed her in the bed the other night Charlotte thought to herself.

"Oh," she heard their patient say, and she rushed around to look at him. He was seeing something for the first time since she had laid eyes on him. He was honestly looking at something and seeing what he was looking at.

Malachi pushed her aside and looked at her parents kissing. "Uncle Allen," he moaned, and she saw tears in his eyes. "Aunt Alicia," he said and reached out to Lang and Holly.

"Daddy!" Charlotte cried out, and her father reluctantly let go of her mother's mouth but still held Holly tightly in his arms.

Lang looked and saw the young man in the wheelchair reaching out to him and his wife, and he moved to where their soldier was pulling his wife with him. "You're all right Malachi, this is my wife," Lang spoke as he knelt before the man seeing that Malachi's gaze wasn't empty. Malachi was looking at Holly.

"Aunt Alicia," the young man said reaching for Holly. "Aunt Alicia."

"This is my wife, Holly Taylor," Lang said gently to Malachi and looked at Charlotte. "We have another clue, his name is Malachi, and he has an Aunt that is like your mother. An Aunt with the name of Alicia."

"And an Uncle like you, Daddy," Charlotte said. "He called you Uncle Allen when you were kissing Mama."

Holly Taylor looked at the man in the chair, the gaze had come back upon him, and he was looking at nothing again. He appeared almost to be blind to Holly Taylor.

"He's someone's son," Holly said. "We're going to take good care of him. But by the grace of God, he could be our own Aaron."

"Aaron is safe at school," Lang said to his wife in a relieved voice thankful that his son had been too young for this war and he prayed there never would be another war such as the one they had just endured. "Let's get him home and out of this cold," Lang insisted, and he saw his best friend Mike coming to help him load the young man and his chair into the wagon. "After all Charlotte and I have done to get him here alive, I want to keep him well," Lang said and saw his wife looking down at her hand.

"He does that Mama," Charlotte said as she gently took Malachi's hand from her mother's hand and placed it on her own.

"Is he able to eat?" Holly asked her husband, and Lang nodded.

"We have to hold the spoon for him, he has horrible tremors, but yes, he can eat."

Charlotte supported Malachi as they took his chair and put it on the wagon and then her father and Mike and a man on the dock helped get Malachi into the wagon. He lay on his back, his legs dangling off the tailgate off of the wagon, the blank look fixed on his handsome face. Charlotte jumped up beside him, covered him with a blanket and reached for his hand and he clung to her hand for dear life as usual.

"We're ready to go home now Daddy," she called out and felt the wagon move. She hoped the trip wouldn't be too hard on him, their patient. And then she felt him pull on her and she was lying down next to him, her hand on his chest. His hand was over her hand, and her head was resting on his shoulder.

"Charlotte," her father called out from his seat in front of the wagon.

"I'm all right Daddy; he's scared I think. And he's cold. He needs comfort." Lang looked at the soldier holding his daughter as though she were his lover, as though they were home alone in bed and he looked at his wife who he knew was thinking the same thing. "He won't harm me, Mama. He's just scared." Charlotte said trying to reassure her mother.

"If he recovers," Holly spoke in a low voice to her husband, "he'll hurt my child unless he falls in love with her."

"What are you talking about?" Lang asked his wife in as low a tone seeing his friend Mike look at Holly in the same way he was.

"It doesn't take but two eyes to see," Holly said still looking at her beautiful daughter lying in the back of the wagon held in the arms of the wounded soldier, "Charlotte has fallen in love with him, and we only know his first name."

"She's his nurse," Lang insisted, and Holly shook her head.

"You, the best lover on the planet and you don't recognize the emotion in your own child?" Holly said softly and laid her head on her husband's shoulder as they headed home. She had missed him more than he would ever know. "No woman would willingly lay with a man as our daughter is with that man unless she had strong feelings for him."

Hearing his wife say this, Lang knew Holly was right. Charlotte had spent a lot of time with this man, she had held his hand many times, and he held hers. There was something there, something growing between them and he wondered, would his daughter help awaken this wounded soldier from the amnesia? From this fugue? Would she break the bound of silence that was his mutism? And had his daughter fallen in love with their patient? Or was she just offering him comfort? Only time and care would tell, Lang knew that and as a doctor, Lang was good at waiting for answers.

Chapter Ten

Lang stood in the doorway of the room off of his kitchen. This use to be the room Holly occupied when he had first arrived here nearly twenty years ago. Now he used the room for patients that needed his care and weren't well enough to go home. He saw the man with no last name, only the first name of Malachi, laying on the comfy bed he had put in this room, and Lang wondered what he was going to do to help the man return to the living. Lang knew this man was lost in his own mind and if left alone, this young man would never find his way out.

"I'm here, Daddy," Charlotte said, and he saw his daughter had on a new dress and her hair brushed out and in a long braid down her back. "I spent some time with Mama. I missed her so much. And Hannah, she's not changed at all. She's still my baby sister." Lang saw the face his eldest daughter made as she pulled up a chair by the bed where their patient lay, and he knew that she was happy to be here with Malachi. If she was tired, she was not too tired to take care of this man.

"Charlotte," Lang said and he saw her huge brown eyes look up into his eyes. "Don't feel too much for him," he nodded to Malachi sleeping on the bed. "He's your patient only. I'm worried you're developing feelings for him."

"Be serious, Daddy," Charlotte gave a little laugh. "Certainly I care for him. I've been with him for weeks now, and I don't want him to die. I want him to get better and have his life back; he deserves that after all he's been through. He's a real hero, Daddy." She looked at her father looking at her with a hard stare, and she got up from her chair and came to stand in front of him. "I'm just like you." She took her father's hand and hugged his him. "You know you care too much. How many babies have you lost to illness and in birth that you came home and clung to mama and cried? And so many patients that you cared for that died, young and old, you came home and clung to mama and cried. And Mama said she was your patient before she was your wife," Charlotte saw the look on her father's face. She saw that he was realizing she spoke the truth. "Yes, I care for Malachi, very much. Look at him, Daddy. He's just a young man, probably not even twenty-five years old. He needs to get well, and I want him well." Charlotte looked back up into her father's eyes. "When we were in England, every man I took care of, I grieved for Daddy, and you did too. They were all young men devastated by a senseless war. We should be loving one another, not hurting one another. Don't worry about me so much, Daddy. I'm your daughter and a lot like you. We feel more than most, and we need too. That's our way."

Lang pulled his daughter close, and he knew that she had his empathy and his compassion. Those emotions were what defined him as the man he was. Those emotions are what had his Uncle bring him here to save his wife who was more lost in herself all those years ago then this man on the bed. Maybe we all need saving in some way, shape or form, Lang thought. He fell in love with Holly. He rescued his wife from the horror she was living in, and she loved him back making him whole and complete and alive. Whatever this man on the bed's future held, Lang knew that his daughter's empathy and compassion could save him if nothing else could.

"Go up to Mama. She's been waiting on you to get him settled for me. She's missed you so much, Daddy." Lang smiled at his daughter and pinched her cheek.

"I need your mother," he said and spun on his heels. Charlotte watched her father take the back stairs two at a time.

Lang opened his bedroom door, and he saw his wife sitting under the covers in the bed. The room was a little cold, and he stopped by the fireplace to add a couple more logs before turning back to Holly and crawling from the foot of the bed to her with a gleam in his eyes.

"I missed you," he almost growled and then lay her down holding her in his arms. "Where's your nightgown?" he asked as he kissed her neck and pulled the covers down staring at his beautiful wife's body.

"On the floor in case one of the girls comes in I can grab it quick," Holly said as her husband's mouth clung to her body, and she cried out. "I missed you more than you'll ever know, Lang."

"I'm not going anywhere without you again, not even down to Jacksonville," Lang said this as his mouth moved further down his wife's body and he heard her gasp. He loved what he could do to her, how he could make her feel. He always took his time with her, always was gentle and caring and tender with her before he ever joined them together. Holly needed his tender care.

"I don't want you to even go out the front door without me again," Holly gasped and tried to say this as her husband made love to her. He knew just what to do to make her beg him to fulfill her. "Lang, I can't wait any longer." She saw him still fully dressed when he lifted his body up from her and together they both started removing his clothes, his shoes kicked off and his shirt losing three buttons in their hurry.

"I love you, Holly," he cried out a few minutes later, his wife gasping beneath him. He wouldn't leave her again ever.

Charlotte sat in the chair looking at Malachi and saw that he had finally closed his eyes and was asleep. He needed to be asleep she thought, the voyage home had been hard on him, the seas rough making him horribly ill and now he felt warm to the touch, she hoped he wasn't coming down with a fever. Charlotte started to move from the chair when his hand shot out from under the covers, and he grabbed a hold of her hand causing her to look down at his grip on her.

"It's all right," she spoke in her gentle way, and she felt his hold on her loosen. "I'm cold. I was going to get a blanket," she spoke softly this time hoping that he would let her go. She really was cold in this room. And then he was pulling her down toward him, those beautiful eyes staring at nothing but he still was aware enough that he wanted her. Charlotte didn't fight him. She lay down on the bed beside him, his arm going around her and she allowed him to pull her close. He obviously needed to do this, she thought. He needed her, and she liked that he did.

He felt her relax against him. Her hand was touching his cheek. She fit in his arms. She belonged in his arms. He wanted her in his arms. He wanted to speak. He had said his Aunt and Uncle's name today. The man and woman that had been with him and this girl reminded him of his family, but they weren't his family, he knew that inside of himself. Yet he wanted them so badly to be his family. He needed his mother. He wanted to tell this girl he held about his home, but his voice was broke, nothing about him seem to be working right. He wanted to cry, but his eyes stayed dry much of the time and inside, in his gut, he was sobbing his heart out, but no one knew. And now he was cold, too cold. His whole body was shaking apart with how cold he was.

Charlotte had dozed off in the arms of their handsome soldier, and she didn't come awake quickly. She felt they were back on the ship. The rocking motion was almost soothing to her. And then the ship was shaking apart, and she forced her eyes open to find the man beside her in the bed still held her close in his arms, and he was shivering apart.

"Oh no," she breathed and felt his forehead. He was burning with fever. "Daddy," she tried to call out for her father but the call came out as a choked whisper.

Charlotte had to pull free of the hold that Malachi had on her, and she left his bed running for the stairs which she did as her father had earlier and took two at a time. She pushed open her parents' bedroom door and nearly fell into the room, the light from the fire giving the room both light and shadows.

"Daddy," she cried out and saw her father sit up in the bed when she did. "He has a fever, he shivering all over." She saw her mother pull the covers up to her chin and her father's pants on the floor and one of his shoes were laying on the floor at the door where she stood and knew she had interrupted them.

"I'm coming sweetie, let me get dressed," Lang said and Holly nodded her head to him and to her daughter.

"Daddy will be down in a minute, Charlotte," her mother added in a calm voice and watched her daughter close the door. "Oh dear," Holly said and fell into her husband's arms as he laughed softly.

"Thank God for covers and a cold night," he said and left the bed pulling on his clothes which were thrown all over the room. "You tore my shirt," he said as he tried to button it up and he couldn't. "I'll put on my robe," he took the shirt off and handed it to his wife as though she were going to sew the buttons back on tonight.

"I didn't tear your shirt,' Holly said and came to her knees on the bed as her husband pulled her close for another kiss.

"Your body is so beautiful," he touched her, and she smiled. All these years later she was still maintaining her figure and for him. "I'll be back," he gave her a long kiss before sitting on the edge of the bed and pulling on his thick socks. "I forgot how cold Florida can get in the night." Holly watched her husband go to the door of their room and glance back at her. He no more wanted to leave her to go downstairs than she wanted him to leave her just to go downstairs. "I'll try and hurry," he said, and she knew if he could, he always hurried back to her.

Lang entered the room and saw his daughter putting another blanket on the man in the bed, and he came to listen to their patient's lungs. Lang reached in his bag for some acetylsalicylic acid and poured the powder into a cup of water before handing the cup to Charlotte. "We need to get this into him. You hold the cup, and I'll hold him," Lang said and moved to the head of the bed. He lifted Malachi's head onto his lap and held him tight as Charlotte put the cup to the young man's lips, but all the medication did was spill out of the side of his mouth.

"What do we do, Daddy?" Charlotte cried in frustration, and her father told her to try again, and again it spilled down the side of Malachi's face. Lang mixed up another powder, and this time he had Charlotte hold Malachi up for him, and his eyes met his daughter's eyes.

"Sweetie, talk to him," Lang instructed, and Charlotte saw Malachi's eyes were open and the handsome young man was awake, he might hear her.

"I need you to drink this for my father, please," she said in her sweet voice, and there was no reaction from the man that she held.

"Speak in a firmer voice," Lang instructed and saw his daughter take a deep breath.

"Drink," she ordered the man in her arms, and she felt him move. Lang nodded as he put the cup to Malachi's lip and he saw their soldier swallow hard several times. "It worked," Charlotte sighed and heard her father sigh along with her.

"You'll need to give him a powder every few hours, Charlotte. Are you sure you can stay up all night after that long trip home? I can come back down in a few hours,"

"Daddy," Charlotte looked at him and then away and blushed. "Go be with Mama," she laughed and hid her face behind her hands. "Don't come back until in the morning. I'm fine. I want you with Mama and happy. You're such a good father." She uncovered her face and saw her father blushing far worse than she was blushing.

"I do need to be with her," she heard her father say, and she pointed toward the door and laughed.

"Go, and I'll knock on your door if I need you."

"Night Charlotte," she heard her father say before she heard him again taking the stairs two at a time. She was still for a long moment and could hear her mother's laughter, and she knew that her parents were the most in love couple on the earth.

His shivering continued. He couldn't get warm. The beautiful girl kept adding blankets to cover him and then he was hot and trying to kick those blankets off seeing the beautiful girl pulling them off of him only to have him cold yet again and shivering with the blankets being pulled back up over him. Finally, he reached for her again, the beautiful girl so like Sarah, and he pulled her down into his arms and he wanted to cry. He felt the tears in his gut, but again they didn't reach his eyes.

"You're going to be all right," the girl said as she put a hand on his chest. "I need to get up. You must let me up so I can give you another of the powders Daddy left you," she pleaded and then gasped as his strong arms lifted her from him and she was able to get the powder. "It would be nice if you would say something," she leaned over him and helped him sit up to drink the liquid powder. He was still burning up despite what she was doing for him, and she was worried. He wasn't breathing deeply in his sleep. His breathing was shallow and labored sounding. There was nothing more her father could do so she didn't go for him. Instead, she laid the man back down and laid beside him again feeling him shive, and despite trying to stay awake, Charlotte felt herself going to sleep, asleep in his secure shivering arms.

"Sarah," he cried out, and the tears came from his eyes at last only he wasn't aware that he was crying. He was lost even more inside of himself than he had been before. "Sarah," he cried out again, and Charlotte sat up seeing the man thrashing around on the bed.

"It's all right," Charlotte said in a soothing voice wondering who Sarah was and at the same time aware Sarah was his wife. No man called out for a woman as this man was calling out for a woman without being in love. A huge sense of disappointment came over her, but at the same time, she had to focus on getting his fever down. He was her patient first no matter that she found him handsome and kept thinking of the kiss that he had given to her.

Malachi felt the cool air hit his body. He felt a damp cloth on his head, and he stopped moving around on the bed, he became still as the warmth spread through him better than the awful shivering had been. He tried to open his eyes, but if they were open, he couldn't see, and he heard her, the voice of an angel talking him down off of the ledge he was on when shivering, making him feel stronger and more secure.

His hands came up and cupped her face as she ran the cool cloth over his face and neck. He wasn't looking at her. He was staring in that blank way that was so much a part of him, Charlotte thought. And then his eyes closed and her hand was still as she looked at him, the cloth held against his cheek. And he was pulling her down to him. She couldn't stop him, she didn't want to stop him. This felt good and right, and despite his calling out for another woman, she only wanted him to kiss her again.

She didn't know how it happened. One moment she was kneeling over him, the next moment she was laying in the bed beside him, the next moment he had come up and over her and he was kissing her. His tongue forcing her lips apart and entering her mouth and she heard him moaning and she moaned with him. She was holding on to him, her hand at the back of his neck and pulling him down to her. She had never been kissed by any man but him, and if this was how kissing felt, she understood why her parents always were touching and kissing. He was making her melt into the bed. She was on fire and burning up underneath him, longing for more and not aware what the more she longed for was.

She shouldn't be doing this, Charlotte thought. He was her patient. He was probably married to this Sarah that he had called out for, or he was engaged to Sarah. She had no right to this man. She shouldn't be letting him touch her. He wasn't even aware that he was touching her. He was sick. Charlotte pushed on him to make him stop, and it did no good. She tried to pull away, and that helped him withdraw his lips from hers, and he rolled over taking her with him held in his arms, his lips now on her forehead, and he clung to her.

"I'm not Sarah," she said, and she felt his hold tighten on her. "You have to let me go," she said using her firm voice that she had used that had gotten him to drink the liquid powder. The firm voice had no effect on him now. He still held her tightly, his lips still on her forehead. He at least wasn't shivering any longer, Charlotte thought, and he wasn't as hot as he had been before. She decided to hold still in his arms and hope that soon he would let her go. But he didn't let her go and the hours stretched on until dawn peeked into the window, and she relaxed, and her even breathing joined his shallow and harsh breathing.

Holly looked into the room where the wounded soldier was, and she saw her beautiful daughter Charlotte curled up into the man's embrace and sound asleep. She knew that she should have been horrified and frantic to find her beautiful child this way, but she was very calm. She remembered how she had been with Lang, how she had needed to control his feelings for her in the beginning of their relationship and then she had learned in time to trust him.

The man on the bed, according to her husband, was the most wounded man to survive the war, he was lost inside of himself as she once had been. He probably needed Charlotte's comfort more than anyone else ever needed anything. She knew how another person's comfort and care could save a lost soul. If anyone knew that, it was Holly Taylor, the wife of Doctor Lang Taylor, the man that has saved her.

"Charlotte," Holly said her daughter's name softly and touched Charlotte's shoulder. "You need some rest. Your father and I will watch over your soldier for you." She saw Charlotte's eyes open and then heard her daughter gasp to have been caught here this way.

"I'm sorry, mama," Charlotte said and stood by the bed. "I didn't mean to fall asleep." She touched the man on the bed's face and felt he was still warm. "I need to give him another powder," she said as she saw the sun shining bright showing that it was morning.

"I'll do it," Holly said and pushed her daughter to the doorway of the room that once had belonged to her. "Go, get your nightgown on and crawl into your bed and I'll wake you up in a few hours." Holly saw her eldest daughter turn to leave as her youngest daughter bounced into the room.

"I'll sit with him," the nine-year-old Hannah said and took her sister's place sitting in the chair next to the wounded soldier. "When I grow up, I'm going off to war with Daddy too and being his nurse," Hannah looked up and smiled at her sister.

"I hope we never have another war like the one we just had," Charlotte said looking at the man on the bed. "And Daddy is never going away from Mama again, he promised." She kissed her mother's cheek and patted her sister's head. "Don't forget to give him the powder, Mama," Charlotte said before turning to the staircase where her father stood with his arms across his chest looking down at her. "What?" she asked him, and he leaned down to kiss her cheek.

"Just in case you don't know," he said in a very serious voice. "I am so proud of you." She smiled, and he pulled her into his arms while she wondered would he be proud of her still if he knew of the kisses she had shared with the beautiful man on the bed? All Charlotte knew was that she longed for that man to kiss her again and she hoped that her father would understand if he ever found out of those shared kisses.

"I'm proud of you too, Daddy," she said before letting go of him and walking up the stairs. She really was tired.

The morning passed with Holly often in the room with the man her husband and daughter had brought home. Her youngest daughter Hannah sat in the chair her sister had placed by the bed swinging her feet and playing with her new doll. Lang was everywhere Holly was. He was beside her while she cooked breakfast. He was beside her while she put eggs on Hannah's plate. He was beside her while she washed the dishes and he was helping her by drying the dishes. He only left her to get wood for the fireplace and stove, and she laughed at how close he was when she turned from putting the butter in the icebox to find him right behind her, less than an inch away.

"Lang Taylor," Holly said with a smile and fell against her husband thankful to have him home and under her feet. "First you were a million miles away from me, and I was dying to have you under foot, and now here you are, and I can't get anything done because you're in the way." Lang tilted her face up to look into his eyes, and she saw the longing there in his eyes as well as his need of her. He had saved her once, and she had saved him every day since. He felt more than most people. Lang felt things down into his soul that others didn't notice and she knew by looking at him that something was wrong. "What it is?" She searched his eyes as his hand touched her cheek.

"I brought him all the way home," Lang nodded his head toward the room where his patient lay, "to die."

"What?" Holly gasped and turned to the room seeing the man on the bed shivering and her little girl beside him hugging her doll.

"His lungs aren't clear," Lang said in sadness. "And we don't even know his full name. We won't even be able to tell his family when and where and how he died."

Holly looked back up at her husband, and she shook her head. "He's not dead yet, Lang. He's survived so much. Maybe he'll survive this too." She moved to the room and beside the bed, her youngest daughter taking her hand. Holly leaned down and very firmly spoke to the man in the bed. "Don't you dare die, young man," Lang almost smiled at his wife ordering his patient not to die. "You have a family that loves you very much. They need you. Don't you think of leaving them." Lang moved to the foot of the bed, and he saw the man turning toward his wife, her voice seem to have reached Malachi.

"Mama," Malachi said in a hoarse way, his voice almost too low to hear.

"Yes, darling," Holly said thinking to herself that she would be his mother if that helped him pull through this crisis. "Come home to me," she said gently and took his hand in her hand. "I need you. Come home to me."

"Mama," he said again, and Holly touched his cheek and told him to rest, she wouldn't leave him.

"If he lives, it'll be because of you," Lang said to his wife. "He needed his mother, and through you, she's here." Holly lifted Hannah from the chair and sat down in that chair putting Hannah in her lap.

"I can see why Charlotte is fighting so hard for him. It's hard to leave him. He's so fragile that he just draws you to him," Holly said hugging Hannah close.

"That's how I felt when I first met you," Lang said looking into the beautiful brown eyes of his wife as she looked up to him with large trusting eyes only for him.

Malachi was in another war; only this one war was within himself. He was fighting off pneumonia. At least he was trying to fight off the pneumonia. The fever raged out of control, and the powders did little to take the fever down. He gasped and had shallow breathing, even wheezing much of the time, and Lang was almost certain that soon he would draw his last breath and leave the torment that he was in and this earth. It was sad really; Lang thought as the doctor tried all that was known to be done to save the young man. Malachi had survived so much, the battle, the war, the injuries, the trip home, only to succumb to illness. This wasn't right, and this wasn't fair.

Someone was with him at all times. Charlotte was staying up in the night, and Holly or Lang was with him in the day. Even little Hannah sat by his bed often just watching over him and calling for help if he began to thrash about or shiver. The family revolved around Malachi as the days wore on and no one expected him to live. He was silent now all the time, never crying for his mother or for Sarah. He was near death, and Lang knew that as did his daughter.

At dawn on the seventh day, Lang came down the stairs and found Charlotte on her knees by the bed. He stopped in the doorway as he heard her sweet voice praying. "Dear God, please help this man. He just needs to get home to his family. He needs his life back and he needs healing. Pleas, God, I'll care for others all the rest of my days and never ask you for anything else again if you'll just bring this man through this. In Christ's holy and loving name I most humbly pray this prayer."

Lang bowed his head, and he knew what he had always known, he had a good daughter. A daughter that was rare and good and kind, and he silently thanked God for her. When he lifted his head, he saw his daughter still kneeling by the bed, her head still bowed in prayer and on the top of her head, rested the hand of their soldier and the young man looked peaceful and still. At first, Lang thought Malachi might have passed away and then he saw the slight rise and fall of the man's chest, there was no wheezing to be heard from a distance and Lang moved into the room.

"Charlotte," he said his child's name, and she looked up at him, the soldier's hand falling away from her head and to the side of the bed. "I need to listen to his lungs," Lang spoke on and his daughter stood and moved aside. "Charlotte," he said a second later as he touched her hand. "His lungs sound clear. I think he's going to make it through this." Charlotte gave out a cry and grabbed her father. He put his arms around her as she began to cry hard. "Remember Charlotte; he's your patient." Her father reminded her gently, but she seemed to not hear him, or if she did, she dismissed his words because she knew, this man was far more than her patient.

"Thank you, God, for helping this man," Charlotte said several times through the tears and Lang patted her back. She really had his empathy and his ability to feel for others, and in a way, Lang wished that she didn't have these things as he did. Having too much empathy was a lot to bear. But she did have his empathy, and she would have to learn to deal with feeling to many emotions for those around her. She was strong like him as well, and Lang knew that. "Soon we'll find out who he is and where he's from. Soon he'll talk to us, Daddy." Charlotte said confidently; her Malachi would live.

May 1919
Fernandina Beach, Florida

The weeks and months since their return from England passed in a lazy manner; Lang stood thinking to himself on a warm spring day. The man they knew as Malachi still wasn't able to talk. The young war hero was making eye contact now, the dazed look that had been constant in Malachi's eyes was now a thing that was coming and going. The young man was almost completely mute. If he made a sound or spoke a word, it was almost always done in an unconscious state. His physical wounds were all healed. Every day he was walking farther and farther on the beach with Charlotte, and he was getting strong. Lang was keeping a detailed account in a notebook on every change in the man hoping to piece together his life, to find some way to learn who he was. And to hopefully help him come back to who he rightfully was and to find his family.

"I'm taking Hannah down to the beach," Holly said this from her husband's office doorway. "Come with us," she reached a hand out to him seeing her husband smile knowing he wouldn't refuse her. "It's a beautiful day," she said as she handed him the picnic basket and grabbed a blanket for them to sit on together. Hannah had a small wooden bucket and a wooden spoon that the girl used to build drip drop sand castles.

"Where is Charlotte and Malachi?" Lang asked as they reached the sand of the beach and he saw Hannah run after the seagulls watching the birds all take flight as his child came near to them.

"There," Holly pointed, and he saw his daughter running down the beach toward them holding onto her hat and Malachi chasing after her. Malachi had a hand out reaching for Charlotte, and Lang heard his daughter's happy laughter. "He may not be able to talk, but those two don't seem to need a language to communicate." Holly watched as her daughter stopped and took their soldier's hand into her own and pulled him toward where her parents' were standing.

"I think Malachi loves the fresh air and sunshine," Charlotte laughed. "He's starting to look so healthy Daddy." Lang stared at the tall man that towered over his small and very beautiful daughter that looked so much like her mother with his hair color and Lang worried of this relationship. The young man and his daughter weren't lovers, but they were getting too close and for all Lang or any of them knew, this man may have a wife and children waiting at home for him.

"He's our patient," Lang said gently to his daughter, and he saw her head raise up, and her huge brown eyes collide with his own.

"I know that Daddy, honestly I do. He's only our patient." Charlotte sat down on the blanket and looked around for her mother. "Where did mama go?" she asked and looked out at the water. "Daddy!" she screamed and saw her mother battling the waves to get to her sister Hannah.

"Oh my God," Lang dropped the basket he had been holding and hit the water. He knew without asking or having seen, that Hannah had gotten caught in the undertow and was pulled out and Holly had seen and gone in after their youngest child. Lang reached his wife and saw her battling to get to Hannah. "I've got her," he yelled and pushed his wife back to shore. But Lang didn't have Hannah. The water was taking her away from him and as hard as he fought Lang couldn't get to his little girl. And then he felt Holly holding on to him and pulling him to shore. "Hannah!" he screamed for his child, and Holly said close to his ear,

"Malachi has her, darling. She's all right now." Lang relaxed in his wife's arms, and they both held still as they watched their wounded soldier swim past them with their small daughter held in his arms. The soldier didn't see them, he was looking toward the shore and when Lang turned, he saw their soldier lift his small child out of the water and standing, the man handed Hannah to Charlotte. Within a couple of minutes, Malachi was back out in the deep water and had Holly in strong, firm arms pulling her to shore as Lang struggled to make it inland. He was swimming as hard and as fast as he could, and he was still battling the waves. Within minutes Lang was very nearly worn out.

"I can walk, Malachi," Holly had said to their soldier as he carried her onto dry land before she looked back at her husband and seeing him struggling to get to shore past the rough waves that had pulled their daughter out and away from the beach. Holly became almost frantic and started to go back into the water to reach her husband "Lang," she screamed his name and Malachi pushed her hard away from the waves and went back into the water soon having a firm hold of Lang's shirt and pulling the Doctor up and onto the beach.

"I use to be that strong," Lang said in a weak and broken voice as he stood on solid ground seeing Charlotte holding Hannah, his littlest daughter giving him a weak wave of her hand. He closed his eyes, and he went to his knees, his emotions overtook him. But for this man, this wounded silent soldier, he would have lost another little girl in his life named Hannah. Only his family knew. Lang Taylor had lost too many he had loved in his life.

"Oh, Lang," Holly came to him and hugged him, his head resting on her stomach and she smoothed his hair. "She's all right darling. Look, our Charlotte has her safe thanks to Malachi. Don't cry. We're all just fine now."

"Holly girl," he looked up at his wife, and she touched his handsome face. "I can't lose another one of my children." She nodded her head in complete understanding. Having seen Hannah snatched from the shore by the wave had taken Holly's breath away, and caused her heart to drop into her stomach and beat like a mad thing.

"Lang, we have to love with all our hearts every second of every single day. You know that none of us are promised the next minute. You and I love one another so much," Holly knelt down in front of him. "And we love our children, and they know that they are loved." Holly looked back at her daughters and saw they're love and understanding for their father's fears.

"I'm sorry, Daddy," Hannah came to her father, and he pulled her close.

"You have nothing to be sorry for, Hannah mine," he kissed her cheeks several times. "You didn't do anything wrong. I'm so thankful for our friend," he looked up at Malachi who held out a hand to him, and Malachi pulled Lang to his feet. "With all my heart, son," he said seriously looking into eyes that were seeing him. "I thank you. And I'll never forget what you did today. You're our family now."

The man standing before Lang nodded his head and smiled in understanding. Malachi kept thinking of another body of water that he had swum in, the current swift and stron, and he closed his eyes and touched his head. There weren't waves where he was within his mind, there was just the fast running current, and he heard a sound, laughter in his memory. He saw her throwing a stone into the water and counting the skips the stone made before it sank. She was beautiful, the woman in his mind and he turned seeing the one that was caring for him, Charlotte, and he thought that he wanted to skip rocks on the water with her. But there was just one problem in his mind, not that he didn't know where he wanted to be to skip those rocks. His problem was this man Malachi, who the hell was Malachi?

Chapter Eleven

Lang's feelings toward their soldier changed after the young man had saved his child from the depths of the Atlantic Ocean. He was grateful to be certain, but he was more than that, he felt that this man was more than a hero. This man was someone that was meant to be a part of their family. Holly had said the man didn't have to talk to communicate with Charlotte, and it was that way with him as well. Lang would go out to chop wood for the stove and find it already chopped. Lang's horses were well cared for, and the man was even exercising them daily. Malachi had a talent with horses and the animals seem to respond to the young man. Lang saw Malachi with Holly one afternoon on the porch, and the next afternoon he came home from seeing a patient and found the young man had painted much of the front of their home. Instead of a soft creamy yellow, the house was now white with a beautiful ocean blue trim. The gingerbread trim that needed replacing had been replaced, and Lang wondered if there was anything this man couldn't do.

Lang saw Charlotte on the beach, standing in the waves with her fishing pole and the soldier was beside her fishing as well. When something pulled his daughter's line, the soldier put his arm around Charlotte's tiny waist and pulled her and the fish on her line up to the shore, Lang could hear Charlotte's laughter, and he caught his wife on the porch watching the young couple.

"They're growing closer and closer every single day," he said, and Holly turned and came into her husband's arms.

"What's wrong with that, Lang? We knew she would fall in love someday. Why not with him?" Holly looked back and saw her daughter running down the beach and Malachi chasing after Charlotte. The young man caught Charlotte quickly as he was so tall he would always outrun Holly's daughter.

Lang saw Malachi tossing Charlotte in the air and catching her. The young man was then holding her close running into the waves pretending that he might drop her. "Remember when we were young?" Lang heard his wife asking him.

"That's the problem," Lang moaned. "I do in fact remember very well when we were young." He looked down at Holly who burst into giggles. "What if he's married? Have you thought of that?" Holly stopped giggling and looked back out at the beach and her daughter standing next to their soldier. The young couple had gone back to fishing and were now holding hands.

"I hadn't thought of that," Holly said and hoped with all of her heart Malachi wasn't married. Then she thought to add, "We're worried about that when the poor man cannot even talk to us. He still has moments where he fades away from us and stares at nothing. He can't even tell us his real name. What if he never recovers? What if he never gets well?" Holly looked up at her husband. "Falling in love with Charlotte and her falling in love with him seems not to matter at all when he might very well live out the next fifty years unaware of who he really is."

"There's truth to what you say," Lang nodded his head and hugged Holly closer. "I've gone through the names of the missing and dead from the Battle of Belleau, and I cannot find one single man named Malachi. I'm not even certain that's his first name."

"Maybe if you read the names of the missing and dead out loud in front of him, he might respond to his own name," Holly suggested, and Lang shook his head.

"Holly girl, there were more than ten thousand Marines killed at Belleau Woods. I can't read all those names to him. That would take days. And he might respond to his friends' names, and I still wouldn't know his name."

"I didn't realize so many men died there," Holly more breathed than spoke. "Ten thousand men," she said this twice.

"All we can do is wait and hope he comes back to himself," Lang said seeing the soldier pull in another fish. "In the meantime, my house is no longer yellow, and I love this shade of blue you chose for the trim. And we're going to have fish for dinner. And by the way, I bought an automobile yesterday. Our new car should be here in a few weeks. We're going to be living like we're in the twentieth century," he teased and saw Holly looking up at him.

"Hannah is still at school. We have a few hours. Why don't we go inside to our room and pretend we're young again." She laughed when Lang took her hand and pulled her into the house at a run and up the stairs, and she laughed in joy that he was her husband.

Charlotte looked back at the house, and she saw her parents were no longer standing on the porch watching her and Malachi. She was glad they were gone. She felt like they were spending too much time watching her with Malachi, and she knew what they didn't know. She had fallen hopelessly in love with him.

"Want to go for a walk before we take the fish up to the house?" Charlotte asked her soldier as she saw they had enough fish for her mother to fry for dinner. He looked at her and put the fish on the line back into the waves to stay fresh while he and Charlotte walked on the sand to nowhere and yet he was happy to be with her.

He took her hand after laying the fishing poles in the powder sand and started down the beach with her alongside of him. With her walking daily with him and his working around her parents' house, he was growing stronger than he thought he might ever have been. He could pick her up with one hand and lift her over his head, and he felt strong and secure in his body again. He closed his eyes and e saw himself bent in the saddle of a horse racing someone and then jumping off his horse in the yard and smiling up at the men on a wide porch of a huge house. He couldn't remember their names. He couldn't remember where they lived. But he saw the white sandy road he had raced down on a horse, and he knew he lived near a shore.

"I wish you could tell me what you're thinking," Charlotte said to him and he stopped forcing her to stop as well because he held her hand. She looked back at hi, and he took a deep breath while looking at her. She had the eyes of a doe dear, he thought. Her skin, despite their living on the beach, was a pale white. Her lips were plump and a deep pink in color and when she smiled, there were two deep dimples in each check.

She was the most beautiful woman he had ever seen. Her golden brown curls were something he had to touch, and he did. His fingers taking a hold of her soft thick hair and getting wrapped up in a curl. He closed his eyes, and he saw another girl with curls. A girl with huge eyes that were a light color so different from the girl before him. He remembered the girl in his mind, seeing her hair that was like the darkest night, her eyes huge and looking trustingly up at him and they were a light sky blue in color. He had skipped rocks with her on the water; he was certain of that. Sarah, he thought, that was all he had in his memory, a beautiful girl named Sarah that he had once loved.

Charlotte saw her soldier looking at her, touching her hair and she wondered what he was thinking. She always seemed to be wondering what he was thinking. With courage, afraid all these months to say the word, Charlotte took a deep breath and said what she must, "Sarah," and she saw him turn his head and stare at nothing.

He wanted to shake his head no. She was not Sarah. He touched Charlotte's chin and shook his head. "Is Sarah your wife?" he heard her asking him, and he closed his eyes. He didn't think Sarah was his wife. He didn't think he had a wife. If he had a wife, he would want this beauty before him as his wife — this beauty with the doe-like eyes. "I cannot feel anything for you knowing you might be married," Charlotte almost broke into tears. And he was shaking his head hard. He might be married, but he wanted her more than his past life. He had to stay here. He closed his eyes and shook his head hard. He had to stay here with her, with Charlotte.

He saw the battlefield within his memory. He saw the man shot. The man that he saw shot was himself. Odd, he thought now as he remembered reaching for the man. He could clearly see his face in the man's face that he was reaching for. "Aaahhh," Charlotte saw the change in Malachi before he screamed, the way his eyes glazed over, and he looked off. And then he grabbed each side of his head letting go of her hand, and he yelled a horrible sound. All he knew was an overwhelming horror of pain. The man in his memory had fallen. The man shot dead was him. He saw himself dead and knew he would never be that man again. He was Malachi, and he loved this beauty before him. The him that he was before knowing he had died on that battlefield near Paris, France.

"You're all right," Charlotte said gently, and when Malachi sat down hard on the sand, she went down with him. "I won't let anything hurt you ever again," she said gently, and she saw him remove his hands from the side of his head and look down into her eyes. His face no longer appeared twisted in an agony of pain. "It's too late you know," she said and leaned into him. "Even if you are married to this Sarah, it's too late for me." Charlotte felt his arms come around her and draw her close. "I'm already in love with you."

He tilted her chin up so that she could look into his eyes and she saw him shaking his head. But Charlotte didn't know what he was trying to tell her. She didn't think he knew what he was trying to tell her. And then he didn't need any words to speak to her. He had her pulled on top of him, and he was kissing her, his hands lost in her hair as he moaned into her mouth.

"More," she begged of him as his mouth came away from her mouth and he moved his lips down her neck and to her collar bone. "What are you doing to me?" she pleaded to know as he came back up to her ear and plunged his tongue in and out and breathed into her ear his hot breath while his hand pulled her hips close to his own and he rolled her over onto her back. "We aren't married," Charlotte said softly, and he lifted off of her. He knew she didn't want to become too intimate with him. "My parents trust me, they have expectations for me, and I cannot fail my Mama and Daddy."

He looked down into her beautiful eyes, and he firmly nodded his head. He wouldn't make her cheap, not her. She was his Princess. He put his forehead onto her chin and breathed onto her neck. He had to remember who he was. He couldn't have her until he knew who he was.

Malachi, he spoke the name in his mind. He was Malachi though he was certain that he didn't know anyone by that name. He tried to see the girl skipping the rocks on the water, and he knew her. He knew he loved that girl. But was she his wife? He feared that she was. He closed his eyes and took a breath seeing Charlotte's parents, and in seeing them, he saw a man he knew was his Uncle Allen, and a woman he was certain was his Aunt Alicia. Beyond those names, he couldn't remember anything else. It was as though his mind were stuck on seeing only those three people from his past and beyond the girl skipping rocks and his Aunt and Uncle kissing; he could remember no one else. He took a deep breath and remembered the water, the sandy road that led to home. And he felt like crying that his mind was so empty when he knew his mind should be full.

He pulled her into his arms and he sat them both up as he looked out over the water. The waves were smashing against the shore nearby, and though almost appearing violent, those waves filled him with peace. What if he never remembered who he was? What if this was all there was in his mind for the rest of his life? He had to find some way to remember who he was so that he could be free to be with her, with his Charlotte for all of his life. He never wanted to know another day without his Charlotte.

Lang sat at the dinner table looking at Malachi who was staring at him, only this time the stare wasn't vacant or void of seeing anything. Malachi was really looking at him, and he felt as though the young man wanted him to read his mind. Lang looked at Holly and Charlotte, both of who were looking at Malachi look at him and Hannah; his youngest child sat sweet and innocent at the table picking at her fish and drinking her milk.

"All right," Lang said standing up from the table and leaving his dinner. "One of us has to talk," he said to Malachi. "My office, now." Charlotte started to stand and go with her father, and her mother took hold of her arm.

"I think this might be a man to man conversation," she said gently, and she saw Charlotte watch her father disappear into his office. Malachi close her father's office door before Charlotte sat back down. "I know you worry over him," Holly said this seeing her daughter look at her with tear filled eyes.

"I've fallen in love with him," Charlotte confessed to her mother. "I love him, Mama. I don't want to live without him. He's everything to me." She leaned on her mother's shoulder, and her mother held her close.

"I understand your feelings," her mother consoled her, "I honestly do."

"I'm pretty certain he's married to a woman named Sarah," Charlotte said in a soft voice. "But he can't remember, and I can see he's frustrated that he can't remember."

"Let's see what your father can do. I know Lang's a miracle worker," Holly said confidently and looked toward her husband's office door hoping and praying that when that door opened again, there would be a miracle return of their soldier's voice.

Lang sat at his desk and watched Malachi pacing around the room. The young man had attempted several times in the past to talk to him, but every attempt had failed. Lang felt like he had failed the young man. He put a pad of paper on the desk and a pencil, and he saw Malachi looking at those items before Malachi finally reached and picked the pad up.

The young man had tried many times to write, but he couldn't hold the pencil for more than a moment due to his tremor in his hands. Even with paper and pencil, he was mute. Malachi reached for the pencil and held the pencil tightly in his grasp. The pencil felt odd in his hand, he couldn't quite hold it like he used to and he saw the tremor that took over his hand. He hated this tremor knowing that when he tried to hold a pencil or a comb or anything in his hand, the tremor happened. That was why he painted the house and fixed the trim on the house. The more he used his hand, the less it tremor. But with a pencil, he couldn't gain control over the tremor, and he looked at Lang with helpless eyes.

Lang was thinking along the same lines as Malachi and knew the paintbrush handle was thick. The hammer handle was thick. The pencil was slim and took more effort to hold. Without warning, Lang snatched the pencil away from Malachi and went to his cabinet for bandages unaware that the younger man was watching him wrap the bandages around the pencil until the pencil was thick like the hammer.

"Try this," Lang said as he shoved the bandaged wrapped pencil at Malachi. The younger man had taken hold of the pencil all bandaged up, the pencil held in his fist much as a small child would hold a pencil.

Lang looked at the paper that Malachi wrote on. First came the name Sarah then the word wife and then a question mark. Then he wrote the names Allen and Alicia and another question mark. Then he wrote the name Lang and then his wife's name Holly. Then he wrote water and current and sandy road, and finally, he looked at Lang and wrote one last word which he underlined several times followed by six question marks.

Malachi watched the older man pick up the pad and read what he felt Malachi was trying to tell him. "You remember a girl named Sarah, and she might be your wife, but you don't know?" He saw Malachi's head nod. "You remember an older couple like Holly and me, maybe parents?" Then Lang remembered at the ferry he had said Uncle Allen, "wait," he looked up at Malachi. "Allen and Alicia are your Uncle and Aunt?" he saw the younger man nod his head.

Malachi took the pad from Lang and put it on the desk pressing with the pencil he wrote the word 'kiss' and then drew a line to the names Allen and Alicia and then turned to Lang pointing to Lang and then to the name Holly causing Lang to laugh out loud.

"Okay, I understand," Lang said still laughing. "Whoever Allen and Alicia are, they kiss a lot like Holly, and I do." He saw Malachi looking at him very seriously and nodding his head. "So this is what you remember of your past? A girl named Sarah, and an Aunt and Uncle that are obviously in love?" Lang saw Malachi pointing to the last word on the pad and looked down at the paper. It was the younger man's name underlined several times and then followed by question marks.

Malachi saw Doctor Lang Taylor looking at the paper with no idea what he was trying to ask, and Malachi felt frustrated all over. He pointed to himself and to the paper and back to himself, and he saw Lang still didn't understand. Lang saw his soldier ball up his fist and try to scream, but nothing came out. Malachi snatched the pad from Lang and went to the door and flung it open going to Charlotte.

She saw his distress. She saw he was beyond upset, and she saw him coming toward her as though she were the only person in the world who could help him and she wanted to help him. With all of her heart, she wanted to help him. She stood up, and she saw her father behind her handsome soldier, and she made eye contact with her father seeing Lang shrug his shoulders. "What's wrong?" Charlotte went to Malachi, and she saw him with the pad of paper. He pointed to his name written in sloppy letters, underlined in squiggly lines and undefined question marks behind his name.

Malachi pointed to his name on the paper, then he pointed to himself and then back to the paper and the question marks. Charlotte looked again to her father and Lang looked helplessly to her. Malachi sat down at the table with the pad of paper and tried to write more, but his hand was shaking too badly. At this point, he couldn't even hold the pencil wrapped in thick bandages.

"Oh, he wants to write but the tremor," Holly said, and she came to him and put her hand under his chin forcing Malachi to look at her. "You want to write to tell us something and you can't because your hands shaking holding this pencil?" Holly looked at the bandage wrapped around the pencil, and she laughed. "This was a good try," she looked at her husband, 'trying to make it fat like the hammer, but there's another way." She pulled Malachi to his feet and told the family to come with her leading them all out the door and down to the sandy beach. "Lang, Charlotte, look for a fat stick of driftwood," she ordered them, and it was Hannah who found a large piece of wood and ran to them. Holly thrust the wood into Malachi's hand, and he breathed a sigh of relief before hugging Holly.

"You're brilliant," Lang said to his wife as he and Charlotte came to stand next to her and Malachi. "Okay son, write your question," Lang encouraged the young man as he watched Malachi bend down to write the words clear with very little shaking.

"Who is Malachi???" he wrote in the sand and Lang smiled at him touching his shoulder.

"You, you're name is Malachi," Lang assured him in a gentle tone of voice. "You have a form of amnesia. About ten percent of our soldiers coming home from the war suffer from this. You have to give yourself time to heal. Then you'll remember who you are and more than just your name."

Their soldier shook his head hard. He pushed on Lang's shoulder and shook his head harder before writing in the sand further. "I am not Malachi. I don't know my name. But I know it's not Malachi."

"Daddy," Charlotte spoke to Lang softly, and her father, mother, and Malachi looked at her. "He didn't have a name. In the hospital, he didn't have a name. And Malachi is the last chapter of the Old Testament. For four hundred years after that chapter, there was silence until Christ came. Since he is so silent and we thought he would die, I thought, we'll he'll see Christ soon. And then that Army office said he couldn't come back to the United States without a name, and he had to have a name. Anyway Daddy, I know I shouldn't have, but I named him Malachi."

"You mean his name isn't really Malachi?" Lang asked Charlotte seeing their soldier's head shaking and Charlotte's head nodding.

"He needed a name, Daddy," Charlotte defended her actions. "And it's a good name." She looked at the man she had named Malachi, and she saw that he was understanding of why she had done what she had done. He even gave to her a smile.

"I understand," Lang said looking at his daughter and then his wife. "But all this time, I've been searching the papers for missing or killed soldiers at the battle of Belleau Woods with the name of

Malachi. I have less of a clue now than I had before to go on," Lang said in a grief-filled voice.

"I know his name," Hannah said skipping to her parents and writing her own name in the sand with a piece of driftwood.

"What?" Charlotte, Lang, and Holly all said to Hannah at the same time. Malachi was looking at the little girl he had saved from drowning.

"He told you his name?" Lang bent down and looked at the little girl that was the spitting image of himself when he had been little. His daughter even had his large purple, blue eyes.

"He didn't tell me," Hannah said in a childish voice looking at her father. "He was having a nightmare, and I went to his room. I was going to try and help him like he helped me get out of the water that day, but he was crying hard." Hannah reached for Malachi's hand. "I'm sorry you're so sad."

"But I don't understand, Hannah," Charlotte said looking down at her little sister. "If he was having a nightmare how do you know his name?"

"Cause he kept yelling it at me," Hannah said simply. "He kept yelling over and over in the bed; I'm a Blackburn. So that's his name, Blackburn."

Their soldier didn't move. He didn't acknowledge that his name was Blackburn or not because he didn't know. He looked at Lang, then Holly and finally Charlotte waiting for one of them to confirm what Hannah was saying, but they all were looking at him as though they were waiting for him to confirm who he was.

"Oh for goodness sake," Lang almost swore and started running to the house knowing that his family was following him. "I have the list of missing and killed in action soldiers from the battle." He threw open his office door and plundered around in his desk. "Here," he put the paper on his desk. The print was too small to read in the room as it was nearly dark outside. "The lights," he waited for Holly to turn on the gas light in the room, and then he bent over the paper and Lang searched out the unusual name, his finger sliding down the newspaper printed list of names. "Found it!" he called out and looked up at their unnamed soldier. "Shaun, Shaun Blackburn."

The former Malachi fell into the chair at Lang's desk, and he didn't move. He saw everyone looking at him as though the name should mean something to him, but he honestly drew no memory from hearing the name. His eyes met Charlotte's eyes, and he shook his head hard. If he was this Shaun Blackburn, that meant nothing to him. For what he knew, his name might as well be Malachi.

"Don't worry," Lang said gently to their soldier who looked very worried. "Tomorrow Holly and I will go to the war office in Jacksonville. We'll request your records and have them mailed here since you probably live out of state. It will probably take a few weeks, but a lot of the men had their photo made for their file. Once we see your photo and your records, then we'll know for certain who you are and where you came from and who your family is."

Everyone followed their soldier out into the dining room where he picked up the pad of paper and pointed to the name of Sarah. He then took Charlotte's hand. Lang and Holly understood what the young man was saying. He needed to know if he was married because he was in love with their Charlotte.

"We'll figure this out," Holly said gently. "I'm going to pack a bag for us. We might have to stay in Jacksonville for the night. Hannah can come with us." She saw Lang shaking his head and put her hand over his lips. "We'll talk upstairs," she said taking his hand and pulling him behind her knowing that he was looking back at their daughter, Charlotte.

"Are you out of your mind?" Lang nearly yelled when Holly closed their bedroom door. "There is no way in hell I'm leaving our daughter alone in this house with him while we go off to Jacksonville." Holly pulled her husband by the hand to the foot of their bed.

"How well do you know our Charlotte?" she asked him as she pulled clothes out of the drawer and put them in a bag. "Keeping in mind that you spent the better part of last year in England with her before you answer my question." She saw Lang go quiet and knew he was thinking. "We can trust her with him. Yes, they are in love, you'd have to be blind to not know that. But Charlotte knows to wait until marriage. You and I raised her right."

"Yeah, us," he hissed, and wife laughed. "As I recall, we didn't wait."

"You know what we did and didn't do, Langston Taylor," Holly laughed and saw him go pale.

"Please, do not make me have the mental vision of my daughter, who is still just a child in my eyes and always will be, doing what you and I did before our marriage." Holly heard him groan out loud and went to him bending down before him.

"Do you want me still that way," she asked him and she saw his head shoot up and his eyes meet hers. "Let me lock our door," she said softly, and he watched her walking away from him and then turn the key in the doorknob before looking back at him. Oh God, he thought, she held his heart in her hand, and she always had, within a moment, she was holding more than his heart in her hand.

"I love you, Holly mine," he breathed, and he didn't close his eyes as he watched his wife make love to him.

Charlotte with Shaun and she was trying her best to think of him as Shaun, took her parents and little sister to the early morning ferry. She hugged her mother, and her father said to her three different times that he trusted her before he hugged her and they left her alone with their soldier.

"We'll telephone you what we find tonight from your Uncle's house," her mother called out, and Charlotte waved a final time before turning and going to the buggy with Shaun.

"Would you like to go down to the beach?" she asked hi, and he nodded his head taking her hand after he had stabled the horse.

Come Save Someone Like Me

"I don't know who you are Shaun. But I do want to tell you who I think you are." Charlotte felt him put his arm around her and pull her close and she let him after they took off their shoes and their bare feet hit the sand. "You're educated," she smiled up at him, "you can read, and you can write when your hand isn't shaking. You can paint a house and repair woodwork. You put a new roof on our huge house," she pointed to her parents' home in the distance with the new tiles shining in the sun that he had put on in the past weeks. "You're very good with horses. You can fix almost anything from the pump in the kitchen to the gas light in Daddy's office."

Shaun stopped walking and looked down at Charlotte shaking his head and then he was looking, and she knew what he was looking for. "Here!" She handed him a large piece of driftwood and followed him down to the sand at the edge of the water. The sand here was made smooth by the waves.

"I am for certain of one thing," he wrote in the hard packed smooth sand. "I'm in love with you." He dropped the driftwood to the ground and grabbed her, and she grabbed him, and his mouth was covering hers.

"I love you too," Charlotte was crying as he lifted her up into his arms and carried her up from the beach and to the house. "My parents trust us alone," she said on a gasp, and he nodded pointing to her lips and then to his own lips. "We'll just kiss?" He nodded his head to assure her.

He laid her on his bed in his small room off of the kitchen, and she lay back against the pillow looking up at him with large trusting eyes. She touched his forehead and ran her hand through his hair and the bangs fell forward and almost reached to his nose. He was beautiful she thought as he began to kiss her. She had never been kissed like this; she thought as his mouth moved from her mouth to her ear and down her throat. She gasped when he kissed her collar bone and moved to where the v neck of her dress was open. He touched her there, and his eyes looked back to her eyes before he opened her dress and his mouth touched her breast. He heard her gasp and then gasp again, and he moved back up to her mouth.

"I don't know how to kiss you," she said in her innocence and felt his hand touching her breast gently before he covered her soft flesh with his mouth again. "I don't know how to kiss you," she gasped again and again and sank lower into the bed. His actions were telling her she didn't need to know how to kiss him. This was what he wanted to do for her right now. He needed to do this for her. "You make me not able to think," Charlotte gasped and tried to think as his hands touched her all over and then in places no hands had ever touched her, and she was crying out, not his name, she wasn't certain of his name, but he knew she was crying out for him.

Charlotte slowly came awake. She hadn't realized that she had fallen asleep until she woke up and then she was shocked that it was so late in the day. She looked down, and she saw that Shaun if that was really his name, had his head on her stomach, his face turned toward her, and his eyes had the thousand-yard stare again, that empty, sightless gaze.

"Shaun," she said his name but he didn't move, and she knew she had to wait, hoping that he would come back to her soon.

"Get behind me," he heard the words being said. "I love Sarah," and he tried to breathe but he couldn't catch his breath. "If you die, I'll go home to Sarah and marry her." Shaun sat up in the bed he lay in with Charlotte lost in time to the memories he didn't want to have. He grabbed a hold of his head. His head hurt worse than he had ever known his head to hurt, even when that German soldier was beating him in the face.

"Shaun," he heard Charlotte saying his name, but he couldn't turn to her, he couldn't look at her. "I'll love Sarah better than you ever did," he heard these words, and he shook his head hard. And then all these months of silence and he finally got a word out, the word loud and clear,

"No," and he shocked himself with saying something at last. "Shane," he breathed the name as though he were saying the name to exhale a breath he had been holding for far too long.

He was being punched in the face. He heard the words, "go to hell." He was looking at his own reflection, only it wasn't his reflection, it was him, and it wasn't him. "No," he cried out again and reached out with his hand as he was falling. He felt the bullet hit him and he was reaching for his brother. He had a brother. "Shane!" he called the name again. He had to get to him, but he couldn't. And he saw, he saw his brother shot down and dying. "Shane!" he cried out maybe only in his mind, maybe to Charlotte, he didn't know. What he did know for certain was that he had seen his twin brother killed in front of his eyes, gunned down by a German soldier.

"It's all right," Charlotte said as she sat up on the side of the bed next to her soldier and took his hands into her hands. "You spoke," she said in her gentle way so similar to her father's gentle way.

"I," Shaun looked at her, and she saw the struggle he was having in talking. "Go home," he finally said, and she knew, she understood what he was saying to her. And at this moment, the phone was ringing in the hall, and she had to leave him to answer the call.

"I'll be right back," she said as she rushed from the room they were in. "Hello," she called outstanding on the stool next to the big box hanging on the wall and the earpiece that was the telephone in her hand. "Daddy," she said and then saw him there in front of her, her soldier, and he took the earpiece from her.

"I have to go home now," he said into the phone and then handed the earpiece back to Charlotte. "I have to tell my parents I'm alive and what happened to my brother. I have to go home now."

"He spoke Daddy," she said into the telephone. "That was Shaun."

"I figured that was Shaun," Lang said to his daughter. "I want you both to get on the ferry at dawn. We'll meet you there and go right to the train station. I'm getting our tickets this evening. We know who he is and where he lives. I need to go Charlotte, but hopefully, he'll tell you everything now that he's able to talk and what we don't know of him, you both can tell us in the morning."

"Daddy," she looked at Shaun while she spoke to her father. "Is he married?" She saw the look on his beautiful face, and Charlotte knew that Shaun still wasn't certain of the answer to this question. But she was because her father had just told her yes.

He stood looking at her, his eyes had at long last filled with tears, and standing on the box by the telephone, Charlotte was eye to eye with him, and she saw the tears drop onto his face. He knew, he was remembering everything in bits and pieces, and he was keeping the memories that he had here, these memories mixing with his past memories. Charlotte knew that it was a part of the shellshock. Her father had explained it all to her and allowed her to read the medical journals.

"Shaun, there is something that happens to soldiers that went into battles like you went in to and survived. It's a type of brain injury I think. I'm not really certain. I don't think the Doctors know yet. But it can steal from you the ability to talk. About seven percent of soldiers became mute, and they suffer from a type of amnesia called fugue. Daddy can explain it best to you. But it happened to a lot of men. Daddy said some men with shellshock just have nightmares and are jumpy and it's not that bad. Other men relive the battle every night in their sleep and re-enact it trying to find a different outcome. But you, you have a lot of the worst symptoms probably because you were shot so many times and left for dead for so long in those woods."

Charlotte saw Shaun listening to her every word, his eyes looking into her eyes and there was no thousand-yard stare. He wasn't talking, but she knew that he could, he had just been silent for so long. "I still love you," he finally said when she had been silent for a minute. "No matter what I have wrong in my head, I still love you."

"Shaun, you're married," Charlotte said and put her face in her hands. "We're not free to love one another. And tomorrow, Daddy says we're going to take you home. Home to your wife and your family."

PART FOUR

SHAUN AND SHANE

Chapter Twelve

Summer 1919
Twin River, Florida

Sarah sat up in the bed, the moon was casting shadows all around the room, and she could clearly see Shane's side of the bed was empty. He might have been in the bathroom, he might have been getting a drink of water, but Sarah knew, he wasn't doing either of those things. Her husband, she knew what he was doing; he was fighting Germans again. She looked around the corners of the room for him, and she didn't see him right away. When she did see him, she saw he was closer than she had known. Crouched down on her side of the bed, so close she could touch him, she heard him talking, maybe to Shaun maybe to Ethan, who knew who he was giving orders too.

"Get down," he said in a serious voice, and she knew it would do no good to wake him up. Her husband wasn't really asleep. He was somewhere inside of himself where no one else was or could ever be. The only person that understood what she was going through was Bethany because Ethan was having this happen to him as well, though Ethan, for some reason had become more calm. Ethan was re-entering the real world of home and leaving the horror of the war behind. Ethan's parents were here with Uncle Allen and Aunt Alicia for the summer. With a father and mother like Levi and Cecily Tucker, it wouldn't be possible for Ethan to not heal, not that she thought Seth and Mary couldn't help Shane. Things were just different for her husband. Shane had lost an identical twin brother in the war.

She rarely thought of Shaun now, Sarah thought. He was a sweet little memory in her head now and then. She no longer had the horrible grief that she had first known when they had lost her husband. She no longer had the empty ache inside knowing that he was gone and he wasn't ever coming back. She remembered the last time she saw Shaun. The last time that they made love. But now, for her, her world was Shane. She loved Shane with all of her being, and he loved her. They had a peace in their lives because of that love. Except on nights like these, Sarah thought as Shane went back to war.

"You won't listen to me," he was saying to no one that was there with him, at least no one that Sarah could see was with him. "I told you to stay down." And then he was looking ahead, and he ducked and then jumped up, and as he did most nights, Shane killed several Germans in his dream with his bayonet and bare hands. He screamed out for Ethan, and then he was reaching, reaching back for his brother.

Sarah saw him fall to the floor and heard his cries and her heart broke for him. He had watched Shaun die all over again tonight, and there was nothing that she could do to protect him from this that was happening to him. She looked out the window and saw the sun just turning the clouds pink off in the distance. Dawn was upon them, and she slipped out of the bed and went to her husband, careful as always not to touch him, but to clearly say his name or he might tackle her and take her down on the floor thinking she was a German soldier.

"Shane," she said his name, and he sat up looking around and seeing the break of day fill the room.

"I did it again?" he asked of her, and she nodded her head in answer. "I'm sorry, Sarah." Shane tried to stand, but he sat still taking a few deep breaths. "Can we go wash the German blood off of me?" he said this in a teasing manner, and she smiled taking his hand and pulling him up and off the floor.

"You're the one that said the river makes us clean." Sarah felt her husband pull her into his arms as they went to the darkened stairwell and started down into the breezeway that was bright with the early light of dawn. "Whenever you and I have a problem, we come into our river," Sarah said looking up at him as they entered their yard and together they saw the river nearby. "You told me that the day we married," she smiled, and he bent and gave her a kiss.

"I wish I could empty my head of the battles I was in and leave them in the river," Shane said before he started to run to their grassy knoll pulling her along behind him, her nightgown lose around her knees.

"We're crazy," she said as she pulled her nightgown over her head and he pulled off his shorts, and they went into the water still holding hands.

"I told you, we're a part of this river, and it's a part of us," Shane spoke low to his wife as he lifted her up against him, her arms around his neck and her legs straddling his hips. "I feel so deep inside of you," he gasped as she clung to him and he made love to her while loving her more than his own life. "Sarah," he breathed her name, and she cried out his name at the same time. Only a water bird was there to hear them as they fell together caught by the river and gently pushed to shore.

Shane was lying on the grassy knoll with Sarah on top of him looking up at the blue sky and the white fluffy fat clouds hanging low above them. "Sarah," he said her name and she lifted up her face to look at him, and she saw whatever he was going to say was serious. "Can we have a baby?" He felt her roll off of him and away from him before she sat up pulling her nightgown on. "What's wrong?" he asked, and she looked back at him.

"Nothing," she said and stood up pulling him to his feet.

"What are you doing? Where are you going?" She reached for his shorts and threw them at him and then turned to run toward the house.

"I'm going to bed and hope my husband hurries up and joins me so we can make that baby!" she called back over her shoulder, and he gave a laugh before he ran after her, his long legs outran her and he caught her on the porch steps, swung her up and into his arms carrying her up the stairs.

"Both of you are late," Levi Tucker said as Shane and Ethan walked up the steps of the house at Riverbend. "Allen and I already inspected the trees and the corn, and we branded three new heifers this morning." Ethan looked at Shane and then came close to his father to speak,

"Bethany told me a secret this morning," he said to his father and saw his wife, Bethany hurry past him and into the house giving him a serious look before she went through the door. "And I can't tell you until she's told her Mama," he said in a serious tone and ran after his wife.

Allen came out of the house looking at Ethan rushing past him, probably going after Bethany, Allen thought as he had just seen Bethany running down the hall. He turned to Levi who was headed for the door he had just come out of, flinching when Levi punched him in the shoulder.

"Come on Grandpa," Levi said and opened the screen door seeing Allen look at him with a dumbfounded look on his face. "Let's go," Levi ordered, and Allen moved through the door with Levi pushing him into the house.

"Did you just call me Grandpa?" Allen asked as Levi pushed him down the hall toward the kitchen talking as they went to where their wives were.

"Ethan just said he has a secret he can't tell until Bethany's told her mama," Levi stopped talking when he heard both Cecily and Alicia cry out. "There, you made us miss them telling their mamas," Levi pushed passed Allen who came close behind him, both men going into the kitchen.

"Daddy," Bethany turned to her father who looked at Levi.

"I'm too young to be a Grandpa," Allen almost moaned.

"I told you not to tell anyone until I told Mama," Bethany slapped at Ethan.

"I didn't tell him, I didn't tell anyone," Ethan defended himself and Bethany looked at her father who pointed to Levi.

"Well, who told you, Daddy Levi?" Bethany asked looking from Ethan to his father.

"I guessed," Levi said in all honestly and went to hug his daughter in law and pat his son on the back. "Now you'll have a new sort of night terror son. You don't know what love is until you're awakened in the nights by the screams of a hungry baby." He looked at Cecily and winked as he knew she was recalling the same memory he was of long ago, "or a ghost in the corner of your bedroom taking care of your infant." His wife came to him and hugged him close.

"One day, we're going to tell him the story of that ghost," Cecily said looking up at her husband and seeing his head nod before he gave her a gentle kiss, and she melted into him. They had fallen in love as children – Levi and Cecily had. And they were still as deeply in love all these years later. He was her Levi, and she was his Cecily. Alone they were only half of who they were meant to be; together they were whole.

"But it wasn't really a ghost," Levi whispered into her ear as he pulled her close. "It was an angel." Levi saw his son looking at him, and he gave his son a wink. He was a proud father, and now soon he would be a proud grandfather. "I love you, Cecily," Levi whispered, and she lay her head on his chest, neither aware that everyone in the room was watching them and smiling.

The train pulled into the station in Tallahassee and Lang sat looking at the man that had been a patient for nearly a year. Shaun had finally found his voice. For months the young man had been mute and unable to recall even a name that was connected to him. And now, everything had all come flooding back to him, and Lang knew that Shaun needed their support. The Taylors were not going to let this man return home alone. He saw his daughter Hannah on one side of him, and his daughter Charlotte on the other side of him and Lang knew that their soldier was comforted in some ways, but not in all ways.

"Our next stop is Woodville," Lang said and saw the look in those grass green eyes that stared at him from the face of Shaun Blackburn. He also saw a look of sorrow and pain.

"I'm coming home without my brother," Shaun said in a voice of agony. "I saw him get shot and I saw him die in front of my eyes," as he said this, he looked down to be sure Hannah was still sleeping and didn't hear his words. "My mother has thought all of this time that I was dead, and now she'll know I lived and it was Shane that died."

"Your mother will be relieved to know you made it home to her," Holly said, and she saw Charlotte holding the folder with a copy of his enlistment records. Because he had been a Marine, all his paperwork had been in the records office in Jacksonville, Florida and not in the state capital of Tallahassee. There had even been a photo of him with a description of him in the records, and they knew he had a twin brother that had been with him. A brother that he had seen killed and had never made it home to their family.

"No matter what, everything will be all right. You'll be home. Think of your mother, Shaun. All this time she's thought she lost both of her sons. And one is coming home." Charlotte took his hand seeing her parents look at one another as she held his hand. He was married. He wasn't free to love her or accept her love, and she was wrong now in touching him.

"I think we should stay the night in Woodville," Shaun said to the Taylor family and turned to Lang. "I don't want to arrive home to my mama in the dark, and I don't want anyone to see me

Come Save Someone Like Me

in Woodville and alert my folks I'm coming home. Would you get the rooms at the boarding house for me? I'll slip in after you tell me our room numbers." Lang nodded his head. Lang understood that this young man wanted to tell his mama and daddy that he was alive himself. He didn't want anyone going ahead of him, and alerting his parents. This was something he had to do.

Charlotte looked up at Shaun. She would always think of him and know him as her soldier, no matter the name given to him. She felt a tear fall onto the back of her hand as she looked down at the folder in her hands and read the names on the folder. Shane and Shaun Blackburn. Who would have thought he was an identical twin? Twins were so rare. She had seen the photos taken of the brothers standing in their uniforms and they looked so alike that she couldn't tell which one of them was the man beside her.

Shaun closed his eyes, and he thought of his brother Shane buried in that mass grave in France that he had escaped. He had stood up after three days and having been shot eleven times; he walked to the stretcher and to safety. Maybe Shane had made it out of those woods alive as well. But if Shane were alive, the war office in Jacksonville had no record stating so.

Doctor Taylor had asked at the war office if they had evidence that Shane and Shaun both had died and the clerk had assured him that one of the twins had to be buried in France, and it wasn't the twin that Doctor Taylor had living with him, because that twin was alive. So they could safely assume it was Shane that was dead.

And Shaun kept remembering. He kept seeing his brother die over and over again when he thought of him. Shaun had clearly seen Shane shot and he had seen him fall almost at the same instant that he had been shot. Even the smallest hope that his brother was home waiting for him faded as they came closer and closer to home and Shaun felt as though he was falling apart.

"Keep your hat pulled low, and no one will recognize you and alert your Mother that you're returned," Holly said to him as she leaned forward to pat his thigh and Shaun nodded his head. "No matter where you go, no matter what you do in this life," she said holding his clear green eyes with her own, "you'll always be a part of our family. We've grown to love you." She then looked at her Hannah asleep in the seat next to him, the little girl's head lying on his arm. "You saved our Hannah," Holly forced a smiled on her face. She would always be thankful that he had been there for them. "We'll never forget what you did for us, Shaun."

"Hey, he pulled me out of the Atlantic too," Lang said teasingly trying to lighten the mood. Tomorrow a son was returning home from the war. At long last, he was coming home, but without his twin brother. He would also be returning to the woman he loved knowing that he was in love with the woman that nursed him all these many months. He would have to say goodbye to Charlotte, and they all knew that he would. Lang frowned and was aware they were all going to lose Shaun tomorrow.

"Doctor Taylor," Lang heard his soldier say his name from the back seat of the buggy and he turned around to look at Shaun. "Can you stop here please?" Lang did as he was asked seeing Shaun looking down a road they hadn't turned on to. "My brother Shane and I, we built our home down there." Lang saw the direction that Shaun was pointing in and turned the horses to go that way. "I should see my mother first," he said in a weak voice and felt Charlotte squeeze his arm. "And Sarah. I should face Sarah."

"We can take a moment to see your home, son," Lang spoke gently as he always did with his patients and he stopped near the house. "Why don't you go look at the place. We'll wait here for you."

Charlotte saw Shaun shake his head and she heard him whisper the word no as he blinked hard. She was thankful the thousand-yard stare had left him. She hoped never to see him with that lost look in his eyes again. But then, Charlotte knew that soon, she would never see him again. He was home, and she would be going back to Fernandina Beach with her parents and without him.

"Sarah might be there," he swallowed hard, and he knew, he couldn't act like a coward now, not when he was finally home. "You're right Doctor Taylor; I need to go take a look." Shaun took a deep breath, and he left the buggy that Lang had rented in Woodville, the horrible tremor was easy to be seen in both of his hands as he climbed down.

He had left here more than two years ago, and the house looked just as he had left it, Shaun thought. The clapboards were all clean and white. The windows were even open, and then he knew, this was Sarah's house too, she was probably living here, why wouldn't she be? He took a deep breath when he realized she might even have remarried and she might have babies of her own now. He had been gone a long time. Too long. He probably wasn't even a memory to her now.

With his heart slamming into his chest, Shaun walked up onto the front porch, and he knew that someone was living in this house. He pulled open the screen door knowing that he was fixing to – at long last, see Sarah again face to face.

"Shane," Sarah said his name in a surprised voice when she saw her husband walk in the front door of their house. "Where did you get that hat?" She saw her husband take off his hat and look at the hat before he then look back at her, at Sarah

"The store," he answered her, and she gave him a soft laugh.

"I thought you were working in the north field with Ethan and Uncle Allen, and here you were at the store buying a hat. You slacker," she teased and came to her husband wrapping her arms around his waist. "I've missed you. I'm so glad you're home."

"Sarah?" he spoke her name as a question, and she pulled away and looked up into his beautiful grass green eyes. "I'm confused," he said simply and again she laughed, and he took a step back away from her, the tremor was worse than ever in his hands, and his head felt like it was cracked open.

"What's wrong Shane?" Sarah had never seen Shane like this. He was distant and acting like he didn't know her. She saw his hands shaking, the look on his face and for a moment she thought of the shellshock that had been such a large part of their marriage. She thought of Shane killing German soldiers in the night and in his dreams trying to protect Shaun.

"Something smells awesome," Sarah frowned and spun around quick seeing Shane coming in the back door with Uncle Allen and Ethan. She took at least four steps back and away from the man in the front hall that she thought was Shane and cried out as the reality of who he was came crashing down upon her, the cry caused the three men coming in the door to look up and rush into the hall where she was.

"Shaun!" Ethan was the first to cry out, and he saw their Uncle Allen move into the hall, Allen reaching for and pulling Shaun close.

Shane looked at his wife and then at his brother then back at his wife. "Oh God," he put his head in his hands and walked out the back screen door. Allen heard his nephew Shane leaving the house and recognized this dilemma for what it was. Shane was married now to Sarah and here stood Shaun, Sarah's husband, not dead and finally home from the war.

"Uncle Allen," Sarah cried when Allen's eyes turned to her eyes and she knew that he knew what she was thinking. "Shane," she called out for her husband and started for the back door seeing him sitting on the step with his head held in his hands. Ethan was standing in the kitchen holding his stomach as though he were going to be sick.

"Ethan," Allen said his son in law's name and was relieved when Ethan looked up at him with clear eyes, the younger man wasn't reliving the moment the twins were shot again as Allen had feared when he had first looked at Ethan and saw his daughter's husband looking pale and stressed. The younger man seemed to be dealing with Shaun's return, though clearly shaken.

"I'm all right," Ethan said looking at Shaun standing silent and looking horribly confused in the hallway of his own home which Shaun hadn't been in for over two years.

"Uncle Allen, I don't understand what's happened," the twin in the hall said seeing Sarah looking from her husband on the back porch who was rocking and moaning and then back to looking at him in the hall. It seemed as though Sarah were trapped between him and his brother.

"We thought you were dead," Allen said to his nephew. "Sarah fell in love with Shane while you've been gone and they married." There, it was out, and it was said, Allen thought and he saw Sarah almost fall and Ethan moved to catch her.

"Uncle Allen," his nephew looked past him and out the back door where his twin brother sat on the porch step. "Uncle Allen, Sarah can't be married to Shane. Uncle Allen, I'm Shane."

Ethan felt Sarah go limp in his arms and he knew that she had fainted and then he heard the moans coming louder from the twin on the back porch that for a year everyone had thought was Shane. "Are you certain you're Shane?" Ethan demanded to know as Sarah revived in Ethan's arms and now clung to his hands for support.

Shane Blackburn looked at his Uncle and then back to his best friend Ethan, and he nodded his head. "I'm sure now. Oh God, I know who I am. I was hurt badly, shot eleven times and almost buried alive. I spent three days on the battlefield before I was found. I didn't know then who I was, but I know now who I am. I'm Shane." As he said, this Sarah moaned and looked at him. "I couldn't talk. I had screamed so long and loud begging for help on the battlefield that when I went to talk nothing would come out of my mouth. And I wasn't able to write because I was shot up, and then this tremor," he held out his hand. "I know who I am now, I know with no doubt in my mind. I'm Shane Blackburn."

"What did you come to my bedroom window to show me that you were going to buy for this house before the war? And what did you tell me?" Sarah stood up and left Ethan's arms going to the man claiming to be Shane Blackburn.

Shane smiled and touched a strand of her hair as Sarah came close to him. "I had the Sears catalogue, and I wanted you to have the best stove. I even ordered it for you. And I told you I couldn't live here with you and Shaun, because I loved you." Sarah Blackburn looked to her husband sitting on the back porch rocking back and forth and moaning out loud, his hands on each side of his head.

"Did you buy a book in Tallahassee near the train station?" Shane shook his head.

"No, if I wanted a book I went to Uncle Allen's office at Riverbend, he has an awesome library there."

"All this time, I didn't even know my own husband," Sarah said in a gasp. "I didn't even suspect." She started to move to the backdoor and Allen put a hand on her arm to stop her.

"Be careful, Sarah," he said softly and went with her out the back door not seeing that Ethan and Shane had followed them both.

She sat down next to her husband, and she felt him fall over onto her, putting his head into her lap and she touched his cheek feeling how wet his face was. She remembered down at the river after Lester had violated her body and the soap, how he had been so caring, so gentle with her. And she remembered their wedding night, how the river had made things fresh and new and clean and right for them both. And she knew that right now he needed from her what he had given to her.

"Shaun," she said his real name for the first time in a long time, and she felt his head nod. "We need to go down to the river," she said in her gentle voice, and she helped him sit up not looking at the three men on the back porch. "Shaun, the river," she said, and he looked down at her nodding his head before he lifted her into his arms and her arms went around his neck.

"What is she doing?" Ethan asked as he moved to the edge of the porch watching Shaun carry his wife down to the grassy bank near their house. He saw Shane beside him and Allen stepping out into the yard.

The three men watched as Shaun walked into the river with his wife and then Sarah turned in his arms and started to kiss him. Shaun was devouring her within a second. "They don't need an audience," Allen said and he pulled Ethan and Shane into the house. "And you need to talk," he said to Shane. "But first," he hugged Shane close, "I'm glad you're home, you've been missed." Allen looked at Ethan and saw Ethan looking at him, "What are you still doing here, son? Get to my house and ring the alarm bell, so everyone within three miles is at my house when I get home with the twins. We might have a wait," he nodded his head toward the river, "so you can walk home and maybe stop and kiss your wife along the way. But tell no one of Shane's return," Allen said firmly to his much-loved son in law. "This is for Shane and Shaun to tell."

Ethan smiled at Shane and slapped Shane on the back. "I'm worried about Shaun, but it seems Sarah knows what she's doing. I'll see you at the house, and you can tell us all how you managed to get here. I want to know where you've been."

"I don't care where he's been, I only care that he's home," Allen said, and he watched Ethan leave the house. "My daughter Bethany has a fine husband," he said, and he saw Shane agree with him.

"Can you excuse me a minute, Uncle Allen?" Shane asked looking out the door to the buggy holding his family. "I'll be back!" He ran down the sandy road waving his hat, "Charlotte! Charlotte!" he saw her stand up in the buggy and then she jumped down and was running to him. "I'm not Shaun! Charlotte, I'm not Shaun! I'm Shane! I'm Shane!" Her arms went around his neck, and he walked with her wrapped in his arms to her parents in the buggy, Hannah hanging over the side with a smile on her face. "Doctor Taylor, Shaun has been here all the time. I'm Shane. I never married Sarah. My brother married Sarah."

"Shane," Lang breathed the name and shook their heroes hand with a smile covering his face. "It's nice to meet you."

"I didn't remember until Sarah called me Shane and then it came rushing back at me who I really am. Can you come to the house? Apparently all this time my brother has thought he was me." Lang nodded his head and turned the horse and buggy toward the house leaving Shane kissing Charlotte in the middle of the road.

Allen Blackburn stood on the porch looking out into the yard as the buggy pulled up and thinking once he had today's facts clear in his mind; he might have a story to tell his grandchildren. "I'm Allen Blackburn," he said taking the hand of a man that was as tall as he was with eyes that looked purple.

"Doctor Langston Taylor and my wife Holly and our daughter Hannah, our other daughter is in your nephew's arms," he teased, and Allen invited them into the house where they sat talking, waiting on the twins to join them.

"I love you," Sarah said as she helped her husband take off his wet shirt and throw it on the grassy bank. He was kissing her neck. He was sliding his hands down her body, and she pushed herself against him as he undid the buttons at the front of her dress. "Only you can make love to me like this. How did I not know that you were my Shaun? I love you so much."

"I love you, Sarah," he breathed her in as the river cleaned them both. The river made everything fresh and new. The river which was a part of them flowed through them, around them, and about them as they made love, Sarah to her Shaun and Shaun to his Sarah.

"Charlotte," Shane said her name now knowing he was Shane and he was free, free to kiss her and make love to her and marry her and grow old with her all the days of their lives. "I haven't asked your daddy yet, but will you marry me? I don't want to live another day without you as my wife." He saw Charlotte chewing on her bottom lip, her arms were still around his neck, and her feet were a good twelve inches off the ground as he held her to him. "Please, say yes," he begged her, and she nodded her head.

"As many times as you want me to say yes," she felt his lips cover her mouth, and she laughed as he held her close. "yes, yes and yes again."

"Can we marry soon? I've been aching for you for almost a year now. When I was lying in that bed all bandaged up, it was your voice that kept me going Charlotte. I knew I had to have you the first minute I heard you; that's why I struggled with all my might to write Yank on that paper for your Daddy."

"I knew I had to be with you too Shane. Only I knew you as the name I gave to you." She heard him laugh and she laughed with him. "Malachi," she said the name out loud.

"Thank goodness I wasn't silent for four hundred years," Shane laughed, and they finally reached the porch, and he took her inside his home, a home that would be her home as well.

"Uncle Allen is ringing the alarm bell," Sarah said pulling on her wet dress and coming up out of the river. "Shaun, we have to get dry and clean clothes on. Shane is really home." She reached back and pulled her husband up and onto the bank as he reached for his pants and pulled them on.

"Sarah, how do I explain?" he asked, and she touched his beautiful face.

"Shaun, let's just take this a step at a time. Let's hear Shane out. You've not even had a chance to talk to him yet." She saw he didn't put on his shirt; he left it on the bank and pulled her dripping wet to the house.

Shane was standing at the back door when Shaun opened it, and the brothers stood staring at one another for several long moments. "I missed you so much," Shaun finally broke the silence and fell into his brother's arms. Sarah looked at Allen in the breezeway, and she saw that they had company. People that she didn't know were standing behind Allen, and she wondered who the company was, but she didn't ask. Shaun and Shane were together again, and that was what she focused on.

"Go change your clothes," Allen said when the brothers came apart. "Shane and I will go saddle up some horses for us all to ride up to Riverbend. Ethan keeps ringing that alarm bell like there is a fire. I didn't tell him to ring it but once." Allen laughed and turned to his new friend Lang. "Well, what are you waiting for, let's go saddle some horses. We can't all ride in that buggy of yours." Allen reached down and picked Hannah up putting her on his shoulders, and Lang looked back at Holly and Charlotte who were smiling at him before he left the house.

Heath Ferrell rode into the yard at Riverbend, and he saw Alicia standing on the front porch. "I don't know what's happening," she called out to her brother in law. "Ethan won't say anything other than Allen sent him to ring the bell to bring everyone here quick."

Heath looked at Ethan pulling on the rope to ring the bell. Bethany was standing next to her husband, and he saw her shrug her shoulders letting Heath know that she had no idea why this ringing of the bell either.

Levi walked to his son with Cecily by his side. "You want to give me a hint to what's happening?" Levi asked his son, and he winked at Bethany who slapped her husband playfully on the shoulder.

"I knew your Daddy didn't guess about our baby," Bethany said to her husband, and Ethan hugged her.

"I honestly didn't tell him, Bethany," Ethan again defended himself while smiling at his father and giving the bell another ring.

"Mama, I see Emily and Heather coming," Bethany pointed into the distance and Alicia wave to her sister in law and niece as the two women galloping toward the house on their horses. As always, Alicia was impressed at how well Emily rode a horse. Emily rode better than a man, but then Emily was one hundred percent, Blackburn. "Oh look," Bethany cried out and pointed down toward the river where Mary and Seth were riding in with their youngest son. "Michael's home from school," Bethany called out loud and waved to her cousin that she hadn't seen in years as he was away getting his law degree.

Jenny and Julie came out of the house and told their mama they had food on the table and Jenny added that she hoped Aunt Mary had thought to bring rolls. "This isn't a party," Alicia said as she hugged Emily who was coming up the steps followed by Heather. "Something serious has happened if Allen has Ethan ringing the alarm bell."

"What's going on?" Seth yelled as his youngest son Michael bounced up the porch steps and hugged his cousins before going to his Aunt Alicia and Aunt Emily who welcomed him home with open arms and wondered out loud if his coming home was the reason for the bell being rung. "Michael surprised us about an hour ago," Seth yelled to Alicia from the front yard assuring her that his youngest son's arrival had nothing to do with the bell sounding. "So you know of no reason Allen is having the alarm sounded?"

"I only know Allen told Ethan to ring the alarm!" Alicia said to her brother in law seeing Seth helping Mary out of the buggy. "Well, Michael's home," Seth said informing them all of what they already knew as Michael was on the porch passing out hugs to his family.

The Taylor family was in the buggy riding alongside Shane who was next to his brother Shaun. Allen turned in his saddle and looked back at Shaun with a worried frown on his face. "You all right?" Allen called out to his nephew, and he saw Shaun lift a hand in a wave holding on to Sarah who was sitting on the horse in front of Shaun.

"I am now," Shaun said this while looking at Shane seeing that Shane was looking at him. "I was trying to reach you," he said to his brother, and Shane nodded in understanding of Shaun's words.

"I saw you," Shane said and reached down in the buggy for Charlotte's hand. Their Uncle Allen was in front of them. "I was mad because you weren't behind me like I told you to be. Then you were shot,"

"I heard you screaming even with that mask over your face," Shaun finished for his brother feeling like it was a healing to talk about this.

"I heard you screaming for me as well," Shane added and saw he Shaun nod.

"You two can finish this conversation at the dinner table. Everyone needs to hear what happened," Allen said as Riverbend came into view and he heard Ethan ring the alarm bell again. "What is that boy doing ringing that bell like that? The whole family is already on the porch."

"He's ringing it and pointing to us!" Shane said. "And there's my Mama and Daddy," Shane looked down at Charlotte, and she let go of his hand and nodded her head with a smile. Allen saw Shane kick his horse and he was waving his hat above his head calling out to his mother. Allen saw Mary turn on the porch and see both of her twin boys galloping toward her, one calling out for her and then she was running, and Shane jumped off of his horse in the yard and picked his mother up in his arms, his father slamming into him and almost knocking him down.

"Shaun!" his cousin Heather called his name, and he saw her leaning over the porch rail right before his brother Michael grabbed him as he held his mother and his father.

There was complete chaos on the front porch. Alicia had turned away and was obviously sobbing. Heather kept saying the real hero was home. Julie and Jenny were hugging their mother, and Bethany was looking from Ethan to Shaun to Shane thinking they had all come home at last. They had all survived the war.

"Shaun, oh Shaun," Mary cried looking up at her returned son. "Where have you been?" Everyone on the porch stopped and held silent when Mary asked this question, all of them leaning over the rail except Alicia who was still crying with her back turned and Ethan who was smiling at Sarah. "Shaun?" Mary said the name again and then looked at her son on the horse holding on to Sarah. "Shaun!" she cried, and everyone looked to Sarah and the brother on the horse. "All this time you've been Shaun!" Mary cried out, and she saw her son nod with Sarah in front of him. "Shane!" Mary screamed and threw herself again into her son's arms as he already held her.

"I don't understand," Heather said looking from one twin to the other.

"I didn't know," Shaun said looking at his family from the horse he sat on with his wife. "I don't know what happened to me," he said louder, his eyes meeting Ethan's eyes from across the porch. "That man kept asking me my name," he looked down at Sarah. "In the field hospital, he kept asking me over and over and over what my name was, and he wouldn't be quiet and leave me alone. And I kept dreaming I was looking for Shane and then I yelled out for Shane to that man that wouldn't leave me alone about who I was, and the next thing I know Ethan was calling me Shane." He saw Ethan nodding his head and saw Ethan step forward on the porch.

"I heard you call out your name as Shane," Ethan said, and the family looked at him. "I thought that you were saying you were Shane." Ethan looked from one twin to the other and stated the obvious, "You look just like Shane."

"I was so confused," Shaun continued. "I kept thinking to myself, even on the voyage home, I'm not Shane, I'm Shaun. But remember fellows?" He looked at Shane and Ethan. "I was seasick on the trip over, but Shane wasn't, and on the trip home, I wasn't seasick in the least. So that made me even more confused, and everyone kept calling me Shane. I really thought I was Shane." He looked down at his wife, "I thought for certain you would know me. But you were mad at me for not bringing Shaun home." Shaun then looked at his parents. "I thought Daddy or Mama would know me. Or even Uncle Allen, but all of you called me Shane. Even you Uncle Heath," he said looking at the Uncle who had been one of his best friends all of his life. He then looked at his brother, and his voice broke when he tried to speak, "I didn't want you to be dead. So I became you, and you weren't dead." Shane was nodding his head to his brother, and he left his parents when Shaun and Sarah got off the horse.

"I really understand, Shaun. I was confused as well. I honestly thought I was you too." Shane looked down at Sarah and smiled. "So in a way, you finally fell in love with me," he laughed and kissed her cheek. "It's good to be home, and this is my fiancée Charlotte."

Shane heard his mother gasp as he lifted Charlotte out of the buggy and turned to help Hannah down while Lang reached up for his wife, Holly.

"We need to go to Mama," Shaun said and smiled at Sarah and taking her hand, he pulled her to his mother followed by his twin who came behind them holding on to Charlotte.

"I can't believe I didn't know you," Mary touched Shaun's cheek and looked into his eyes. "I can only tell you two apart when you're together."

"Mama, I hope you brought your rolls," Shane said, and she laughed hugging him again and loving that he was hugging her right back

"I didn't, but I have some at home," she said, "And who is this?" Mary asked reaching for Charlotte and taking both of the young woman's hands.

"My fiancée if her parents approve of me as a son in law," Shane said turning to Lang and Holly. "Mother, Father, this is the Doctor that found me in the hospital in England and brought me home. His daughter Charlotte nursed me back to health. They saved me, Mama."

"How do we ever thank you," Seth stepped forward and took Lang's hand, and hugged Holly.

"Your son saved our little girl from drowning, so we're even," Lang said, and he turned to Shane. "Shane, I've long admired you for the hero that you are, Holly, and I welcome you as we did almost a year ago into your family. You'll always have our love and support. Yes, you may marry our daughter." Holly hugged Shane and then looked at Shaun before saying

"They really are identical."

"Come inside everyone," Alicia said and opened the door while Ethan rang the alarm bell again and laughed at the murderous look Allen gave to him before he ran into the house behind his wife putting his arms around her from behind and lifting Bethany playfully off of the floor.

"I feel like the war really is over," Ethan whispered into Bethany's ear, and she turned in his arms.

"Welcome home, Ethan. We're all complete again. Shane is here." She laughed and stood on tiptoes when Shane came to her and hugged her close before introducing his Charlotte. "She's beautiful," Bethany said, and Shane pinched Bethany's cheek.

"Bethy," he used her nickname, the nickname that only he used for her, and she realized that all these months, the twin they thought was Shane had never once used that nickname because Shaun never did, it was Shane's special nickname for her.

The plates were on the sideboard; the food spread out on the table. Everyone was talking at once and then finding their seats and passing the food to one another. "Well I want to hear where Shane's been all this time," Allen said when plates were full, and everyone was eating. All eyes turned to Shane who was sitting beside Charlotte, her mother on the other side of him with Lang next to Holly, their daughter Hannah was in the kitchen eating at the children's table with Julie and Jenny and Levi and Cecily's three young daughters. Shane looked at his Taylor family, saw Lang head nod and put down his fork ready to tell of his journey home with Lang's support and silent offer of any help.

"I was shot when Ethan and Shaun were shot. I know you all know that part of what happened to me. And the battle went on around me while I lay still. I must have moved or something, because a German soldier came at me and beat me in the face with the butt of his gun. After that, I decided I would be best to just lay still. Medics came out into the woods, and they were gathering up all the injured, but they didn't get me. No one realized I was alive. I was so hot in that gas mask that I couldn't get the thing off, and too, my face was swollen from the beating I took by that German. I had screamed so loud and long for Shaun and Ethan too, that I couldn't talk anymore. My throat was closed up and so dry. I laid there waiting for help, and no one came. I watched the sunset three different times and rise the same amount of times, but no one came for me. And then when they did come for me, it was to bury me. I couldn't talk. I couldn't make any noise at all. But I moved, and finally, I forced myself to sit up. I didn't want to get buried alive, and someone called out they had a live one. They brought a stretcher, but they couldn't get it to me, too many bodies were in the way, so many bodies." Shane fell silent looking down at the food on his plate. He reached for his glass and drank some of his Aunt Alicia's sweet tea. He looked up and saw his brother Shaun and then Ethan. "I thought you fellows were in the crowd of those dead bodies," his voice broke, and he took another sip of the tea feeling Charlotte touch his arm and he covered her hand with his own.

"How did you get to the stretcher?" Heather asked, and Shane looked at her, he had known for a long time that his cousin Heather didn't like him. She compared him to Shaun and thought he fell short in all areas. He wondered what she must think of him now, sitting here at the table telling what happened to him and seeing he was about to break down in tears. She probably thought even less of him. He looked away from her and at Lang and then Holly and finally at Charlotte. It didn't matter what Heather thought of him. He looked around the table at his family, and he knew he was loved and respected.

"I got up, and I walked out," Shane said, his eyes locking for a moment with Heather's eyes. "I was shot eleven times. They said I was the most heavily bandaged man in the hospital, and no other man survived being shot as many times as I was." He stopped talking, and he smiled while looking down at Charlotte. "And then she found me," he said softly and heard her soft laugh as Charlotte leaned against him. "For months I laid in a hospital in London, England. Doctor Taylor and Charlotte took care of me. I couldn't talk, but I somehow wrote on a paper that I was a Yank and when they left England to come home to Florida, they brought me home with them." Shaun looked at Lang, "Would you explain to them?"

"I'm Doctor Lang Taylor for anyone that might have missed who I am," he smiled to everyone at the table. "When we found Shane, he was suffering from shellshock. I think our Shane wasn't the only one suffering from that," he looked at Shaun and then Ethan too. "About seven to twenty-one percent of the troops returning from the war suffer from mutism. They can't talk, and most of those men also have a form of amnesia, like both Shane and Shaun had. Shaun had all of his memories, except he didn't know which brother he was, and he was dependent on others that knew them both to help him know who he was. When everyone called him Shane, he thought that was who he was. And Shane, who was living with us, had no idea who he was, no memories at all of his past. When he did remember, like his brother, he was confused over which brother he was. All Shane could remember while living with us was Sarah," Lang nodded to Shaun's wife. "When my wife and I went to the war office and received his records we saw Sarah listed as his wife. Shane had no wife. So we all assumed that Shane was Shaun and that Shane had died in France.

"And Shaun," Lang spoke to the twin that was always Sarah's rightful husband. "We had some rough seas on the trip home with Shane, and he was very seasick. You probably were more sensitive on your first voyage whereas your brother wasn't. But he was seasick in rough waves on the crossing home. I cannot fathom how you must have felt not knowing for certain who you were. But you survived, and you made it through, and now you're home with your loving family."

"Can you please tell us more about this shellshock?" Bethany asked, and Lang nodded his head.

"Some of the men that have shellshock have tremors, like our Shane. Some men can't walk or sit up; they lose all mobility. Others might have night terrors and worse. The list of what these war heroes suffer from shellshock is long. And a man may have one symptom, or he might have them all. It's going to be years of research following this war before we know for certain what causes shellshock and we might never know. We need to focus on not having another war again, that will be the cure for shellshock."

"Some might relive the battle in their bedroom several nights a month," Sarah said taking Shaun's hand into her own.

"That's very common, I'm sorry you have that happening," Lang said to both Sarah and Shaun.

"Will they get well?" Bethany asked seeing Ethan leaning forward and knowing that was the question her husband wanted to ask.

"They are finding that over time the men are getting better. Lots of love and comfort and understanding," Lang said looking at Bethany. "This is hard on the families too, but if we all pull together, and I know my family will join your family, and support and love these heroes, then yes, there should be a recovery."

"Doctor Taylor," Allen said looking at his wife and seeing her nod her head, "our home is your home for as long as you would like to stay. And please, know that our door is always open and we accept your family as our family."

"And thank you for saving my son," Mary said looking from Lang to Holly.

"Wait until everyone sees us together in church on Sunday," Shaun laughed, "it's not the Reverend Farmer's Sunday to come out. Which of you two want to explain to the congregation how Shane came home and how Sarah didn't marry Shane, but she married me twice?" Shaun looked from his Uncle Allen and then to his father.

"I was always the one that spoke well," Seth said looking at his older brother Allen. "But as the years have passed, my brother has grown into a great communicator. I'll pass the pulpit to him on Sunday."

Allen looked around his large dining table. Levi and Cecily were at one end with their son Ethan and his daughter Bethany to their side. His sister Emily and her husband Heath were on the other side with their daughter Heather by their side. He saw Shaun and Sarah seeming to only have eyes for one another next to his brother Seth and Seth's wife Mary, and their youngest son Michael was next to his wife Alicia who was holding their baby son Shaun Allen on her lap. He looked to the other side of the table, and he saw Shane with his fiancée Charlotte and Charlotte's parents, Lang and Holly Taylor, and he could hear the younger girls, his daughters Jenny and Julie and Lang and Holly's daughter Hannah and Cecily and Levi's three daughters in the kitchen talking.

"So Shane," Levi Tucker spoke, and Shane looked up at him. "Are you coming home to work this place? We could sure use you. I have the sawmill working seven days a week, and we need all the help we can get to keep this place planted in trees.

"If it's all right with Charlotte," Shane looked down into her beautiful eyes, and he knew he would do whatever she wanted. "I would like to live at Twin River," he looked over at his brother when he saw Charlotte nod. "If it's all right with you two," he spoke to Shaun and Sarah.

"We built that house, you and me, to grow old in together with our families. We've always been together Shane and truth be told, being away from you for over a year, I don't want us to ever be apart for long ever again. The only problem is, I've thought all this time that I was you and I've been living on your side of the house." Shaun saw his brother laugh and shake his head.

"That's not a problem, Charlotte and I will move into the side we built for you. We'll make this work," he said looking back down at his wife.

"There is one thing I need to get from my old room," Shaun said, and Sarah saw him turn red and look down at her. "A book," he saw her hand cover her mouth.

"A book?" Shane looked at Sarah and remembered she asked him about a book back at the house a bit ago. "I think I would like to see this book." Sarah burst out into giggles, and Shaun told Shane where to find the book in his room.

"It's a good book," Shaun assured his brother and gave him a wink.

"I can't believe I have my sons back," Mary started to cry, and Seth pulled her close rocking her in his arms, their joy was endless.

"Mama, you can cry all you want, after you make your yeast rolls for me, I've missed them, Mama," Shane said winking at her and Shaun agreed causing their mother to laugh, she was known for making the best yeast rolls in all of the county.

Darkness had fallen, and Alicia had opened up all the bedrooms upstairs, the younger girls were all sleeping in one room so that the married members of the family could have their own room to sleep in. No one was going home tonight. On the back of the warm stove, the yeast rolls were rising that Mary had made for everyone to enjoy with breakfast in the morning while Cecily, Holly, and Alicia sat at the kitchen table talking and enjoying the evening together.

Heather Ferrell stood on the porch looking at Sarah and Shaun on the porch swing so wrapped up into one another that they didn't notice anyone else was out on the porch with them. On the other end in a rocking chair, Ethan was holding Bethany on his lap, and they were rocking back and forth totally unaware Heather was watching them. She saw her cousin Shane come out of the door, and he sat down on the top step with Charlotte beside him not seeing Heather near him.

She had been wrong. All these years she had thought of him as a coward because he lost to Shaun. He lost to Shaun in everything, and he didn't mind. He had made her think that he was weak and she had been so certain when the brothers went off to war that to trust Shaun to care for Shane was certain death for Shaun because she knew that Shane failed at everything he did. Heather sat down on the porch rocking chair thinking about their childhood and knowing the truth. Shane never really failed. Shane just did things differently than Shaun. Shane didn't mind losing to Shaun. He didn't care if he won or not. And he was the hero of the war. He may not have saved Shaun, but he tried just as Shaun had tried to save him. And he had been shot eleven times.

"It's all right to feel as you do, Heather," Shane said softly and turned to look up at his little cousin who he had grown up with and loved all of his life. "You were right in a way when you told me the day we left for the war that I was a coward."

"Shane, I'm sorry about what I said," Heather was quick to say and left the chair to move onto the porch step next to him seeing Charlotte listening closely to their conversation.

"Heather, the truth is, every battle we went into I nearly wet my pants," Shane laughed when he said this though he was serious. "Inside I was a coward, so you were right. And I know you always favored Shaun and that's all right. I love you even though you never loved me." He put his arm around her, and she leaned into him.

"I was so wrong about you," she said softly. "You were shot eleven times?" she asked this in a horror-filled voice.

"It wasn't that bad," Shane said lightly. "Three times in the arm and three times in the leg and five times in the side and just next to my ribs. The worst was that German soldier that wanted to make sure I was good and dead and beat me in the face with the butt of his gun. I was swollen up so badly that I couldn't hardly swallow."

"Oh Shane," he heard his Aunt Emily say behind him. "All I keep thinking is how glad we are to have our boys home and not what all three of you went through." Heath came up behind his wife, Emily and within a few seconds, he was sitting on the step next to Shane, Charlotte, and Heather.

"Remember when you boys and I climbed that huge and mighty oak down by the river near our place and we got to the top and we all agreed we could see the Gulf of Mexico?" Shane nodded his head seeing Shaun and Sarah were now with them, and Bethany and Ethan were standing at the porch rail. "I'm glad we all grew up together," Heath said to the younger ones on the porch. "Allen and Seth and I grew up on the banks of that river with our daddies watching over us. Then you younger ones came along," he looked at Sarah and Shaun, Heather and Shane and Bethany and Jenny and Julie, "and Allen and Seth and I got to grow up all over again with you bunch of kids. Allen is right, that river is in our families' blood. The river is a part of us, and who we are, it's what makes us whole."

Sarah leaned back into Shaun's arms and reached up to hold his face, "a whole new generation is coming for you to grow up with all over again Uncle Heath," Sarah said, and she put Shaun's hand over her abdomen. "We won't have to wait long," she said, and she heard Shaun gasp before turning her around and pulling her close.

"A baby," Bethany said looking up at Shaun. "We'll have our babies at the same time, Sarah," Bethany smiled. "We may not have twins, but we'll have babies that will grow up together."

"Charlotte and I will make sure we have one on the way soon as well," Shane said, and he hugged Charlotte close hearing her gasp. "Why aren't you old and married, Heather?" Shane turned and teased his cousin not seeing how quiet she had become.

"The love of my life died at Camp Leon before he even went to war," she spoke softly, and everyone went still and silent to hear what she was saying. "James Jerald, he got sick in the camp and died before you boys even signed up."

"I didn't know you were in love with James," Bethany said, and she saw Heather nodding her head.

"There's no one else for me," Heather said firmly.

"You never know, Heather," Allen said coming out onto the porch with his little son Shaun Allen in his arms and Seth and Lang with him. "I swore I would never marry Alicia Steel," he saw his wife coming toward him with the other women, and Alicia was smiling at him. Allen reached for her hand, and he pulled her close. "I'm so thankful I did marry her, and I would marry her a million times over."

"And I would let you, Allen Blackburn," his Alicia said before he turned and kissed her not caring that his son was between them and the whole family was watching what they were doing. He would set the example of a devoted loving husband to the younger ones.

"Now I see why you thought my parents were your Uncle Allen and Aunt Alicia," Charlotte said looking at Shane.

"You thought the Taylors were us?" Alicia asked Shane, and he nodded his head.

"The first time I laid eyes on the two of them together, he was jumping off the ferry and into her arms," Shane pointed to Lang and Holly. "And they were behaving like you two," Shane laughed looking to his Aunt and Uncle while hugging his Charlotte. "Don't worry. I hope everyone confuses me for you both one day real soon as well. You have a true love that can stand up to anything." Shane looked to Lang and nodded his head, "Your daughter and I will have the same deep love you and your wife have. I give you my word."

"I'm honored you saw and admired my love for my wife and want to give that love to my daughter," Lang said pulling his Holly close, her hand coming up to touch his face before he kissed her.

"The only thing that lasts besides the river," Allen said looking around the porch at his family, "is the love we hand down to our children. The example of love we set and share with one another that our children learn from. Thank you, Shane, for seeing that deep love in the Taylor's and thinking of your Aunt Alicia and me."

"So, can someone ride to Woodville tomorrow and send a telegram to the Reverend Farmer to come out and marry us?" Shane asked, and he heard Lang groan. "You're not losing a daughter,

Doctor Taylor, you're gaining a son," Shane laughed, and Lang laughed with him.

"Yes, I need another son." Lang looked at Levi Tucker holding his wife Cecily close and thought there was another man that set the example on how to love. Levi Tucker's wife was leaning into him, and he only had eyes for her. "While he was recovering, Shane put a new roof on my house, he painted the whole place top to bottom, and he replaced some of the gingerbread trim that had rotted." Lang turned to Shane and saw him smiling with pride. "Every few months you and Charlotte have to come home so you can fill up my wood box," Lang teased, and Shane assured Lang that they would come home.

"What river do you live on, Lang?" Allen asked, and he heard Shane laugh.

"We don't live on a river, Allen. We live on the Atlantic Ocean near Fernandina Beach. You'll have to come over and visit. All of you will have to come over. Our doors are always open to our family."

"Honestly, we would love to have you come stay with us," Holly said looking from Cecily to Alicia, to Mary, Sarah and Bethany, and finally Charlotte. "Family means the world to us." She felt Lang pull her into his arms from behind her and he leaned into him. When he found her all those years ago, she never dreamed that she would be a part of something like this. Lang had changed her whole world.

"Levi just took Cecily to bed," Lang whispered into Holly's ear and he pointed to Allen walking into the house with Alicia and up the stairs. "We'll see everyone in the morning," Lang said to the family left on the porch.

"Lang," Holly cried out as he picked her up in his arms and started for the door of house looking back at Shane.

"I may need your help fishing me out of the ocean, Shane. But I can still carry my wife upstairs." He winked at Shane right before he and Holly disappeared into the dark house, and Shane heard him call out, "Charlotte, you're sleeping with Hannah!"

"Yes, Daddy," his daughter answered looking up into Shane's eyes aware that she would have him forever now.

Shane Blackburn had finally and at last, come home...

The churchyard was full as the families arrived. The Reverend Farmer had come out to marry another Blackburn, and they had to spend time explaining the return of Shane and Shaun. The Reverend was honest and told everyone that he really didn't understand but when he saw both twins, he was thrilled. Alicia had organized with the ladies in the area to bring food, and they would have dinner on the grounds after services. The smell of fresh made pies and rolls and meats filled the church as everyone came in.

In the past week, Allen found that he had a new best friend in Lang Taylor. And Holly and Alicia had grown very close. They already had made plans with Levi and Cecily to get together the first week of September at Lang and Holly's house on the beach for a week.

Lang took his wife by the hand and sat with Levi and Cecily in the church watching Allen herd in the large family. "I don't know about you Levi," Lang said, "but I feel like we're a part of something larger than ourselves."

"They call themselves a clan," Levi laughed. "I personally call us all together, a crowd." Cecily laughed and leaned into her husband

"Family, by blood, by marriage, doesn't matter, we're still a family," Cecily said seeing her handsome son Ethan come into the church and she felt certain that he was going to be all right. She and Levi didn't have to worry about Ethan anymore. Their son had, at last, survived the war and come home to his family.

"I'm going to be sick," Sarah said to Shaun, and he thought she didn't sound herself. Morning sickness he was coming to learn was not a good thing. "I need to step outside." Her husband took her to the doors of the church, and she fanned herself in the fresh air as she looked and saw her parents and Eddie coming toward them. Shaun raised his hand and waved as Eddie came running to him.

"Shaun," Eddie said and hugged him, and he looked at Eddie realizing that ever since he had returned home, Eddie had called him Shaun. They had corrected Eddie over and over telling the sweet young man that he was Shane.

"He knew," Shaun said to Sarah who was looking at Eddie. "All this time, Eddie knew who I was."

"Shaun," Eddie said again and then bounced into the church with his parents.

The Reverend Farmer married Shane to Charlotte after services. Shaun with Sarah were going home with Bethany and Ethan for a week to give the newly wedded couple some time alone. Sarah watched Shane riding away with Charlotte in front of him on the horse, and she remembered the two times she had married Shaun. Two times they had made love anew.

"I still cannot believe I didn't know you," Sarah turned into Shaun's arms and looked up at him. "I've loved you for as long as I can remember and I didn't know you were you the second time we married and made love." Her husband smiled down into her eyes and gave her a long deep kiss before raising his head and looking into her eyes again.

"I gave the book to Shane."

"Oh you did not," Sarah said looking back down the road and seeing Shane and Charlotte were out of sight.

"Oh yes I did," Shane laughed out loud. "You and me. Shane and Charlotte. Bethany and Ethan, and babies on the river. A whole new generation of Blackburns."

"I love you, Shaun." Sarah looked up into his eyes and smiled. "Forever and ever and ever."

Shane was humbled by the fact that this beautiful girl had married him. She had nursed him when he was near death, changed his bandages, and cleaned his wounds, and she stood by him, even giving him a name when he had none. And now she was leaving her home, her parents, and her sister to start a whole new life here. He knew she was special. He knew that he would love her for ten lifetimes.

"I promised your daddy I'd bring you home for at least two weeks to visit every three months," Shane said as he lifted Charlotte from his horse and lowered her to the ground. "If you need to go more often than that, I'll understand and make sure we go when you say." Charlotte put her arms around his neck and laid her head on his chest knowing that she had married a very good man.

"Can we go and kiss some more now?" she asked, and she saw his smile seconds before he swung her up and into his arms.

Shane went up the steps on the porch and looked back down the road. Shaun was going to stop by and put up his horse for him; after that, no one was going to come for days. They had this place to themselves. He was home, Shane thought. He had come home with the woman that he had loved for months, and she was his wife. "I'll be gentle with you," he whispered as he went up the stairs and into their new room.

"I trust you," she said as he lowered her onto their bed.

"Remember the day?" he saw her nod her head and reached to undo the buttons of her dress and saw her breathing heavy as he was also. He looked into her beautiful brown eyes and swallowed hard as she touched his face gently.

"What are you thinking, Shane?" she asked him as she saw him pull her dress free of her shoulders and look at her lying still before him.

"I'm thinking that you came to me, that you found me, and that you saved someone like me," Shane answered his wife before he lowered his head to her breast, his intent to spend the night making love to her and later, much later, he would thank his brother for the book.

"I love you, Shane…"

The End

She saw me hurt and wounded,
Lying on the bed.
She tried to ease my suffering,
My tears I could not shed.
I only wanted to hold her,
In my arms she belonged to me.
But I was bound to another,
For her I was not free.
Then the war that harmed my soul,
The battle last at an end.
The truth came down upon me,
A lifetime with her I could spend.
For eternity and forever,
With her I will always be.
For she came into my arms at last,
She came and saved someone like me.

To read more of the Blackburn family:
Come Love Someone Like Me – Allen and Alicia's love story
Come Tame Someone Like Me – Ethan and Bethany's son Tucker's love story
A Return of Innocence – Lang and Holly's love story
No Sound the Silence Makes – Levi and Cecily's love story
Cherish the Lights Burning Low – Levi's parents Lilly and Ethan's love story